LABOR HISTORY ARCHIVES IN THE UNITED STATES

LABOR HISTORY ARCHIVES IN THE UNITED STATES

A Guide for
Researching and Teaching

Edited by
DANIEL J. LEAB and **PHILIP P. MASON**

 WAYNE STATE UNIVERSITY PRESS   DETROIT

99 98 97 96 95 94 93 92   5 4 3 2 1

Library of Congress Cataloging-in-Publication Data

Labor history archives in the United States: a guide for researching and teaching/
    edited by Daniel J. Leab and Philip P. Mason.
       p. cm.
Includes bibliographical references and index.
ISBN 0-8143-2388-X (alk. paper).—ISBN 0-8143-2389-8 (pbk. : alk. paper)
1. Labor—United States—Archival resources. 2. Working class—United States—
Archival resources. 3. Archival resources—United States. I. Leab, Daniel J. II.
Mason, Philip P. (Philip Parker), 1927- .
Z7164.L1L28 1992
[HD8066]
026'.331'0973—dc20   91–38550
                                                                                   CIP

Cover photo courtesy of Labor Archives and Research Center, San Francisco State
University.

Some of the material in this volume originally appeared in *Labor History*, Vol.
31, nos. 1-2 (Winter-Spring 1990), *Labor History*, Vol. 32, no. 1 (Winter 1991),
and *Labor History*, Vol. 32, no. 2 (Spring 1991). Reprinted by permission.

CONTENTS

Introduction   *Daniel J. Leab*   9
Labor Archives and Collections in the United States   *Philip P. Mason*   12
Labor Holdings at the Schlesinger Library,   *Eva Moseley*   18
    Radcliffe College
Labor Material in the Collections of   *Clare M. Sheridan*   27
    the Museum of American Textile History
Labor History Sources at the University   *Ken Fones-Wolf*   33
    of Massachusetts at Amherst
The Connecticut Labor Archives   *Randall C. Jimerson*   41
Sources for Business and Labor History   *Mary K. Witkowski*   46
    in the Bridgeport Public Library
Labor History Resources at New York University   50
    1.) The Tamiment Institute/
        Ben Josephson Library   *Dorothy Swanson*
    2.) The Robert F. Wagner Labor Archives   *Debra E. Bernhardt*
Labor Archives in the University at Albany,   *Geoffrey A. Huth*   61
    State University of New York
Sources on Labor History in the   *Richard Strassberg*   67
    Martin P. Catherwood Library
Sources on Labor History at the   *Erwin Levold*   75
    Rockefeller Archive Center
Labor History Resources at the Rutgers   *Ronald L. Becker*   83
    University Libraries
Labor Collections at the Urban Archives   *David M. Weinberg*   87
    Center, Temple University Libraries
Labor Archives at Indiana University   *Eileen Mountjoy Cooper*   93
    of Pennsylvania
Historical Collections & Labor   *Peter Gottlieb and*   97
    Archives, Penn State University   *Diana L. Shenk*
The UE/Labor Archives, University   *Mark McColloch*   102
    of Pittsburgh
Labor History Sources in the Manuscript   *John E. Haynes*   105
    Division of the Library of Congress
Labor History Sources in the National Archives   *Tab Lewis*   114

Labor and Social History Records at the   *Nelson Lichtenstein*   121
   Catholic University of America
The Joseph A. Beirne Memorial Archives   *Bruce P. Montgomery*   125
Labor Union History and Archives: The   *Lauren Brown*   129
   University of Maryland at College
   Park Libraries
The George Meany Memorial Archives   *Katharine Vogel*   133
West Virginia Labor Sources at the West   *Ken Fones-Wolf*   140
   Virginia and Regional History Collection
The Southern Labor Archives   *Robert Dinwiddie and*   146
                                           Leslie S. Hough

Labor History Resources at the Ohio   *Dan Ashyk and*   155
   Historical Society   *Wendy S. Greenwood*
The Debs Collection at Indiana State   *David E. Vancil,*   161
   University   *Robert L. Carter, and*
                                          Charles D. King
The Archives of Labor History and   *Philip P. Mason*   167
   Urban Affairs, Walter P. Reuther Library,
   Wayne State University
The Labadie Collection in the University   *Edward C. Weber*   177
   of Michigan Library
Labor History Manuscripts in   *Archie Motley*   185
   the Chicago Historical Society
The Ozarks Labor Union Archives at   *J. David Lages and*   190
   Southwest Missouri State University   *Neal Moore*
Labor History Resources in the University   *John N. Schacht*   195
   of Iowa Libraries, the State Historical
   Society of Iowa/Iowa City, and the
   Herbert Hoover Presidential Library
Sources for the Study of the Labor   *James P. Danky and*   203
   Movement at the State Historical   *Harold L. Miller*
   Society of Wisconsin
The Immigration History Research Center   *Joel Wurl*   212
   as a Source for Labor History Research
Labor Collections in the Western   *Cassandra M. Volpe*   219
   Historical Collections, at the University
   of Colorado, Boulder
Labor Resources at the Nevada State   *Guy Louis Rocha*   224
   Library and Archives
The Texas Labor Archives   *George N. Green*   229

Sources on Labor History at the Southern   *Sarah Cooper*   235
    California Library for Social Studies
    and Research

The Urban Archives Center at California   *Robert G. Marshall*   240
    State University, Northridge

The Labor Archives and Research Center   *Lynn A. Bonfield and*   248
    at San Francisco State University   *Leon J. Sompolinsky*

Index   257

INTRODUCTION

The Fall 1982 issue of *Labor History* surveyed in some detail the holdings of 13 diverse American institutions.[1] These institutions contained a wide variety of resources for those interested in writing or researching the many-faceted history of the American working class. That issue, because of its contents, was in great demand and quickly went out of print. Because of the continuing interest in the material described in that issue and in later articles on archival holdings,[2] the editorial board of *Labor History* deemed it important to resurvey the field. The Winter-Spring 1990 issue of the journal dealt with over 30 institutions, archives, and historical societies whose holdings contained "labor material."[3] That double issue also quickly went out of print.

This book is a revised and expanded update of that issue and describes the holdings of 40 libraries, archives, and historical societies. Indexing has further enhanced the utility of these descriptions; it is now possible to ascertain easily which institutions have holdings on such diverse subjects as labor education, the CIO, radical women groups, and various construction workers' locals. Many of these institutions have only recently established collection programs dealing with the working class, labor organizations, and related areas, but all contain material valuable to those interested in American labor history.

These institutions are large, small, and medium-sized. Some are under-funded and some are well-housed and fully staffed. All wish their resources were greater. Some contain a great deal of original material unique to the specific institution and others hold a great many microforms to be found in a variety of places. These institutions are scattered around the United States, but modern technology has made the task of the researcher much easier as original sources are copied in one format or another and made available in various locations.

[1] *Labor History*, 23 (Fall 1982).

[2] See, for example, James Gilreath, "Labor History Sources in the Library of Congress Rare Book and Special Collections Division," *Labor History*, 25 (1984), 243–51; Maurice A. Crane, "Labor History Materials in the G. Robert Vincent Voice Library, Michigan State University," *Labor History*, 26 (1985), 288–90; Stephen Schwartz, "Holdings on the 1934 West Coast Maritime Strike in the San Francisco Headquarters Archive, Sailors Union of the Pacific," *Labor History*, 27 (1986), 427–30.

[3] *Labor History*, 31 (Winter-Spring 1990).

RLIN is a recently established tool which can help to find this material. Some of these institutions belong to RLIN; others do not. Most researchers can obtain access to RLIN. A few words about RLIN (pronounced ar-lin), which is an acronym for Research Libraries Information Network, a data base that eases access for its users to the various collections that participate. RLIN is a service sponsored by the Research Libraries Group that began in 1984. RLIN members and users enter bibliographic information about their institution's holdings into the network's data base. Currently, over 200 libraries, archives, historical societies, and other institutions participate. RLIN contains nine files of different bibliographic formats which can be searched: these formats include books, serials, visual materials, recordings, and machine-readable data files.

As regards archival material, the description (or "record") provided by RLIN to the searcher usually includes a variety of information such as the availability of the material, its dates, and a brief description. Such a "record" generally deals with a whole collection but can also refer to a single manuscript item or to a group. Public access is usually on a fee basis (i.e., a user search charge). For information on access, contact the RLIN Information Center, 1-800-537-RLIN. For other information about RLIN, contact the Research Libraries Group, Inc., 1200 Villa Street, Mountain View, CA 94041-1100. As of this writing, although rumors about the restructuring of RLIN are flying, it remains in operation and promises to continue for the foreseeable future. In any event, should RLIN ultimately cease to function as now constituted, its data bases will be operated by another facility.

Labor History, under the editorship of my able predecessors (Norman Jacobs and Milton Cantor) and myself, has for more than three decades paid considerable attention to the multitude of resources available to scholars and others interested in the history of the American working class and its organizations. The annual bibliography, various bibliographical essays, and the 1982 and 1990 issues surveying holdings are manifestations of that continuing commitment. Philip P. Mason—administrator, archivist, historian, teacher, and veteran *Labor History* board member—has ably coordinated, with me, the reports which comprise this survey. He has also provided an informed, comprehensive, and succinct overview of the past achievements and future prospects of archival programs of the United States concerned with collecting, preserving, and making accessible the materials necessary for researching and writing American labor history.

In preparation of this survey, the net was cast very wide. Unfortunately some institutions ignored repeated inquiries and thus are not represented. I very much regret our inability to include them. But the institutions responding include the most important collections, and range from coast to coast (as well as north to south), and represent thoroughly the different kinds of collecting philosophies and materials. The respondents include not only archives and libraries whose holdings deal predominantly with workers and unions, but also institutions concerned with gathering and preserving material on various subjects—such as immigration, radicalism, social welfare, philanthropy, and urban affairs—all of which are areas important to anyone dealing with American labor history.

No attempt has been made editorially to impose a standard format on these reports, except in so far as each includes a contact person, a telephone number, and days and hours of access. The diversity and size of the holdings as well as the mood and inclination of the authors (as they responded to our inquiries) obviously played a large part in the form and substance of their responses. The reports are published by region beginning with New England. Our cutoff date was October 31, 1991.

Labor History remains eagerly interested in publishing reports about bibliographical and archival resources. The journal remains wide open for such contributions and welcomes them. I very much hope that anyone reading these comments who has such a contribution to make will get in touch with me. And I would also appreciate any comments that readers may wish to make on this survey. I would like to give special thanks for their assistance in the preparation of this book to Alberta Asmar, Philip Mason's secretary, and to Susan Stoessel, my former assistant, as well as Arthur Evans, the director of the Wayne State University Press.

Daniel J. Leab
Tamiment Library
New York University

LABOR ARCHIVES AND COLLECTIONS IN THE UNITED STATES

by
Philip P. Mason

The establishment of archival institutions whose primary objective is to collect and preserve the records of labor unions, labor organizations and the personal papers of labor leaders and workers is a relatively recent development in the U.S. and Canada. Prior to 1950 there were five major archival programs specializing in labor history: the John Commons Collection of the State Historical Society of Wisconsin, the Labadie Collection of the University of Michigan, the Tamiment Library — now at New York University, the Catherwood Library at Cornell University, and the labor collections at Catholic University of America. The National Archives established in 1934 also has extensive public records relating to government and labor, as do a number of state archival programs. In addition, scattered labor-related collections were found in regional and local archives in all parts of the United States. But, for the most part, up to 1950, collections relating to the labor movement were not given priority by the major archival institutions which concentrated their collecting priorities on the "white male elite" in the U.S.

The 1960s witnessed a change in this emphasis, resulting in the establishment of new archival programs devoted to specialized subject areas such as immigration, social welfare, women, minorities, native American Indians, and urban America. Special attention was given to the labor movement, encompassing not only the records of trade unions and the personal papers of their officials, but also the papers and accounts of rank and file workers. In this category are the Southern Labor Archives at Georgia State University, the Texas Labor Archives at the

Philip P. Mason is Professor of History and Director of the Walter P. Reuther Library of Labor and Urban Affairs, Wayne State University. He has served on the editorial board of Labor History _since 1974._

University of Texas at Arlington, the Pennsylvania State University Labor Archives, and the Archives of Labor and Urban Affairs at Wayne State University. Also, many traditional archives associated with state and regional historical societies as well as the numerous, newly established university archives actively solicited labor records. The archives at the University of Maryland, the Ohio State Historical Society, Rutgers University, the University of Pittsburgh, Radcliffe College, the University of Iowa, and the University of Colorado at Boulder are typical of those institutions which have acquired labor collections as a part of their overall holdings. In 1989 plans were announced for the establishment of two more labor archives programs, one in Humboldt County, California, and a second at Florida International University.

Several international unions have established archival programs to preserve their own records, rather than placing them in an archival institution. The International Brotherhood of Teamsters, the National Association of Letter Carriers, the Communication Workers of America, and the American Postal Workers Union have such programs, although access to non-union researchers is often limited.

Two major archives programs have been established since 1982. The AFL-CIO opened the George Meany Memorial Archives in 1987 on the campus of the George Meany Center for Labor Studies in Silver Spring, Maryland. The collecting scope of the Meany Archives is now being developed, but the core of the Archives' holdings are the historical files of the AFL-CIO, of a selected group of affiliated institutes, and of defunct international unions as well as the personal papers of current officers and leaders of the Federation. A second significant labor program is the Labor Archives and Research Center at San Francisco State University which opened in 1986. This archive, which concentrates on the records of the labor movement in northern California, has, in just a few years, acquired many important labor collections and serves as a model of its kind.

In addition to new labor archives programs, existing archives have expanded their labor holdings since 1982. These programs are included in this book although there will inevitably be some institutions overlooked in this account. The role of Canadian archival institutions in collecting and preserving labor records is not included. The 1988–89 issue of *Archivaria*, the official Journal of the Association of Canadian Archivists, contains detailed accounts on such holdings.

Despite the progress made since 1982 in preserving records of the labor movement, the same serious problems exist now, as they did at that time. Financial resources available for the establishment of new archival programs and the support of existing ones remain limited, and in many instances funding has been sharply reduced. Federal grant funds for archival programs have declined and international labor unions, coping with declining memberships have been reluctant to support archives, or related projects such as oral history programs.

Huge gaps remain in the archival documentation of the American labor movement. Approximately 70 international unions have no current plans to preserve their historical files, either internally or by depositing their historical records in an existing archive. Some union officials are anxious to preserve their historical files, but lack the expertise to develop a program to accomplish their ends. Few of the 50 state federations of labor and only a handful of the more than 700 AFL-CIO local central bodies have systematic programs to preserve their records. Even more dismal is the future for the preservation of the records of over 60,000 affiliated local unions. Such records have not been actively collected and preserved by local and regional archives in the United States.

This lack of archival capacity and facilities is compounded by the sharp increase in the volume of current records. As unions run out of office and storage space for records, older files are often discarded indiscriminately in order to make room for current files. Furthermore, organized labor's increasing use of computers has not reduced the volume of records, nor resulted in paperless offices. On the contrary, the computer has facilitated the creation of paper records in size and format not consistent with filing equipment. The quick copy and FAX machines, now in widespread use in union offices, combined with the concept of a "participatory democracy" have created a glut of paper records. In 1988, for example, the UAW and AFSCME, two large international unions, created more paper records than they had during the previous three years combined. Such an influx of records has resulted in a breakdown of filing systems and caused a crisis in retrieving needed records.

The "paper explosion" has not only created a serious problem for labor unions and their staff, but also has hampered the archivists who collect and preserve the records of labor unions and the personal papers of individuals. On the average, only about 2-5% of a union's inactive records qualify for permanent preservation in an archive. This process of identifying and determining which records have enduring value — called "appraisal" by archivists — has become far more difficult because of the sheer volume of union records and the chaotic condition of many filing systems.

For the past decade archivists have been grappling with the problem of appraisal standards for labor records. At one level archivists are trying to determine whether records from *all* major offices and departments of an international union should be selected for preservation – or just those of the president, the secretary-treasurer, and other key officers. Should the records of regional offices and affiliated local unions, for example, be appraised and preserved? It may not be possible to preserve the records of all local unions; nevertheless, some criteria for a selective sampling of local unions can be adopted. Archivists face similar problems in appraising the various types of records created by unions. Grievance records, for example, represent the largest important source of information on the operation of a local union, on standards and issues relating to women, and on minorities and ethnic groups. It is not possible, in most cases, to retain all grievance records because of their volume; yet a valid sampling procedure must be adopted to enhance their research value.[1]

The issue of competition between labor archives is no longer the problem that it was 20 or 30 years ago when the "scarcity" theory of collecting dominated the field. Archivists now recognize that not only are there enough important and valuable collections for all archives to share, but indeed, the existing programs cannot begin to collect and preserve the available union sources. Cooperation has replaced competition among labor archivists.

There is some disagreement, however, between those archives that collect materials on a national basis and those that concentrate on regional areas. An archive which is the official depository for the inactive records of an international union may, by agreement or policy, also collect the records of affiliated regional or state offices and local unions. The reason for such grass-roots interest is obvious and enhances the value of the archival holdings of the international union. On the other hand, the records of local unions may have particular interest to a regional archive and the locale in which the local union operated. There is also friction between archives in Canada which specialize in labor materials and their counterparts in the U.S. Many Canadian archivists and researchers are opposed to the transfer of any Canadian union records to depositories in the U.S., even though such records are a part of an international union, with headquarters in the U.S. Greater attention must be given to this problem by archival institutions.

Access to labor union records is another perplexing issue facing archivists. The history of unions in the U.S. has involved many violent and controversial strikes and vicious internal factional struggles, inter-

---

[1]See Richard Kesner, "Labor Union Grievance Records: An Appraisal Strategy," *Archivaria*, 8 (1979), 102–114.

union battles, and activities which border on violation of the law. Understandably, union leaders are cautious about making these sensitive materials available to outside researchers, regardless of the historical value of the material.

In order to assure that such confidential records are preserved, archivists have had to accept some restraints upon access to these files. Access agreements usually provide that official union records remain closed or restricted for a specified number of years. And records of a more recent period may be used only with special permission of the designated union official. Usually there is a provision whereby records of a particularly sensitive nature, such as personnel records or internal investigations, may be restricted for longer periods of time.

Some researchers have been critical of such restrictions; indeed, some have maintained that archival institutions should not accept collections that contain any restrictions upon accessibility.[2] Experienced archivists who deal with union leaders recognize that reasonable restrictions upon access are necessary if union records are to be deposited in an archives. Without such restrictions, it is likely that unions and other donors would refuse to place any of their records in an archives or they might even destroy such records.

Despite the serious problems facing labor archives, some concerted action can be taken within existing resources to consolidate the gains of the past 30 years and, indeed, to increase the research value of labor sources. Archivists can exchange finding aids and other guides to their collections with other labor and interested archives. Such widespread distribution of guides will be of great assistance to researchers who will be able to easily locate other relevant sources at a variety of archival centers. Such information will also enhance archival contacts with respective donors who may not have selected a depository for their records.

Another problem facing students of labor history is the absence of archival programs to preserve the records of municipalities and local units of government (such as police agencies, courts, and social welfare agencies). Local public records often are vital as a supplement to official union records in the study of labor history, working conditions, and the treatment of workers. Although most states have state archives to preserve public records, virtually nothing is being done to systemat-

---

[2]The question of access to archival collections was the main theme of a conference sponsored by the American Historical Association, the Organization of American Historians, and the Society of American Archivists. See Philip P. Mason, "The Archivists' Responsibility to Researchers and Donors: A Delicate Balance," *Access to the Papers of Recent Public Figures: The New Harmony Conference* (Bloomington, IN, 1978).

ically preserve the public records of municipalities, townships, and other local units of government. A few large cities have established municipal archives in the last decade, but most smaller communities have not taken any action, creating a situation which has been described as a "national public scandal." The quality of research will eventually suffer from the lack of availability of this source of information on workers and their unions.

Also impeding the task of historians of the labor movement is the lack of records relating to business firms, public agencies, and other organizations which deal with labor unions. Except for the files of some units of government, most of these records are not retained and if they are, are not available to historians or other researchers. For example, there is a wealth of material available on the unionization of the automobile industry as a result of the action taken by the UAW to preserve its historical files. There are practically no records available from the automobile companies dealing with unions and workers. Those records that have not been systematically destroyed by the automobile companies have been closed to research. Thus, there is a serious gap in the historical record.

In looking forward to the coming decade, it is obvious that it will be increasingly difficult to find suitable archival depositories for union records. The difficulty of obtaining financial support from foundations, Federal granting agencies, and unions, as well as archival institutions themselves will force many archives to restrict their collecting activities. Perhaps the best hope is for researchers and other users of union records to encourage exisiting archives to expand their collecting scope to include the files of unions and the personal papers of union leaders and workers.

LABOR HOLDINGS
AT THE SCHLESINGER LIBRARY,
RADCLIFFE COLLEGE

by
Eva Moseley

The Arthur and Elizabeth Schlesinger Library on the History of
Women in America was founded in 1943 when Radcliffe College accepted the Woman's Rights Collection (WRC). The gift of alumna Maud
Wood Park (class of 1898), the WRC documents several women's suffrage organizations and includes the papers of Park and other women
active in the movement. But it does not end with 1920, the year the
federal suffrage amendment was ratified, and it includes the library's
first labor collection: papers of Frances Perkins, U.S. Secretary of Labor,
1933–45, and the first woman in the Cabinet. Thus, despite the emphasis on suffrage and women's political and legal rights, labor issues –
women working, women organizing, the rights and conditions of
working women – from the beginning have been an integral part of the
Schlesinger Library (until 1967 known as the Women's Archives).

At about the time the WRC arrived at Radcliffe, President Wilbur
K. Jordan and Professor Arthur M. Schlesinger, Sr., of the Harvard
history department decided to make it the centerpiece of a growing
research library on women, rather than a static memorial to the suffrage movement. Soon after, in December 1945, another major labor
collection arrived: the papers of Leonora O'Reilly (1870–1927). She was
born in New York City, went to work in a collar factory at 11 and at
16 joined the Knights of Labor. That same year she started the Working
Women's Society, which attracted the attention of Josephine Shaw
Lowell and led to Lowell's founding the New York Consumers' League
in 1890. O'Reilly, continuing to work 10 hours a day in garment factories, met and impressed many reformers, and became vice-president
of the Social Reform Club. She later taught sewing – first at a Brooklyn

Eva Moseley is Curator of Manuscripts at the Schlesinger Library.

settlement and then at the Manhattan Trade School for Girls, hoping that skilled workers would more readily join unions. When the National Women's Trade Union League (NWTUL) was founded in 1903, O'Reilly became a board member. She drew Mary Dreier and Margaret Dreier Robins to the NWTUL. A lifetime annuity from Dreier enabled O'Reilly to work for the league full-time. She was an inspiring orator, traveling throughout the U.S. and speaking almost daily. She was also a founder of the NAACP (1909), an active socialist and suffragist, and the NWTUL delegate to the International Congress of Women (The Hague, 1915) and the International Congress of Working Women (Washington, DC, 1919).

O'Reilly's papers (7 linear feet) make up one major series in the micropublication, *The Papers of the Women's Trade Union League and Its Principal Leaders*, a project sponsored by the Schlesinger Library (SL), edited by Edward T. James with assistant editors Robin Miller Jacoby and Nancy Schrom Dye, and published by Research Publications, Inc. in 1981. Four other SL collections were included: the papers of Mary Anderson (1872–1964), first director of the Women's Bureau of the U.S. Dept. of Labor (1920–44); the autobiography of Mary Kenney O'Sullivan (1864–1943), first woman organizer for the AFL and a founder of the NWTUL; and records of the Boston WTUL and the NWTUL. The Library of Congress filmed its NWTUL records in conjunction with this project.

It was Mary E. Dreier who gave the SL the O'Reilly papers. Dreier (1875–1963) was president from 1906 to 1914 of the New York Women's Trade Union League and an active member till it disbanded in 1950. Her background was very different from O'Reilly's, the Dreiers being a well-to-do German-American family in Brooklyn. Margaret Dreier Robins (1868–1945), first president of the NWTUL (from 1907 to 1922), was the oldest sister; two others, Dorothea and Katherine, were artists. The sisters, a brother (Henry Edward), and sister-in-law Ethel (Valentine), as well as the NYWTUL, are well represented in Mary's papers. Numerous letters discuss not only labor activities but also current events, health, family news, modern art, and spiritualism. Mary's long-time companion was Frances Kellor (1873–1952), a social reformer who was a founding member and from 1926 to 1952 vice-president of the American Arbitration Association, dedicated to efficient, fair settlement of industrial and international disputes. During Mary's protracted visits to the Robinses in Florida or her summer home in Maine, she and Frances exchanged frequent letters.

Margaret Dreier Robins (whose papers, at the Univ. of Florida, are a major series in the NWTUL project) was president of the short-lived International Federation of Working Women. The library has one file box of papers from its three congresses: Washington, DC, 1919; Geneva, 1921; and Vienna, 1923. Also reflecting international labor interests are the papers of Frances Perkins (1880–1965) referred to above. These papers document much of Perkins's work, first as New York State Industrial Commissioner and then as Secretary of Labor; a major portion consists of correspondence, reports, and other papers concerning International Labor Organization (ILO) conferences and its governing body. It is well known that Franklin D. Roosevelt, having appointed Perkins in New York, persuaded her to follow him to Washington. Less well known is that she evidently persuaded him to have the U.S. join the ILO.

At least two other women with papers at SL were involved in labor issues internationally: Frieda Miller (1889–1973) and Ethel McLean Johnson (1882–1978). Both worked as special assistants to Ambassador John G. Winant in England during World War II. Miller had been Industrial Commissioner of New York State (1938–43) and was later director of the Women's Bureau (1944–53); she had begun representing the U.S. at ILO conferences in 1936 and went to work there full-time after leaving the Women's Bureau. Johnson had been Minimum Wage Director of New Hampshire (1933–35) while Winant was governor, and had worked for him at the ILO (1935–39) and at the ILO's Washington office (1939–43). Johnson's papers measure 5.5 feet, document her work in New Hampshire, England, and Massachusetts, and include many speeches and articles, while Miller's (7.5 feet) document her work in New York, nationally, and internationally. Perkins, Miller, and Johnson, unlike O'Reilly and the Dreiers, represent leaders in labor and other causes whose activities and reputations led to their appointment to official positions at various levels of government.

From 1924 until her death Miller shared a New York apartment with Pauline Newman (1890?–1986). Unlike Miller, who came from a comfortable Wisconsin family and had done graduate work at the Univ. of Chicago, Newman came to the U.S. from Lithuania in May 1901 and by September was working at the Triangle Shirtwaist Company. She soon joined the Socialist Party, the ILGWU, and the NYWTUL. From 1924 until her retirement she was Education Director for the ILGWU's Union Health Center. The library has more than 4 feet of her labor and personal papers.

An earlier example of a worker who, like O'Reilly and Newman, became a leader is Harriet (Hanson) Robinson (1825–1911), a Lowell mill girl from the age of 10 until her marriage at 23, then an abolitionist, and after the Civil War, founder of the National Woman's Suffrage Association of Massachusetts and promoter of women's clubs. An occasional contributor to the mill girls' magazine, the *Lowell*

Offering, Harriet while only 11 years old persuaded other young girls to join a strike of older workers protesting a wage cut. She documented her life and interests in correspondence and in 66 diaries and scrapbooks, which are available on microfilm.

Most of the SL's earlier labor holdings — like the Dreier papers — are papers of leaders or reformers rather than of working women themselves. Many repositories find it necessary to collect more or less indirect evidence of the lives of working people. Elizabeth (Gardiner) Glendower Evans (1856–1937), for instance, was born into a prominent Boston family — which later turned its back on her for her radical views and activities. She learned about social and political issues from her husband and after his early death (1886) became an advocate for workers and prisoners, a suffragist, civil libertarian, and outspoken supporter of Sacco and Vanzetti. Her appearance on the picket line at the second Lawrence textile strike (1919) and her publicity about police brutality there helped the strikers win. Evans's papers are available on microfilm.

In 1929 Harvard President A. Lawrence Lowell fired 19 scrubwomen working in Widener Library because of a dispute about their pay between the university and the Massachusetts Minimum Wage Commission. Corliss Lamont of the class of 1924 tried unsuccessfully to organize alumni to sign an open letter of protest; he did raise contributions equivalent to the women's lost wages. This episode in Harvard's history is documented in two file boxes of Lamont's papers, including a few letters from scrubwomen.

Also involved in the scrubwomen affair was the Consumers' League, an organization dedicated to improving conditions for working women; Margaret Wiesman, executive secretary of the Massachusetts league, interviewed the scrubwomen and kept in touch with Lamont. A founder and first president of the National Consumers' League was John Graham Brooks (1846–1938), Unitarian minister and for many years an investigator of strikes for the U.S. Dept. of Labor. Four file boxes include letters from many well-known people and a small amount of material on the league, which is more fully documented in other collections: for instance, the records of the Connecticut league (1.5 feet; 1902–50) and the Massachusetts league (12.5 feet; 1891–1955). The league's minutes, reports of investigations, etc., document sweatshops, child labor, homework, industrial poisons, wages and hours, and the like. A third significant Consumers' League collection is the papers, 1890–1938, of Maud (Nathan) Nathan (1862–1946), a wealthy "lady" who was a tireless champion of the New York and National Consumers' Leagues and wrote about them in *The Story of an Epoch-Making Movement* (New York, 1926).

Besides Lamont and Brooks, another man whose papers are at the library is Alexander Lincoln, a Boston lawyer and president (1927–36) of the Sentinels of the Republic. In this case, the primary connection with women's history is the Sentinels' opposition to a Federal child labor amendment, purportedly on the grounds of individual and states' rights. The Sentinels were among the radically anti-communist groups that sprang up after the Russian Revolution.

Equating labor activities and protection of workers with communism, and red-baiting of labor leaders, are themes that appear in several other SL collections as well. The Consumers' League of Massachusetts records, for instance, include a folder on "Communists and Red Baiting," the FBI investigated Mary Dreier, and Congressman J. Parnell Thomas wanted Frances Perkins impeached. Adelaide Schulkind Frank was executive secretary of the League for Mutual Aid, founded in 1920 to provide loans and advice to liberals and labor activists. Two boxes of her papers include letters from David Dubinsky, A. Philip Randolph, and Mary Heaton Vorse. Florence Luscomb (1887–1985) appeared before the Massachusetts Special Commission to Study and Investigate Communism and Subversive Activities and Related Matters in 1955. Among the activities that made her suspect was an attempt in the 1930s to organize clerical workers in Boston.

Traditionally resistant to unionizing, clerical workers have more recently organized in 9to5: Organization for Women Office Workers, founded in Boston in 1972. With sister organizations in other cities, 9to5 sponsored a national group, Working Women, in 1977. The SL has more than 22 feet of partly restricted records documenting campaigns against the banking, insurance, and publishing industries and universities, as well as membership, fundraising, and such issues as child care, minority women, and health and safety. Another valuable source for the recent history of clerical workers is a series of interviews conducted by Jean Tepperman with women employed in the Boston area by private corporations, universities, and state and local governments. Much of this material was used in her book, *Not Servants, Not Machines: Office Workers Speak Out* (Boston, 1975).

Long before women were clerical workers, many resorted to the "oldest profession." Only in recent decades have prostitutes in the U.S. organized, notably in COYOTE (Call Off Your Old Tired Ethics). Most of its 35 feet of records are temporarily closed or restricted. Earlier evidence of the economic function of prostitution is found in the records of a "vice study" carried out by the Women's Educational and Industrial Union (WEIU) of Boston in 1909. A woman who might earn $12 a week in a factory could earn $100 or more on the street. There are reports and other papers about "white slavery" in the papers of New

York suffragist Harriet (Burton) Laidlaw (1873–1949). And Rutland Corner House, founded in Boston in 1878 as the Temporary Home for Working Women, had as a thinly veiled goal keeping women off the streets; prerequisites for admission were "poverty, respectability, and ability to work."

Rutland Corner House, the WEIU, and similar agencies in Boston and elsewhere aimed not only to protect women against "vice" but also to offer them alternative ways to achieve economic independence. The WEIU's concern with domestic workers and immigrant girls at times reflected the needs of employers more than those of working women, but the union also sponsored such projects as a study of the income and expenses of women workers, published in 1911 as *The Living Wage of Women Workers.* The questionnaires, account books, and drafts are in the papers of Louise Marion Bosworth (1881–1982), who participated in the study and published the results.

As new industries spawned new occupations, vocational guidance became a concern of social agencies and itself a new occupation. About 3.5 feet of the office files of North Bennet Street Industrial School, a Boston trade school and settlement house founded in 1879 and still active, document the school's vocational guidance and placement efforts, including syllabi of courses on vocations from the 1910s. The Vocational Adjustment Bureau for Girls operated in New York at about the same time; founded and headed by Blanche Ittleson, it aimed to evaluate and place "maladjusted girls" in suitable jobs.

The Bureau of Vocational Information addressed a different group — college-educated women — and investigated opportunities and actualities in such varied occupations as agriculture, home economics, law, personnel work, and statistics. Nevertheless, about one-third of 9.5 feet of records (1908–32) document clerical work. Opportunities are laid out in government, university, and trade association publications and employer questionnaires; for a look at actualities, there are hundreds of questionnaires from women working in the various fields.

The labor education movement was for both women and men a way to widen mental horizons, to occupy limited leisure time constructively, to bolster — or create — the self-respect that semi- or unskilled, repetitive, ill-paid work tended to destroy, and perhaps even to open up new vocational opportunities. Hilda Worthington Smith (1888–1984) was the first director of the Bryn Mawr Summer School for Women Workers in Industry, and in 1927 a founder of the American Labor Education Service. The library has one of several collections (13 feet covering the years 1900–75) documenting her family and her work; others are at Bryn Mawr, Cornell, the Franklin D. Roosevelt Library, Rutgers, and the State Historical Society of Wisconsin. Esther Peterson (b. 1906) was an instructor at the Bryn Mawr Summer School, a labor organizer in Boston, and later an advocate for women workers as head of the Women's Bureau under President Kennedy. She is best known as vice-chair of the President's Commission on the Status of Women and as a leading consumer advocate. Her papers, still growing, now occupy more than 60 feet. Also active in labor education was Margaret (Earhart) Smith (1902–60). In 1943 in Detroit she was co-founder of the Special Services Committee, which initiated and supported workers' education programs, and in 1949–53 she chaired the Labor Participation Committee of United Community Services of Metropolitan Boston.

Doubly oppressed, and doubly elusive to the historian, are black women. Many, if not most, have of course worked outside the home (outside their own homes, that is, though often in those of other people), and some have organized or otherwise assisted workers. Four such women were interviewed for the SL's Black Women's Oral History Project. Frances Mary Albrier (b. 1898) in the late 1920s organized porters, waiters, and maids working for the Pullman Company. Melnea Cass (1896–1978), a Boston civic leader, was herself a domestic worker for several decades and later president of the Women's Service Club, which provided training, counselling, and housing for young black women seeking domestic employment. Mae (Graves) Eberhardt (b. 1915) was a union activist for almost 35 years, as a laundry worker, an electronics worker, and as civil rights director of District 3 for the IUE; as executive vice-president of the New Jersey Industrial Council she was the first black woman to be elected an officer of a state labor organization.

Maida Springer Kemp (b. 1910) was also an interviewee and has given the library one linear foot of her papers, with more to come. Both sources document her leadership in various garment industry unions. The main emphasis, however, as with Johnson, Miller, and Perkins earlier, is on international activity. Kemp has represented the AFL-CIO in many countries, but her primary focus has been Africa, where she has attended trade union and other congresses and advised labor and political leaders.

Depending on one's definition of "labor" — how much one emphasizes industrial employment, organized union activity, or simply people working — other sources suggest themselves. The records of the Home for Aged Women (1849 to the present) include some quantifiable information on residents; many were domestics or other workers. The papers of the Lydia E. Pinkham Medicine Company (1859–1968; more than 130 feet) include payroll records for the years 1877–1961. The North

Bennet Street Industrial School records mentioned above also document vocational training for girls and boys, women and men, work relief programs during the Depression, and recreation for workers. A scattering of diaries and account books gives at least glimpses of individual women supporting themselves as teachers, milliners, and so on, and the papers (1911–   ; 21 feet) of Clara (Mortenson) Beyer (1892–1990) document her long career with government labor agencies, especially with the Bureau of Labor Standards of the U.S. Dept. of Labor. She was interviewed for the library's Women in the Federal Government Oral History Project, as were Mary (Dublin) Keyserling (Women's Bureau), Alice Angus Morrison (Dept. of Labor), and Aryness Joy Wickens (Dept. of Labor).

A researcher wishing to look at any of the collections described or find other holdings of interest can browse through the finding aids at the library or at a distance. The library's finding aids have been published by Chadwyck-Healey as part of the *National Inventory of Documentary Sources* (1990), a microfiche publication. The catalogs for the books, periodicals, and manuscripts, and the manuscript inventories, were published by G. K. Hall in 10 volumes in 1984. SL manuscript collections are briefly described in 657 entries in *Women's History Sources*, edited by Andrea Hinding, *et al.*, and published by Bowker in 1979. Many manuscript holdings are reported to the *National Union Catalog of Manuscript Collections*, published periodically by the Library of Congress (LC). Most up-to-date are entries in the Research Libraries Information Network (RLIN), available online at member libraries throughout the U.S. Books and many of the periodicals (not described in this article) are cataloged in OCLC. Most entries in RLIN and OCLC also appear in the Harvard On Line Library Information System (HOLLIS), a local database.

The SL has always applied subject cataloging to descriptions of manuscript collections and in recent years has increased the number of name and subject headings used so as to enhance intellectual access to the holdings. Having earlier used Library of Congress (LC) headings with modifications, since joining RLIN it has conformed to LC usage, sometimes suggesting changes. It is therefore possible to determine what manuscript sources are available on a given topic, or by or about specific organizations or individuals, without visiting the library. It is also possible to borrow microfilms of manuscript collections on interlibrary loan. Several such collections (Evans, Robinson, etc.) are mentioned above; a list and information on borrowing are available from the library. While making information about holdings, and some holdings, available to researchers unable to visit, the library of course welcomes visitors.

Access: the Library is open to the public 9 am–5 pm, Monday–Friday, throughout the year, with some evening hours for printed materials during the fall and spring semesters. There are no scholarly or other qualifications. Before visiting, reseachers do well to check on such matters as holidays, the availability of specific holdings, and restrictions on use of recent collections. When visiting, they should allow time for a reference interview; staff can often point out little-known holdings or unexpected research tracks. For further information contact Eva Moseley, Schlesinger Library, Radcliffe College, 10 Garden St., Cambridge, MA 02138; phone: (617) 495-8647.

LABOR MATERIAL IN THE COLLECTIONS OF THE MUSEUM OF AMERICAN TEXTILE HISTORY[1]

by
Clare M. Sheridan

The Museum of American Textile History (MATH) was established in 1960 by Caroline Stevens Rogers, a descendent of Nathaniel Stevens who founded in 1813 what was to become one of New England's largest woolen companies. The Stevens woolen and worsted mills were finally closed in 1972 and the original site in North Andover was razed in 1974.[2] The records of the company, scattered by vandals, were removed from a building on the company's premises and now form the core of the museum's manuscript collection. Mrs. Rogers had also inherited a collection of spinning wheels, handlooms, and tools which she and her husband donated to the new museum to form the basis of its artifacts collection. Industrial textile machinery, textiles, books, prints, photographs, and ephemera were subsequently added. The museum now collects from all regions of the U.S.

The museum's policy is to collect and preserve objects and information that promote an understanding of the history of textile production in this country and to encourage the study of its technological, social, labor, decorative arts, and business history. For a number of years, the museum has had to counter a reputation for management bias in its collecting. In fact, throughout its history, MATH staff has conscientiously collected labor-related material and has been encouraged to present labor's role in exhibits and publications. Consequently, the scope of the Museum's collecting encompasses the industry's management and labor history, decisions, and strategies.

Clare Sheridan has been Librarian of the Museum of American Textile History since 1983.

---

[1]Formerly, the Merrimack Valley Textile Museum.

[2]J. P. Stevens & Co. had originally been formed as the selling agent for Moses T. Stevens & Sons Co. of North Andover. JPS & Co. expanded to include the selling of cotton fabrics and invested heavily in southern mills. In the 1940s, the two companies merged. The mills of MTS & Sons became the woolen and worsted division of JPS & Co., Inc.

A researcher's visit to the museum often begins and ends in the library with an introductory tour of the gallery where the machinery and manufacturing process are demonstrated and their social and economic context described. To fully utilize MATH's resources, however, a visit should also include an interview with one or both curators and an examination of the collections. Collaboration between the researcher and the staff can provide for a more informed picture of worker, machine, and product.

The collections of tools, machinery, and textiles support research into labor history in significant ways. While attention to artifacts should not displace documentary research, an examination of these objects helps to ensure that the researcher fully comprehends the day-to-day experience of the workers themselves, their role on the shop floor, the relationship between management's definition of skilled and unskilled work, the changes which alterations and repairs in machinery or the introduction of new machinery made, and the physical activity needed to produce a particular type of fabric. Labor research is enhanced by understanding how the equipment works and by examining different types of cloth — some coarse, some fine, some easy to produce, and some requiring complicated production techniques.

The museum operates an 1827 carding machine, an 1864 spinning mule, a c.1870 loom, and a 1930 "automatic" loom. These machines provide direct information about the tasks of their operatives. Hundreds of other machines, while not operational, are available for study and reveal the ways in which the work experience was altered by purposeful developments flowing from the goals of management and through alterations to machines which occurred on the shop floor and are not otherwise recorded. This parallel approach to examining labor and technological history has assisted research on machinists, mulespinners, weavers, and other workers.[3]

The textile collection includes examples of finished cloth, both factory-produced and handwoven, as well as cloth samples which number in the millions. As a rule the museum does not collect cut and sewn objects, which excludes clothing and quilts, although research on workers' clothing is regularly done by examining fabrics and the library collections. Specific pieces in this collection that may interest historians of labor include union banners, ribbons commemorating workers

---

[3]Laurence F. Gross, "Wool Carding: A Study of Skills and Technology," *Technology and Culture*, 28 (1987), 804–827, "Research Outside the Library: Watkins Mill, A Case Study," *Industrial Archeology*, 7 (1981), 15–28.

outings and union meetings, and mulespinners' and weavers' aprons.

A study of textiles, as with an examination of tools and machinery, can be a rewarding experience for labor historians. A study of American printed textiles by textile curator Diane L. Fagan Affleck has shown how the design process was divided between the management hierarchy and shop, floor operatives by controlling differences in the gender, level of skill, and ethnicity of the workers.

The library collects manuscripts, printed materials, images, and ephemera. Within these categories, there is a wide range of material: union and company records; prints, photographs and stereocards showing workers, managers and mills; technical handbooks and mechanics manuals; trade periodicals, employee magazines and house organs; trade catalogues and handbills; architectural drawings and studies of factory design and worker housing; patent records and insurance maps; songs, poetry, novels, juvenile literature; postcards, cloth labels and other advertising ephemera — anything, in fact, that was produced or used by workers, businessmen, engineers and architects employed in the textile business. Research and theses that reflect past and current interpretations of labor history are also part of the collection.

The book collection contains many titles from other countries that bear upon the history of labor and manufacturing in the U.S. Not surprisingly, British material occupies a prominent place: government documents regulating imports and exports and the dissemination of trade secrets, commentaries on factory labor and workers' "combinations," and technical literature that enjoyed a wide circulation among American mechanics.

The library also has a large selection of the late 18th and early 19th century pamphlet literature debating the virtues and evils of manufacturing and related tariff issues. It is also strong in portraying the early period of manufacturing in lower New England. The writings of mill operatives, visitors from home and abroad, and other commentators on the social scene form much of this period's literature on the working force, interspersed, with "factory tracts," newspapers, and the legislative inquiries and petitions inspired by the Ten Hour Movement. Much of what we know subsequently about the labor history of the textile industry and working-class life in mill communities is derived or inferred from sources familiar to social historians: housing and sanitation reports, child labor investigations, legislative hearings on hours of work, newspapers and periodicals, directories and census reports, factory regulations and time-tables, dime novels, comparisons of British and American mills, reports of and responses to mill disasters, com-

pany records, letters of operatives to family and friends, labor petitions, strike broadsides, notices of mill and machinery auctions, as well
as local histories of textile cities and towns celebrating the foundation
of their economic wealth, and the subscription-supported biographies
of a region's "eminent" manufacturers.

Workers' varied responses to their workplace are also illustrated
in the hundreds of photographs the library collects showing men,
women, and children in and out of the mill. Most early images are
company-sponsored group photographs or studio portraits showing
workers with the tools of their trade in hand. Later photographs are
intended as exposés, others are unintentionally revealing. Yet others,
clearly promotional, try to simulate the model factory with operatives
tending machines in their Sunday best. But the bulk fall somewhere
in between — workers interacting with the machines they tend or posing
as a group on the factory floor for the company photographer or one
of their own hire. Stereocard series and a few examples of shop-floor
tours on motion picture film or video help to convey the work process
but the tone is more educational than spontaneous. The museum also
owns several early images of workers, one of which is said to be the
oldest known photograph of a woman tending a power loom (c.1850).
In addition, we have a large collection of postcards from the first half
of the 20th century. These views of mills and milltowns were souvenirs
of an industrial landscape that has since disappeared or been trans-
formed by developers.

Yet another record of working life is the correspondence of mill
workers. One of our most frequently used collections is the Metcalf-
Adams papers, consisting of 325 letters relating New England family
life from 1796 to 1866. Many of those from the 1840s and 1850s were
written by younger members of the family, recounting the work and
social life of Lowell operatives.

MATH was also fortunate to obtain TWUA/ACTWU files from
the New England area office from 1939 to 1980 including the records
of the Joint Boards of Greater Boston, Lowell, and Lawrence and the
minutes of several locals. They are of particular interest as they chronicle
the union's struggles in a period of industrial decline.

Company records provide both obvious and subtle information
about the labor force. Records in the museum's collections offer evidence of labor unrest, blacklisting, Taylorism, social welfare work, company housing and company towns, recreational activities, speed-ups
and stretch-outs, etc. Of our 2800 linear feet of company records and

personal papers, the bulk of which fall between 1830 and 1930, we have the following categories that may be of interest to labor historians: cotton and woolen worsted mills; flax, jute and silk and knitting mills; trade associations; engineering and consulting firms; machinery manufacturers; dyeing and finishing firms; weavers' account books. There are also oral history tapes. Most of the larger collections contain job applications, petitions, contracts and indentures, pension plans, accident reports, payrolls, time books, personnel files, and production records. These business records are arranged in a uniform pattern based on a scheme devised by Harvard University's Baker Library which allows for a comparison of similar series across collections.[4]

Several trade associations have files of interest in addition to their published transactions: the National Association of Wool Manufacturers (1864–1970) with information mainly from 1930 to 1970 on industrial relations and wages, Walsh-Healey, and the NRA Code Authority; the files of the National Assn. of Cotton Manufacturers/Northern Textile Assn. (1896–1970) containing information, chiefly after the late 1920s on strikes, wages, the TWUA, arbitrations and contract negotiations, New Deal legislation, Taft-Hartley, etc. In addition, we have acquired consultants' reports from Barnes Textile Associates from 1925 through 1971 which give a candid picture of mills and their managers in a particularly stressful period. Most, but not all, of these reports apply to New England mills.

There are other institutions in the New England area that collect material complementary to our own: the manuscript collection in the Baker Library, Harvard University, which contains voluminous records of New England textile firms chiefly from the 19th century through the 1930s, with some later exceptions. Lowell's textile history is a special focus of the Univ. of Lowell's Special Collections, and the Univ. of Massachusetts at Amherst collects union records, some of which are from the textile industry in this region. The Slater Mill Historic Site in Pawtucket, RI, and various historical societies and public libraries throughout New England also have important resources.

Although we try to present a balanced picture of the industry by collecting artifacts and information from all areas of the U.S., researchers seeking further regional information are best served by comprehensive resources in the Philadelphia/Delaware area for the Middle Atlantic states, and by the Southern Labor Archives and the several university archives in the South that have recognized the urgent need to collect

---

[4]See Helena Wright, ed., *Merrimack Valley Textile Museum: Guide to the Manuscript Collections* (New York, 1983).

in that region. The major archives of the Midwest are also important
sources for textile labor history. These and other institutions of value
are listed in a general bibliography of American textile history which
can be purchased from the MATH library ($4.20 plus postage).[5]

The museum encourages the study of American textile manufacturing through a yearly program of fellowships (for information, write
to the Director). It also sponsors and underwrites publications in the
field, co-sponsors conferences like the Lowell Conference on Industrial History, and has hosted a series of Textile History Conferences.

Access: The Museum Library is open 9 am–4 pm, Tuesday–Friday.
Other collections by appointment. For further information contact Clare
Sheridan, Museum of American Textile History, 800 Massachusetts
Avenue, North Andover, MA 01845; phone: (508) 686-0191.

---

[5]Clare Sheridan, "Textile Manufacturing in American History: A Bibliography," *Textile History, 18 (1987), 59–86.*

LABOR HISTORY SOURCES AT THE UNIVERSITY OF MASSACHUSETTS AT AMHERST

by
Ken Fones-Wolf

Massachusetts workers have engaged in some of the most important struggles in American labor history. From the strike of Lynn shoemakers in 1860 to the "Great Vacation" of Fall River textile workers
in 1875, to the Lawrence "Bread and Roses" Strike (1912), the conflicts
played out in Massachusetts have frequently held the attention of the
entire nation. Yet, until recently, there has been no systematic attempt
to document the Bay State's labor organizations. Instead, the primary
sources for these dramatic events have either been scattered throughout
the country or lost to posterity. The Archives & Manuscripts department of the Univ. of Massachusetts at Amherst hopes to ensure that
the state's more recent labor history will not suffer a similar fate.

The industry at the center of much of Massachusetts labor activity
was textile manufacturing. While Harvard's Baker Library and the
Museum of American Textile History held considerable company
documentation, little from the labor side existed, except in the labor
press, before current collecting began in 1984. The Univ. of Massachusetts previously had eight volumes of minutes (1900–1917) and
dues books (1895–1907) of the Loom Fixers Association of Fall River,
a small, elite craft union in the industry, and a minute book for the
Fall River Yarn Finishers Union (1919–1922). But the paucity of labor
records reflected both the lack of interest by repositories and the sporadic
strength of textile unions until the rise of the CIO.

In 1986, the University acquired the records of the New Bedford
Joint Board of the Textile Workers Union of America (TWUA), documenting the resurgence of New England textile unionism from 1940
through its decline in the 1970s. The records deposited include Joint
Board executive board minutes (1947–1967), some local union minutes,

Ken Fones-Wolf was an archivist in the University Library, University of Massachusetts at
Amherst, and currently is Manuscripts Curator at the West Virginia and Regional History
Collection at West Virginia University, Morgantown, WV.

correspondence with TWUA officers, and subject files. Also of note for a more detailed look at shop-floor conditions in New Bedford are files, arranged by companies, of arbitrations, grievances, and wage-stabilization board cases covering the years 1942 to 1977.

Equally valuable for studying the textile workers are the papers of J. William Belanger and Solomon Barkin. Belanger, whose labor career began when he received an organizer's commission for the AFL's United Textile Workers in 1932, eventually became the New England Regional Director and International Vice President of the TWUA, the second president of the Massachusetts CIO, and the first president of the combined state AFL and CIO in 1958. Particularly useful are four oversized scrapbooks which cover Belanger's career from 1934 through his final position as Director of the Massachusetts Dept. of Employment Security. These scrapbooks are especially enlightening on labor's political activities and, supplemented by pamphlets in the collection, document the state CIO's success in thwarting anti-labor referenda in 1948, the efforts to expel Communists from the labor movement, and the state labor movement's efforts on behalf of civil rights and of liberal politicians (including John F. Kennedy). Belanger's papers also contain some 150 photographs, many capturing Belanger with such important labor and political figures as Kennedy, Alben Barkley, George Meany, Philip Murray, and Walter Reuther.

Solomon Barkin's papers document a different level of labor leadership, that of a national labor intellectual. Barkin began his career in 1929 as an economist for the New York State Commission on Old Age Security. In 1933 he joined the Labor Advisory Board of the National Recovery Administration. Four years later, he became Director of Research for the TWUA, a position he held until 1963. Barkin also served on the National Planning Association, the War Production Board, and the CIO Fair Labor Standards Committee, among many other organizations. The papers consist principally of his voluminous writings on issues of importance to the labor movement. Included are TWUA internal memoranda, position papers, union-related publications, government testimony, and writings for popular magazines and scholarly journals. The breadth of subjects in Barkin's writings are equally impressive, ranging from deindustrialization, government planning, and old-age security to automation and his 1961 monograph, *Decline of the Labor Movement.*

In 1976 the TWUA merged with the Amalgamated Clothing Workers of America (ACWA). The university has acquired several relevant collections of ACWA in New England. The records of Boston Joint Board 1916 (1940–1979) include minutes (1942–1979) of the Board and several locals, financial records, contracts, and price lists for Boston area firms. Also included are three large scrapbooks covering the career of Joint Board president Joseph Salerno. An Italian immigrant, Salerno came to Boston in 1907 at age 10, participated in his first strike in 1911, and became an ACWA organizer in 1920. A second relevant collection is the records of ACWA Local 125 which undertook a major effort to organize New England's shirt workers in 1933. Local 125 was based principally in the shirt-making plants of Connecticut. Its records contain very thorough minutes of the executive board and the shop delegates council meetings (1928–1980), subject files, and several scrapbooks which contain organizing fliers, meeting notices, and other union communications (often printed in several languages) spanning the years 1933 to 1955. Finally, the university has acquired the collective bargaining files of the ACWA's New England Joint Board which had responsibility for clothing centers outside of Boston (principally Lawrence, Lowell, New Bedford, and Fall River) as well as some files from the New England Joint Board of the combined Amalgamated Clothing and Textile Workers Union created by the 1976 merger. Several of these collections have photographs documenting strikes, union picnics, informational picketing and boycotts, and union conventions.

Building trades unions have frequently been the backbone of Massachusetts organized labor when other workers found it difficult to unionize. In recent years, however, the building trades have come under attack from contractors. Witness, for instance, the 1988 election referendum seeking to repeal the state's prevailing wage law, originally passed in 1914. The Archives has been actively involved in documenting labor's successful campaign to defeat this threatening measure.

Taking advantage of the interest sparked by Mark Erlich's excellent history of Massachusetts carpenters, *With These Hands* (1986), the university acquired records of the carpenters unions of Western Massachusetts. Included are the records of the Holyoke District Council, United Brotherhood of Carpenters and Joiners of America (UBCJA) and its affiliated locals. These records span the period 1906 to 1976 (the date of the Council's merger with the Springfield District Council) and contain District Council minutes (1917–1972) and the minutes of Local 1881 (1923–1933), Local 656 (1942–1976), Amherst Local 1503 (1948–1976), and the French-speaking Holyoke Local 390 (1906–1975). Membership ledgers, agreements, financial ledgers, and some correspondence round out the collection, which comprise 10 boxes. The Greenfield (#549) and Northampton (#351) locals are a separate collection, making up what was formerly the Pioneer Valley District Council, with minutes and dues ledgers spanning the years 1899 to 1978.

Even more substantial and enlightening for the history of the UBCJA are the records of the Springfield District Council and Affiliates, totalling 23 linear feet. District Council minutes (1906-1968) and correspondence (1920-1968) offer insight into the attitudes of building trades unions toward New Deal programs, the housing boom of the post-World War II era, and the more recent assault on the union by contractors. These minutes and correspondence also give some idea of how the carpenters interacted with other unions in and beyond the building trades. Subject files document such developments as new technology, jurisdictional disputes, and the health and welfare fund. Also contained in the Springfield District Council records are the minutes and dues books of Chicopee Local 685 (1900-1968), Springfield English-language Local 177 (1916-1968), French-language Local 96 (1885-1959), and Westfield Local 222 (1952-1968). Taken together, these collections provide comprehensive documentation for the UBCJA in the Connecticut River Valley of Massachusetts.

For no other building trade union does the university have such coverage. The records of Northampton Local 36 of the International Brotherhood of Electrical Workers detail similar issues but only since the 1930s. One particularly intriguing part of those records is the documentation of a local debate over the merits of nuclear energy, especially since Local 36 members were employed at several of the power plants in the region. One other building trade union collection merits mention — the records of the Granite Cutters International Association (GCIA). The university, through the good offices of the George Meany Memorial Archives, acquired the fascinating minute books of the Quincy, Massachusetts-based GCIA's executive board spanning the years 1886 to 1954 as well as the union's monthly circulars (1886-1973), its newspaper (the *Granite Cutters Journal*, 1877-1978), and three over-size membership registers (1906-1932).

Of prime importance to the economy of the western part of the state until recently has been the machine-tool industry. The university acquired two important collections from one of the principal unions in the industry, the International Union of Electrical, Radio and Machine Workers (IUE). The records of Local 206, which represented over 1200 workers at the American Bosch plant in Springfield, span the years 1942 to 1986 and include executive board, membership, and union association meeting minutes (1947-1965), correspondence (1947-1979), contracts and negotiation files (1942-1985), grievances and arbitration cases (1948-1985), and publications from both the union and the company. In the 1970s American Bosch sold its interests to United Technologies which closed the plant in 1986 but not before sparking a lively effort to prevent the shutdown, some of which is documented in the 15 linear-foot collection.

The records of IUE Local 278 chronicle a similar fate for the region's machine-tool industry. Local 278, which at its peak represented some 400 workers at the Chapman Valve Company, suffered through a buyout of the company by the Crane Company of New York which eventually closed the plant in 1983. The union's minutes (1942–1983) provide a detailed look at Local 278, its relations with other unions, the tensions between the AFL and the CIO, and the local conditions which caused the local to abandon the left-wing United Electrical, Radio, and Machine Workers for the IUE in 1949. Also included is a history of Local 278's founding, written by its last president, Dennis Riel, who was a son of one of the union's pioneers. Finally, the university has a small collection from IUE Local 213, which represented workers at the Van Norman Machine Company in the 1950s.

The university has only begun to collect records related to public-employee collective bargaining. Through commission-member Harvey Friedman, files (1969–1973) of the Massachusetts Commission on Collective Bargaining came to the Archives. This commission wrote the state's public-employee collective bargaining law. Another important collection documents the University of Massachusetts Employees Association, an affiliate of the Massachusetts State Employees Association, which represented the university's clerical and technical workers from 1964 until 1977 when it was decertified and succeeded by the current union, an affiliate of the Massachusetts Teachers Association (MTA). The records include correspondence, minutes, newsletters, collective bargaining files, and subject files. Smaller and less comprehensive collections document the other campus unions, including the Massachusetts Society of Professors/MTA (1977–1988), AFSCME Local 1776, and the local of the American Federation of Teachers which lost its battle to represent faculty at the university.

The Archive's other holdings are grouped more by location than by industry. For the Connecticut River Valley region, the holdings include the Northampton Labor Council minutes (1933–1985), some records of the United Food and Commercial Workers Union Local 1459 (1950–1986), and contracts and arbitrations for International Brotherhood of Teamsters Locals 170 and 404. More substantial are the records of Local 48B of the Graphic Communications International Union (1951–1985), which represented about 1500 bindery workers at several Holyoke establishments. Noteworthy in the Local 48B records are materials dealing with a 1970s rank-and-file movement that eventually captured control of the union. The movement won support by raising

issues of importance to women and about occupational safety and
health, American foreign policy, and other progressive causes. For
scholars interested in the growth of rank-and-file activism in the 1970s,
this small collection offers some fascinating insights. Also dealing with
progressive issues are the records of the Center for Popular Economics,
a collective of radical economists and local community and labor activists. The Center's correspondence, curriculum materials, and research
files (1978-1986) chart the educational programs aimed at providing
a wide variety of activists with the basic tools for alternative economic
analysis and planning.

Another body of material that provides a unique viewpoint are the
records collected by United Paperworkers International Union activist
Raymond Beaudry, deposited at the university in 1985. Beaudry saved
not only some records from UPIU Eagle Lodge #1, but also the historical files of the American Writing Paper Co. (AWP), the trust formed
by several independent Holyoke-based paper industry firms in 1899.
Included are incorporation papers, board minutes, executive committee
minutes, executive files, and reorganization plans of this troubled company. Of greater importance for the purposes of labor history are the
"master labor files" of the company. AWP created a position for a "labor
czar" in 1937 to enable a single individual to negotiate with the unions
at each of its subsidiary plants which had maintained a good deal of
autonomy under the original trust agreement. These "master labor files"
include correspondence with the unions, contract negotiations, company surveys on wages and benefits, grievances, and background information on the various unions in the industry. They are fairly complete for the period from 1937 until AWP shut down its Holyoke
operations in the early 1960s. Also of interest are issues of the company's magazine, *Eagle A. Unity*, established in the era of welfare
capitalism (1918-1921).

The university's holdings of local business archives, in general, complement its labor holdings for the region. Two substantial collections
cover the local cutlery industry — the Northampton Cutlery Co. records
(1868-1986, 48 linear feet) and the Clement Co. records (1880-1956,
40 linear feet) — documenting wages, working conditions, the labor force,
and technological change in the local industry as well as the two principal efforts of local workers to organize: the first occurring in the era
of the Knights of Labor; the second (more successful) directed by UE
Local 274 in 1968. Other significant collections are the records of the
Rodney Hunt Co. (1865-1940, 120 linear feet), an Orange, Massachusetts
textile machinery and turbine manufacturer, and the records of the
George H. Gilbert Co. (1841-1931, 36 linear feet), a Ware woolen

manufacturing firm. Both collections provide data for the study of wages, working conditions, and the success of several family-owned, rural manufacturers in keeping their plants union-free.

Scholars, inspired by the innovative uses of account books by such historians as Mary Blewett and Thomas Dublin, are becoming increasingly aware of the insights contained in these sources. The university has a very interesting collection of account books and ledgers that complement substantial collections at the Essex Institute, the Henry Flynt Library at Deerfield, and several other repositories. Of particular interest are the ways that account books document the use of labor in what has become known as the period of protoindustrialization. The Archive's holdings cover the wages and conditions of work in such 18th and 19th century industries as palm-leaf hatmaking, shoemaking, agricultural labor, codfishing, and tanning leather. Taken together, these snippets illuminate the economic transformation of the Massachusetts countryside in the first century after independence.

Finally, the papers of two intellectuals document issues of importance to labor history in the 20th century. The papers of Harvey Swados (1936–1972, 23 linear feet) trace the thought of an important writer attempting to deal with the problem of worker alienation in the modern industrial era. His writings about assembly-line work influenced a generation of unionists and intellectuals, as evidenced in his correspondence with such people as Richard Hofstadter, C. Wright Mills, Irving Howe, Stan Weir, Ben Seligman, and James T. Farrell.

The papers of W. E. B. Du Bois shed light on the long and tumultous relationship of blacks and organized labor. Du Bois was one of the first scholars to document and denounce the role of unions in excluding blacks from economic opportunity. He repeatedly sought to place the plight of the black worker on the agenda of American trade unionism, and his writings effectively demonstrate the long-term harm effected by organized labor's shortsightedness on issues of race, beginning with the era of Reconstruction and continuing into the 1950s. His papers (1877–1963, totalling more than 170 linear feet) are a testament to one person's fight against the exclusionary mentality of American labor.

The holdings of the University of Massachusetts at Amherst have begun to provide the raw material for the story of the Bay State's labor history. There are yet many gaps to fill — Boston's important labor history is as yet largely undocumented; maritime workers are underrepresented, as are the furniture workers of Gardner, the steelworkers of Worcester, and the state's printers, among many other trades. Other repositories in the state, however, are also awakening to the task. The Immigrant City Archives in Lawrence has collected some of that city's labory history; the Baker Library has records of Lynn shoemakers; the Univ. of Massachusetts at Boston has records of United Packinghouse Workers Local 10 (1937–1968) and the Brockton Boot and Shoe Workers (1895–1930); the Massachusetts Historical Society has the minute books of the Boston Central Labor Union (1886–1917); and the Schlesinger Library has several collections relevant to female labor activism in the state. Perhaps when the next labor archives update is offered by *Labor History*, we will have an even better story to tell.

Access: The Archives & Manuscripts Dept., University of Massachussetts at Amherst is open 8:30am-5pm, Monday–Friday, and at other times by appointment. Inventories are available for nearly all the collections mentioned above. For further information contact Linda Seidman at the University Library, Univ. of Mass. at Amherst, Amherst, MA 01003; phone: (413) 545-2780.

THE CONNECTICUT LABOR ARCHIVES

by
Randall C. Jimerson

The Connecticut Labor Archives at the University of Connecticut Library is the only state-wide program to preserve historically significant records of Connecticut labor unions and individuals. The collecting policy emphasizes local unions and labor leaders within the state. These collections form part of the Historical Manuscripts and Archives Division's broad documentation of Connecticut history, particularly focusing on economic, industrial, social and political developments since about 1850. The Connecticut Labor Archives thus documents labor history as an aspect of state and local history, more than as part of vertically-integrated national and international union history.

The history of the labor movement in Connecticut had received little scholarly attention prior to 1980. A major reason for this neglect was that few labor records had been collected, preserved, or made available in archival repositories. Prior to 1979, when the Historical Manuscripts and Archives Division was founded, only the Bridgeport Public Library actively collected Connecticut labor records. Labor records soon became a top priority for Historical Manuscripts and Archives. The preponderance of business records among its early accessions made collection of labor sources essential in order to present a balanced perspective on economic development and industrial relations in Connecticut.

The Connecticut Labor Archives developed as part of a labor history consortium at the University of Connecticut. The consortium includes the Labor Education Center, the Center for Oral History, and the Historical Manuscripts and Archives Division, which cooperate in sharing information and resources in order to document the work and union organizing experiences of laboring men and women in Connecticut. Starting in 1980, the consortium began a major labor history ini-

---

Randall C. Jimerson is director of the Historical Manuscripts and Archives.

tiative that has included collecting labor records, conducting oral history interviews, and teaching labor history to union members. Each of these three projects received funding from separate programs in the National Endowment for the Humanities. Together, the three programs constitute an extensive effort.

The basic goal of the Connecticut Labor Archives Project, conducted from 1983 to 1985, was to develop a state-wide research center to serve labor unions and researchers. Supported by a major grant from the National Endowment for the Humanities, the project was designed to enable the Historical Manuscripts and Archives Division to develop closer ties with labor leaders and organizations, to locate historical labor records, and to preserve and process available materials through a depository arrangement. The decision to collect labor records on a geographical, rather than vertical, basis derived from our archival collecting policy and from the premise that locally-created records of any segment of society have special significance for the community and state in which such organizations conduct their public activities.

The Connecticut Labor Archives now provides scholars with an extensive collection of historical materials from labor leaders, unions, and workers. These archival records are the essential primary sources for any scholarly research on the history of the Connecticut labor movement. The Labor Archives grant project provided the necessary resources for the university to strengthen both its own research program and the ties of cooperation between the academic and labor communities. The project staff included a half-time labor historian, Cecelia Bucki, whose major responsibility was to establish contacts with labor leaders and unions, and a full-time labor archivist, Daria D'Arienzo, who assisted in field work and supervised processing.

Outreach to the labor community remained the top priority during the first few months of the project itself. On July 20, 1983, the executive board of the Connecticut AFL-CIO voted to endorse the project's goals, to encourage local unions to cooperate in preserving labor records, and to begin negotiations to deposit state AFL-CIO records in the University of Connecticut's Labor Archives. At the September 1983 Connecticut State AFL-CIO convention, the project staff set up an exhibit booth which included a small photograph display and project brochures. The State AFL-CIO executive board sponsored a resolution endorsing the project, which the convention delegates adopted after hearing a brief presentation by the project director.

The project's main success in acquisitions was with district and local unions of the International Association of Machinists and Aerospace Workers (IAM) and with the Connecticut State AFL-CIO office. Through personal contacts and negotiation, the labor historian secured a deposit agreement with the state's largest Machinists local in East Hartford. This opened the door to deposit agreements with IAM District 91 and with three other locals. These inter-related collections constitute a valuable core of records for one of the most influential unions in Connecticut.

Securing a deposit agreement with the state AFL-CIO required lengthy discussions and negotiations. During this time, we were able to inventory records in the attic and basement storage areas of the headquarters building. This collection is extremely valuable, both for its wealth of information about the Connecticut labor movement and as the symbolic center of the Labor Archives collections. It ensures an ongoing relationship between the state AFL-CIO leadership and the Labor Archives staff. The state AFL-CIO staff continue to make yearly deposits of archival records.

The Connecticut Labor Archives Project enabled the University of Connecticut to build an important research collection of primary sources relating to the labor movement in Connecticut. During the project, the Archives acquired 15 collections of union records and five collections of personal papers of labor leaders. Most of these collections were fully processed by the project archivist and student assistants during the grant period. Other labor collections continue to be added to this nucleus. The Connecticut Labor Archives thus represents an important new resource for labor historians and others interested in labor-management relations in Connecticut.

The Connecticut State AFL-CIO deposited its headquarters office files in the Labor Archives in 1983, with additional materials deposited yearly. These files, which include some state AFL materials as far back as 1938, date mainly from the merger and formation of the Connecticut State Labor Council, AFL-CIO, in 1957. The nearly 150 linear feet of records include files of Joe Rourke, John Driscoll, Betty Tianti, and other AFL-CIO officials.

Central labor councils are represented by records of the Greater Hartford Labor Council, AFL-CIO (GHLC). This collection of records includes files of the Hartford Central Labor Union-AFL (1947–57), the Greater Hartford Industrial Union Council-CIO (1948–57), the GHLC (1957–82), the Royal Industrial Union (1946–77), and the Greater Hartford Building and Construction Trades Council (1967–78).

The most significant grouping of local labor union records consists of records from local lodges of the International Association of Machinists and Aerospace Workers. These include records of Aeronautical Industrial District Lodge 91 and four IAM locals. District 91 records include 95 linear feet of materials (1947–82), including voluminous legal records and court proceedings resulting from a 1960 strike against United Aircraft Corp. (now the Pratt and Whitney division of United Technologies Corp.). Records of Lodges 743 (Windsor Locks) and 1746 (East Hartford) also contain strike information. Other collections include records of Lodge 700 (Middletown) and Lodge 707 (North Haven).

The Labor Archives contains records of several other local unions. The United Association of Plumbers and Steamfitters is represented by records of two locals: Local 76 (Hartford) (1909–83), 9 linear feet; and Local 305 (New London-Norwich) (1934–64), 2 linear feet. Building trades unions also include records of the Brotherhood of Carpenters and Joiners. AFL-CIO, Local 210. This Stamford union has preserved minutes of meetings and other records from 1901 to 1984. The Bakery, Confectionery and Tobacco Workers International Union, AFL-CIO, is represented by records of the Waterbury chapter (1892, 1921–77). The only item obtained from the United Telegraph Workers International Local 47 (East Hartford) is the union's 1942 charter.

Two small union collections from the turn of the century, both transferred from the Connecticut State Library, include a minute-book (1896-1905) of the Allied Printing Trades Council of Hartford, and a small quantity of records (1901–04) from the International Union of Steam Engineers, Local 62, of Danbury.

Labor education groups include two important organizations. Records of the Diocesan Labor Institute (1944–65) indicate the involvement of Catholic leaders in labor activities. Records of the University of Connecticut's Labor Education Center (1947–70) indicate the extent of activities of this important program to support workers' education.

These records of labor organizations and local unions are supplemented by personal papers of labor leaders. These collections sometimes include official files of local unions, but they usually also contain a more personal and, therefore, sometimes richer perspective on the labor movement. Personal papers of labor leaders in the Connecticut Labor Archives include: Henry Becker, organizer for the Amalgamated Clothing Workers of America and the Machinists; Merlin D. Bishop, labor educator with the United Automobile Workers; Roger N. Borrup, official with the Hartford Typographical Union, ITU Local 127; Andrew Frank Daniels, sub-district director of the Sheetworkers union, Fairfield; and Jeremiah Driscoll, president of Royal Industrial Union, UAW (Hartford).

Other labor leaders' collections include the personal papers of: Daniel J. Gallagher, Eastern Connecticut regional director of the Textile Workers Union of America; Ralph J. Pancallo of the New Britain

Typographical Union; Eugene J. St. Pierre, an official with the International Brotherhood of Electrical Workers; Joseph Sposato, president of Local 110, Textile Workers of America; and Nicholas J. Tomassetti, international representative of the United Electrical, Radio and Machine Workers Union.

The Connecticut Labor Archives has one major collection of oral history. The Connecticut Workers and Technological Change project, sponsored by the Center for Oral History at the University of Connecticut, compiled 152 interviews, which have been transcribed and indexed.

An unpublished listing, "Labor Records in Historical Manuscripts & Archives," is available through the Archives. One guide has been published: Michelle Palmer, ed., *Catalogue of Interviews: Connecticut Workers and a Half Century of Technological Change, 1930–1980, Oral History Project* (Storrs, CT 1983).

Most collections in the Connecticut Labor Archives have been deposited under an agreement based on the national AFL-CIO model deposit agreement. In most cases, materials are restricted for 15 years from date of creation. Grievance and arbitration files and similarly confidential materials are subject to more stringent restrictions. Other materials more than 15 years old are open for research use.

Access: during the academic year, Historical Manuscripts and Archives is open Monday–Friday, 1–4:30 pm. Summer and vacation hours are somewhat reduced, but appointments can be made in advance. Copying services are available, for a modest fee. For best service and assistance, it is advisable to write or call in advance. Contact Randall C. Jimerson, Historical Manuscripts and Archives, Box U-205, University of Connecticut, Storrs, CT 06269; phone (203) 486-2893.

SOURCES FOR BUSINESS AND LABOR HISTORY
IN THE
BRIDGEPORT PUBLIC LIBRARY

by
Mary K. Witkowski

In 1977 a project was initiated at the Bridgeport Public Library Historical Collections to collect labor and business records of local Bridgeport industries. The project, funded through a grant from the National Historical Publications and Records Commission, was administered by David Palmquist, former Head of the Historical Collections, and Marc Stern, labor records specialist. Throughout the next year, local labor unions and companies were contacted, and labor and business records were requested. The resulting collection comprises manuscript materials on an area of Bridgeport history that had been lacking in the Historical Collections. Many labor historians have since used the collection, and have admired the foresight that the Bridgeport Public Library used in securing these records.

Bridgeport Public Library Historical Collections is probably the only institution in the U.S. to house both a labor history collection and a circus collection. The focus of the latter, P. T. Barnum, resided in Bridgeport most of his life and helped develop Bridgeport as an industrial city. The 1851 project that was initiated by Barnum, and his friend, William Noble, still sets the scene for Bridgeport today. It was Barnum's idea to establish East Bridgeport, lay out streets, build housing, a new park, and attract businesses into the area. Companies such as Wheeler and Wilson Sewing Machines and Elias Howe's factory moved into East Bridgeport.

This early development of East Bridgeport prompted other factories to set up in Bridgeport. Many of these companies, such as Bridgeport Brass (1865), Warner Brothers (1874), Bullard Co. (1880), Union

Mary K. Witkowski is Dept. Head, Historical Collections.

Metallic Cartridge Co. (1867), have donated papers that are now housed in the library's collection.

World Wars I and II helped to build the munitions and defense industry in Bridgeport. Remington Arms and Union Metallic Cartridge Co. grew enormously during the first World War. The Locomobile Co. producing Riker trucks and the Lake Torpedo Boat Co. were just two of the companies that thrived during this period. World War II helped to provide Bridgeport companies with many defense contracts, and contributed to the growth of Sikorsky Aircraft and other companies.

The manuscript collections housed in the Bridgeport Public Library Historical Collections reflect the changing face of labor in Bridgeport. As Palmquist stated in a 1977 article in the *Bridgeport Post*, "the primary purpose of the project will be to save important business records from loss, deterioration, and destruction. There has never been a program to collect these specific materials in Bridgeport. The library's project, will, therefore, launch the first comprehensive drive to locate and accession these records and to continue that process once the initial project is finished."

The project channeled a surge of 20th century material into the Historical Collections, and while the pace of accessioning these materials has slowed, the cataloguing of the collections will continue into the next decade.

The following is a partial list of the business and labor records housed in the Historical Collections:

1) Business Records
   — Bridgeport Brass Co., 1865–c.1980, comprises approximately 27 linear feet of papers, including correspondence, catalogues, advertising art, and photographs.
   — The Warner Corset Co. (Warnaco, Inc.) Collection, 1874–1980 (unprocessed), contains account books, advertising art, publicity, photographs, and other miscellaneous papers.
   — Coulter & McKenzie Machine Co. collection (machinists), 1878–1984, contains approximately 5 linear feet of photographs, and 4 linear feet of account books and stock books.
   — Bullard Co. (machine tool manufacturers), 1874–1985, contains minute books (1894–1968), 3 linear feet of advertising department records, 12 linear feet of photographs of machines, 7 linear feet of product information.
   — Sprague Meter Co. (gas and special meter manufacturers), 1915–1927, 3 linear feet of materials, including factory notes (1915–1927).
   — Locomobile Co./Riker Trucks, c.1900–1928, this collection contains 20 linear feet of correspondence, advertising, and photographs.
   — A. W. Burritt Co. (lumber), c.1890–c.1980, 1½ linear feet, includes Ar-

ticles of Association, salary records, and operating statements, plus miscellaneous materials.

2) Labor Records

Many of these records were collected in the Labor History Project. Although the following listing is not comprehensive, it includes small collections that may be of interest to researchers:

— Central Labor Union, 1914–1954, includes constitution and list of affiliated unions.
— Mine, Mill and Smelter Workers International Union, Local 623, 1940–1950, includes Local 320 (Bridgeport Brass, 1944–1950), Local 601 (Belknap Manufacturing, 1946–1947), Local 719 (unidentified employer, 1950).
— Louis J. Santoianni (United Electrical Workers, Local 203, and International Union of Electrical Workers, Local 203, General Electric Company), 1945–1975, 1 linear foot of pamphlets and agreements.
— Carpenter's District Council records, 1905–1919, includes financial receipts of Carpenter Locals 115, 1013, and 1520.
— Brass Worker's Federal Labor Union, Local 24411, 1955–1976, includes financial reports and agreements with Bridgeport Brass Co.
— Records of the International Association of Fire Fighters, Local 1426 (Fairfield Fire Dept.), including minutes and financial records, 1962–1973.
— Bricklayers Union, Local 2, c.1890–c.1930.

3) Organizational Records

The following are some organizational records that would be of interest to business and labor historians:

— Bridgeport Area Chamber of Commerce, 1915–1960, 4 linear feet.
— Stratford Chamber of Commerce, 1950–1974, 5 linear feet.
— Manufacturers Association of Southern Connecticut, 1906–1984, 12 linear feet, includes bulletins, 1906–1968, wage reports, 1919–1926, and other materials.
— Connecticut Foreign Trade Association, 1920–1977.

4) Personal Papers

In the collections are the papers of local Bridgeport citizens who were influential in local business and labor organizations:

— Herman W. Steinkraus (businessman; president, Bridgeport Brass Co.; president, U.S. Chamber of Commerce), c.1930–1974.
— Arthur Clifford (businessman; president, Burritt Lumber Co.; chairman, Redevelopment Agency), 1921–1983.
— DeVer H. Warner (businessman; president, Warner Brothers Co., corset manufacturers), 1901–1911 (unprocessed).
— Jasper McLevy (Socialist Mayor; candidate for Governor and Congress), c.1900–1906, c.1930–1961.

We are fortunate in having a large collection of photographs of factories, workers, products, and other Bridgeport scenes. Photographs such as those of workers in Remington Arms, the Locomobile, Bullard Machines, and Warner Corset Co. are available for researchers.

There are several runs of Bridgeport newspapers available, 1795 to date, many of which are on microfilm after 1861. Among the microfilmed newspapers is the *Bridgeport Herald* (1890–1973), which devoted many articles to labor unions. A project is currently underway to film the *Bridgeport Times Star* (1918–1941), which was also sympathetic to the working class. A large newspaper clipping file on Bridgeport and Fairfield County (c.1935–1977), containing background information on Bridgeport companies, politics, and ethnic groups is located in the collection.

A *Brief Guide to the Historical Collections* is available free upon request.

Access: Hours of service are currently Monday and Wednesday, Noon–8 pm, Tuesday and Thursday, 10 am–6 pm, and Friday, 9 am–5 pm; also Saturday, 9 am–5 pm during fall and winter months. Reference inquiries about the Bridgeport Public Library Historical Collections should be directed to Mary K. Witkowski, Bridgeport Public Library, 925 Broad St., Bridgeport, CT 06604, phone: (203) 576-7417.

LABOR HISTORY RESOURCES AT NEW YORK UNIVERSITY

1.) The Tamiment Institute/Ben Josephson Library

by
Dorothy Swanson

The Tamiment Institute/Ben Josephson Library, America's first library devoted to collecting material for the study of socialism, was begun in 1906 as the library of the Rand School of Social Science and continues operations today, a vital repository of rare socialist and trade union documents, books and periodicals. Renamed the Tamiment Institute Library in 1963 (after the Rand School's summer camp that underwrote the library's expenses for many years), the library was incorporated into New York University library's system and in 1973 physically moved into NYU's Bobst Library complex.

Although the Rand School was virtually the first workers' school (Ruskin College at Trenton, Missouri, also had been founded in 1906 but failed shortly thereafter), it was not a new idea. The founding of the Rand School was the natural culmination of a number of activities by socialists — open-air meetings, soap-box addresses, study groups, literary societies, and the discussion of "live issues" during the internal struggles of the Socialist Party. The Rand School was named for its benefactor, Carrie Rand, a wealthy widow who was sympathetic to the socialist cause and turned SP leaders' dream of opening a school into reality by bequeathing a trust fund for such a purpose to the American Socialist Society. The New York socialists were mostly well-educated, articulate German and Eastern European Jewish immigrants who placed a high value on education and felt that the way to gain political advan-

Dorothy Swanson is Director of the Tamiment/Ben Josephson Library.
Debra E. Bernhardt is Archivist of the Robert F. Wagner Labor Archives, and Head of Archival Collections, Bobst Library, New York University.

tage was to extend socialist education to as large a part of the public as possible.

From the very first the library was an important component of the school. In the first year the library committee was given permission to select books at a total cost of $1000 and periodicals not to exceed the sum of $125 annually. This was a considerable expenditure from the Rand trust fund whose income never exceeded more than $5000 to $6000 annually. In addition to the books purchased, individuals participating in Socialist Party functions at the Rand School donated pamphlets, works of Marx, and efforts by their preferred socialist theoreticians. The library's primary audience was envisioned as Rand School students composed of SP members, working people, and immigrants, especially the Jewish immigrants who had been flooding into New York at the turn of the century at the rate of over 100,000 persons each year. One of the great events in the life of the Jewish working-class community on the Lower East Side was the election to Congress of socialist Meyer London, in 1914 and again in 1916 and 1920. In 1936, ten years after his death, the Rand School Library was renamed the Meyer London Memorial Library.

Socialism was a topic of immediate importance to the working-class patrons of the library. They were working 10 hour days in sweat shops, and then trying to improve themselves with classes by night. The library tried to meet this demand by actively soliciting periodicals and books representing the diverse range of socialist thought in the early 1900s. A healthy heterodoxy was encouraged from the first at the Rand School Library, so holdings grew eclectically mirroring the full panorama of contemporary radical tendencies. Home grown radicals Eugene Debs, Edward Bellamy, Clarence Darrow, and, New Yorker Morris Hillquit were included on the shelves. The works of Karl Kautsky, August Bebel, and other German Social Democrats were also promoted by the library: one of the Rand School's aims was to study in depth the socialist theories then developing on the European continent.

By 1917, the Rand School had outgrown its 19th Street headquarters and took over a six story building at 7 East 15th Street vacated by the Young Womens' Christian Association. Dubbed a "People's House," it was modeled after the center in Brussels, Belgium, with an auditorium, bookstore, and cafeteria; space not needed for school operations was rented to sympathetic organizations. The original concept of the Rand School was expanded to include adult school general studies classes, trade union shop stewards training, popular lectures, choral singing, dramatic and musical productions, and functions usually associated with a settlement house. A communications line was run from the People's House to the Socialist Party's radio station, WEVD (the acronym stands for Eugene Victor Debs), so that lectures and concerts could be broadcast live from the new Debs Auditorium.

With the transition to the new scope of activities under way at the People's House, America's first socialist library broadened its holdings to include all of the social sciences, and many other works of general interest as well. The American Socialist Society instructed the Publication Department to supply the library with copies of all books and pamphlets published by the Rand School Press. The library also made energetic efforts to acquire pamphlet literature. In the early years of the Rand School pamphlets often provided the only available English translations of works by Kautsky, Plekhanov, Lenin, and the leading Marxist theoreticians of continental Europe and Russia. Throughout its 84 year history to date, the Library has attempted to collect works on socialism from every conceivable point of view. Communist writings and newspapers were impartially collected even in the years when the Communist International had branded rival socialist organizations as "Social Fascists." For this breadth of vision, the Rand School was rewarded by the government with harrassment.

In 1919 New York State Senator Clayton R. Lusk's Committee, having been voted $50,000 to investigate what it considered "subversive activities," targeted the Rand School. A stated aim of the Committee was to show that "whereas in Europe there is a wide split between the Bolshevik elements and the big bulk of the Socialist Party, in the United States the split is in theory rather than in practice and all are working for a common end — establishment of a Soviet government in America." The first "official" attack was the result of an anti-war, anti-draft, anti-Liberty loan pamphlet written by Scott Nearing titled "The Great Madness" and published by the Rand School Press in August 1917. Six months after the pamphlet's publication, Nearing and the society were indicted under the Espionage Act. The ASS was fined $3000 and after a series of appeals which failed, friends of the school raised the money in three days by each contributing $1.00. Launching a second attack, the Lusk committee armed with a search warrant raided the Rand School on Saturday, June 22, 1919. The raiding party numbered 55 men, including three squads of uniformed police and ten state police. Three rooms had been reserved for the operation at the nearby Prince George Hotel and the raiders had the foresight to bring three moving vans. Government harrassment eased as the Red Scare ended.

Starting in the 1920s, and into the 1930s, first under the directorship of Alexander Trachtenberg and later Solon De Leon, the Rand School Library augmented its labor holdings through the Research

Department's publishing activities: the *American Labor Year Book* (1916–32); a monthly index of labor periodicals (1926–1955); and the *American Labor Who's Who* (1925). The year book included summaries of contract negotiations and trade union conventions, and reports on regional and horizontal coordination and cooperation among unions. The *Index of Labor Periodicals* provided a listing of unions publishing newspapers as well as a guide to specific articles appearing in the labor press. Throughout this period, the library was collecting materials of an archival nature as well: Socialist Party records, the papers of American labor figures, pamphlets, and newspapers that would otherwise have been lost. The Rand School had always sought to establish close ties with the labor movement. William Green, Samuel Gompers' successor as head of the American Federation of Labor, was personally close to or politically allied with some of the key supporters of the Rand School.

The cost of operations, however, perennially exceeded the school's assets. In 1920, the Rand School's financial situation was especially desperate. The school had just waged and won a costly two-year battle against the New York State Lusk Committee's attempt to close the school by injunction. With operating capital at an all-time low, fundraising was a major concern. The school had been surviving financially through various means, partly supported by the bookstore, the Rand School Press, the cafeteria, and various donations. At that time, it was customary for unions to maintain resorts for the use of their members. In the summer of 1919, Bertha Mailly, executive secretary of the school from 1912 onward, visited Unity House, a resort owned by a local of the International Ladies Garment Workers Union in Bushkill, Pennsylvania. While there, she learned of an adjacent 2106 acre tract of land for sale. She immediately made a deposit on the property and started an ultimately successful fund drive to purchase and build a camp. Called after an old Indian name for the area, Tamiment Camp opened in the summer of 1921. Beginning with its first season, the camp contributed substantially to the Rand School.

Never self-supporting, the school came to rely increasingly on Camp Tamiment for its survival. From 1937 until the school's demise in 1956, Camp Tamiment paid from 50–75% of the school's yearly expenses. A large part of the Camp's success was due to the fact that it had tax-exempt status based on the Tamiment Institute's educational and cultural programs. Since 1936 the Tamiment Institute had been sponsoring symposia and conferences principally at Camp Tamiment. It also conducted college essay contests, a publications program, and in 1950 inaugurated an annual book award.

The Tamiment Institute gave immediate priority to revitalizing the library and keeping it open to the research public. The annual reports from its first two years of operation speak of acquiring a professional staff, publishing a monthly *Library Bulletin*, and cooperating with other libraries to pool resources and microfilm complete runs of old socialist and labor newspapers before they disintegrated. An ad hoc committee was set up in the metropolitan area in a project aimed at preserving trade union materials for scholarly uses and the library was "becoming nationally recognized for the research services it offers to students and scholars." During this period the Library acquired the material assembled by the Fund for the Republic on the operations and ideology of the American Communist Party. Daniel Bell's scholarly investigation of communist subversion of American trade unions also assembled books, interviews, and investigative reports on the subject, which the author donated to the library.

In the 1950s the government began challenging the camp's tax-exempt status. In February 1963, after several appeals, the People's Educational Camp Society lost its case with the IRS. Camp Tamiment was eventually sold to a commercial conglomerate. The library, now named the Tamiment Institute Library, was given, together with a commitment of continued support, to New York University Libraries. The university agreed to maintain the collection as a separate entity and to keep the collection open to the public.

It is as a research collection that the library is best known today. But for roughly its first 30 years the Rand School Library saw its primary objectives as twofold: 1) to serve as the reading room of preference for Socialist Party members, trade unionists and working people, generally; and, 2) to serve the New York City labor movement, by providing vital facts, figures and the accumulating practical experience of unions nationally and internationally. A third function, now paramount in importance, evolved over many years, namely, to serve scholars by collecting political material that the great majority of even university libraries considered ephemera. Pamphlets and periodicals focusing on labor questions were always very much in demand. Aside from the ephemera—the newspapers, pamphlets, leaflets—the library also built up a sizable non-circulation book collection. During its early days, noted intellectuals visiting the school—Charles Beard, John Dewey, John Strachey, Sidney Hook—began the practice of donating first editions and autographed volumes of their work to the Rand School Library. Accumulating and increasing in value over time, the pamphlets, the extensive labor periodical collections, the treasures (Eugene Debs scrapbooks, among them), and the personal papers donated to the library gave it within a very few years sufficient credibility to begin attracting trade union donors. By the late 1930s it was for its labor collection, not its superb depth in works on socialism, that the Rand School Library was most widely known. The building, 7 East 15th Street, had always housed labor and related organizations. The editorial office of the *New Leader*, which continued the old *Socialist Call*, had offices there. The American Labor Conference on International Affairs, a research organization established in 1943 by a "group of internationally-minded American labor leaders and progressives," allied itself with the school. Including American and European scholars as well as representatives of the European labor movement residing in the United States during World War II, the conference engaged in research on international economic and political problems for the benefit of the American labor movement. After World War II the American Labor Archives and Research Institute was established at the Rand School and included among its sponsors William Green of the American Federation of Labor and Philip Murray of the Congress of Industrial Organizations. When the Tamiment Institute began operating the library it built up the collections to new research strengths. Ever eager to play a role in the preserving of labor union records, a conference was initiated by the Tamiment Institute in November 1958 which was instrumental in the passage of the 1959 AFL-CIO resolution in support of labor union archives. In 1960 *Labor History* was launched and still shares the library's premises. These earlier attempts at becoming a repository for labor union records came to official fruition in April 1977. Stephen Vladeck, labor lawyer and secretary-treasurer of the Tamiment Institute, was instrumental in bringing the New York City Central Labor Council and New York University together in the founding of the Robert F. Wagner Labor Archives.

The first step in making the Rand School's collections more widely available to the research community had begun as soon as NYU acquired the library by incorporating cataloging records for the books into the catalogues of the university's libraries. With the increasing growth of computerization, and the inclusion of non-book materials in data-bases, the existence of many of the library's "rarer" holdings are being brought to the attention of researchers and students. In 1984 a U.S. Department of Education Title II-C two year award for cataloging books and serials began. To date the library's non-circulation book collection of over 20,000 has been cataloged, as has approximately half of the library's 5000 serial titles. A National Endowment for the Humanities grant to the Research Libraries Group enabled NYU to add 136 manuscript and archival records to the RLIN data base. The library currently receives approximately 800 current serials and maintains an extensive vertical file collection containing 500,000 pamphlets, leaflets, and internal documents from labor and left organizations. The personal papers of a number of leading radicals, communists, and labor officials are also maintained. Recent significant acquisitions include the personal papers of Max Shachtman, Elizabeth Gurley Flynn, and Mark Starr. In response to the increased interest in non-print documentation the library has begun strengthening its oral history collection. In 1981, the Jacob and Bessye Blaufarb Videotape Library of the American Labor Movements was established with the goal of preserving the personalities and memories of American labor activists and radicals.

Tamiment Institute President Ben Josephson, Bertha Mailly's assistant at Camp Tamiment and then successor, spent his retirement at the library. It was his efforts which were principally responsible for preserving the Rand School Library and effecting its transfer to NYU. In recognition of the 50 years of service he gave to Tamiment his name was added to the library's in 1981.

2.) The Robert F. Wagner Labor Archives

by
Debra E. Bernhardt

The Robert F. Wagner Labor Archives was founded in 1977 to preserve and disseminate the history of labor in New York, the city Samuel Gompers called "the cradle of the modern labor movement." A special project of the Tamiment Library of which it is a part, the Wagner Archives was jointly initiated by New York University, the Tamiment Institute, and the New York City Central Labor Council (AFL-CIO). The Archives is named for the late New York Senator whose papers are not located at the Archives, but who, as chief sponsor of the 1935 National Labor Relations Act, played an important role in the histories of the unions whose records are located there.

The development of the Wagner Labor Archives collection benefitted from the National Historical Publications and Records Commission (NHPRC) funded New York City Labor Records Survey, conducted as a cooperative project with the George Meany Memorial Archives and Cornell's Labor-Management Documentation Center.

Between 1984 and 1986, Wagner field archivists visited over 400 metropolitan-area labor organizations to collect their organizational histories and to inventory existing records. Summaries of the information gathered by the survey will soon be available to scholars across the country through the Research Library Information Network (RLIN) and the New York County guides of the Historic Documents Inventory.

The survey provided the basis for a rational, cooperative, and ongoing "documentation strategy" of New York labor: the records of over 75 organizations were designated for permanent preservation at either NYU or Cornell. A grant from New York State allowed the Archives to microfilm a large number of historically important union minutes identified by the survey, copies of which have been deposited at NYU, Cornell, and the George Meany Archives. Current state funding extends the work of identifying and preserving significant labor documentation upstate in Rochester and Utica and downstate in the Long Island and Lower Hudson counties.

As a result of these activities and of the cooperation of organized labor, the collections of the Robert F. Wagner Labor Archives over its first decade have grown to reflect the importance and diversity of the city's labor movement. The Archives serves as the repository for the records of many of New York's central bodies and labor coalitions including the New York State AFL-CIO (1938–1983), the New York City Central Labor Council and its AFL and CIO predecessors (1933–1983), the Jewish Labor Committee (1933–1980) founded first as a relief and rescue operation by the needle trades after Hitler came to power, the Union Label and Service Trades of Greater New York (1911–1980s), and the New York Committee on Occupational Safety and Health.

Other strengths of the collection reflect New York's unique economy and arenas where its trade union movement has broken new ground such as performing arts unionism. The city's entertainment industry is the focus of a number of collections: in legitimate theater through the rich and voluminous records of Actors' Equity Association, dating to the union's founding in 1913; the Actors' Fund, established for the mutual benefit of sick and indigent actors in 1882; Equity Library Theater, a showcase for young talent; the United Scenic Artists, Local 829, Brotherhood of Painters and Allied Trades (1918–1975), representing set and lighting designers, costume and make-up artists; the archives of the American Guild of Variety Artists record a membership so diverse as to include go-go dancers, stand-up comics, circus and ice-capade performers. The Archives has microfilmed minutes of the following performing arts unions which are now or will soon be available at NYU as well as at the George Meany Archives and Cornell's Labor-

Management Documentation Center: Actor's Equity Association (1913–1982); American Federation of Musicians Local 802 (1922–1985); American Guild of Musical Artists (1936–1980); Associated Actors and Artistes of America (1919–1985); Musical Mutual Protective Union (1863–1910); Screen Actors' Guild; United Scenic Artists. Finally, the collection of The Labor Theater dramatizes, through scripts and business records, the activities of a small union-oriented performing troupe in the early 1980s.

Public employee collective bargaining is another strength in the Wagner Labor Archives collection. In 1984 the Archives acquired 500 linear feet of records from the Transport Workers Union documenting its growth from 1933 to the present. The collection includes the records of both NYC transit Local 100 and the national union it fostered. The life and work of the union's founder and colorful president, Michael J. Quill—including his councilmanic papers and the radical Irish immigrant organizations he supported—leap from the pages deposited at the Archives. Over 300 cans of film and 500 reels of audiotape attest to Quill's astute use of the media in the early years of television. The collection as a whole is an untapped lode for the history of the CIO, ethnicity, labor, and politics.

Public employee organizing on the Federal, state, and local levels can be researched through several other Archives' accessions: the records of the New York Metro Area Postal Union (1907–1981); the microfilmed minutes of the pioneering Civil Service Forum (1931–1968); the records of the Union of State Employees (1937–1983). The oral history interviews and materials Bernard and Jewel Bellush collected in researching their book, *Union Power and New York: Victor Gotbaum and District Council 37*, microfilmed minutes of District Council 37 (1959–1968), and the records of a number of American Federation of State, County, and Municipal Employees (AFSCME) affiliates round out the history of municipal labor.

Public employee unionism overlaps into another area of research strength: white collar unionism. Among the records of AFSCME District Council 37 affiliates at the Wagner Archives are those unions representing librarians, social workers, architects, and engineers. The first sortie of the Communications Workers of America (CWA) into the public sector, Local 1180, represents managers and supervisors who work for the city of New York. The work lives of public school teachers and university professors are richly documented in the records of the United Federation of Teachers, Local 2, AFT (1938–present) and the Professional Staff Congress (1938–1980). The records of two organizations, Engineering and Professional Guild, Local 66, and the Engineers

Association of ARMA, IUE Local 418, document engineers in the private sector. Microfilmed minutes of pink collar office and communication workers are available for the Office and Professional Employees International Union and Local 153, its New York affiliate (1941-1981), as well as telephone workers at AT&T Longlines organized by CWA Local 1150 (1940-1978).

Craft union records constitute another strength of the Archives collection. Documenting the building trades are microfilmed minutes of the influential IBEW Local 3 (1902-1982), minutes of Tunnelworkers Local 174 (1939-1975) and Paperhangers Local 490 (1884-1952), and the personal papers of painters union activists Louis Weinstock (1925-1978) and Frank Schonfeld (1945-1973). Labor in the city's printing industry is represented in the microfilmed minutes of the Allied Printing Trades Council of New York State (1897-1985), Eureka Lodge 434 of the IAM representing machinists who produced, maintained or repaired printing machinery (1908-1977), and Mailers Local 6 (1896-1954). The records of the Lithographers and Photo-Engravers Local 1-P (1904-1975) include complete membership and apprenticeship files which will enable social historians to trace the changing ethnic composition of a craft beleaguered by technological change. The personal papers of Betsy Wade (1975-1984) cover the years of her "insurgent" leadership of Newspaper Guild Local 3. Finally, the Wagner Archives is repository for the NYC chapter of the National Writers Union.

The extensive files of District 65 UAW (1933-1970) are a rich source for the history of the CIO in New York in the wholesale and retail industry. The political and social milieux of this left-wing ethnically diverse organization are also captured in over 50,000 photonegatives taken between 1939 and 1968 by rank and file members of the union's camera club. An even more voluminous collection of over 100,000 photonegatives represents the opus of Sam Reiss who served as photographer for many NYC unions between 1948 and 1975. Another collection of 7000 photonegatives documents the history of teacher collective bargaining between 1947 and 1977.

In addition to these photonegative collections, the combined nonprint holdings of the Tamiment Library and the Wagner Archives comprise 43 photo collections including approximately 87,000 prints, over 800 reels of film, some 3000 audio tapes, and several thousand posters, scrapbooks, songbooks, buttons, and ephemera. A preliminary guide summarizes photo holdings. The largest single audio collection is the Oral History of the American Left including over 750 interviews spanning the political spectrum (a published guide is available for purchase from the Tamiment Library, $5 for institutions, $3 for individuals). In the early 1970s, students of Herbert Gutman went to nursing homes and union retiree associations to search out interviewees for the NYC Immigrant Labor History Project: the resulting 285 interviews are available at the Archives. Another collection of over 150 interviews with working New Yorkers resulted from the Archives' production of an 8-part documentary radio series for National Public Radio, broadcast in 1981: the resulting "New Yorkers at Work: Oral Histories of Life, Labor and Industry" curriculum unit is now available with accompanying study guides for classroom use (for $27 including postage) and forms the catalyst for an innovative archival outreach program which has linked over 90 local unions with 123 public high schools in NYC. Other major oral history collections include those commissioned by the United Federation of Teachers, the American Federation of Teachers, the Civil Service Technical Guild, and the New York City Central Labor Council.

A collection of over 60 videotapes on labor history and radical politics including vintage films from the 1930s and documentaries and drama produced since the 1960s were acquired with a grant from the New York State Council on the Arts and funding from the Jacob and Bessye Blaufarb Endowment. These films can be viewed at the Avery Fisher Center for Music and Media in NYU's Bobst Library. The Blaufarb Endowment also provides seed money for independent video productions on left and labor topics.

Unpublished finding aids have been prepared for most Archives' collections; machine-searchable inventories exist for some of the more voluminous collections. Bibliographic records in the MARC-Archives and Manuscripts Control format appear in the Research Libraries Information Network (RLIN) data-base. The Archives published a selected bibliography of New York City labor history compiled by Robert Wechsler which is available for purchase ($3 by mail). In addition, the Archives publishes an occasional newsletter, *New York Labor Heritage*. A poster/brochure and library bulletin summarizing the Archives' program and holdings is also available.

Access: During most of the school year the library and archives are open to the public Monday and Thursday, 10 am–9 pm, Tuesday, Wednesday, and Friday, 10 am–5:45 pm, and Saturdays, 10 am–5 pm. Because hours vary with the academic calendar, researchers are advised to write or call in advance. For the library contact Dorothy Swanson, for the archives contact Debra Bernhardt, both c/o of the Tamiment Library or the Robert F. Wagner Labor Archives, 70 Washington Square South, NYC, NY 10012; phone: (212) 998-2640.

LABOR ARCHIVES IN THE UNIVERSITY AT ALBANY, STATE UNIVERSITY OF NEW YORK

by
Geoffrey A. Huth

The University Libraries' department of Special Collections and Archives has been seeking labor records for its Archives of Public Affairs and Policy since 1986. These growing archives include papers of individuals and records of organizations concerned with New York State public policy issues, especially since 1950. Preservation or accessioning of labor history records began in earnest in 1989 when the University Libraries were funded through the ongoing Harry Van Arsdale, Jr., Labor History Project (along with New York University's Robert F. Wagner Labor Archives and Cornell University's Labor-Management Documentation Center) to survey and preserve labor records from the Empire State's Capital District (that is, the Albany-Schenectady-Troy metropolitan statistical area, with a population of approximately 830,000). While there are approximately 450 public- and private-sector labor unions and related organizations in this area, the survey has been expanded geographically in recognition of the New York State Department of Labor's broader definition of the "Albany District," which includes the industrial cities of Glens Falls, Gloversville, Hudson, Johnstown, Plattsburgh, and Poughkeepsie. This wider area encompasses more than 850 labor organizations from the Mid-Hudson Valley to the Canadian border. Coordinated by archivists Don C. Skemer and Geoffrey A. Huth, the two-year Capital District Labor History Project has resulted in improved archival documentation on New York State labor

Geoffrey A. Huth is former field archivist of the Capital District Labor History Project of SUNY, Albany.

history through the accessioning or preservation microfilming of the records of over 30 labor unions.

Despite the long history of organized labor in the Capital District, there has been little serious historical scholarship on unionism in the area. The monographs and dissertations that have been produced give insight into reasons for the successes and failures of organized labor and examine unions in a few trades, but much of the labor history of the region remains unknown.[1] Part of the problem has been the dearth of accessible union records. Much of the historical record of labor has been lost through fire, flood, or neglect, and what archival documentation has survived is often stored in the attics or basements of union offices or the homes of its officers and is unavailable to all but the most persistent and tireless of researchers. By amassing records of organized labor that document almost a century and a half of activity, the Capital District Labor History Project makes accessible the points of view of a broad range of unions in this area. It is hoped that these records will give more breadth to studies which have relied primarily on local newspapers or the surviving records of employing companies.

The history of organized labor in the Capital District begins in 1850 with the founding Albany Typographical Union, No. 4. Before that time, printers in Albany had belonged to fraternal societies more interested in fostering camaraderie within the trade than in protecting the interests of their members. Local workers in other trades had joined together to strike for higher wages or shorter work days, but there had been no formal organization of workers in the Capital District before 1850. The Albany Typographical Union, typical of most typographical unions throughout its history, was founded when printers worked 54- and 60-hour weeks, and the union strove for decades to reduce the work week just as it struggled for the right to determine the number of apprentices allowed per journeyman as a means of regulating the profession. The Albany union was a founding member of the National Typographical Union (which became the International Typographical Union after the inclusion of Canadian locals in 1869). Since the 1950s the Albany Typographical Union has merged with a number of locals over a broad geographical area, replicating the widespread consolidation of unions on the local and national levels during these years. The

---

[1]Monographs include Brian Greenberg, *Worker and Community: Responses to Industrialization in a Nineteenth-Century American City, Albany, New York, 1850–1884* (Albany, 1985); Ronald W. Schatz, *Electrical Workers: A History of Labor at General Electric and Westinghouse, 1923–60* (Urbana, 1983); and Daniel J. Walkowitz, *Worker City, Company Town: Iron and Cotton-Worker Protest in Troy and Cohoes, New York, 1855–1884* (Urbana, University of Illinois, 1978).

records of the Albany Typographical Union (1850–1988) held in Special Collections and Archives document over a century of activity in Albany, as well as the union's response to technological change.

The records of several other unions in the printing trades are housed in Special Collections and Archives. These include the Newspaper Guild of Albany, Local 34 (1934–89); Graphic Communications International Union, Local 10-B, a bookbinders' local (1909–89); the records of two typographical unions that merged with the Albany union, Columbia County Typographical Union, No. 896 (1927–68) and Fulton County Typographical Union, No. 268 (1893–1989); and local unions representing pressmen, lithographers, photoengravers, electrotypers, and stereotypers in the Capital District. Together these records provide rich documentation of union activity within a single industry.

One of the earliest trades to organize after the printing trades was the building and construction industry. The oldest records of a building trades union preserved by Special Collections and Archives are those of the International Union of Bricklayers and Allied Craftsmen, Local 16, of Schenectady. These records include minutes and contracts and begin in 1886, the year the local was organized probably in reaction to the large-scale building program begun by Thomas Alva Edison after he moved his Edison Machine Works to the city that year. Also noteworthy are the records of Local 83 of the Sheet Metal Workers' International Association (1892–1989), which include an almost complete set of minutes from its beginning in 1892. One of the largest and oldest collections is the records of the Hudson Valley District Council of Carpenters (1887–1989), which include over a century of minutes, dues ledgers, and contracts documenting the activities of union carpenters in the lower Hudson Valley of New York State. This manuscript group includes records of a predecessor district council and of dozens of affiliated carpenters' locals. The department of Special Collections and Archives also holds the records of locals of painters, laborers, plumbers, and electrical workers from Albany, Schenectady, and Troy.

Two sizable collections of records document labor activity in the clothing and textile industry. The Hudson Valley Area Joint Board of the Amalgamated Clothing and Textile Workers Union (ACTWU) represents scores of textile workers' locals located throughout New York State's Hudson Valley. These records (1919–89) document the activities of the joint board and its predecessors in organizing shops, negotiating contracts, and managing strikes. Along with the records of dozens of locals of textile workers, the records of the Hudson Valley Area Joint Board also include the records of four predecessor joint boards, the records of officers of the Textile Workers Union of America who were working out of these joint boards, and the records of four industrial union councils and labor councils from the Hudson Valley. Together these provide a broad picture of textile unionism and its cooperation with other unions. The records of the Glove Cities Area Joint Board of ACTWU (1935–89) center on a smaller geographical area, primarily the leather-tanning and glove-making cities of Gloversville and Johnstown. These records include virtually complete sets of minutes, often quite detailed, which shed light on labor unrest in these cities during the 1930s and 1950s. Also included with these records are those of the Capital District Joint Board, which represented clothing workers in Troy and vicinity.

Union activity in manufacturing is represented by the records of a few locals. The most important of these is Local 301 of the International Union of Electronic, Electrical, Salaried, Machine and Furniture Workers (IUE), which represents workers at General Electric's first plant, in Schenectady. Included in these records (1949–89) are minutes, contracts, and audio tapes providing insight into the management of this pioneering local, which negotiated an agreement in 1941 guaranteeing pay equity for women and which as a part of IUE successfully used the courts to contest unfair labor practices at General Electric during the 1960s. Another affiliate of IUE, Local 379 was a match workers' union which represented workers in that specialized trade in Hudson, and which began as Federal Labor Union No. 24122. The AFL directly chartered federal labor unions to provide workers with the benefits of unionism in industries no international union cared to organize. These records (1944–87) provide a detailed account of the activities of the union through minutes and contracts, and sample agreements from other match workers' unions allow a glimpse into the organization of this industry.

Since Albany is New York State's seat of government, many statewide public-sector unions and locals maintain their headquarters in the city. With the passage of the New York State Public Employees' Fair Employment Act (the Taylor Law) in 1967, all public employees in New York were guaranteed the right to collective bargaining at the same time they were prohibited from engaging in strikes. Until 1968 employees of the state belonged to employee associations which had limited power to realize improvements in the working life of their membership. One of the earliest of these associations was the Civil Service Employees Association (CSEA), which was formed in 1910. The records of CSEA (1933–89) document the association's relationship with the state of New York and its transformation, after the implementation of the Taylor Law, into the largest public employees' union in the state. CSEA affiliated with the American Federation of State, County and Municipal Employees (AFSCME) in 1978 and has become the largest local of any union in the country, representing approximately 250,000 workers across New York State. Another large public-sector union is Council 82, Security and Law Enforcement Employees, which is the exclusive bargaining representative of over 22,000 of New York's law enforcement personnel. In 1979 Council 82 struck for 16 days and was fined $2,500,000 for contempt of court under the Taylor Law. Files on the hearings held after this strike are some of the most significant records of Council 82 (1968–89). Also surveyed were the records of United University Professions (UUP), which is Local 2160 of New York State United Teachers (NYSUT), the state affiliate of the American Federation of Teachers (AFT). The largest higher-education union in the country, UUP represents some twenty thousand faculty and professional staff throughout the State University of New York system. It is hoped that the records of UUP (founded 1974) and its predecessors (1967–74) will be accessioned within a year.

Besides the records of local and regional labor unions, the department of Special Collections and Archives holds the records of labor councils, trade councils, and other labor organizations. Included are the records of AFL-CIO central labor councils in Glens Falls (1959–90), Schenectady (1921–88), and Troy (1942–89). Additionally, the records of the Hudson Valley Area Joint Board include the records of AFL-CIO central councils in Newburgh (1960–65) and the Upper Hudson area (1956–84) and of CIO industrial union councils in Troy (1948–60) and the Upper Hudson area (1952–58). The accessioned records of trades councils include those from a number of trades, such as the Albany Allied Printing Trades Council (1909–90), and the Schenectady Building and Construction Trades Council (1960–78). Other labor organizations include labor coalitions and single-trade associations such as the Empire Typographical and Mailer Conference (1919–90), which includes typographical unions across New York State. These records help illuminate how unions have cooperated with each other as well as how they have handled differences among themselves.

The Capital District Labor History Project has accessioned and microfilmed the records of local and regional organizations and has surveyed the papers of unionists and others involved in the labor movement. The focus of much of the project, however, has been the preservation of records of labor union locals, which are often not retained by the unions themselves and which are often ignored by large labor archives. Included in the records of labor organizations held by the University at Albany are records of over one hundred affiliated and predecessor bodies, giving added depth and breadth to the collection. Special Collections and Archives intends to continue accessioning records of labor organizations to its Archives of Public Affairs and Policy after the completion of this project.

Access: Holdings are available for use in Special Collections and Archives, Monday through Friday, from 10 a.m. to 3 p.m. and by appointment. Bibliographic information on labor archives in the University at Albany is available online through the Archives and Manuscripts Control (AMC) database of the Research Libraries Information Network (RLIN). For further information contact Don C. Skemer, Head, Special Collections and Archives, University at Albany, State University of New York, 1400 Washington Avenue, Albany, NY 12222; telephone (518) 442-3544.

SOURCES ON LABOR HISTORY IN THE MARTIN P. CATHERWOOD LIBRARY

by
Richard Strassberg

The Martin P. Catherwood Library at Cornell is the largest academic collection on labor and industrial relations in the United States. With 170,000 volumes and 8000 current and noncurrent serial titles, this research facility is a major resource for the study of contemporary issues in industrial and labor relations. Such holdings, when combined with the 813 manuscript accessions and 230,833 documentary items held by its Labor-Management Documentation Center, make the Catherwood Library an especially rich source for the study of labor history.[1]

The Library of the New York State School of Industrial and Labor Relations was founded in 1945. It was renamed in 1971 to honor Martin P. Catherwood, second Dean of the School (1949–1958), who subsequently served as New York State Industrial Commissioner (1959–1970). Although its primary purpose has always been to support the instructional, research, and extension functions of the academic unit of which it is a part, the Catherwood Library has, as well, developed a world-wide reputaton for the quality of its holdings in the areas of collective bargaining, labor law, labor union administration, labor economics, income security, human resources, personnel administration, and, of course, labor history.

The book, periodical, and government document collections housed in the Catherwood's open stacks include convention proceedings, officers' reports, and journals for every major and most minor 20th century labor unions. If publications about workers and labor organizations are not available in hard copy, the library attempts to obtain

Richard Strassberg is Associate Director of the Martin P. Catherwood Library and Director and Archivist of the Labor-Management Documentation Center at Cornell Univ.

[1]This article is an updated version of one which appeared in the Fall 1982 issue of *Labor History*.

them in microfilm. Thus, the Catherwood Library has an excellent collection of microfilm editions of early work-related newspapers. These include the *New Harmony Gazette* (1825–1828), *The Mechanic's Free Press* (1828–1831), the *Working Man's Advocate* (1829–1835, 1844–1845), *Young America* (1845–1847), *Republik Der Arveiter* (1850), *Fitcher's Trades Review* (1863–1866) the *Workingman's Advocate* (1864–1877), *Der Sozialist* (1885–1888), *New Yorker Volkzeitung* (1878–1899), *John Swinton's Papers* (1883–1887), the *Journal of the Knights of Labor* (1890–1917), and the *Voice of Labor* (1902–1905). The Library also maintains American government documents in its subject areas and has amassed respectable holdings of international labor association and foreign union publications. Of special note are the Catherwood's resources for the study of the International Labor Organization and the World Federation of Trade Unions.

Information on Library holdings of specific monograph titles acquired after 1976 is available online through the RLIN database. Information on currently-held serial titles is likewise available through RLIN. All the monographic and serial titles included in the Martin P. Catherwood Library have recently been entered into the Cornell University Online Catalog which is available for remote searching. Information as to how to obtain telephone access to the Online Catalog via computer modem is available by calling (607) 255-2184.

Bibliographic access to the resources of the Catherwood Library had been previously facilitated by G. K. Hall's publication of the Library catalog through 1979.[2] As well as listing the monoraphic acquisitions of the Library, the published *Catalog* and cumulatives also indexed approximately 100 core journals which represented the scholarly disciplines central to the research in labor and industrial relations. The Catherwood Library also publishes "Library Acquisitions List" which is available by subscription.

The special collections held by the Catherwood Library are located in its Labor-Management Documentation Center. Founded in 1949 to house and service the wide variety of fugitive and limited edition pub-

[2]Cornell University Libraries. *Library Catalog of the New York State School of Industrial and Labor Relations, Cornell University* (Boston, 1967), 12 vols; Cornell University Libraries. Martin P. Catherwood Library, *Cumulation of the Library Catalog Supplements of the New York State School of Industrial and Labor Relations, Cornell University* (Boston, 1976) 9 vols; *First Supplement to the Cumulation of the Library Catalog Supplements of the New York State School of Industrial and Labor Relations, Cornell University* (Boston, 1977) 1 vol; *Second Supplement to the Cumulation of the Library Catalog Supplements of the New York State School of Industrial and Labor Relations, Cornell University* (Boston, 1978) 2 vols; *Third Supplement to the Cumulation of the Library Catalog Supplement to the Cumulation of the Library Catalog Supplements of the New York State School of Industrial and Labor Relations, Cornell University* (Boston, 1979) 2 vols; *Fourth Supplement to the Cumulation of the Library Catalog Supplements of the New York State School of Industrial and Labor Relations. Cornell University* (Boston, 1980) 2 vols.

lications characteristic of industrial relations literature of that period, the Center has grown into a major repository of primary source documents of every description. These are maintained in the current document and the manuscript sections of the Center.

At the present time, the Current Document Section consists of five extensive files: the Union File, Organization File, Labor Relations Board File, Informaton File, and Foreign Union File. The Union File contains constitutions, by-laws, collective bargaining agreements, health and pension plans, political literature, and union histories, as well as many other kinds of information produced by American unions.

A large sample of the Fortune 500 corporations is represented in the Organization File in the form of company histories, employee newsletters, employee benefit plans, personnel practice manuals, performance appraisal forms, affirmative action policies, training brochures, job descriptions, and career development programs as well as national trade association documents and recruitment material.

The Labor Relations Board File holds American Arbitration Association decisions including Arbitration in Schools and Arbitration in Government as well as the decisions of the Assistant Secretary for Labor Management Relations, the Federal Labor Relations Authority, the CT Labor Relations Board, and the National Mediation Board.

The Foreign Union file includes printed information produced by the International Confederation of Free Trade Unions, the World Confederation of Labour, the World Federation of Trade Unions, and their sub-divisions which coordinate the activities of a variety of trades. Also found in this collection are English language publications from national trade unions and centers around the world.

Miscellaneous pamphlets, reprints, and legislative committee prints on a variety of issues of interest to students of labor and industrial relations are to be found in the Center's Information File.

With the exception of the Board File, which contains materials of strictly contemporary interest, each of these collections has been divided into current circulating files (current plus the nine preceeding years) and non-circulating retrospective files. The latter have been extremely useful for research in labor history. The retrospective union files, for example, contain over 40,000 collective bargaining agreements which span the 20th century and union constitutions which date from the Knights of Labor. In all, these union pamphlet collections occupy 480 linear feet of shelf space. The Center's historical Organization File varies in size from company to company and may range from a single pamphlet on the Crescent Steel Co. dated 1880 to two linear feet of documents pertaining to Standard Oil for the years 1910–1985. This file also subsumes the contents of a similar collection that originally was housed at the Univ. of Michigan at Ann Arbor. Finding aids for each of these document collections are available for interlibrary loan.

Coincidental with the establishment of the current document files in 1949, the Labor-Management Documentation Center began to collect historical manuscripts. The early years of manuscript acquisition efforts in the Center have been chronicled elsewhere.[3] Suffice it to say that the Center is currently the repository for the original records of labor unions, seven lobbying and education groups, and several local labor unions and associations. These large accessions are supplemented by the more intimate papers and oral history reminiscences of 350 individuals prominent in the field of industrial and labor relations. The subject areas of main collecting interest to the Center include transportation, the garment industry, public sector unionism, New York State industrial relations, labor legislation, labor education, arbitration, and, most recently, management theory.

Center acquisition efforts in transportation have centered on the railroad industry. Major accessions include the AFL Railway Employes Dept.-Records, 1917–1970 (180 feet); Brotherhood of Locomotive Firemen and Enginemen-Records, 1901–1968 (169 feet); Brotherhood of Railroad Trainmen-Records, 1883–1968 (158 feet); Brotherhood of Railway, Airline and Steamship Clerks, Freight Handlers, Express and Station Employees-Records, 1906–1979 (987 linear feet); Illinois Central Gulf R.R., Industrial Relations Dept.-Selected Records, 1918–1949 (22 feet); *Labor*-Editorial Files, 1917–1975 (27 feet); A. E. Lyon (president, Brotherhood of Railroad Signalmen of America) reminiscences (3 reels microfilm); National Railway Labor Conference-Records, 1907–1955 (63 reels microfilm); Order of Railway Conductors and Brakemen-Records, 1881–1969 (22 feet); Railway Labor Executives' Association-Records, 1935–1983 (247 feet); Switchmen's Union of North America-Records, 1894–1971 (390 feet); United Transportation Union (UTU) Records, 1969–1888 (61 feet); and Oral History Project on the Founding of the UTU (143 interviews), among others.

Some of the most significant manuscript collections which document the history of the American needle trades are housed at Cornell. These include: Amalgamated Clothing Workers of America-Records, 1910–1975 (175 feet); International Fur and Leather Workers' Union-Records, 1912–1953 (35 feet); and the Joint Board of Fur, Leather and Machine Workers-Records, 1933–1970 (203 feet). Clothing Workers records subsume the papers of Dorothy Bellanca, Bessie Hillman, Sidney Hillman, Jacob Potofsky and Joseph Schlossberg. The papers of

---

[3]J. G. Miller "Labor Resources in the Cornell University Library," *Labor History*, 1 (1960), 314–326.

Abraham Feinglass, Ben Gold, Morris Kaufman, and Pietro Lucchi are to be found among the International Fur and Leather Workers materials, while Joint Board records contain substantial materials documenting the careers of Sam Burt, Henry Foner, Leon Strauss, and Ben Woolis.

In 1987 the Archives of the International Ladies' Garment Workers' Union were deposited with the Center. These records, totaling 1809 feet, had been gathered under the union's own archival program since 1973. In addition to the records enumerated in an article on the ILGWU Archives which appeared earlier in *Labor History,*[4] the Archives now include the papers of President Emeritus Sol C. Chaikin and Executive Vice-President Wilbur Daniels.

Public sector unionism and New York State labor history are documented by American Federation of Teachers, Local 2-Records, 1923–1957 (21 feet); Assembly of Governmental Employees, Records, 1963–1984 (8 feet); Paul Frederick Brissenden-Labor Injunction in New York State, Study Files, 1928–1936 (6 feet); Drug and Hospital Workers Union-Records, 1950–1974 (240 feet); New York State AFL-CIO Central Councils-Records (which include Auburn, 1891–1919; Binghamton, 1941–1960; Buffalo, 1936–1953; Elmira, 1899–1936; Geneva, 1907–1964; Oswego, 1916–1924; Lockport, 1936–1955; Peekskill, 1936–1972); New York State Public Employment Relations Board-Records, 1968–present (910 feet); New York State Board of Mediation-Case Files, 1937–1962 (150 feet); New York State United Teachers Union — Records, 1869, 1928–1972, (248 feet); Teachers Union of the City of New York-Records, 1948–1964 (40 feet); and U.S. National Labor Relations Board-Oral History Project (44 interviews) and Selected and Photocopied Files, 1935–1950 (14 feet).

Among the significant Documentation Center resources on labor lobbying and labor education are The American Association for Labor Legislation-Records, 1905–1943 (71 reels microfilm); American Association for Social Security-Records, 1920–1944 (160 feet); American Labor Education Service-Records, 1927–1962 (225 feet); Consumers' League of New York-Records, 1943–1958 (22 feet); National Institute for Labor Education-Records, 1957–1971 (60 feet); Lawrence M. Rogin (activist and labor educator)-Interviews, (27 recordings); Isaac M. Rubinow (physician, Social Security activist)-Papers, 1913–1936, (18 feet); Theresa Wolfson (labor educator)-Papers, 1919–1970 (35 feet); and Workers Education Bureau of America-Records, 1921–1950 (3 feet).

---

[4]Robert E. Lazar, "The International Ladies' Garment Workers' Union," *Labor History,* 23 (1982), 528–533.

The Center's holdings of arbitrators' records are probably the most extensive in the nation. Key collections in this area include the National Academy of Arbitrators-Records, 1940–1983 (41 feet); Paul Abelson-Papers, 1903–1953 (43.2 feet); Gabriel Alexander-Papers, 1940–1986 (110.5 feet); David Cole-Papers, 1942–1976 (89.2 feet); I. Robert Feinberg-Papers, 1946–1975 (64.5 feet); Clara Friedman-Arbitration Files, 1975–1984 (8 feet); James Gross-Arbitration Files, 1975–1986 (15 feet); James Hill-Papers, 1942–1985 (94 feet); E. E. Hilpert-Papers, 1948–1975 (138 feet); Jean McKelvey-Papers, 1950–1986 (90 feet); Jacob Seidenberg-Papers, 1935–1985 (89 feet); Peter Seitz-Arbitration Files, 1974–1983 (25 feet); Ralph T. Seward-Papers, 1949–1986 (47.8 feet); Morton Singer-Papers, 1942–1969 (19.5 feet); William E. Simkin-Papers, 1942–1986 (18 feet); S. Herbert Unterberger-Papers, 1946–1976 (53 feet); Saul Wallen-Papers, 1945–1969 (176 feet); Benjamin Wolf-Papers, 1952–1985 (74 feet); Sidney Wolff-Papers, 1949–1980 (69 feet); Louis Yagoda-Papers, 1961–1983 (8 feet); and Arnold Zack-Papers, 1960–1982 (100 feet). Arbitrators' papers typically contain files which include decisions and the arbitrator's notes on each case, as well as transcripts and employer and union exhibits for more complicated arbitrations. Many of these collections contain other professional and personal papers as well.

The acquisition of records relating to management theory is a relatively new project for the Documentation Center. With the cooperation of the Management History Division of the Academy of Management, the Center collects the records of organizations and individuals who have made major contributions to the development of management thought, particularly as it relates to industrial and labor relations. Included among the collections thus far acquired are Academy of Management-Records, 1947–1985 (76.5 feet); Edward Wight Bakke-Papers, 1932–1971 (48 feet); Dearborn Conference Group-Records, 1951–1971 (1.6 feet); Harrington Emerson- Files, 1873–1931 (5 feet); Richard A. Feiss-Files, 1910–1953 (3.0 feet); Keppele Hall-Files, 1894–1926 (5 inches); Ordway Tead-Papers, 1917–1969 (18 feet); and Sanford E. Thompson-Papers, 1892–1949 (8 feet).

In the course of the history of the Labor-Management Documentation Center there have been significant acquisitions which fall outside the core areas which generally define our development parameters. Collections in this category include: Committee for Industrial Organization-Minutes, 1935–1936 (1 reel microfilm); John H. Cornehlsen (industrial psychologist), 1950–1969 (59 feet); Engineers and Electrical Society-Records (19 feet); Glass Bottle Blower's Association of the United States and Canada-Records, 1890–1940 (2 feet); Industrial Workers of the World-Collected Documents, 1905–1971 (8 feet); Insurance Workers of America, Vice-President Simon Helfgott-Papers, 1951–1957 (1 foot); International Brotherhood of Pulp, Sulphite, and Paper Mill Workers-Records, 1906–1957 (284 reels microfilm); International Workers Order-Records, 1917–1954 (37 feet); Vernon Jensen, Collector-International Union of Mine, Mill, and Smelter Workers and the Western Federation of Miners-Documents (4.5 feet, 7 reels microfilm, 3 audio tapes); James O. Morris, (educator), Labor and Politics Primary Source Files, 1905–1935 (35 feet); Serafino Romualdi (AFL-CIO Latin American Representative)-Papers, 1936–1967 (10 feet); William L. Standard (General Counsel, National Maritime Union)-Papers, 1937–1947 (12 feet); Steel Workers Organizing Committee-General Meeting Minutes, 1937–1938 (2 bound volumes); Philip Taft (labor historian)-Research Files, 1939–1970 (19 feet); Telecommunications International Union-Records, 1949–1986 (76 feet); George Tichenor (labor journalist, editor)-Papers, 1939–1959 (2 feet); United Brotherhood of Carpenters and Joiners, Selected Records, 1881–1979 (2 feet, 8 reels microfilm); United Mine Workers of America, District 12-Records, 1899–1928 (7 reels microfilm); National War Labor Board-Region 2 Case Files, 1941–1945 (55 feet); President's Commission on Pension Policy-Commission Members' Files, 1970–1980 (1 foot); Ralph Winstead (Federal labor official)-Papers, 1935–1947 (5 feet); World Federation of Trade Unions-Minutes and Publications, 1945–1973 (12 feet, 2 reels microfilm).

Beyond its responsibility for the collections of manuscripts and fugitive documents, the Documentation Center serves as the archival repository for about 100 feet of official School archives. The Center houses the personal and professional papers of the following School faculty members: Leonard Adams (1955–1963); Robert Aronson (1970–1974); Martin P. Catherwood (1935–1980); Alice Cook (1955–1978); George Hildebrand (1949–1978); Vernon Jensen (1945–1980); Milton Konvitz (1940–1987); John McConnell (1952–1973); Robert McKersie (1977–1980); Albert Martin (1952–1966); Maurice Neufeld (1946–1980); Eric Polisar (1923–1968); and William F. Whyte (1942–1985).

The Center has generated over 350 original history interviews relating primarily to the National Labor Relations Board; the Drug and Hospital Workers Union, 1199; the International Ladies Garment Workers Union; and the union merger which formed the United Transportation Union. A substantial collection of recordings of labor songs is also held by the Center. The audio-visual collections in the Center have grown immensely in recent years. Photographic collections held by the Center relate largely to the garment industry, but more general labor themes are to be discovered, as well, among its 120,000 prints and 102,000 negative images. An important recent accession in this area is the labor cartoons of John Baer who illustrated the railroad union publication *Labor* between 1922 and 1970.

The Center is a repository for a substantial number of micropublished manuscript collections. These include: *American Federation of Labor Records. Part I, Strikes and Agreement File, 1898-1953* (Frederick, MD, 1985); *American Federation of Labor Records. Part II, President's Office Files, Series A: William Green Papers, 1934-1952* (Frederick, MD, 1986); *William Green Papers, 1891-1952* (Columbus, OH, 1981); *Cigar Makers International Union Records, 1860-1873* (College Park, MD, 1983); *The John R. Commons Papers, 1859-1967* (Madison, WI, 1982); *International Workingmen's Association Papers, 1868-1877* (Madison, WI, 1972); *John L. Lewis Papers, 1879-1969* (Madison, WI, 1970); *United States Commission on Industrial Relations, 1912-1915* (Frederick, MD, 1985); *Records of the Women's Bureau of the U.S. Department of Labor, 1918-1965* (Frederick, MD, 1986).

Further information on the majority of the original manuscript accessions listed above is in the form of published and unpublished finding aids available on interlibrary loan or by purchase from the Center. A narrative guide to the holdings of the Center prior to 1980 may be purchased. Narrative information about Center holdings is also available in updated form on-line in the Research Library Group's AMC database which is available in a number of major libraries around the nation. Information on the collections held by the Center also is available through the use of Cornell's Online Catalog.

Access: the Martin P. Catherwood Library is open 12 months a year except for legal holidays and the eight days between Christmas and the New Year. During the academic year, the Library is normally open seven days a week. Labor-Management Documentation Center hours are 8 am–4 pm, Monday–Friday.

Visiting researchers are encouraged to write for specific information about any of the Center's holdings to Martha Hodges, Reference Archivist, Labor-Management Documentation Center, 144 Ives Hall, Ithaca, NY 14853-3901; phone: (607) 255-3183.

SOURCES ON LABOR HISTORY AT THE ROCKEFELLER ARCHIVE CENTER

by
Erwin Levold

The Rockefeller Archive Center (RAC), a division of the Rockefeller University, was founded in 1974 and brought together the archival collections of the various institutions founded by members of the Rockefeller family, as well as the personal papers of John D. Rockefeller, Sr. and John D. Rockefeller, Jr. Since 1974 the founding institutions—the Rockefeller family, Rockefeller Foundation, and the Rockefeller University—have added material to their archival collections, and non-Rockefeller institutions such as the Commonwealth Fund, Russell Sage Foundation, and the John and Mary Markle Foundation have deeded their archives to the Center. The records housed at the RAC date from the late 19th century to contemporary times. A wide range of topics can be researched at the RAC, including agriculture, the arts and humanities, Black history, economic development, labor, medicine, public and industrial health, religion, science, the social sciences, social welfare, and women's history. The Center holds approximately 27,500 cubic feet of records, with a complementary photograph collection of about 250,000 items, and also 3500 films.

The archives of the Rockefeller Foundation (6200 cubic feet) and the Rockefeller family (2500 cubic feet) offer the largest selection and concentration of material relating to the study of industrial enterprises, work, and workers. What follows can only serve as a brief introduction to the varied holdings at the RAC and the many labor-related topics in the records. *A Guide to Archives and Manuscripts at the Rockefeller Archive Center* (1989), which fully describes all the RAC collections; and *A Survey of Sources for the History of Labor and Industrial Relations at the Rockefeller Archive Center* (2nd ed., 1989), which contains

---

Erwin Levold is archivist at the Rockefeller Archive Center.

a complete box and folder list of relevant files, are available from the RAC.

The Rockefeller Foundation (RF) was established in May 1913 by John D. Rockefeller "to promote the well-being of mankind throughout the world." The archives consist of a number of record groups (RG), all of which contain varying amounts of labor-oriented material. Access to these files is through a comprehensive name index. RG 1.1 and 1.2, the project files, hold the majority of material. These files are arranged according to country and program, with each series or subseries arranged alphabetically by grant recipient. RF records more than 20 years old are open for research. The RF was active in the U.S. and throughout the world. Grantees include the Free Trade Union Committee, National Child Labor Committee, Working Women's Protective Union, the Social Science Research Council, and the Watts Labor Community Action Committee. The following examples of RF grants only hint at the array of material available in the project files, which generally include correspondence, grant actions, RF officers' reports, and final project reports.

In April 1949 the RF approved a grant for $5000 to the Dept. of Education and Research of the Congress of Industrial Organizations (CIO) to be used in bringing a small number of trade unionists from Germany and Austria to the United States to participate in the CIO's summer schools. These trade unionists were assigned to the South, to Michigan, and to the CIO Department of Education and Research. During their stay in the U.S., they visited CIO summer schools for two months and spent a month in an industrial community assigned to a CIO union.

The American Federation of Labor (AFL) benefited indirectly from RF support. In 1948 a grant of $5500 to the Free Trade Union Committee in Germany and Austria enabled them to send a delegation to the U.S. These leaders of Germany's revived labor movement studied how organized labor lived and functioned in America. The visitors spent six weeks in the United States examining labor management relations, meeting and conferring with officers of trade unions, visiting factories, and observing representative American industrial centers. They also spent time living with "typical" Americans. The delegates came from the western zones of Germany and the non-Russian sectors of Berlin and Austria, and were selected by the trade union bodies from the respective zones with the assistance of the AFL representative in Germany. The group arrived in October of 1948 and stayed through the mid-November 1948 AFL convention. Their visit promoted a better understanding between the free trade union movements of the U.S. and Germany.

Since its founding in 1913, the RF has generously supported unemployment relief and industrial welfare. In 1931 the RF appropriated $75,000 to the University of Minnesota to help underwrite the university's economic and social study of unemployment in Duluth, St. Paul, and Minneapolis. This study was part of a general unemployment relief program sponsored by the Tri-City Employment Stabilization Committee. Prior to the RF's involvement in 1931, Minnesota unemployment already had been studied for two previous years by the university with the support of the councils of the three cities. The result was a detailed index on regional unemployment. The collected data were utilized in local unemployment relief programs, and plans for a long-term program of prevention had been developed by the Tri-City Employment Stabilization Committee, which comprised the chief officials of the three cities and various members of the university faculty. The RF grant supported the implementation of this prevention program. The resultant analysis of the Minnesota labor situation included the study of the specific cause of the present unemployment of individual workers; complete case histories of the unemployed; tests of the individual aptitudes and abilities of the workers; an accurate and practical study of the employment possibilities of the workers under study; experiments with reeducation and vocational readjustment of workers who shifted to lines of work other than those which they had been following; experiments in the more effective operation of placement bureaus and employment offices serving the local committees; and the general adoption of programs of employment stabilization.

Industrial hygiene is another area in which the RF actively supported programs. RF officials in 1919 did not think that industrial hygiene was an appropriate field, but they altered this policy after World War II and made a number of grants to individuals in Finland, England, and the U.S. The early files on industrial hygiene are quite illuminating, since it is as interesting to see why grants were not approved as well as why others were. On November 14, 1919 the Yale Club in New York City hosted a Conference on Industrial Hygiene that was attended by more than 20 prominent practitioners in the field and several RF representatives. Already by 1919, close to 900 corporations employed about 1500 doctors and industrial hygiene had become an increasingly important phase of public health work, involving the proper safeguarding of factories and working conditions against accidents, disease, and fatigue; the treatment in industrial dispensaries or elsewhere of those suffering from accidents or disease; the fostering of preventive measures with respect to diet, exercise, recreation, and forms of community development. Questions regarding workmen's compensation, compulsory health insurance, and functional reeducation were also addressed at the 1919 meeting. The RF policy report that was generated after the conference stated that government, state, and municipal agencies were studying industrial hygiene; that a number of municipal clinics for industrial diseases had been established; and that courses or lectures were being given at several major universities, e.g., the Cincinnati Medical College, Harvard-Massachusetts Institute of Technology, the Johns Hopkins School of Hygiene and Public Health, the Museum of Safety in New York City, Rush Medical College, Ohio State University, the University of Pennsylvania, and Yale University. Despite the merits in the study and promotion of industrial hygiene, RF officers concluded that the field was "so new and so large that the activities undertaken by various groups in different parts of the country have not been working toward a thorough, comprehensive development of the field, nor in fact toward clear realization of what it involves," and therefore opted in 1919 not to get involved in the funding of industrial hygiene programs.

These examples are the just the tip of the archival iceberg of labor-related material in the RF archives. Additional material is available for studies of grants pertaining to labor, unemployment, industrial hygiene, and industrial psychology. RG 2 (General Correspondence) and RG 3 (Program and Policy) also contain further information. Since the RF files are not limited to the U.S., and many grants were awarded to individuals or institutions in Europe, Asia, Latin America, and Africa, the RF files also present a unique window on the development of labor movements abroad. Of special note are the files of the Mexico Field Office (RG 6.13).

The archives of the Rockefeller family, while primarily documenting the careers and activities of three generations of the Rockefeller family beginning with John D. Rockefeller (1839–1937), are also extremely rich in their documentation of American labor history. RG 1 of the Rockefeller Family Archives documents John D. Rockefeller's (JDR) activities during the 19th century. His actions during the 20th century are recorded in the files of RG 2 (Office of the Messrs. Rockefeller-OMR, see below). Series C in RG 1 includes business-related correspondence for 1879–1894. The JDR Letterbook Series (1877–1918, 394 volumes/200,000 letters) contains copies of handwritten or typed correspondence sent by JDR, JDR, Jr., or office staff on their behalf. Corresponding incoming letters may be found in Series C of RG 1 or in RG 2. Subjects documented in the letterbooks include the individual and cooperative business endeavors of JDR and JDR, Jr. and their charitable and philanthropic activities.

"Business Interests" and "Economics Interests," two series within RG 2, are of particular note. Boxes 11–26 of "Business Interests" contain material on the Colorado Fuel and Iron Company (CFI) and the multitude of union and labor activities associated with the company. These records include UMW and IWW material, CFI company bulletins and annual reports, information on the Colorado Industrial Plan and welfare work; documents from the United States Industrial Commission, the Committee on Mines and Mining Hearing (U.S. House of Representatives/63rd Congress); State of Colorado material, the reports of the Committee on Unemployment and Relief (1916), the military occupation of the Coal Strike Zone (1914), State Supreme Court briefs regarding voting cases (1915) and documentation on JDR, Jr.'s industrial relations plan. Correspondents include J. F. Welborn, W. L. MacKenzie King, and Robert DeForest. Three boxes of files relating to the strikes, unemployment, and labor situation in Colorado are located in RG 3 Series 900 (General Program and Policy), with three additional folders in Series 200 (U.S.) RG 1.1, of the Rockefeller Foundation archives.

For the most part, the material in the "Business Interests" series concerns Rockefeller family investments in a variety of companies and consequently these files are not as rich in labor-oriented material as the CFI files. The Standard Oil records represent a number of Standard Oil companies, but do not include any corporate records; therefore the majority of the records do not relate to the day-to-day operation of the companies, but emphasize the investment side of the businesses. The file on the Midwest Refining Company is an exception: here the documents present wonderful insight into the firm's daily activities in the Elk Basin region of Wyoming and Montana. These records address the issues of working conditions, management-labor relationships, and the implementation of an eight-hour workday. A central issue in these files is the controversy engendered by the publication of R. S. Lynd's "Done in Oil" in the November 1922 *Survey Graphic*. This article was highly critical of the working conditions in the oil fields and prompted John D. Rockefeller, Jr. to call for a private investigation, the findings of which convinced Rockefeller that the seven-day work week and 12-hour day needed to be abolished. "Business Interests" also holds a small amount of material concerning the labor contracts during the construction of Rockefeller Center.

The documents in the "Economic Interests" series reflect the Rockefeller family's efforts in economic and social reform. Among the organizations and topics represented in these files are the American Association for Labor Legislation (1910–1961); national, state, and local chambers of commerce; the Industrial Relations Counselors Program (1926–1958); the Commerce and Industry Association of New York, Inc. (1900–1961); the National Consumers League (1920–1953); the

National Employment Exchange (1909–1931), a private philanthropic employment agency; the New York Household Placement Association (1939–1947), an association of domestic employment agencies in New York created to protect employers and employees from unfair practices; the Bureau of Part-Time Work (1922); and the Farmers Federation (1926–1956), an organization designed to improve farm conditions in the Appalachian Highlands, and which inaugurated the "Lord's Acre" program. Also included is general material on unemployment relief, retirement, and industrial relations consultants (1919–1958). Specific files on the National Industrial Conference Board (1917–1956); the President's Mediation Commission of 1918; the Washington Industrial Conference of 1919; the National Bureau of Economic Research (1920–1961); and testimony to the United States Industrial Commission in 1915 by John D. Rockefeller, Sr., John D. Rockefeller, Jr., Ivy Lee, W. L. MacKenzie King, and J. F. Welborn is also available.

Labor-related material in RG 2 of the family archives is not limited to these two series, since additional files are located in "Welfare–General" and "Welfare–Youth" series, as well as the series on "Civic Interests" and "Educational Interests." A separate JDR, Jr. Speech File also contains a number of talks addressing industrial or labor questions. Name indices for both the JDR letterbooks and the material in RG 2 OMR are available. Many other collections housed at the RAC contain documents on labor history, but none are as extensive as the Rockefeller Foundation archives or the Rockefeller family records. The concluding paragraphs will briefly summarize the holdings of some other collections at the RAC.

The Rockefeller University was created in 1901 by John D. Rockefeller as the Rockefeller Institute for Medical Research. In 1954 the Institute became part of the University of the State of New York and in 1965 was renamed the Rockefeller University (RU). There is a small amount of material on labor relations at the RU, including a file on the Women's Educational and Industrial Union (1912–1913). The Commonwealth Fund, established in 1918 with an endowment of $10 million from Mrs. Stephen V. Harkness for "benevolent, religious, educational and like purposes," gave grants and supported programs in child welfare, public health, rural hospitals, medical research, and medical education. The Commonwealth Fund Grants series contains a file on the Industrial Personnel Problem Conference (1919–1921), and the Legal Research Program series includes material on a study on workmen's compensation laws (1928–1940). The General Education Board (GEB), founded in 1903 by John D. Rockefeller, sought to aid education in the U.S. "without distinction of race, sex or creed." Support went to major universities and small colleges throughout the U.S. for a variety of projects and studies. Included are grants for an industrial art survey (1919–1951), and support of the Affiliated School for Workers, Purdue University, for a farm work simplification study (1942–1949); the Workers Education Bureau; and Duke University, for a study of Southern industries. Industrial research at both the University of Alabama and the University of Arkansas (1945–1949) received assistance, as well as the American Council on Education—American Youth Commission, Employment and Adjustment Program (1937–1940), and the Southern Conference for Education and Industry (1915–1916). The GEB also funded agricultural and home economics extension work. A name index to the GEB files is available.

The International Education Board (IEB), chartered in 1923 by John D. Rockefeller, Jr., and dissolved in 1938, supported the "promotion and advancement of education throughout the world," funded fellowships to hundreds of individuals, and gave grants to institutions in 39 countries. The JDR 3rd Fund, established in 1963 by John D. Rockefeller, III "to stimulate, encourage, promote and support activities important to human welfare," supported the National Child Labor Committee during 1972–1973. A major program of the JDR 3rd Fund, the Youth Task Force, was created in October 1970 to promote collaborative efforts between the youth of the 1970s and leaders in business and the professions. The Laura Spelman Rockefeller Memorial (LSRM), incorporated in 1918 for general philanthropic purposes, had as its goal the overall improvement of public welfare before its merger with the Rockefeller Foundation in 1929. LSRM Series 3.6 (Social Studies) includes a number of files on industrial research conducted at the University of Pennsylvania, the National Institute of Industrial Psychology, and Harvard University. LSRM Series 3.7 (Social Welfare) holds material on the National Child Labor Committee, the President's Conference on Unemployment, and the Women's Educational-Industrial Alliance.

The Russell Sage Foundation (RSF), established in 1907 by Margaret Olivia Sage "for the improvement of social conditions in the United States," undertook research and educational programs in social welfare and also funded the work of other organizations active in those fields. The records of the RSF's Department of Industrial Studies, the institutional base for Mary Van Kleeck, and individual files on the National Employment Exchange and the United States Commission on Industrial Relations are of special interest. The Spelman Fund of New York, incorporated in 1928 from a $10 million grant from the LSRM, supported programs designed to improve technical knowledge, promote the exchange of knowledge, and devise better methods of organization. The Fund was dissolved in 1949. Its files document support for the Industrial Commission of Minnesota; the Pennsylvania Department of Labor and Industry, for general unemployment relief; and the United States Employment Service, for a study on job specifications. The Rockefeller Brothers Fund (RBF), begun in 1940 by John D. III, Nelson A., Laurance S., Winthrop, and David Rockefeller, makes grants to a broad spectrum of local, national, and international organizations dependent on general public funds. Areas of concentration have been civic improvement, cultural advancement, education, religion, public health, civil rights, and welfare. Grant files are arranged alphabetically by grant recipient, and material more than ten years old is open to researchers.

In addition to the corporate collections, small amounts of labor-oriented material can be found in the personal papers of Frederick T. Gates, a close business and philanthropic associate of John D. Rockefeller; Mark M. Jones, a management consultant and economist whose papers contain further documents on the Colorado Fuel and Iron Company; and John H. Knowles, a physician, who served as general director of the Massachusetts General Hospital (1962–1971) and president of the Rockefeller Foundation (1972–1979). Series 2 of the Knowles papers contains documents on hospital unions.

This brief review can only serve as an introduction to the many files at the RAC pertaining to the study of labor relations and work. Those seeking more specific information regarding the availability, extent, and scope of the records should either request the RAC publications mentioned above or submit a research inquiry outlining their particular interests or projects.

Access: The Rockefeller Archive Center is open 9 am–5 pm, Monday–Friday. Researchers are encouraged to contact the Center in advance of their first visit. For further information contact Erwin Levold, Rockefeller Archive Center, 15 Dayton Ave., Pocantico Hills, North Tarrytown, N.Y. 10591-1598; phone: (914) 831-4505.

LABOR HISTORY RESOURCES AT THE RUTGERS UNIVERSITY LIBRARIES

by
Ronald L. Becker

Although Rutgers Univ. was founded in 1766 and has been in the process of building library collections for over two centuries, the concept of building manuscript and archival holdings in an organized fashion dates back less than 50 years. Rutgers' Special Collections and Archives now includes approximately 3000 manuscript collections and the largest and most comprehensive collection of New Jersey books, pamphlets, newspapers, maps, broadsides, and pictorial materials. Although the major focus of the collection has been New Jersey and its history, significant 20th century holdings have been developed in such areas as the consumer movement, social welfare policy, and women's history — all areas that have collections relating to labor history. There are records of trade unions, political organizations, and consumer associations. Also included are the papers of people involved in labor activities and in the study of labor history, collections of printed materials, and the resources of the library at the Institute of Management and Labor Relations.

The Rutgers Library serves as the official repository for the archives of the International Union of Electrical Workers (IUE). To date, over 500 cubic feet of records relating to the union and its activities have been received. The papers, which date from the 1930s, include United Electrical, Radio, and Machine Workers of America (UE) files and document the split of the IUE from the UE during the late 1940s. Also included are district and local organizing files, company files, and the correspondence of IUE presidents James Carey and Paul Jennings, as well as extensive legal files which document hundreds of cases before the National Labor Relations Board and the courts. Minutes of meetings,

Ronald L. Becker is Head, Special Collections, Rutgers University.

convention materials, correspondence, photographs, and other topical files round out the collection.

The library has recently acquired over 105 cubic feet of records (1936–1980) of the National Maritime Union of America. Of particular interest are extensive photograph files depicting elections, hearings, strikes, ships, crews, and other maritime workers' scenes. Also included are organizational files, contract files, research department files, trial committee records, correspondence, and minutes of meetings and conventions. The trial committee records, which contain charges, disposition of cases, and personnel files, are restricted. Permission to use them must be secured from the union.

In addition to the records of these two unions, the library also holds the records of several NJ local chapters of national unions. The largest of these are the archives of Locals 56 and 195 of the Amalgamated Food and Allied Workers Union, founded as the Amalgamated Meat Cutters and Butcher Workmen of North America. Approximately 150 cubic feet of records include correspondence of presidents Leon B. Schachter and Leo Cinaglia (1941–1981), vice-president Joseph C. Nettleton (1962–1978), minutes of the executive board, general membership and stewards' meetings (1941–1982), and other records relating to finances, health and welfare concerns, contracts, strikes, publications, memorabilia, and photographs of these Southern New Jersey/Philadelphia locals. Also represented are the records of the Scholarship Fund Committee of the International Brotherhood of Teamsters, Chauffeurs, Warehousemen, and Helpers, Local 560 of Union City, NJ, including minutes and correspondence (1962–1965).

Other New Jersey labor organizations represented are the CIO, Industrial Union Council of NJ and the NJ State Federation of Labor. The former includes correspondence and other papers of numerous union executives (1951–1957) and materials relating to the CIO Political Action Committee (1952–1955) and the Women's CIO League of New Jersey (1953–1955). The State Federation of Labor collection includes transcripts of annual convention proceedings (1901–1973), proceedings of the Joint State Labor Board of New Jersey (1918–1920), and tape recordings of five interviews with veteran Federation members.

The library also has transcripts of and exhibits used in the dispute between the New Jersey Bell Telephone Co. and the Telephone Workers Union of New Jersey (1947) before the NJ Statutory Board of Arbitration. Hundreds of other labor-management arbitration records (1948–1965) are found in the Monroe Berkowitz papers.

Civil rights issues in the labor movement are documented in the papers of Ernest Thompson, which include files relating to his service on the National Negro Labor Council (1951-1956) and the UE Fair Practices Committee (1944-1958).

There is abundant material for the study of labor history to be found in the records of political parties and interest groups. Rutgers holds the records of NY's American Labor Party (1947-1956) and the New Democratic Coalition of New York (1959-present). These collections include election campaigns, issues files, organizing files, correspondence, and numerous subject files relating to the labor movement. The records of the NJ League of Women Voters (1913-1961) document such issues as child labor, women in industry, migrant labor, and other related concerns.

Also at Rutgers are the papers of over 20 NJ politicians who have served in the U.S. Senate and House of Representatives, dating from William Paterson's term in the Senate (1789-1790) to former Congressman/now Governor James J. Florio. Most of the collections are recent and document the issues that were of most concern to the office holders and their constituents. These papers contain much material on farm labor, child labor, minimum wage, labor law reform, workmen's compensation, and numerous other related concerns. Of particular importance for the study of labor history are the papers of Harrison A. Williams, Jr., who served long terms in the House (1953-1957) and Senate (1959-1982). Extensive files relating to his service as chairman of the Senate Labor and Human Resources Committee document the research, framing, and passage of such legislation as the Employee Retirement Income Security Act, the National Labor Relations Act, the Occupational Safety and Health Act, and the Federal Mine and Safety Act of 1976. The papers of Congresswoman Mary T. Norton include correspondence (1920-1959), speeches (1927-1952), and an unpublished autobiography. Norton served in the House for 35 years (1924-1959) and was chairwoman of its Labor Committee (1937-1946). Among the legislation passed during her leadership were the Wages and Hours Act and the Fair Labor Standards Act, both in 1938. Norton also supported (1944-1951) unsuccessful legislation to establish a permanent Fair Employment Practices Commission to combat racial discrimination.

The 20th century consumers movement in the U.S. has dealt with labor related issues throughout its history. Rutgers holds the records of the Consumers League of New Jersey (1913-present) which includes documentation on child labor, minimum wage, industrial health and safety, equal pay for equal work, industrial homework, workmen's compensation, and other allied issues. Another major collection is the archives of Consumers Research, Inc. (1927-1980) which documents the bitter strike of 1935 resulting in the founding in 1936 of Consumers

Union by the strikers and their supporters. Rutgers also has the papers of several consumer advocates, most notably Sidney Margolius (1940–1980) and Erma Angevine (1957–1984). A prolific writer and speaker, Margolius served on a number of government and private commissions and committees including the National Commission on Product Safety. Angevine's distinguished career is highlighted by her service (1977–1982) as president of the National Consumers League.

The archives of the Rutgers Institute of Management and Labor Relations (IMLR) includes materials relating to the Bryn Mawr labor schools' activities such as the Barnard School (1920s and 1930s), the Bryn Mawr Summer School (1920s and 1930s), and the Hudson Shore School (1920–1950). Other files include the official records of the IMLR and its many programs, workshops, and seminars such as the Union Leadership Academy, Center for Human Resources, New York–New Jersey Port Authority Employment Relations Panel, and occupational safety and health workshops. IMLR also has extensive files of contracts, union constitutions, periodicals, newspapers, and other printed and manuscript material, and the papers of a number of faculty members active in the labor movement in NJ and elsewhere. The IMLR Library also serves as the repository for the records of the New Jersey Public Employment Relations Commission. As such it holds extensive bargaining agreements between state agencies and public employees as well as arbitration decisions covering NJ police officers and firemen.

Access: The Rutgers University Libraries Special Collections and Archives are open to the public 9 am to 5 pm, Monday–Friday. During the academic year (Sept.–May) the hours are extended to include Saturday, 1–5 pm. Information concerning these collections, restrictions, and finding aids should be directed to Ronald L. Becker at Special Collections and Archives, Alexander Library, Rutgers Univ., New Brunswick, NJ 08903; phone: (908) 932-7006.

LABOR COLLECTIONS AT THE
URBAN ARCHIVES CENTER,
TEMPLE UNIVERSITY LIBRARIES

by
David M. Weinberg

The Urban Archives Center at Temple University was established in 1967 by a member of the History Dept. to document the lives of common urban dwellers in Philadelphia. Temple and a number of other universities — usually located in the cities — initiated centers like the Urban Archives to document the life experiences of everyday people living their everyday lives. Instead of collecting the papers of well-known figures, these new social history archives acquired manuscript collections that represented services provided to working-class people. Typical collections include the records of housing, minority, educational reform, social welfare, and labor organizations.

The Urban Archives Center began as an archival program of Temple University's History Dept. and was transferred to the University's library system in 1969 as a unit of the Dept. of Special Collections. Currently, the Urban Archives Center serves as the research base of the newly established Center for Public History which is jointly administered by the library system and the History Dept. The Archives is one component of the Center for Public History, which also offers courses in applied history through the History Dept., programs with the Philadelphia Board of Education, and conferences on various aspects of public history.

Labor collections became a central part of the Urban Archives Center's collections after receipt of a grant from the National Endowment for the Humanities (NEH). This grant enabled the Urban Archives Center to acquire and process the records of more than two dozen

David M. Weinberg, *formerly assistant curator at the Urban Archives Center, since 1988 has been curator, Center for the Study of the History of Nursing, School of Nursing, Univ. of Pennsylvania.*

labor unions. These collections now form an integral part of the Urban Archives Center's overall collecting responsibility. The Urban Archives Center acquired various collections under the NEH grant and reported its holdings in the 1982 *Labor History* special issue.[1] This article updates the 1982 report and focuses on some of the new acquisitions of the Urban Archives Center.

One of the Center's most important acquisitions of the last few years is the records of the Pennsylvania Railroad Co. Acquired through the Center's participation in the Penn Central Railroad Appraisal Project,[2] the collection now comprises one of the largest collections of organizational records housed at Temple Univ. Consisting of 754 cubic feet of records, it clearly documents the Pennsylvania Railroad's (PRR) presence and impact on the Philadelphia region. Additionally, it includes the work histories of its 20th century employees through the Railroad's Voluntary Relief Department (VRD). The VRD was, in essence, a sick and death benefit plan whereby the company and its employees contributed to a fund which gave benefits to workers who took ill, or in the event of the employee's death, to the family. The plan was first introduced by management, and, after some employee modifications, was put into effect in February 1886.

VRD "death files" consist of 643 cubic feet of material, arranged in death date order. These files provide complete work histories of every VRD member who died between 1900 and 1968. The earliest files, especially of those employees who worked for the PRR for many years, document work opportunities as far back as the mid-19th century. In general, these death cases are excellent primary sources for studying occupational opportunities, health standards over a broad geographical area, and occupational mortality. The types of information that can be gained from these files obviously vary from packet to packet, but typically each contains the age, occupation, rate of pay, and tenure of the employee; the location and division where the employee worked within the PRR system; the cause of death (i.e., accident or natural causes); the employee's general health conditions; the names of the beneficiaries; and the amount of benefits paid.

The 19th century fatalities are summarized in the death ledger books (1886–1955), since the death files for that century no longer exist. VRD minute books (1886–1954) provide insight into the operations of the

[1]Ken Fones-Wolf. "Sources for the Study of Labor History in the Urban Archives, Temple University," *Labor History*, 23 (1982), 520–525.

[2]Michael Nash and Christopher T. Baer, "Final Report on the Penn Central Railroad Appraisal Project, April 1, 1984–October 15, 1986," unpublished report to the National Historical Publication and Records Commission.

VRD, relations with the PRR, and disputes that came before the respective advisory committees from railroad workers.

Related material in the Pennsylvania Railroad records include the Employe's Provident and Loan Association (PLA), whose records consist of death ledger books (1923–1941) and 32 cubic feet of death cases (1925–1938). Like the VRD program, the PLA was popular with employees, attracting 18,434 members in its first year of operation. The Pension Dept. records consist of 12 cubic feet of minute books (1899–1938) and 13 cubic feet of the Board of Managers "sustaining papers" (1900–1943), providing insight into the detailed workings of the board for all cases brought before it.

Another of the Center's recent collections is the worker surveys of the Philadelphia Labor Market Study (PLMS), commissioned by the Work Progress Administration's National Research Project. Gladys Palmer, an economist at the Industrial Research Dept. of the Univ. of Pennsylvania's Wharton School, directed this important project to investigate re-employment and employer selectivity during the Depression. Palmer and her colleagues examined how such factors as age, sex, skill level, and specialization affected employment opportunities by selecting and studying four occupational groups. Specifically, the PLMS surveyed workers in 1) a growing industry — 686 radio and production workers, two-thirds of whom were male and comparatively young; 2) a stable industry — 683 machinists, millwrights and tool makers, who tended to be older, highly specialized, and exclusively male; 3) a declining industry — 357 weavers and loom fixers in the carpet and rug, woolen and worsted, and upholstery trade, who were mostly older men; and 4) a unionized industry — 673 hosiery workers of the American Federation of Hosiery Workers, Branch 1, where worker opportunities were strictly divided by sex.

These surveys provide detailed accounts of each worker's career, employment opportunities, period of unemployment, length of residence in Philadelphia, and location of employment. In addition to more than 30 demographic variables, each survey presents rich qualitative information: worker narratives that provide insight into the tenor of the time. For example, discussing one unemployed punch-press operator a surveyor reported:

> From 1919 to 1926 Mr. F did "huckstering" with his father and occasionally he went out alone with a push-cart. Mr. F secured his jobs by standing outside of a factory or plant and then making applications when help was needed for a particular job that he thought he might be able to do.
>
> Mr. F mildly likes punch press operating, but claims that it is very tedious. He says he would like a job as a night watchman "better than anything."

Mr. F was on the "Welfare" about six months last Winter before being placed on the W.P.A. He made many derogatory and scathing remarks about the "New Deal," and believes he was fired from the W.P.A. because he was a Republican.[3]

In addition to two cubic feet of surveys, the Urban Archives Center has eight volumes of the PLMS final report summarizing the findings of Gladys Palmer and her colleagues.[4] The interviews are particularly valuable because they document worker opportunities and worker perceptions during a very unsettling time in Philadelphia's and the country's history.

Some recent acquisitions of union records include the American Federation of Musicians, Local 77 (AFM), and the Textile Workers Union of America, Philadelphia Joint Board. The former represents the expansion of union activities into the realm of the white collar employee. The AFM collection contains 15 cubic feet of records (1898–1982), primarily minutes of the general membership and executive committee, correspondence, subject files, and publications. The records show how the AFM grew to become one of the strongest AFL unions in the city. The records document, for example, a bitter 27 month strike that ended in 1944 which successfully sought to give royalties to members for recorded music broadcast on radio stations. The members of the AFM ranged from musicians in small bands that played at corner restaurants to the Philadelphia Orchestra. Additionally, the records include extensive material about the world-renowned conductor, Leopold Stokowski, who elevated that orchestra into a world-class organization. Men of Stokowski's stature, as well as common AFM men and women, are equally documented in this largely unknown history of Philadelphia's music establishment.

The Textile Workers Union of America, Philadelphia Joint Board (TWUA), on the other hand, was typical of the large industrial unions. Organized in 1937 as the Textile Workers' Organizing Committee under CIO direction, its membership grew to over 10,000 members of diverse ethnic backgrounds, reflecting the composition of the city of Philadelphia. The TWUA records (1921–1980) chronicle the role the union played in forging liberal politics within the city's Democratic Party. The records detail labor education classes, political action, recreation programs, and social events. The collection consists of administrative files, primarily composed of minutes; subject files of correspondence and printed

---

[3]Philadelphia Labor Market Studies, Urban Archives Center, Temple University Libraries, radio industry, folder 2, case 0167.

[4]*National Research Project on Reemployment Opportunities and Recent Changes in Industrial Techniques*, Philadelphia Labor Market Studies, Reports P-1–P-8, 1937.

matter; union and company agreements, consisting of 10 cubic feet of materials; proceedings and financial records; and the records of local unions that predate the founding of the TWUA. In 1976, the TWUA merged with the Amalgamated Clothing Workers of America, Philadelphia Joint Board, to form the Amalgamated Clothing and Textile Workers of America, Philadelphia Joint Board.[5]

Representing the work of a union arbitor are the personal papers of J. Hazen Hardy (1903–1984). Hardy's professional career with a wide range of unions is documented in the 18 cubic feet of arbitration case files from 1946 to 1980. Most notable are the Teamsters, the Transport Workers Union of Philadelphia, the United Automobile Workers, and the United Steelworkers of America. The remaining five cubic feet of manuscripts consist of Hardy's work with the American Arbitration Association, the American Institute of Banking, and Temple Univ., where Hardy taught several courses in its School of Business and Public Administration.

Temple University Libraries acquired the news clipping and photograph libraries of the *Evening Bulletin* after that Philadelphia newspaper closed in 1982.[6] The *Evening Bulletin* began in 1847, and unfortunately few of its 19th century materials survived. Although not a labor collection, the *Bulletin* material, consisting of 230 ten-drawer filing cabinets of news clippings and 250 filing cabinets of photographs, is very rich in documenting nearly every facet of everyday life in Philadelphia. Literally thousands of labor related issues are covered in this vast resource. For example, filed under "Strikes-Transit" are 139 packets of news clippings measuring 29 inches.[7] Of these, seven packets relate to the infamous 1944 transit strike that halted production of critical war-related products when white transit motormen refused to work with recently promoted black motormen.[8]

Information about these and other collections is disseminated through "Urban Archives Notes," the Center's bi-annual newsletter.[9] In addition to describing a noteworthy collection in each fall issue, the major manuscript holdings are listed under broad subject headings in order to provide an easy survey of related collections. Hence for labor

---

[5]The Amalgamated Clothing Workers of America, Philadelphia Joint Board records were described in the 1982 issue of *Labor History*.

[6]Its motto once proclaimed that "in Philadelphia, nearly everyone reads the *Bulletin*."

[7]This excludes transit operations in NJ, NYC, and the Philadelphia Suburban (Red Arrow) lines. Appropriate "see" references are included.

[8]The four inches consist of seven packets. The titles that follow are illustrative of the depth and breadth of the collection: "Strikes-Transit-1944 Phila.-Aug. 1 & 2," "Strikes-Transit-1944 Phila.-Aug. 8 & Later," "Strikes-Transit-1944 Phila.-Probe-Miscel.," "Strikes-Transit-1944 Phila.-Probe-Report & Indictments."

[9]Available upon request by writing to the Urban Archives Center.

historians, one could check the 34 collections listed under "Labor" or the 49 collections listed under "Business and Economic Development." Each spring issue includes brief comments about recent acquisitions by the Center as well as a description of yet another important manuscript collection. Three past issues of "Urban Archives Notes" describe in detail the labor collections which the Urban Archives Center accessioned at that time.[10] The Urban Archives Center's staff is also entering bibliographic descriptions of its holdings into the Research Libraries Information Network (RLIN). This enables scholars to obtain summary information, historical sketches, and other pertinent information about the collections. Outreach efforts such as these help inform scholars of the available resources at the Urban Archives Center.

The labor collections at the Center represent one important aspect of Philadelphia's social history. Closely allied are the records reflecting the city's ethnic groups, education, the legal system, housing, and social welfare organizations. Many of these "non-labor" collections are usually very fruitful for labor historians and should be consulted when examining the important role that Philadelphia played in the history of the labor movement.

Access: the Urban Archives Center is located in the Paley Library of Temple Univ. Its hours are 9 am–5 pm, Monday, Tuesday, Thursday, Friday, 9 am–8 pm, Wednesday. Researchers are encouraged to schedule an appointment for their first visit. Telephone inquiries are also welcomed. Contact Margaret Jerrido, Head, Urban Archives Center, Temple Univ., 13th and Berks Streets, Philadelphia, PA 19122; phone: (215) 787-8257.

---

[10]Urban Archives Notes, No. 23, Sept. 1982 (Philadelphia Federation of Teachers, Amalgamated Clothing and Textile Workers of America, Philadelphia Joint Board, Upholsterers' International Union, and the Federation of Telephone Workers of Pennsylvania); No. 24, Feb. 1983 (unions from the building trades and industrial workers); and No. 25, Sept. 1983 (white collar and professional sector unions).

LABOR ARCHIVES AT INDIANA UNIVERSITY OF PENNSYLVANIA

by
Eileen Mountjoy Cooper

Within the past two years, Indiana University of Pennsylvania (IUP) has significantly added to already existing archival collections with the addition of several important groups of labor-related materials.

In 1986 due to the expansion of its present office structure and the creation of an in-house computer center, the Rochester & Pittsburgh Coal Co. (Pennsylvania's largest coal producer) donated many of its corporate archives to IUP. This collection, consisting of 420 linear feet, constitutes one of the most complete groups of coal company records in the East. Probably the most significant group of papers consists of the presidential files of R&P and of its several predecessor companies.

Lucius Waterman Robinson (1889–1919) left papers rich in labor history and the industrial heritage of Western Pennsylvania. B. M. Clark (1919–1933) and his son, Heath S. Clark (1933–1948), both served as president during periods of industrial expansion and labor-management strife, and these are reflected in their surviving correspondence. In addition, Heath S. Clark served for many years as president of the National Coal Association.

Dr. Charles J. Potter, who recently celebrated his 50th year with R&P, served both as president and as chairman of the board. He was Deputy Solid Fuels Administrator under Harold Ickes during World War II, and is still an internationally significant figure in the coal industry. His correspondence illuminates many labor-related issues in the U.S. and abroad from 1948 to 1970.

H. Vernon Fritchman's papers cover the company's growth from 1970 to 1972; many of his earliest materials show the development of the freight-rate system for coal transportation as well as the transfor-

---

Eileen Mountjoy Cooper is Historical Collections Specialist at the Stapleton Library, Indiana University of Pennsylvania.

mation of R&P from a group of over a dozen independent coal and land-holding companies into today's corporation.

The R&P collection also contains a unique group of early financial ledgers which document the founding of the company's 17 mining towns, beginning with the parent company's incorporation in 1881. Included too are the ledgers of several railroads and pig iron furnaces owned by the earlier companies, engineering records, records of shipments, and company store files. A group of approximately 150 photographs, including images of mining town life, mining technology and its development, and historic views of R&P's mining plants document the period 1881–1950.

Complementing the R&P collection, IUP has within the past year and a half acquired two important groups of materials from two district offices of the United Mine Workers of America (UMWA). The first and most complete, are those of District 2, presently headquartered in Ebensburg, PA. Earliest records in this collection date from 1899–1917 and are comprised of agreements, convention reports, financial records, and other printed materials.

The papers of John Brophy, president of District 2 from 1917 to 1927, document in detail the struggles to unionize the miners of central Pennsylvania during the years leading up to World War I, and the period of economic hardship created by the subsequent lack of coal markets after the Armistice. Especially strong are files in the collection which contribute fresh insights into the coal strikes of 1919 and 1922, the beginnings of the conflict between Brophy and John L. Lewis, rank and file activities in District 2, organizational tactics on a local level, and the development of Brophy's thoughts on mine nationalization.

Highlighted among Brophy's papers are also an exchange of letters between the District 2 president and Mother Jones when the fabled labor leader came to Indiana, PA, to speak at a Labor Day rally in 1921. Several local organizers are also introduced through the medium of Brophy's correspondence. In various files, the daily activities of previously anonymous figures such as Dominick Gelotte, Stanley Hudzinski, and David Irvine are brought vividly to life.

The papers of James Mark, who served for half a century as vice president and later as president of District 2, form the largest part of the collection's correspondence. His papers, dating from 1918 to 1952, chronicle, in particular, the process of gradual mine mechanization and its resulting change in the workplace, the implementation of the miners' Health and Welfare program, early black lung and mine safety legislation, and the awarding of vacation and back pay for mine workers.

The remainder of the collection is comprised of: correspondence files of International Board members; receipts and expenditures of District 2 from 1947 to 1969; commissioners' cases, workers' compensation cases, grievances, and other legal documents relating to District 2.

Death certificates for miners and their wives and dependents, dated 1912–1928, provide detailed information on each applicant, including age, place of birth, work record, and cause of death. There are also more recent files listing and identifying local coal companies who signed contracts with District 2 from 1950 to 1970.

The second UMWA District collection, that of District 5, is still in the process of being transferred to IUP from its present location at the District's headquarters near Pittsburgh. Although more recent in scope than the District 2 collection, and less complete, due to this District's several relocations, these materials are comprised of several important groups of materials. Included are grievances (1947–1975); District Commission reports (1960–1974); office correspondence covering workers' insurance plans; wage agreements; international and District 5 minutes and proceedings (1909–1968); Welfare and Retirement Fund materials (1945–1972); ledgers and financial documents from a related District (#3); check-off records from local coal companies (1948–1959).

Two boxes of District 5 materials are particularly rich in the history of the Pittsburgh labor scene, and include recent union election materials, documentation of election proceedings, and the resulting cases of indictment and various court hearings (1970–1977).

IN addition to IUP's coal industry-related archival materials, the university is also the repository for an important collection of United Steel Workers of America records, those of Local 1397, headquartered in Homestead, PA. This group of papers was acquired in June 1977, when the local was forced to disband due to the closing of many of Pittsburgh's steel mills. This group is comprised of 59 boxes of materials, dating mainly from 1970 to 1987.

Arbitration proceedings and awards, weekly production reports, grievances, tonnage statistics, departmental schedules, job bids and awards, and pension files are included. Also present are materials on the Mon Valley Grievance Council, the Steel Valley United for Economic Development Group, the Military Spending Peace and Justice Campaign, job elimination programs, and the Steel Valley Authority. The grievance and arbitration reports are invaluable for their detail, listing individual workers, their age, work record, complete descriptions of each case, its progression through the arbitration system, and its eventual resolution.

The Local 1397 materials have also documented first-hand the struggles of workers to survive in the midst of the economic disaster that hit Pittsburgh's steel industry. This local, under the leadership of Ron Weisen and Mike Stout, played a crucial role as critics of both the United States Steel Co. and the national officers of the United Steel Workers of America. The local also established a food bank and undertook other programs to assist the unemployed.

The collection also includes materials from the Tri-State Conference on Steel, a community organization composed of clergy, workers, and activists, which turned to eminent domain and other unique and innovative techniques to restore elements of the steel industry and revitalize steel towns.

As well as printed materials and photographs, IUP's labor archives also features a collection of oral history tapes, including 60 hours of interviews with Western Pennsylvania coal miners and their families. Several faculty members in the Dept. of History, in addition, have done extensive work in this field, collecting oral interviews with working women in Indiana County, McCreary Tire and Rubber personnel, and World War II veterans.

Due to the availability of trained student workers, IUP has the ability to process collections with relative rapidity. Archival holdings are inventoried in detail; inventories are, at this time, being computerized for eventual printed finding aids. The labor archives are housed in an area of maximum security, with archivally correct environmental controls. There is a reading room available, and copying of documents is permissible in most cases, usually done for the researcher by a trained student worker. Negatives of photographic images may also be obtained.

IUP's collections are available for research by all serious students in the field of labor history and other related academic disciplines, although the university's agreement with District 2, UMWA, requires prior approval by a District 2 officer.

Access: IUP's Special Collections and Archives are open during regular school terms, 9 am to 4:30 pm, Monday–Friday, and by appointment on weekends and during periods of university breaks and vacations. For more information interested researchers may phone Eileen Mountjoy Cooper at (412) 357-3039, or write to Special Collections, 302 Stapleton Library, IUP, Indiana, PA, 15705.

HISTORICAL COLLECTIONS & LABOR ARCHIVES, PENN STATE UNIVERSITY

by
Peter Gottlieb and Diana L. Shenk

Penn State's Historical Collections & Labor Archives (HCLA), a unit of the University's Pattee Library, began in 1958 as a special collection of historical source material concerning Pennsylvania. In the mid-1960s, the staff initiated a labor archives project in cooperation with Penn State's Labor Studies Department to collect archival records, manuscripts, and oral histories primarily on the labor movement in Pennsylvania. In the roughly 20 years since the beginning of its labor archives project, HCLA has acquired a variety of sources that document both working class institutions as well as the lives of workers themselves.

The labor movement in Pennsylvania is the focus of HCLA's labor collections. HCLA has the records of state-wide labor federations, central bodies, and local unions. These records include the Pennsylvania Federation of Labor (1938–1960), the Pennsylvania Industrial Union Council (1937–1960), the Pennsylvania AFL-CIO (1960–1980) and some of the allied political organizations of these groups, notably Labor's Non-Partisan League of Pennsylvania (1936–1940). In addition to these core collections, there are also roughly two dozen local union and central body collections from all parts of the state and from both craft and industrial unions.

The largest single group of records in HCLA is the United Steelworkers of America Archive (1936–1983), which covers the union's membership throughout the U.S. (though not in Canada) and documents the internal and external activities of every hierarchical level of the organization. While these records go back to the founding of the Steel

---

Peter Gottlieb is the archivist at Penn State University's Historical Collections & Labor Archive.
Diana L. Shenk is the archivist for the NEH-funded Steel Workers Project at HCLA.

Workers Organizing Committee in the mid-1930s they fall mostly in the years from the mid-1940s to the early 1980s.

The main components of the USWA Archive are the record groups of the International Executive Board, elected officials, staff departments, and district and local union offices. The verbatim transcripts of the Executive Board proceedings provide insight into the Steelworkers' second highest policy-making body; office files of the International President, Vice-President, and Secretary-Treasurer reveal the union's relations with the labor movement, state and Federal governments, as well as the daily administration of the organization. Records of 13 district offices contain valuable documents on organizing, contract negotiations, grievances, and political action at the regional and local levels. There is extensive and particularly valuable information for Districts 1 (New England), 19 (Pittsburgh), 23 (WV), and 36 (AL). District records also offer useful information on Steelworkers local unions, and there are minute books, financial records, and detailed grievance files for several important union locals, including Local 1211 (Jones & Laughlin's Aliquippa, PA mills).

The roles played by the USWA professional staff emerge fully from the files for 11 staff departments: Arbitration, Civil Rights, Contracts, Education, Housing, International Affairs, Legal, Legislative, Public Relations, Research, and Safety and Health. Record groups for each department have reports, correspondence, memoranda, meeting minutes, and speeches that trace the relationship among the staff and the elected officials and constitutionally mandated bodies of the union. Careers of several notable USWA staff (e.g., Lee Pressman, Arthur Goldberg, Otis Brubaker, Emory Bacon, Meyer Bernstein) can also be studied in these files.

In addition to 2750 cubic feet of files, the USWA Archive contains 554 reels of microfilm, and an additional 7500 items, including photographs, sound recordings, and movie film. The photograph collection documents many important aspects of the USWA, though it mostly reflects formal activities within the union. It is a valuable source for individual or group photos of important officers and staff that have served the union through the years. There are also photographs of individuals closely associated with the union and others concerning labor organizations and activities in which the Steelworkers were involved. District and local union meetings and conventions are included in the sound recordings collection, and the movie films include footage of David McDonald's monthly TV spots, International Convention tapes, and labor education films.

HCLA staff, supported by funds from the National Endowment

for the Humanities and the USWA, are improving finding aids to the most important portions of the union's records, including the Executive Board proceedings, the President's and Secretary-Treasurer's office files, and several staff department record groups. The past 20 years of material in all Steelworkers records is restricted. Executive board proceedings from 1942 to 1952 are available to all researchers, but those from 1953 to 1964 may be examined only by application to HCLA.

Like the USWA Archive, the Graphic Communications International Union records (1975–1985) extend beyond the boundaries of Pennsylvania. A combination of formerly independent printing trades unions, the GCIU has transferred to the HCLA its own documents as well as those of predecessor unions, including the Graphic Arts Industrial Union, the Amalgamated Lithographers of America (1943–1964), and the International Photoengravers' Union of North America (1905–1964). Other labor records that range beyond Pennsylvania are those for the International Union of District 50 (1961–1972), the Amalgamated Association of Iron, Steel, and Tin Workers (1915–1942), the Aluminum Workers of America (1933–1944), and the Wallpaper Craftsmen and Workers of America (1904–1952).

Manuscript collections donated by labor leaders, organizers, activists, and industrial relations experts complement the records of labor organizations at HCLA. These collections reflect a wide range of involvement in the labor movement, from that of itinerant steel worker and coal miner organizers like George Medrick and Howard Curtiss to national labor figures and union leaders like Philip Murray, David J. McDonald, and I.W. Abel. Collections from labor intellectuals and mid-level officials are even more important. They include personal correspondence, diaries, reports, research files, and memorabilia of Clint Golden, Harold Ruttenberg, E.J. Lever, Meyer Bernstein, and Frank Fernbach of the United Steelworkers; Louis Leonard of the Amalgamated Association of Iron, Steel and Tin Workers; Michael Kosik and William Mitch of the United Mine Workers; Harry Block of the United Electrical Workers, the International Union of Electrical Workers and the Pennsylvania AFL-CIO; Martin Grayson of the Amalgamated Lithographers of America; and labor activist Father Charles Owen Rice. The papers of Socialist Party official Darlington Hoopes should be mentioned with this group of collections as well.

Oral histories provide another vital set of documents about organizing campaigns, formation of union policy, rank and file movements, mergers of unions, and the formative experiences of labor leaders. Of a total of 293 oral histories, nearly 200 are interviews with current or former officers and members of the United Steelworkers. The remainder of the oral histories are with their counterparts in the Graphic Communications International Union, the Philadelphia Federation of Teachers, the International Union of Mine, Mill, and Smelter Workers, the United Electrical Workers, and the Bakery and Confectionery Workers. General subjects like workers education, trade union women, and labor radicalism are the themes of the remaining oral histories. All interviews are transcribed and individually indexed.

Because records of industrial corporations contain important sources for the study of work relations, the labor process, technology's impact on labor, workers' communities, and strikes, HCLA collects business records that contain significant documentation for research about workers and their organizations. HCLA has recently acquired both corporate archival records and manuscripts of business executives to broaden its holdings. Of these acquisitions, a group of records from the Pennsylvania Railroad and the New York Central Railroad are the most extensive, covering the years from the 1880s to the 1960s. The railroads' archives have files on workers' housing, wages, strikes, strikebreakers, and labor legislation, especially for the years 1900–1930. Several important collections provide information about coal mining employment and coal miners' unions, notably the payroll records of the anthracite industry's Hudson Coal Co. The payroll records cover the years 1871–1932 and reveal the company's compensation schemes for men and boys during the transition from union to non-union labor. A similar kind of information for the early iron industry can be found in the financial ledgers and daybooks of several 18th and 19th century Pennsylvania iron furnaces.

The papers of Harrington Emerson (1853–1931) are the most important of the businessmen's manuscript collections available for labor research. The Emerson papers include consultants' reports to major U.S. corporations on training, methods of payment, work habits, housing and other personnel matters. These reports, in conjunction with Emerson's voluminous correspondence, constitute a vital source for studying the impact of scientific management and managerial reform movements on workers.

Researchers can investigate labor topics in the published monographs and periodicals, government documents, and microfilmed collections at HCLA and in Pattee Library. HCLA holds approximately 300 titles of non-current labor journals and newsletters, for some of which there are current issues in Pattee Library's Periodicals Department. The Microforms Department has union newspapers as well as numerous labor manuscripts and archival records on microfilm. U.S. and Pennsylvania government documents in Pattee Library contain vast stores of information about the labor movement. Annual reports and bulletin series of the Commonwealth of Pennsylvania's Bureau of Labor and Industry, Bureau of Mines, and Dept. of Welfare can support research on a wide range of subjects.

Descriptions of HCLA's labor records and manuscripts can be found in the Library of Congress's National Union Catalog of Manuscript Collections. HCLA is also entering collection descriptions into Penn State University Libraries' on-line catalog—the Library Information and Access System—which is available at Penn State campuses throughout the state. This information is also being added to the bibliographic data base of the Research Libraries Information Network (RLIN). Researchers may obtain finding aids to individual collections by contacting HCLA directly. A general information brochure about HCLA is available, and those interested in receiving a semi-annual newsletter with information about current projects and recent acquisitions may request to have their names added to the newsletter mailing list.

Access: HCLA is open from 8 am–5 pm, Monday–Friday except for national holidays. All researchers are welcome to examine its collections, but since some materials are restricted and others require advance notice to prepare for examination, it is important to write in advance for information about the particular documents and collections needed. Unless restricted or fragile, documents and photographs can be copied and mailed for a fee. Further information about the copying service, collections, and travel/lodging arrangements in the local area can be obtained by calling Peter Gottlieb at (814) 863-2505 or by mailing an inquiry to him at HCLA, W313 Pattee Library, Penn State Univ., University Park, PA 16802.

THE UE/LABOR ARCHIVES, UNIVERSITY OF PITTSBURGH

by
Mark McColloch

The UE/Labor Archives (UELA) is a division of the Archives of Industrial Society at the University of Pittsburgh. The UE/Labor Archives was established in 1975. It is the official repository for the records of the United Electrical, Radio and Machine Workers of America (UE) and its geographic districts in the U.S. It is also the home for dozens of other collections about labor in Western Pennsylvania, including labor union records, corporate employment and personnel files, the records of labor attorneys, labor activists and organizations associated with the labor movement.

The largest single collection in the UELA are the UE records. The following UE record groups have been organized and opened for use by scholars:

— UE District/Local Series: these are records maintained by the UE National Office about its constituent districts and locals. They are organized in numerical order by local and district, covering the period 1935-65. They consist of constitutions, contracts, officers records, minutes, correspondence, financial records, publications, and memoranda. This material is about 81 cubic feet in volume.

— UE Publications Series: these are publications files maintained by the UE National Office. They include mimeographed letters, periodicals, convention publications, pamphlets, leaflets, radio broadcast transcripts, newspaper clippings, press releases, etc. They cover the period 1935-65. There is about 14 cubic feet of material in this series.

— UE Organizers Series: this series consists of UE National Office files for most of its national organizing staff for 1935-50. It includes correspondence, reports and other material. It is organized alphabetically, by organizer. It consists of about 21 cubic feet.

Mark McColloch was archivist at the UE/Labor Archives and is now Associate Professor of History, the Univ. of Pittsburgh, Greensburg.

—UE Conference Board Series: these are UE National Office files for most of its industry conference boards. Those opened include Westinghouse, Remington Rand, Sylvania, General Electric, International Harvester, General Motors, and RCA. The files include minutes, negotiations records, publications and files on the constituent locals of each conference board. The files cover the years 1935–65 and are about 50 cubic feet in volume.

The UE collection is also the repository for the records of all current UE districts in the U.S. The records of Districts 2, 6, 7, and 11 are open, and those of District 1 are partially opened. The files consist of records which each district maintained about itself and its constituent locals. They are about 18 cubic feet in volume and cover the period 1935–60.

Please note that the above material is open to scholars, provided that it is more than 25 years old. Currently, therefore, material through 1965 is open. As new series are processed over the next several years, additional records will become open, including General Executive Board minutes and the files of the UE's Washington Office. There are about 550 cubic feet of material in this unprocessed and unopened category. The UELA also holds about 1500 UE photographs, which are available for use by scholars.

Two closely related collections in the UELA are the papers of Thomas Quinn, a former UE activist and current director of the Pennsylvania Bureau of Mediation and Conciliation, and Margaret Darin Stasik, a former UE activist and staff member. These collections focus on the history of UE locals 601 and 610. They cover the period 1935–60.

The UELA is also the home for a number of local union records from the Western Pennsylvania area. These include Service Employees International Union Local 565 (clerical, technical and service workers), and SEIU Local 668 (public employee caseworkers and social workers). The UELA also holds the records of several locals of the United Brewery Workers and its Pennsylvania Joint Council, American Federation of Teachers locals at the Univ. of Pittsburgh, Community College of Allegheny County, Robert Morris College and five public school district locals based in Allegheny County. Other records housed at the UELA include material generated by the Federation of Telephone Workers of Pennsylvania (now a local of the Communications Workers of America), and the Iron City Legal Assistance Workers (District 65, UAW). The UELA is the repository for a large collection of Teamster contracts from Western Pennsylvania, covering 1940–1970 and the quite substantial Gaston Le Blanc papers (Le Blanc was the final president of the United Stone Workers of America, now merged into the United Steelworkers). Several AFL-CIO federal locals in the beer bottling, beer transportation, and beer brewing industries have their records in the UELA, as do the Environmentalists for Full Employment, a joint project of the Sierra Club and the Steelworkers. These records cover the 1979–84 period. The UELA is also the repository for the archives of the Beaver Valley Labor History Society (containing a large number of oral interviews with steelworker activists of the 1930s), the Mon Valley Unemployed Committee, and the Steel Valley Unemployed Council.

Finally, the UELA hosts some major corporate labor relations and personnel card collections. These include the personnel cards of the A.M. Byers Company (24,000 detailed cards spanning the years 1895–1960), the personnel cards of the LTV Steel Corporation for the former Jones and Laughlin plants in Pittsburgh (195,000 cards, covering the period 1900–70), and the USX Corporation's (formerly U.S. Steel) labor relations files and payroll ledgers from 1905 to 1970.

The UELA has prepared detailed guides to most of this material. For the UELA collections there is an item-by-item inventory of all open items, with notations indicating subject matter. There are also summaries, describing each record group in more general terms. The summaries are available from the UELA upon request, for the cost of their photoduplication. Most of the other collections described above are cataloged at the file folder level. In most cases, finding aids are available upon request for the cost of their reproduction.

Access: except for Christmas week, the UELA is open year round. Hours are 8:30 am–5 pm, Monday–Friday. Special hours can sometimes be arranged. Unannounced patrons will generally be welcomed, but because of the small staff it is best to write or call ahead, so that your research visit can be a productive one. Contact David Rosenberg. His telephone number is (412) 648-7099. The mailing address for the UE/Labor Archives is 363 Hillman Library, Univ. of Pittsburgh, Pittsburgh, PA 15260.

LABOR HISTORY SOURCES IN
THE MANUSCRIPT DIVISION OF THE LIBRARY
OF CONGRESS

by
John E. Haynes

The Manuscript Division of the Library of Congress seeks to preserve personal papers and organizational records that document the course of America's national experience. Its more than 10,000 collections with more than 40,000,000 manuscript items touch upon every aspect of American history and culture. The Manuscript Division's holdings are strongest, however, in the areas of American national government, the Federal judiciary, diplomacy, military history, women's history, and black history. Collections containing labor-related material are considerable and constitute a major archive for labor history research.

Organizational Records

American Federation of Labor (AFL) Letterbooks. These letterbooks of outgoing correspondence span the years 1883–1925 and are an indispensable source for studying the development of the American labor movement. Principally written by Samuel Gompers and to a lesser degree William Green, John McBride, and James Duncan, the letters deal with every aspect of the trade union movement. Microfilm edition available.

American Friends Service Committee Work Camp Diary. Detailed typescript diary kept in the summer of 1933 by a Quaker community-organizing team in a coal mining town in Kentucky. The diary conveys a significant amount of information on the psychological attitudes of mining families and the impact of early New Deal legislation.

John E. Haynes is editor of the Historians of American Communism Newsletter *and a Specialist in 20th Century Political History at the Library of Congress.*

Brotherhood of Sleeping Car Porters. The Brotherhood's records (41,000 items) span the years 1939–1968, with most material dating after 1950. The largest part of the records consists of files on agreements with major railroads, conventions, relations between the headquarters and local branches, and the Brotherhood's relationship with other rail unions and with the AFL. The records also include several short series consisting of the personal papers of Benjamin F. McLaurin, Ashley L. Totten, and A. Philip Randolph. The latter's series contains files on his interest in organizing farm workers.

Massachusetts Textile Strike List, c. 1900–1926. Labor spy report of unknown origin regarding an unidentified textile strike in Massachusetts.

National Association for the Advancement of Colored People. The NAACP records contain files on the relationship of black workers and various trade unions. A related collection is the *NAACP Legal Defense and Education Fund.* These extensive records, however, were recently acquired and have not yet been processed. The *NAACP Washington Bureau* papers discuss NAACP dealings with Washington area labor unions. Access to all NAACP collections is restricted.

National Association of Railway Postal Clerks. Typescript extracts of convention proceedings (1880–1901) of the union and its predecessors.

National Child Labor Committee. The records (2800 items) chronicle the campaign in the early decades of this century to eliminate child labor. NCLC records include official proceedings, minute books, correspondence, press clippings, and campaign literature as well as detailed reports on child labor conditions, arranged by industry and state.

National Consumers League. The records (75,000 items) of the NCL span the years 1882–1973 with most for the period 1920–1950. The NCL was concerned with the conditions under which products were made and not with the products themselves. It sought comprehensive legislation regulating wages and hours, requiring sanitary working conditions, and prohibiting child labor. Microfilm edition available.

National Urban League. The League's records include exhaustively documented studies of the economic and industrial conditions of black Americans. These records, which begin in 1910, are without peer in understanding the changing role of black workers in the American economy. Related collections are the *National Urban League Southern Regional Office* and the *National Urban League Washington Bureau.* Access to all NUL records is restricted.

National Women's Trade Union League of America. The records (7400 items) span the years 1903–1950. Originally concerned with promoting the unionization of women, NWTUL soon turned its attention to protective labor legislation. Microfilm edition available.

People's Legislative Service. Contains speeches, printed matter, and correspondence from the labor-backed 1924 presidential campaign of Senator Robert M. La Follette.

Pinkerton's National Detective Agency. Contains reports from the early 1870s on the agency's infiltration of the Molly Maguires. Microfilm edition available.

United States Work Projects Administration Federal Writers' Project and Historical Records Survey. These WPA records (400,000 items) contain a variety of folk, ethnic, and social data of interest to labor historians. Microfilm edition of printed matter available.

Personal Papers

Allen, Henry J. Allen was governor of Kansas, 1919–1923. His papers document Kansas's unique Court of Industrial Relations, Allen's debate with Samuel Gompers over government regulation of labor relations, and activities in Kansas of the Industrial Workers of the World.

Beyer, Otto S. Beyer was a consulting engineer and labor-management relations specialist. The 30,000 items of his papers span the years 1915–1948 with most dating after 1929. During World War I, Beyer developed a successful program of union-management cooperation at army arsenals. Following the war, he worked as a consulting engineer for various unions, industrial firms, and railroads. During the New Deal, he served as labor relations consultant to the Tennessee Valley Authority, chairman of the National Mediation Board, and member of the War Manpower Commission. His papers reflect his involvement in a wide variety of strikes, lockouts, and personnel disputes.

Billings, Warren K. Billings, a labor militant, was convicted with Tom Mooney for exploding a bomb during the San Francisco Preparedness Day parade in 1916. The papers (2600 items) span the years 1914–1973, but most concern his 1920–1939 campaign to win release from prison.

Borah, William E. Borah was a U.S. Senator from Idaho during the years 1907–1940. His papers contain a limited amount of material on Idaho labor matters, Federal labor legislation, and the post-World War I Red Scare. The Library's Borah papers span the years 1905–40, with most material dating after 1912. The collection contains little regarding Borah's prosecution of William Haywood of the Western Federation of Miners for conspiracy to murder an Idaho governor. The Idaho State Historical Society houses a collection of papers relating to Borah's activities from 1890 to 1907.

Carnegie, Andrew. The collection chronicles Carnegie's extensive involvement in late 19th century industrial development and early 20th century philanthropy. His business correspondence often touches upon labor conditions at Carnegie Corporation facilities.

Clark, Samuel H. Clark headed the Association of Colored Railway Trainmen and Locomotive Firemen. His papers' 250 items contain scattered documents on union affairs from the 1930s to the 1950s as well as a detailed file for 1945–49 from the union's Norfolk & Western Railroad grievance committee.

Cortelyou, George B. His papers contain correspondence and subject files for his 1903 tenure as the first Secretary of the U.S. Department of Commerce and Labor.

Darrow, Clarence. Darrow's papers include material on his role in the Woodworkers' Conspiracy Trial, Haywood's Idaho conspiracy case, the Darrow Bribery Trial growing out of the McNamara case, and the 1902 Anthracite Coal Strike Arbitration Commission.

Davis, James J. His papers contain very little correspondence for his tenure as U.S. Secretary of Labor (1921–1930); a number of speeches and articles on labor questions are present, however. Also present is a 1941 draft of an unpublished book entitled "The History of Strikes."

Draper, Ernest G. Draper served on the National Labor Board and as Assistant Secretary of Commerce during Franklin Roosevelt's presidency and on the board of governors of the Federal Reserve System from 1938 to 1950. His papers contain numerous speeches and articles about unemployment.

Frankfurter, Felix. Frankfurter was a key figure in progressive and liberal politics from World War I until his appointment to the Supreme Court in 1939. His extensive correspondence with political figures and government officials often touches on issues of labor and industrial legislation, particularly during the New Deal. Microfilm edition available.

Frey, John P. Frey headed the Metal Trades Dept. of the AFL from 1934 to 1950. His papers total 28,000 items and include extensive correspondence and subject files dealing with all aspects of the trade union movements. Frey developed extensive files on topics of special interest, including concentration in the banking industry, craft unionism versus industrial unionism, Communism, and the Communist role in the CIO. The papers include Frey's "Trade Union Experiences," a manuscript narrating the development of the AFL.

Garfield, James R. Garfield was commissioner of corporations (1903–1907) in the Dept. of Commerce and Labor. His diaries, letters, and subject files contain detailed information on labor conditions in the meat-packing, petroleum, and railroad industries.

Gleason, Arthur H. The papers of this reformer and journalist include files on his work with John Brophy of the United Mine Workers and the Bureau of Industrial Research in 1921–1923. Microfilm edition available.

Goodman, Leo. Goodman pioneered the labor movement's concern with radiation safety and was secretary of the AFL–CIO's Atomic Energy Technical Committee from its establishment until 1967. His papers are not yet processed, and no finding aid has been prepared.

Harriman, Florence J. These papers contain a limited amount of material concerning Harriman's membership on the Federal Industrial Relations Commission (1913–1916) and the AFL Committee on Women In Industry (1917–1919).

Harriman, W. Averell. Harriman's papers include material on labor relations at his Merchant Shipbuilding Corporation and Union Pacific Railroad and his perspective on relations between the Roosevelt administration and business during his chairmanship of the Business Advisory Council of the U.S. Dept. of Commerce in the late 1930s. Harriman's political files also contain material on labor politics in New York and elsewhere in the 1950s. Access restricted.

Harrison, Nancy Blaine. These papers, part of the Gilbert Harrison Papers, document Nancy Harrison's career as a union organizer in North Carolina in the 1940s.

Hines, Lewis G. Hines held a variety of union and public posts. His papers (13,800 items) are especially useful for studying Pennsylvania labor politics in the 1930s. Hines supported Republicans through the 1930s and Wendell Willkie in 1940. He vigorously opposed the CIO and Communism, and his files document his close attention to the CIO and his effort as head of Pennsylvania's Dept. of Labor and Industry to discharge those aligned with the Communist-led CIO union of state employees. His files for his tenure as national AFL legislative representative (1943–1949) deal with the AFL's interest in conscription, veterans' benefits, wage and price controls, labor standards, health insurance, and the Taft-Hartley Act. Files for his later career as AFL special representative (1949–1958) include material on the importation of farm labor.

Ickes, Harold L. The voluminous diary Ickes kept during his tenure as Secretary of the Interior (1933–1945) includes conversations with hundreds of New Deal officials, politicians, and union leaders about political topics. Ickes's diary and memoir are available on microfilm.

Kingsbury, John A. Kingsbury held key positions in the State Charities Aid Association (1907–1911), the Association for Improving the

Condition of the Poor (1911–1914), and the Public Charities of New York City (1914–1918). His papers reveal much about the condition of the most hard-pressed levels of American society.

Kroll, Jack. Kroll directed the CIO's Political Action Committee from 1946 until the 1956 merger with the AFL. His papers (3600 items) contain many speeches dealing with the CIO's political views and its electoral strategy.

La Follette Family. This collection includes the papers of Wisconsin governor and U.S. Senator Robert M. La Follette, Sr., U.S. Senator Robert M. La Follette, Jr., Wisconsin Governor Philip F. La Follette, other La Follette family members, and the records (1911–1912) of the National Progressive Republican League. The papers contain extensive correspondence on political and legislative matters with numerous trade union officials and progressive politicians as well as extensive files on labor legislation.

Land, Emory S. Adm. Land headed the War Shipping Administration during World War II, and his papers document his frequent clashes with unions over personnel policies.

Landis, James M. One container of Landis's papers is devoted to his role as a special trial examiner for the U.S. Dept. of Labor in its attempt to deport Harry Bridges of the West Coast longshoremen's union.

McAdoo, William G. McAdoo, President Woodrow Wilson's Secretary of the Treasury, ran the nation's railroads during their seizure for military purposes in World War I. His correspondence and subject files document his experiences with rail labor relations.

McGranery, James P. McGranery was assistant to the U.S. Attorney General, 1943–1946, U.S. district judge, 1946–1952, and Attorney General, 1952–1953. His papers include legal files on labor racketeering and the legal status of certain types of union political activity. Access restricted.

McKelway, Alexander J. McKelway served as southern secretary of the National Child Labor Committee in the early decades of the 20th century. His papers (2500 items) contain numerous speeches on labor conditions in the South and extensive correspondence regarding child labor legislation.

Neufeld, Maurice F. Neufeld's diaries contain accounts of conversations with leading figures in labor relations and labor politics, including Francis Perkins and Herbert Lehman. Access restricted.

Olney, Richard. Olney's papers contain correspondence and other material dealing with his role, as President Grover Cleveland's attorney general, in the use of U.S. troops in the 1894 railroad stikes. Microfilm edition available.

Pinchot, Amos R. E. The papers of this earnest progressive touch on all aspects of reform in the period from 1910 to his death in 1944. Included in his papers is correspondence with union officials and labor politicians as well as files on labor legislation.

Pinchot, Cornelia. Contains considerable material on the National Women's Trade Union League.

Pinchot, Gifford. The files for his two terms as Pennsylvania Governor (1923–1927 and 1932–1935) frequently discuss labor and economic conditions. His diaries and scrapbooks are on microfilm.

Randolph, A. Philip. Randolph's long career as a labor and civil rights leader is documented in the 13,000 items of his papers. In addition to correspondence, speeches, and writings, Randolph's papers contain subject files on the Brotherhood of Sleeping Car Porters and the U.S. Fair Employment Practices Committee, as well as material regarding his interest in the treatment of black members by various unions. The papers include files on the March on Washington Movement, the Negro American Labor Council, the Socialist Party, and the National Negro Congress. Microfilm edition anticipated.

Rauh, Joseph L. Rauh, a labor lawyer, leading liberal, and civil rights activist, was attorney for the United Auto Workers in the 1950s. His papers contain extensive files concerning UAW legal affairs and his work for many other union clients. Rauh's files also document his legal work on behalf of the Edward Sadlowski insurgency in the United Steel Workers and on behalf of the anti-Tony Boyle caucus of the United Mine Workers in the 1970s.

Ryan, Joseph P. This collection contains a dozen letters exchanged between Ryan, leader of the International Longshoremen's Association, and various U.S. officials concerning ILA cooperation with the war effort in World War II.

Sampson, William. Sampson's letters contain references to his role as attorney in the 1810 landmark case of the journeymen cordwainers regarding the legal status of the closed shop.

Schofield, John M. Gen. Schofield was the commanding general of the U.S. Army, 1888-1895. His papers contain extensive correspondence on the use of troops during the railroad strikes and labor unrest of 1894.

Schwellenbach, Lewis B. Schwellenbachs' papers include speeches and statements on postwar labor problems he delivered when he was Secretary of Labor, 1945–1948.

Sifton, Paul F., and Sifton, Claire G. The Sifton papers (15,550 items) contain files on Paul Sifton's work as national legislative representative for the United Auto Workers (1948–1962). Also document his work in the 1930s in New York's unemployment compensation system and the U.S. Wages and Hours Division. Other files cover his post-1941 activities with the National Farmers' Union, the Union for Democratic Action, and the War Manpower Commission. The Siftons' papers also contain a number of playscripts for social dramas authored by one or both of them. Present as well is an unfinished exposé of John L. Lewis written by Paul Sifton.

Straus, Oscar S. Straus was Secretary of Commerce and Labor, 1906–1909, and chaired the arbitration commission to settle the dispute between eastern railroads and their engineers in 1912. His diary and his correspondence discuss labor controversies of the era.

Taft, Robert A. Senator Taft's legislative files document his lengthy battle to modify the National Labor Relations Act as well as his work on numerous other pieces of labor legislation. Taft's political files also contain background information on union political activity.

Thompson, Huston. Thompson's papers contain some material concerning his membership on presidential boards investigating railroad labor disputes during the Roosevelt and Truman administrations.

Wallace, Henry A. The Library's Wallace papers (about 24,600 items) are chiefly from his Vice-Presidency. His correspondence and political files contain many letters with union officials and labor politicians. The University of Iowa and the Franklin D. Roosevelt Library also maintain large Wallace collections. Microfilm edition available.

Presidential Papers. The Library's Manuscript Division holds the main body of the papers of 23 presidents spanning from George Washington to Calvin Coolidge. Labor historians may find items of interest in one or another of these collections. The papers of *Theodore Roosevelt* and *Woodrow Wilson*, for example, include files relevant to a variety of labor controversies during their administrations. All of the Library's presidential collections are available on microfilm.

Judicial Papers. The Manuscript Division holds the papers of 31 justices of the Supreme Court, 32 U.S. attorneys general, several solicitors general, and a number of appeals court judges. Files regarding key court cases bearing upon the legal position of workers and unions often can be found in the relevant judicial papers.

Other Library of Congress Collections

In addition to its manuscript collection, the Library of Congress maintains other large collections of value to labor historians. Researchers may wish to consult "How to Find Materials on *Labor* at the Library of Congress," a 1985 publication of the Library's *General Reading Rooms Division*. This publication describes the Library's bibliographic resources and how to use them to find labor-related material. The Library's main book collection contains hundreds of volumes of bound union convention proceedings as well as thousands of other books and bound serials on labor topics. The *Microform Reading Room*'s collection of microfilmed documents, publications, and dissertations is vast. The *Prints and Photographs Division* maintains (to name just three collections of interest to labor historians) Lewis Hine's dramatic child labor photographs from the early 1900s, Dorothea Lange's photo-documentation of rural and migrant workers in the 1930s, and the photographic collection of the National Women's Trade Union League. The Library's holdings of labor-related broadsides and pamphlets are described in James Gilreath, "Labor History Sources in the Library of Congress *Rare Book and Special Collections Division,*" *Labor History*, 25 (1984), 243–251. The *Motion Picture, Broadcasting and Recorded Sound Division* maintains a large collection of feature films, newsreel footage, and contemporary news broadcasts for those wishing to use this type of source. The *Archive of Folk Culture* of the American Folklife Center has compiled bibliographies of labor and industrial songs, and recordings of many of them can be found in the Motion Picture, Broadcasting and Recorded Sound Division.

Access: The Manuscript Reading Room is located in room LM 101 of the Library's Madison Building at 101 Independence Ave., Washington, DC, and is open from 8:30 am to 5 pm, Monday–Saturday. All collections discussed have finding aids unless otherwise noted. Security regulations prohibit bringing personal property into the reading room and lockers are provided for researcher use. Coin-operated copy machines are available. Microfilm editions of manuscript collections usually may be borrowed on interlibrary loan. Reference services are available in person or by correspondence. Requests for informational brochures or other questions may be addressed to John E. Haynes, Manuscript Division, Library of Congress, Washington, DC, 20540; phone: (202) 707-5387.

LABOR HISTORY SOURCES IN
THE NATIONAL ARCHIVES

by
Tab Lewis

The National Archives was established in 1934 as the repository for the permanently valuable records of the U.S. In the intervening years, it has become a system consisting of three records facilities in the Washington, DC area, 11 regional archives, and 8 presidential libraries.

The Washington, DC area facilities alone contain almost 1,200,000 cubic feet of textual records, over 17,000,000 photographs, audiovisual items, maps, artifacts, machine readable records and almost 18,500,000 microforms. The textual records of agencies cited herein include but are not limited to correspondence, reports, conference and meeting proceedings from agency committees and boards, memoranda, press releases, copies of speeches, and hearing transcripts. Documents published by the Government Printing Office are maintained according to their Superintendent of Documents classification in RG 287.

Many of the records in archival repositories operated by the National Archives and Records Administration (NARA) relate to labor issues in some way. These records are maintained in record groups (RGs) on the basis of the creating agency. A short essay such as this can only touch upon relatively few of the records that relate to labor in the vast archival holdings of NARA.[1] The purpose here is to describe Federal records that document activities of the Federal government relating to

Tab Lewis is Archivist, Civil Reference Branch, National Archives, Washington, DC.

[1]For a detailed examination of specific labor-related record items in the National Archives, see two articles by Meyer H. Fishbein: "Business History Resources in the National Archives," *Business History Review*, 38 (1964), 232-57, "Labor History Resources in the National Archives," *Labor History*, 8 (1967), 330-50. For a survey of labor archives, including the National Archives, as they relate to the history of the modern state, see Robert H. Zieger, "Labor and the State in Modern America: the Archival Trail," *Journal of American History*, 75 (1988), 184-96.

the labor movement and working-class life, and to highlight published guides and other finding aids to these records.

Various types of finding aids to National Archives records are available to researchers. "Guides" give a general overview of records in NARA's archival repositories. They can be comprehensive, like the *Guide to the National Archives of the United States* (1977), or specific, such as the *Guide to Cartographic Records in the National Archives* (1971). In addition, individual finding aids are available for each record group. These vary in sophistication, from "location registers" to printed inventories.

Because archival practice requires that the original order of records be preserved, the organization of labor-related materials within a record group varies with the filing practices of individual agencies. One widely used arrangement system is a variation of a decimal classification or numerical system, whereby all records created or received in the agency are filed together. Some agencies use an alphabetical system which uses letters as the subject designator. Use of such filing systems is usually noted in finding aids, and explanations of systems in use often appear therein as appendices. In many cases a filing manual is available. In addition, records are often indexed by subject, file number, and/or names.

NARA has labor archives created by each branch of the government, but most labor materials are in the records created by executive branch agencies and departments. These will receive the most attention here. However, as the Congress is responsible for fundamental labor law at the national level, this is where our description of labor-related archives begins.

Most congressional records relating to labor are in RG 233, Records of the U.S. House of Representatives, or RG 46, Records of the U.S. Senate. The pertinent records are those of committees concerned with labor matters. These include several House, Senate, Select, Special, and Joint Committees. The Committee on Education and Labor (1867–1883, 1946–present, named the Committee on Labor, 1883–1946) of the House of Representatives has jurisdiction over most labor matters. Their Senate counterparts are the Committee on Labor and Public Welfare (1869–1870, 1947–present) and the Committee on Education and Labor (1870–1947). The Subcommittee Investigating Violations of Free Speech and Labor (1936–1941) and the Subcommittee on Employment, Manpower, and Poverty (1965–1968) were two significant subcommittees of the Senate's full committee which studied labor issues. The free speech and labor subcommittee is of special interest in that it investigated employer tactics used in some industries to prevent collective bargaining with unions.

The House and Senate both occasionally create "Select" or "Special" committees to investigate labor problems of immediate concern. The House's primary contribution here was the Special Committee on Postwar Economic Policy and Planning, established in 1944 to plan the transition to a peacetime economy after World War II. The Senate Select Committee on Improper Activities in the Labor or Management Field (1957–1960) studied the extent of criminal and unethical activity in labor-management relations.

These are a few of the committees that have created records relating to the fundamental labor laws of the nation. In addition, several "joint" committees have been established over time to oversee labor laws and activities. Furthermore, other standing committees have sometimes dealt with labor issues that fall more appropriately under their domain; an example is farm labor as a concern of the agriculture committees. The best sources of information about records at the National Archives resulting from the work of all these committees are two recently published guides to Congressional records, *Guide to the Records of the United States House of Representatives at the National Archives, 1789–1989* (1989) and *Guide to the Records of the United States Senate at the National Archives, 1789–1989* (1989).

The records created by the executive branch of the government reflect the varied ways in which it is involved in labor matters. Such government activity includes continuing supervision of labor regulations, efforts to resolve labor problems during economic and military crises, analysis of working-class life, and studies of labor problems affecting specific segments of society or specific industries. Records relating to all of these are in the National Archives.

Agency records in the National Archives pertaining to government's continuing direct responsibility in labor matters are those of the Dept. of Labor (RG 174), the National Labor Relations Board (RG 25), and the Federal Mediation and Reconciliation Service (RG 280). The Dept. of Labor is the most prominent of these.

Labor Dept. records currently at NARA (in RG 174) include the records of most Secretaries of Labor from William B. Wilson (1913–1921) to Raymond J. Donovan (1981–1984). These files also include the records of numerous under-secretaries, assistant secretaries, and divisions of the department. An important series in these records is the main numerical series or the "Chief Clerk's" files (1907–1942). These records cover many labor topics including radicalism, unions, industries, labor conditions at home and abroad, legislation, and various aspects of working-class life.

The depression and the world wars are examples of crises in this century which affected the working public and required action beyond the mandate of established agencies. New agencies were established as a result, and many of their records are now in the National Archives.

The Great Depression began in 1929, and its effect upon labor was devastating. Numerous agencies were created during President Franklin Roosevelt's "New Deal" to put people to work and restore the nation's economy. The records pertaining to labor-related New Deal agencies include the records of the Work Projects Administration (WPA) and the records of its predecessors, the Civil Works Administration, and the Federal Emergency Relief Administration, all in RG 69.

The rural equivalent of the WPA was the Civilian Conservation Corp. Its records are in RG 35. Records of the Office of the Secretary of Agriculture (RG 16), of the Bureau of Agricultural Economics (RG 83), and of the Federal Extension Service (RG 33) also contain materials related to farm labor.

Records of the National Recovery Administration (NRA) chronicle depression-era economic recovery efforts that affected labor in specific industries. The NRA regulated industry through fair competition codes. "Labor boards" within the NRA monitored the status of bituminous coal miners and steel, automotive, and textile workers, while the NRA's Labor Advisory Board provided guidance regarding labor policy. Records of the NRA and these boards are in RG 9.

Military crises, such as world wars, often provoke strong reactions to organized labor. The manpower needed to fight a war must be balanced with the manpower needed to produce armaments. Civilian and military authorities share responsibility for meeting these needs. All the while, "subversion" of the war effort, often attributed to radical unionists or others on the Left, must be stopped. All of these factors have combined to prompt the creation of many Federal records relating to American labor.

There are guides available to assist in the identification of records of all types created during World Wars I and II. These are the *Handbook of Federal World War Agencies and Their Records 1917–1921* (1943), and *Federal Records of World War II* (2 vols. 1951). These describe records of the numerous agencies created in the war emergencies as well as the relevant records of established agencies. Many, but not all, of the records described in these guides are housed in NARA's archival repositories.

Agencies were created during both world wars to coordinate manpower needs of the war effort. In World War I, the War Labor Policies Board and the National War Labor Board (NWLB) were established to coordinate labor policies of Federal agencies and to mediate labor disputes. The records of these agencies are in RG 1 and RG 2, respectively. Their counterparts in World War II were the War Manpower

Commission (with records in RG 211) and another National War Labor Board (with records in RG 202). The World War I NWLB was established after two Labor Dept. mediation attempts failed. Records of these earlier efforts, the U.S. Commission of Industrial Relations (1912–1915) and the President's Mediation Commission (1917–1918), are in RG 174 and, along with the NWLB records, are available commercially from University Publications of America (UPA), Frederick, Maryland, as microfilm publications in its "Research Collections in Labor Studies" series.

The records of three military agencies concerned with labor in the armaments industry are in the National Archives. The intelligence divisions of these agencies monitored subversive activities against the war effort. These agencies also had a role in formulating manpower policy for armaments construction. The agency records that chronicle these activities are the general records of the Dept. of the Navy (RG 80), the records of the War Dept. General and Special Staffs (RG 165), and the records of the Office of the Provost Marshall General (RG 389). Indexes to records in RG 80 and RG 165 are available as NARA microfilm publications.

Subversive activity, particularly in peacetime, is generally the responsibility of the Dept. of Justice (with records in RG 60) and the Federal Bureau of Investigation (with records in RG 65). The subject files of the Justice Dept. contain records relating to general labor subjects, such as the eight-hour day and specific labor laws, as well as records pertaining to strikes. FBI records relating to investigations of suspected labor radicals and radical unions, such as the Industrial Workers of the World, are included in the "Investigative Case Files of the Bureau of Investigation, 1908–1922," available as a NARA microfilm publication. The records of the Pardon Attorney (RG 204) include files on suspected subversives such as Eugene V. Debs. The records of the Post Office Dept. (RG 28) contain case files relating to subversive activity during the world wars, many of which contain copies of radical publications.

Numerous federal agencies concerned with labor, including suspected subversive labor activity, in specific industries have been created. In maritime labor matters, these agencies include the U.S. Shipping Board (with records in RG 32), the Maritime Labor Board (with records in RG 157), and the Shipbuilding Stabilization Committee (with records in RG 254). Important federal agencies concerned with railways included the National Mediation Board (with records in RG 13) and the U.S. Railroad Administration (with records in RG 14). The Bureau of Mines (with records in RG 70) and two bituminous coal commissions—one in the U.S. Fuel Administration, another during the 1930s—regulated the mining industry. Records of the commissions are in RG 67 and RG 150, respectively.

The labor problems of specific segments of the population have also received their share of government attention. The records of the Bureau of Indian Affairs (RG 75), the Women's Bureau (RG 86), the Children's Bureau (RG 102), and the National Youth Administration (RG 119) show that all were created as units within other agencies to assist specific groups in the population. Reports, conference proceedings, articles, and copies of speeches by officials of the Women's Bureau are available on microfilm from UPA in its "Research Collections in Women's Studies" series.

Many records dealing with labor in the National Archives cited herein document the labor experience of blacks. *Black History: A Guide to Civilian Records in the National Archives* (1984) describes many of these records in detail. These include the records of the Committee on Fair Employment Practice (RG 228) specifically concerned with discrimination against blacks in the labor force.

The President of the U.S. occasionally appoints panels to investigate subjects of immediate interest. The records of these panels in the National Archives are in RG 220, Records of Presidential Committees, Commissions, and Boards. Panels investigating labor-management policy, equal employment opportunity, employment of the handicapped, state workmen's compensation laws, and employment and unemployment statistics are just a few of these bodies. Descriptions of their records are included in the *Guide to the National Archives*, and in guides available from individual presidential libraries. A privately published source (1985) that includes these latter records, *A Guide to Manuscripts in the Presidential Libraries* by Dennis Burton, James B. Rhoads, and Raymond W. Smock, is available from the College Park, MD Research Materials Corp.

The records of two agencies include data on the labor market and the spending habits of wage earners. Records of labor market surveys conducted by the Bureau of Employment Security during World War II (in RG 183) describe the labor supply for states and major municipalities therein. Consumer purchase surveys conducted by the Bureau of Labor Statistics in the mid-1930s (in RG 257) provide information on the effectiveness of New Deal programs.

The National Archives also has labor-related records of certain nongovernment agencies. The American Red Cross occasionally provided relief during labor disputes. Red Cross records relating to some of these efforts have been transferred to the National Archives.

The labor situation in other countries often affects the economic situation in the United States. The Bureau of Foreign and Domestic Commerce maintained records (now in RG 151) relating to strikes and lock-outs in other nations as well as the U.S. Reports of commercial attaches in this record group analyze the economic status of other nations, which may affect American labor. The *Guide to Materials on Latin America in the National Archives* (1974) describes records relating to labor conditions in Central and South America.

Regional records of Federal agencies, as well as the records of the U.S. District Courts in RG 21, are in 11 NARA regional archives, thereby remaining in the region of the country in which they were created. Regional archives holdings are described in *The Archives: A Guide to the National Archives Field Branches* by Loretto Szucs and Sandra Luebking (Salt Lake City, 1988).

Occasionally, labor-related issues arise in the district courts and eventually come before the Supreme Court for a final decision. The files pertaining to such cases, as well as related dockets and opinions, are in RG 267.

Non-textual records — photographs and motion pictures — are also available. They are in the custody of NARA units equipped to care for them, physically separated from the textual records of the creating agency but considered part of the same record group.

In the last 100 years, the U.S. government was involved in labor matters many times, especially when this involvement was thought to serve the best interests of the people. The records cited in this broad survey are only some of the numerous labor history sources in the National Archives that document the many forms that involvement has taken.

Access: There are various finding guides available. For further information about such aids and the location of collections write to the Civil Reference Branch (NNRC), National Archives, Washington, DC, 20408. You can also call Tab Lewis at (202) 501-5395. The Archives building in Washington, DC, at Constitution Avenue and 8th St., is open for researchers 8:45 am–10 pm, Monday–Friday, 9 am–5 pm on Saturdays, except for Federal holidays.

LABOR AND SOCIAL HISTORY RECORDS AT THE CATHOLIC UNIVERSITY OF AMERICA

by
Nelson Lichtenstein

For more than 100 years the American labor movement has been heavily Catholic, both in its rank and file composition and top leadership. In the half century extending from the 1880s to the 1930s waves of immigrant Catholic workers, first from Ireland and Germany and then from Poland, Italy, Hungary and Mexico swelled American trade union ranks. Before World War I and then again in the 1940s Catholics certainly composed a plurality, if not an outright majority, of all organized workers. Top trade union leadership may well have been even more heavily Catholic during these years. But unlike continental Europe the U.S. never had a separate Catholic labor movement; instead the hierarchy of the Catholic Church and a corps of "labor priests" long found the trade unions a social movement upon which the Church could have a distinct social and political impact, one designed both to moderate free market capitalism in the light of such Papal encyclicals as *Rerum Novarum* (1893) and also to stem the tide of socialism and secularism that seemed so dangerous during the first half of the 20th century.

From its inception in 1948 the Dept. of Archives and Manuscripts at the Catholic University has therefore devoted a substantial portion of its holdings to collections in the field of American labor history. Many of these collections were acquired with the help of clerical faculty who had themselves been important figures in early 20th century social reform. The most important of these are those of John Ryan (25 feet) and Joseph Haas (50 feet). As the author of *A Living Wage* and *Distributive Justice*, Monsignor Ryan was one of the most important Catholic social thinkers of the Progressive era, and as head of the Social Action Department of the National Catholic Welfare Conference,

Nelson Lichtenstein is Professor of History at the University of Virginia.

he provided one of the important bridges between labor reform ideas of the World War I era and the New Deal, in which he held important labor relations posts. Monsignor Haas was also an influential New Deal mediator and arbitrator, active in the Minneapolis Teamster strike of 1934, the New Jersey textile strikes of 1937, and the Allis-Chalmers conflicts of 1938 and 1941. His papers reflect his service on the first National Labor Board (1933-1934), the Fair Employment Practices Committee in World War II, and the Michigan Committee on Civil Rights just afterwards.

The records of the National C. nference of Catholic Charities (200 feet), the Catholic Interracial Council of New York (40 feet), and the National Council of Catholic Women/National Council of Catholic Men (140 feet) contain much material on Church welfare work, Catholic social programs, and efforts to influence government social and economic policy. The National Catholic War Council (1917-1931) (100 feet) undertook extensive social surveys among the Catholic urban population with particular emphasis on the conditions of women and child laborers, extent of immigrant citizenship and health conditions at home and in the armed service camps. The Social Action Department of the U.S. Catholic Conference (formerly National Catholic Welfare Conference) (100 feet) emerged out of the Church's World War I-era commitment to the investigation and ameloriation of working and living conditions among its huge urban constituency. The Social Action Dept. is a particularly rich source, reflecting the work of such important "labor priests" as Ryan, Raymond McGowan, and George Higgins during the New Deal and post–World War II eras.

The key labor collections of the pre-World War I era include the papers of Terence Powderly (90 feet) and John Hayes (25 feet), which together offer a remarkable portrait of the Knights of Labor, including much correspondence, minutes of the General Executive Board (1870–1905), and proceedings of national and some district assemblies. These papers, which include Powderly's years with the U.S. Immigration Commission, 1897–1921, have been microfilmed and indexed by University Microfilms. The John Mitchell Papers (100 feet) offer turn of the century resources for a study of the United Mine Workers (UMW), and include important material on the Anthracite Strike of 1902, the American Federation of Labor, the National Civic Federation and the New York State Industrial Commission. These papers are also available from University Microfilms.

Two additional small collections of this era include the clippings and scattered letters of Charles Patrick Neill (2 feet), the second Commissioner of the Bureau of Labor; and Mary Harris "Mother" Jones (8 inches), the legendary UMW tribune.

Catholic University was the first academic archive to receive manuscript collections bearing on the organization and political/economic life of the Congress of Industrial Organizations (CIO). Much material is sporadic and routine, and possibly purged of letters and memoranda bearing on the Communist issue, but the 200 feet of boxes and clipping books also contain significant sources on internal union politics, jurisdictional disputes, efforts to influence government economic policy, and civil rights.

The John Brophy papers (25 feet) is the most consistently useful of the CIO holdings. These papers contain diaries, speeches and scrapbooks, and pamphlets, especially in the 1919–1923 period when he was an important political opponent of John L. Lewis in the UMW and after 1936 when Brophy was a CIO official. The collection contains most UMW proceedings from 1912 to 1940, including those of District Two from 1904 to 1927. There is also a 1000 page autobiography.

In the CIO papers themselves (50 feet) Brophy's activities are further recorded in the series devoted to the state and local Industrial Union Councils, which Brophy supervised in the late 1930s. CIO files covering national and international affiliates are almost exclusively devoted to the organizing years 1935 to 1939. Correspondence is not continuous, but can be rich, especially covering the smaller unions in need of national CIO assistance during their early organizational efforts. Internal CIO jurisdiction disputes are often well covered, including the politically important FE-UAW conflict and the fight between UMW District 50 and the Transport Workers Union. The CIO Central Office correspondence is disappointing, consisting of random letters sent in by individuals; likewise the material in the files of Labor's Non-Partisan League, although both sub-collections might well be used to capture something of the popular mood and political language of labor politics in the late 1930s.

The Philip Murray Collection (90 feet) covers the period 1943 to 1952 when Murray was simultaneously president of the CIO and United Steelworkers of America. Murray's persona is largely absent here, and the CIO's original filing system is awkward, but these papers are quite useful for an understanding of United Steelworkers' District grievances and negotiations, War Labor Board politics, postwar economic policy, steel industry problems, and jurisdictional disputes among CIO affiliates. Some Political Action Committee material is present, as is occasional, but quite revealing memoranda on race relations, especially in the Steelworkers' Southern District files. A collection of 100 newspaper clipping scrapbooks records CIO activities on a daily basis during the 1940s and early 1950s.

Two small but rich collections contain important material on Catholic anti-Communism in the CIO. The Richard Deverall Papers (12 feet) reveal this former UAW Education Director, Association of Catholic Trade Unions (ACTU) activist, and AFL-CIO foreign affairs operative to be a remarkable correspondent. His 10 volumes of letters and memoranda, first to the Office of War Information (1942–1943) and then to the AFL's Jay Lovestone (from Japan, India and the Far East, 1946–1959), reveal Deverall as a hyper-political but often keen observer of labor politics and social trends. The Harry Read Papers (10 feet) reflect the work of an important behind the scenes figure who, as executive assistant to CIO Secretary-Treasurer James B. Carey, helped mobilize anti-Communist sentiment within the postwar CIO. A Chicago newspaperman, Read was an ACTU activist, Newspaper Guild leader, and editor of the *Michigan CIO News*: and all these activities are reflected in his collection.

The papers of George Higgins (56 feet), postwar director of the U.S. Catholic Conference's Social Action Department, reflect the Church's renewed interest in social activism in the 1960s and 1970s. Here are several boxes on the United Farm Workers' struggle in California, material on the effort to organize J. P. Stevens in the 1970s, and copies of Higgins' many columns and speeches in support of organized labor. Higgins' service for more than three decades on the UAW Public Review Board is reflected in this collection, as is his interest in the corporativist reorganization of industry, whether derived from the tradition of European social democracy or Catholic social doctrine.

The Joseph Keenan Collection (8.5 feet) is less rewarding, but the papers of this Chicago-born International Brotherhood of Electrical Workers official and AFL-CIO executive board member contains extensive correspondence on the effort to unionize the Kohler Company in the 1940s, efforts to resolve the United Farm Workers-Teamsters dispute in California, and accounts of Keenan's foreign affairs work for the AFL and the AFL-CIO. The latter includes his work with General Lucius Clay in the reconstruction of unionism in postwar Germany, representation of the AFL-CIO in international labor organizations, and an important 1967 trip to South Vietnam on behalf of the AFL-CIO and the U.S. government.

Access: The Dept. of Archives and Manuscripts is housed in crowded conditions in the basement of Mullen Library and is open 9 am–5 pm, Monday–Friday. Most collections are unprocessed and have no finding aids. For further information contact Anthony Zito, Dept. of Archives and Manuscripts, The Catholic University of America, Washington, DC 20064; phone: (202) 635-5065.

THE JOSEPH A. BEIRNE MEMORIAL ARCHIVES

by
Bruce P. Montgomery

On Labor Day 1974, the founding father of the Communications Workers of America (CWA), Joseph A. Beirne, passed away after more than 30 years in the vanguard of the labor movement. During his tenure, Beirne reshaped a fledgling union on the edge of ruin into a strong, progressive organization that eventually won the grudging respect of the powerful Bell System. After his death, the union decided to honor the memory of its founding leader by initiating a three-part program, including an archives, museum, and written history, as a testament to CWA's many achievements under his administration. The project is being sponsored by the Joseph A. Beirne Memorial Foundation, which was created in 1975 to support programs devoted to the advancement of education and other social concerns.

The archives was initiated in 1986, when CWA hired an archivist to organize the Joseph A. Beirne Memorial Archives. The original scope of the project encompassed primarily the processing of the Beirne papers and the renovation of an area in the CWA headquarters building in Washington, DC into an archival facility. Since then, however, the role of the archives has expanded considerably to include the preservation of the important records of the entire union and the establishment of an oral history project, which will update an earlier project conducted by the Univ. of Iowa's Center for Labor and Management between 1968 and 1972.

The Beirne archives consists of six major collections, which include records relating to the administrations of Joseph Beirne and his successor, Glenn Watts, as well as to the National Federation of Telephone Workers (NFTW) and the International Typographical Union (ITU). The largest collection comprises the Joseph Beirne papers (1942–1974),

---

Bruce P. Montgomery is in charge of the Joseph A. Beirne Memorial Archives.

amounting to approximately 250 cubic feet and including mostly correspondence, speeches, proceedings, minutes, scrapbooks, tapes, and films. Beirne seemed to be keenly aware of his standing as a leader within the labor movement and so made sure his many activities were recorded. The collection consists of numerous tape recordings of Beirne's participation in labor rallies, press conferences, interviews, congressional testimony, conventions, radio broadcasts, executive board meetings, and other activities. The records mostly relate, however, to the rise of CWA as a successful and effective organization in opposition to the largest corporation in the world. The collection also contains information regarding CWA's predecessor union, the NFTW, which comprised a loose and generally ineffective federation of independent and autonomous telephone unions. The NFTW was organized in 1938, and Beirne served as its president from 1942 until the federation's demise in 1947 after a ruinous nationwide strike against the Bell System.

In addition to chronicling collective bargaining and strike activity, the records document the formation of the CWA and its affiliation with the CIO, interunion warfare with the International Brotherhood of Electrical Workers and the International Brotherhood of Teamsters, organizing drives, legislative and political action, and the union's involvement in community and international affairs. Two of Beirne's abiding concerns, the achievement of national bargaining with the Bell System and the impact of new technology on job composition and work patterns, are reflected in the records. AT&T had always maintained the fiction that the local Bell companies operated as wholly independent and autonomous corporate entities, although it was abundantly clear from the beginning that the companies acted under the direct control of AT&T. This negotiating stance forced the union to bargain separately and at varying time periods with each of the 22 local operating companies and AT&T. CWA finally won national bargaining, however, in 1974, just months before Beirne died.

Workplace problems stemming from technological advances was a major concern for the telephone union as far back as the NFTW days, when the Bell System accelerated the pace of conversion from manually operated telephones to dial telephones. By the end of the 1930s, for example, fully 56% of all Bell System telephones were dial operated, which meant that one dial switchboard operator could do the work of six manual switchboard operators. In ensuing decades, operators continued to decline as a proportion of the total workforce, despite the enormous increase in use and number of telephones. Since the Bell System represented one of the world's most highly automated industries, the union was compelled to constantly assess the effects of such technology on members and their jobs.

Although incomplete, the Glenn Watts records (1974–1985) reflect a transitional phase for the union from a membership based largely in a regulated monopoly to one struggling in a newly deregulated, market-oriented environment. Watts succeeded Beirne as CWA president in 1974 and served in that capacity until his retirement in 1985. During this time period, the union witnessed a progressively deregulated environment fostered by the FCC and attempts by the U.S. Congress to pass new legislation governing the telecommunications industry. More important, the Justice Department's 1974 anti-trust suit against AT&T grew more ominous with time and presaged the dramatic restructuring of the Bell System and the telecommunications industry in the 1980s.

Unfortunately, a sizable portion of the Watts records relating to this transitional period in the 1970s and early 1980s was destroyed before the commencement of the archives project. Scattered documentation, however, does exist, mainly in the form of speeches, general correspondence, convention proceedings, and bargaining council records. The bargaining council records serve as the richest source of information with respect to union attempts to negotiate new ground-breaking employment security provisions and joint labor-management committees with the Bell System, governing such things as quality of work-life, the introduction of new technology, and training and retraining programs. As with many other unions, the issue of employment security became CWA's number one concern in the 1980s as the tempo of competition increased dramatically in the telecommunications industry and workforce reductions became more common.

The Watts records also contain material regarding his cornerstone achievement, the CWA Committee on the Future. Formed in 1981, the committee's purpose was to chart the union's future course amidst the rough waters of increasing worldwide competition and rapid technological advancement. The underlying imperative for creating such a committee was that CWA had to adapt itself to the winds of change of the new market environment or else . . . .

Three small collections relating to the NFTW include the records of Ray Hackney, the Telephone Guild of Wisconsin, and the United Brotherhood of Telephone Workers. The Ray Hackney records (1920–1958) comprise information primarily on affiliated unions of the NFTW, but also contain material on Bell Systems employee associations and CWA. Originally a member of the NFTW's Southwestern Telephone Workers Union, Ray Hackney came to serve as one of CWA's vice presidents. The collection consists of six cubic feet and includes scrapbooks, contracts and agreements, correspondence, jurisdictional dispute files, charters, journals, proceedings, constitutions and bylaws, and information regarding the Bell System's employee pension plan. The subject of pensions represented one of the major issues of contention between the NFTW and management.

The records of the Telephone Guild of Wisconsin and the United Brotherhood of Telephone Workers also relate to the NFTW. Both organizations were members of the federation and eventually became part of CWA. The collections comprise correspondence, annual convention reports, executive board minutes, general council proceedings, charters, and constitutions and bylaws.

Another major collection, amounting to about 200 cubic feet, consists of the records of the International Typographical Union (ITU). Formed in 1852, the printer's union became the first labor union in the U.S. to be recognized by an entire industry. But what was once a strong craft union considered to be among the aristocracy of the skilled trades became a virtual quasi-industrial union by the 1980s as rapid technological innovation eliminated the need for the skilled printers' craft. The new automated workplace devastated the ITU to such an extent that the union lost approximately two-thirds of its total membership between 1970 and 1985, compelling it to seek refuge by merging with the communications workers in 1986.

The ITU records, albeit incomplete, comprise a wide variety of material, including correspondence, convention proceedings and pamphlets, published journals and books, letterpress books, scrapbooks, cash books and ledgers, strike information, executive council rulings, local charters, photographs, and film. A portion of the records were destroyed when the union moved its headquarters from Indianapolis to Colorado Springs in the early 1960s. The ITU's newspaper, the *Typographical Journal*, and the convention proceedings represent the best source of information regarding the union's role in spearheading the formation of the American Federation of Labor in 1886 and the union's many feuds with the AFL hierarchy over the issue of autonomy. The records also contain information concerning ITU's nonprofit corporation, Unitypo, Inc., which was established in the 1940s to employ striking members in commercial enterprises set up to compete in business with offending employers. Such enterprises were never meant to be profit-making ventures, but rather a means to apply economic pressure to force employers to resolve strike or lockout disputes in the union's favor. In addition, the records document the issue of technological change and its impact upon the union.

Access: The Joseph A. Beirne Memorial Archives is open 8 am–3 pm Monday–Friday. Requests for information should be directed to Bruce Montgomery, Joseph A. Beirne Memorial Archives, CWA, 1925 K Street, NW, Washington, DC, 20006; phone: (202) 728-2568.

LABOR UNION HISTORY AND ARCHIVES:
The University of Maryland
at College Park Libraries

by
Lauren Brown

The University of Maryland at College Park, the state's land grant institution, is located approximately 10 miles to the northeast of Washington, DC, in suburban Maryland. Several international unions which have national offices in the greater Washington, DC area have sought assistance in preserving their archival records. The proximity of the College Park campus to their headquarters is one of the reasons it has proved attractive to these unions. A combination of developments also contributed significantly to the creation of a labor archives program at College Park: the formal establishment of what is now called the Historical Manuscripts & Archives Department by the Libraries at the University of Maryland at College Park in 1972 and the commencement of the Samuel Gompers Papers Project at the College Park campus in 1973. During the last 15 years professional archivists at College Park have benefited from the advice and assistance of Stuart B. Kaufman, editor of the Gompers Papers and currently consultant to the George Meany Memorial Archives at the AFL-CIO's George Meany Center for Labor Studies in nearby Silver Spring, MD.

The first major archival collection to arrive at College Park was the records of the Industrial Union of Marine and Shipbuilding Workers of America (IUMSWA) in 1967. Mr. A. G. Delman, then research and publicity director of the union, sought and received assistance from university officials in finding an archival repository for the records of the Shipbuilding Workers. The union has continued its archival relationship with the campus as the library system hired professional archival staff in the following decades. At present IUMSWA records are open to researchers with prior approval of the union.

Lauren Brown is Curator, Historical Manuscripts & Archives Department, the University Libraries, University of Maryland, College Park.

IUMSWA originated in the ferment of the labor movement of the 1930s; by 1938 it claimed a membership of over 100,000. The archives located at College Park provide in-depth documentation on the origins of the union, its contact with civilian and military agencies during World War II, labor and race relations during the war, and the union's efforts to combat the decline of the shipbuilding industry during the late 1940s and 1950s. IUMSWA's archival files contain extensive correspondence between the national office and various locals, organizer reports and political action committee campaign files documenting the union's promotion of the shipbuilding industry. The archives, occupying approximately 150 linear feet of shelving, is in the process of being properly arranged and described at the present time. A preliminary inventory is available and the collection is being consulted heavily by researchers who are studying not only the shipbuilding industry but also local and national trends in labor and social history.

The archives of the Cigar Makers International Union were deposited with the University of Maryland in 1974 after the union merged with the Retail, Wholesale and Department Store Workers. The Cigar Makers Union was formed in 1864 and was chartered by the AFL in 1887. Samuel Gompers was appointed International President in 1877 and figures prominently in the history of this union. The collection is approximately six linear feet and spans the years 1864–1974 although the bulk of the material falls within the mid-1930s. Over the years the union was in existence, it campaigned for sick, death, and out-of-work benefits, a shorter workday and trade-union group insurance, and fought against prison contract labor and child labor. The records are divided into administrative files, locals, financial proceedings and publications. Samuel Gompers, William L. Green, Joseph Lewis, George Meany, and Claude Pepper are correspondents in these files.

The Tobacco Workers International Union (TWIU), originally founded in 1895 as the National Tobacco Workers Union, deposited its archives at College Park during the 1977–1979 period as it merged with Bakery & Confectionery Workers International Union in 1978. The archives, 120 linear feet in size when accessioned, is now a combination of original and microfilmed records. Documentation covers the years 1896 to 1979. The union's long history includes campaigns for the union label as a symbol of independence from the tobacco industry and major organizational campaigns in Kentucky, Virginia, and North Carolina. Relationships with major tobacco firms such as R. J. Reynolds are documented in the TWIU Archives and researchers also have access in this archival collection to extensive runs of tobacco union newspapers and a significant number of photographs.

Shortly after 1978 the Bakery, Confectionery & Tobacco Workers International Union also concluded a deposit agreement with the Univ. of Maryland. Archival records arrived at College Park in 1980 and 1981. This union traces it origins to 1886 when representatives from independent unions organized to form the National Union of Journeymen Bakers of North America. Many of the locals in the early years were dominated by German immigrant bakers. By the turn of the century the union had clearly developed a national base and identity; it became known as the Bakery & Confectionery Workers International Union of America in 1903. Later in the 20th century the union split into two competing factions due to charges in 1957 of misconduct on the part of its then president, James Cross. Reunification of the union was accomplished in 1969.

The fractious period of the 1950s and 1960s is well documented in the archives through correspondence, publications and legal documents as well as files generated by the Committee to Preserve Integrity. Unfortunately very little documentation from the union's formative years has survived. However, early minutes of the general executive board cover the years 1898 through 1918. There are voluminous files documenting locals and their activities during the 1940s, 1950s, and 1960s.

Recently the staff of the Historical Manuscripts & Archives Department at the University of Maryland and the research and publicity divisions of the B, C & T headquarters staff have embarked on a cooperative project to survey and identify those office records meriting retirement to the archives. It is hoped that the anticipated transfer of a new generation of records to the archives and the establishment of records retention schedules for BC&T offices will prove of immense benefit to the research community in future years.

One of the most notable recent accessions in labor history at the university is the acquisition in 1988 of the papers of the late Andrew A. Pettis, former president of the Industrial Union of Marine and Shipbuilding Workers of America (IUMSWA). Pettis joined the union in 1942 and rapidly progressed through the ranks as president of Local 50 (Portland, ME) and president of the New England region. During the 1960s and 1970s, Pettis occupied the highest positions of leadership at the national level. The 40 linear foot collection contains grievance files, shop steward reports, organizers reports, conference proceedings, union publications, and photographs; it spans the years 1942 to 1978. A preliminary inventory is available to guide researchers through this extensive collection which serves to complement the previously-accessioned IUMSWA archives.

Access: Researchers who wish to consult labor collections at the

University of Maryland at College Park should visit the McKeldin Library at the center of the College Park campus. The Maryland Room, located on the fourth floor, serves as the reading room for the use of these holdings. The hours of the Maryland Room are noon–5 pm, Monday–Friday, and noon–5 pm on Saturday by prior appointment. Guides to specific archival collections such as the records of the Bakery, Confectionery & Tobacco Workers International Union are available via mail or by personal request at no cost. Although the archival records do not circulate, a limited amount of photoduplication can be requested. Researchers can also make arrangements for the photoduplication of microfilm and photographic components of the archival collections. Those who wish to obtain more information about labor history resources at the university may write to Mr. Lauren Brown, Curator, Historical Manuscripts & Archives Dept., McKeldin Library, Univ. of Maryland, College Park, MD 20742-7011; phone: (301) 405-9059.

THE GEORGE MEANY MEMORIAL ARCHIVES

by
Katharine Vogel

On August 17, 1987, the new building for The George Meany
Memorial Archives was dedicated on the campus of the George Meany
Center for Labor Studies in Silver Spring, MD, ending the formative
years of the Archives and creating a national center for the study of
the American Federation of Labor and Congress of Industrial Organizations. As a memorial to Meany, the first president of the merged AFL-
CIO, the building complements his vision to build a national campus
for the American labor movement. The Archives is a 33,000 square
foot facility consisting of a five-story central storage area surrounded
by three stories devoted to exhibition, learning, and administrative work
areas. A rear lobby opens to the interior of the campus and, together
with two classrooms, integrates the building with the campus.

The Archives was established in 1980 by the AFL-CIO executive
council, and was funded by the unanimous vote of the 1981 AFL-CIO
Convention approving a per capital tax increase to provide for construction of the building. Additional funding from the National Endowment for the Humanities, both for planning and for the processing
of collections, provided support for the program during its first three
years.

The Meany Archives serves as the official archives of the AFL-CIO
and has defined as its collecting scope the records of the federation
and its predecessor organizations, the constitutional trade and industrial departments, affiliated institutes and selected personal papers of
AFL-CIO officers and staff. The Archives does not collect records of
its affiliates, but assists these unions in developing programs for disposition of their historical records. Nor does it collect records of its
state and local central bodies; it encourages them to deposit their records

Katharine Vogel is chief archivist at The George Meany Memorial Archives.

in an appropriate archival depository in the geographic region in which they were created, following the policy announced by then-Secretary-Treasurer Lane Kirkland in 1979. While the Archives does not collect these archival records, it does attempt to secure copies of finding aids to such collections in order to be able to better guide researchers to scholarly resources. It is the plan of the Archives to eventually become a national clearing house for information about labor-related archival collections through participation in the Chadwick-Healey micropublication *The National Inventory of Documentary Sources in the United States* and through cooperation with the Labor Archives Roundtable of the Society of American Archivists.

Another "clearing house" function provided by the Meany Archives is, of necessity, a result of the checkered history of the disposition of its records by the federation. Several scholars have written about the fate of records that would otherwise be expected to be held by the Meany Archives, and a description of their disposition appears in the introduction to volume 1 of *The Samuel Gompers Papers*.[1] To briefly summarize: between 1926 and 1969 several significant records series of the AFL, the CIO, and the AFL-CIO were sent from federation headquarters to different institutions, among them the New York Public Library, the State Historical Society of Wisconsin (SHSW), the Library of Congress, Duke Univ. and The Catholic Univ. of America. Records sent to SHSW and Catholic Univ. had been previously screened, winnowed and microfilmed by staff members of the federation's General File Room in a well-meaning records management program that was adopted by the federation in 1952 and produced a 16mm microfilm that is of poor quality and at many points unreadable. Unfortunately, many other series of correspondence had been filmed and the originals destroyed before the State Historical Society of Wisconsin secured an agreement to receive records after filming, with the result that these series survive only on the original film. The following descriptions of processed collections available for research at the Meany Archives will make reference to the source of original documents in cases where the Archives holds only microfilm. Reference to this film will include "16mm mf" and the number of reels in the description. The records available for research are:

1) *American Federation of Labor and American Federation of Labor and Congress of Industrial Organizations*: Most extant records of the Gompers era of the AFL (1881–1924) are reproduced in the three

---

[1]Stuart B. Kaufman, ed., *The Samuel Gompers Papers*, Vol. 1: "The Making of a Union Leader, 1850–86," (Urbana, 1986), pp. xviii-xxi.

micropublications available at the Meany Archives as well as several other institutions. Two of these editions were produced by the Samuel Gompers Papers project: *American Federation of Labor Records: The Samuel Gompers Era* (a joint project with the SHSW; published in 1981 by the Microfilming Corporation of America, 144 reels), and *The American Federation of Labor and the Unions: National and International Records from the Samuel Gompers Era* (published in 1985 by the Microfilming Corporation of America, 5 reels). The *American Federation of Labor Records* reproduces most of the Gompers-era records of the federation that existed uniquely on microfilm as well as most of the records of this period that were sent to the State Historical Society of Wisconsin. The third collection, *Letterpress Copybooks of Samuel Gompers and William Green's Outgoing Correspondence, 1883–1925*, was filmed by the Library of Congress after the original copybooks were donated by the federation in 1966 and 1969.

AFL records series held by the Meany Archives (some of which overlap the subsequent tenure of presidents William Green and George Meany) supplementing these micropublications include: AFL, Account Books, 1886–1925, 42 cu. ft.; AFL, Dept. of Research, Convention Files, 1909–1952, 16mm mf, 26 reels (originals at SHSW for 1947–1952); AFL, Charter Books, 1897–1956, 2 cu. ft.; AFL & AFL-CIO, Dept. of Legislation, 1906–1978, bulk 1945–1965, 86.5 cu. ft.; AFL & AFL-CIO, Office of the President, Strikes and Agreements, 1898–1953, 16mm, 9 reels (originals) at SHSW and subsequently refilmed by University Publications of America (UPA) in Melvin Dubofsky, ed., *American Federation of Labor Records, Part 1: Strikes and Agreement File, 1899–1953* (1986, 55 reels); and AFL & AFL-CIO, Office of the President, Charter Files, Directly Affiliated Local Unions, 1900–1965, 16mm mf, 12 reels.

From the 1880s to the AFL-CIO merger in 1955, the AFL chartered 24,958 local federal labor unions (known. after the merger as "DALUs" or directly affiliated local unions), which were numbered sequentially as chartered. An undocumented change in records-keeping in July 1933 indicates that a decision was made to throw out all records of these local unions if they were no longer extant on that date. Charter records were kept, however, for all other locals and were subsequently microfilmed in this series, which contains charter information and occasional correspondence about activities. The Meany Archives also holds the originals filmed for *The American Federation of Labor Records*, including the minute book of the legislative committee of the Federation of Organized Trades and Labor Unions of the United States and Canada (FOTLU); the Gabriel Edmonston Papers, 1881–1912, .35 cu. ft., AFL, Office of the Secretary-Treasurer, Frank Morrison, 1911–1914, 1920, 1924, 1 cu. ft., and AFL, Executive Council, Minutes, Vote Books and Correspondence, 1892–1955 (filmed only through the Gompers era for *The American Federation of Labor Records*). The latter collection just recently has been transferred to the Archives and is available for research. One other collection, the copy books of Secretary-Treasurer Frank Morrison for the years 1904–1925, was donated to Duke Univ. in 1969.

As with Gompers-era records, most of the AFL archives for the period during which William Green served as president, 1924–1952, are either not held by the Meany Archives or exist only on microfilm. Several large groups of records of the Office of the President were sent to the State Historical Society of Wisconsin under its agreement with the AFL, and other records from the Dept. of Research were also transferred there unofficially by the economist of the AFL, Boris Shishkin. Many of the Green files at SHSW have been commercially published in a UPA microfilm edition, Melvin Dubofsky, ed., *American Federation of Labor Records, Part 2: President's Office Files Series A: William Green Papers, 1934–1952* (1986, 38 reels). This collection is not presently available at the Meany Archives, but the material was filmed by the AFL before it was sent to Wisconsin, and these 16mm films are available for research.

The Meany Archives does hold the following additional collections in the original, some of which overlap George Meany's tenure as president of the AFL and the AFL-CIO: William Green Papers, 1909–1952, 11.35 cu. ft. (microfilmed by the Ohio Historical Society in 1981); AFL, Office of the President, William Green, 1909–1952, 12 cu. ft. [contains official files that complement holdings at SHSW]; AFL, Office of the President, William Green, 1940–1952, 8.25 cu. ft. (two series: Government Boards, Agencies, and Correspondence with National and International Unions, returned from SHSW in 1967); AFL, Office of the Secretary-Treasurer, George Meany, 1940–1952, 7 cu. ft.; George Meany Papers, 1935–1960, 2.5 cu. ft.; Boris Shishkin Papers, 1927–1951, 8 cu. ft.; AFL & AFL-CIO, Dept. of Civil Rights, 1943–1967, 7 cu ft.; AFL, CIO, AFL-CIO, Committee on Political Education (COPE), Research Files, 1944–1973, 54 cu. ft.

The following records from the Office of the President are on AFL microfilm, but are restricted for research after 1960: AFL & AFL-CIO, Office of the President, Copy Books, 1925–1968, 63 reels; Speeches and Addresses, 1924–1952, 3 reels (originals at SHSW); State Governments, 1941–1951, .5 reel; U.S. Government Depts. and Staff Depts., 1940–1968, 17 reels; International Affairs, Correspondence, 1949–1951; International Affairs and International Affiliations, 1949–1967, 10 reels. Open for research without restriction are copy books from the Secretary-Treasurer's Office on 16mm microfilm, 1925–1968, 65 reels.

Beginning in 1952 and up to the present, records of the AFL and the AFL-CIO held by the Meany Archives are fairly complete, and a vigorous records management program conducted by the Archives assures that all noncurrent records of the AFL-CIO will come to the Archives in the future. Collections of this period not mentioned previously that are now available are: AFL & AFL-CIO, Office of the President, George Meany, 1952–1960, 63 cu. ft.; AFL-CIO, Assistant to the President, Merger Files, State and Local Central Bodies, 1955–1962, 3 cu. ft.; and AFL & AFL-CIO, Office of the Secretary-Treasurer, William F. Schnitzler, 1952–1980, bulk 1955–1962, 12 cu. ft. (Executive Council files are restricted until 1999).

2) *Congress of Industrial Organizations*: Memos in the archives of The George Meany Memorial Archives between 1958 and 1962 in part document the disposition of the CIO records that were in federation headquarters after the merger. In a memo of April 1, 1958, for example, E. Logan Kimmel, supervisor of the General File Room, indicates that 15 drawers of correspondence to local and state industrial union councils were reduced to three, and 25 drawers of local industrial unions were reduced to 10, preparatory to microfilming.[2] According to this memo, the AFL-CIO transferred seven drawers each of records of the Steelworkers and Mine Workers and 20 drawers of records of Philip Murray's office to Catholic Univ., as well as the originals of the four series it filmed (16mm, now at the Meany Archives): CIO, National Office, National and International Unions, 1935–1955, 3 reels; State Industrial Union Councils, 1935–1955, 2 reels; Local Industrial Councils, 1935–1955, 5 reels; and Local Industrial Unions, 6 reels. The Meany Archives also holds the minutes of the CIO Executive Board, 1942–1955.

Most heavily used of the Meany Archives research collections is the still photograph collection, which numbers approximately 60,000 images, most from the mid-1930s to 1978. In addition to the still photographs, in 1983 Frank Alexander, major photographer of labor from the 1940s to the present, donated his collection of over 18,000 negatives to the Archives, documenting major labor events of the period. The Archives has a small collection of graphic images, over 10,000 audio tapes, and a small but growing collection of film and videotape.

The Archives is not conducting interviews at this time, but among the few oral history interviews it holds are those of the AFL-CIO Merger Oral History Project, 1978–1980, funded by the National Endowment for the Humanities and directed by Alice Hoffman. She and others

---

[2] E. Logan Kimmel to Wes Reedy, April 1, 1958, unprocessed file in the archives of The George Meany Memorial Archives.

interviewed 44 prominent labor leaders about the merger between the
AFL and CIO in 1955, and their transcripts are available.

The limited printed collection of the Meany Archives reflects the
fact that the Archives is located in a geographic area with superb library and archival resources; the Archives concentrates on collecting
a complete set of the publications of the AFL, CIO, and AFL-CIO.

Since 1987 the Meany Archives has undertaken several new outreach programs, most prominent being the launching in January 1989
of a new quarterly, *Labor's Heritage*. This is a scholarly based, heavily
illustrated magazine, with the editorial objective being to bring public
attention to the rich and varied heritage of American workers and to
resources and exhibits for the further exploration of this subject.

In February 1988 a "Cooperative Library Program Agreement" between the Archives and the U.S. Dept. of Labor (DOL) gave the Archives the authority to identify titles from the DOL library's general
circulation collection which are related to the labor movement's history and which would benefit from being placed in an environment
with appropriate climatic and security controls. To date 1322 items have
been removed to the Archives where preservation work such as poly-
ester encapsulation of fragile broadsides and pamphlets has been carried out. They comprise the basis of The United States Department
of Labor Collection at the Meany Archives, and under the agreement,
the DOL retains ownership of the collection.

Two other activities have begun and will be part of the on-going
outreach program of the Archives. In cooperation with the AFL-CIO
Dept. of Education and the National Capital Area Trade Union Retirees
Club, the Archives conducts a "Labor in the Schools" program in which
classes of high school and junior high school students visit the Archives,
are divided into small groups and guided through Archives exhibits
by retired trade unionists. And, on September 22, 1989, the Archives
initiated its annual symposium series with a one day symposium, "American Labor and World War I," in which seven scholars presented work
in progress and senior scholars commented on the presentations.

The Meany Archives has a strong commitment to making records
available for research, but cannot do so until they are processed. A
survey of 130 cubic feet of records of the Civil Rights Dept. has recently been conducted and plans call for the processing of this collection to begin during 1990. Other significant collections in the holdings
include records of: AFL & AFL-CIO, Railway Employees Dept., 1909–
1980, 700 cu. ft., complementing the collection at Cornell Univ.; AFL-
CIO, Industrial Union Dept., 1955–1974, 99 cu. ft.; AFL & AFL-CIO,
Building and Construction Trades Dept., 1890s–1974, 300 cu. ft.; AFL

& AFL-CIO, Metal Trades Dept. 1908–1983, 170 cu. ft.; and the National Joint Board for the Settlement of Jurisdictional Disputes in the Construction Industry, 1948–1982, 350 cu. ft.

Access: The Archives are open 9 am-4:30 pm, Monday-Friday. Information on availability of collections, restrictions, finding aids, and research assistance can be obtained by contacting Lynda DeLoach or Robert Reynolds, The George Meany Memorial Archives, 10000 New Hampshire Ave., Silver Spring, MD 20903; phone: (301) 434-6404.

WEST VIRGINIA LABOR SOURCES AT THE WEST VIRGINIA AND REGIONAL HISTORY COLLECTION

by
Ken Fones-Wolf*

Although dominated in the popular imagination by the famous coal field wars, West Virginia labor history is far more complex. For five decades, curators at the West Virginia and Regional History Collection (WVRHC) have attempted to collect primary sources for the study of labor in all its varieties in the Mountain State and in Appalachia generally. This description of the Collection will attempt to highlight the most substantial groupings of the WVRHC's holdings.

The logical starting place for a survey of the WVRHC's labor holdings is with collections relating to the coal industry. Glimpses of organizing efforts, as well as the tremendous barriers to unionization erected by men of wealth and power, are found in the papers of many of the major politicians in the state. Among some of the most useful collections are those of John J. Cornwell (Governor during the mine wars after World War I) and Henry D. Hatfield (Governor during the 1912–13 strike at Paint and Cabin Creeks). The WVRHC houses the papers of many other prominent state politicos—Harley Kilgore, Matthew Neeley, Rush Dew Holt, Clarence Edwin Smith, Stephen S. Elkins, Henry Gassaway Davis, *et al*—which inevitably touch on labor matters.

Early campaigns of the United Mine Workers of America (UMWA) to breach the anti-union wall in West Virginia are represented in small collections in the WVRHC on the Paint Creek-Cabin Creek strikes, the Matewan "massacre," and the "treason" trials of local UMWA leaders in the Logan County strikes of 1921. These collections include letters, speeches, trial transcripts, hearing testimony, petitions, and reports of investigations by representatives of the U.S. Dept. of Labor and the judge advocate general's office. Noteworthy among these papers

Ken Fones-Wolf is Manuscripts Curator at the West Virginia and Regional History Collections at West Virginia University, Morgantown, WV.

are some letters and speeches of Mary Harris "Mother" Jones, including her two-part typescript memoirs, part one of which closely follows the 1925 *Autobiography of Mother Jones* (Chicago: Charles H. Kerr & Co.). Also relevant to this period of West Virginia labor history are the memoirs and papers of Fred Mooney, one of the UMWA leaders targeted by the "treason" trials.

The struggles of the UMWA in the 1920s is represented principally in the papers of Van Bittner, dating from his years as president of UMWA District 5 and as a UMWA international representative. Bittner's collection, comprising 6 linear feet, includes correspondence, legal papers, pocket diaries, photographs, clippings, and printed material, and is particularly rich concerning his pre-CIO activities.

There are several collections in the WVRHC concerning the opposition to John L. Lewis's leadership of the UMWA. Particularly noteworthy are the records of the Progressive Mine Workers of America (PMWA), an organization of rebellious miners in Illinois which began in the 1930s. The PMWA's records total 23 linear feet and include minutes, convention proceedings, negotiation conference proceedings, president's office files, local union correspondence, grievance case records, and the union journal. The records are especially strong for the post-World War II decade. In addition, there are some 30 oral histories in the WVRHC concerning the PMWA, its activities, and coal mining in Illinois. In Appalachia, opposition to Lewis came from the left-wing National Miners Union (NMU). Among the materials in the WVRHC for the study of the NMU is the manuscript of a thinly-disguised autobiographical novel written by Tom Meyerscough, an NMU activist in Harlan County, Kentucky. There are also a number of oral histories with former NMU members conducted by Paul Nyden, Linda Nyden, and Keith Dix. Finally, more recent rank-and-file opposition in the UMWA is represented by 16 tapes in the WVRHC sound archives of speeches, meetings, and interviews involving activists in Miners for Democracy in the early 1970s.

Contributing to the volatile labor relations in the coal industry was the dangerous nature of coal mining. One collection focusing on the occupational hazards of mining is the Monongah Mine Relief Fund records. The 1907 Monongah Mine explosion took the lives of 361 miners. Citizens formed the relief fund to provide assistance to the victims' families. Included in the 7 linear feet of records are a valuable series of case files containing information on each of the victims. Another side of mine safety is found in the West Virginia Dept. of Mines records (1916–32), available on 113 reels of microfilm. The Dept. investigated accidents, filed routine inspection reports, and prosecuted safety law violations.

Of even greater importance for the study of mine worker safety and health as well as the recent history of the UMWA are the records of its Health and Retirement Funds. The Funds had their origins in Lewis's demand for pension and medical care programs for miners in the UMWA's 1946 contract negotiations. The records of the Health and Retirement Funds comprise 156 linear feet, spanning the years 1946 to 1974. They include trustee correspondence files, memos, reports, construction plans for hospitals, minutes of trustee meetings, and extensive records on the creation and implementation of hospitalization and medical care policies for the nation's first industry-wide pension and medical care plans for coal miners and their families.

Another vantage for studying labor in the coal industry comes from looking at the local scene in West Virginia. The WVRHC houses the records of Local 6046 in Lochgelly (1943–66), and District 29, headquartered in Beckley. Complementing these are extensive records from coal companies. Included in various collections is information on wages, safety, price fixing, labor conditions, the operation of company stores, and, of course, labor relations. Especially notable for labor history are the papers of coal mine operator Justus Collins, which document his long tenure (1911–34) as a leader of the Smokeless Coal Operators Association in the Pocahontas fields.

Glass manufacture never rivaled coal mining in importance to West Virginia's economy, but glass workers contributed mightily to the labor and socialist movements in the state. The WVRHC holds the records of one of the longest-lasting craft unions in the industry, the Window Glass Cutters League of America, which traced its history from Local Assembly 300 of the Knights of Labor in the 1870s. The more than 200 linear feet of records contain virtually complete sets of minutes, correspondence, apprenticeship records, financial records, publications, contracts, working rules, negotiations, arbitrations, statistical reports, membership records, and photos from the League's founding in 1923 until its demise in 1975. Included also are minutes and some correspondence of the League's many predecessor organizations, including materials from Local Assembly 300, the Window Glass Cutters and Flatteners Protective Association, and the National Window Glass Workers Union.

One of the League's presidents, Glen McCabe (a West Virginian), played a major role in the formation of the Federation of Flat Glass Workers, a union representing the industrial workers in the window glass industry. The WVRHC holds the records of McCabe's Clarksburg Local 2 of the Flat Glass Workers, which eventually became the United Glass, Ceramic and Silica Sand Workers of America. Local 2's archives contain detailed minutes (1934–74), correspondence, grievance records, negotiations files, and membership materials, and document an important CIO affiliate in the window glass industry. Together with files from the Window Glass Cutters League, Local 2's records shed a good deal of light on the competition between craft and industrial unionism in the industry.

Window glass manufacture was only one branch of the industry that thrived in West Virginia. Northern West Virginia was also home to the pressed glass tableware industry and to locals of the American Flint Glass Workers Union (AFGWU). The WVRHC has records from Locals 10 and 507 of the AFGWU which represented workers at the Fostoria Glass Company factory in Moundsville. Included in the 10 linear feet of records are minute books dating from 1894, correspondence dating from the 1930s, contracts, wage lists, reports, convention proceedings, and circulars. Complementing the records of the Moundsville locals are several collections documenting glass making in Morgantown. The WVRHC has the archives of Local 536 of the AFGWU (1939–80), totaling 3.5 linear feet, and company records from Seneca Crystal, Inc. The collection (1891–1985) includes company board minutes, correspondence, appraisals, wage scales, blueprints, and materials dealing with AFGWU locals 501 and 540, which represented workers at Seneca. Rounding out the Morgantown glass making sources are oral histories and even the poetry of a local glassworker.

An example of glassworker political activism is evident in the records of the Glass Workers' Protective League. Founded in West Virginia in 1946, the League was a national alliance of glass unions for the purpose of opposing the importation of cheap foreign glass products. The three-box collection includes minutes of the West Virginia League (1947–72), political and organizational correspondence, and files focusing on tariff bills and the Burke-Hartke law.

The political activities of the West Virginia labor movement more generally are evident in the WVRHC's holdings of state-wide labor federation archives. The five feet of records of the West Virginia Federation of Labor (WVFL) contain executive council meeting minutes, proceedings, and the correspondence of the principal officials. Especially for the 1940s and 1950s, there is correspondence between the WVFL and such prominent West Virginia and national politicians as Robert C. Byrd, Harley Kilgore, and Arch Moore, among others.

Following the secession of industrial unions in the 1930s, the WVFL was no longer the state's sole voice of labor. The WVRHC also holds the records of the West Virginia Industrial Union Council, the state branch of the CIO. The 21-foot collection comprises correspondence, legal papers, and proceedings, documenting the industrial union movement in the state from 1939 to 1951. Included is information on the

Steel Workers Organizing Committee, Operation Dixie, the Taft-Hartley Act, the fair employment practices law, and the CIO Political Action Committee. A sample of correspondents includes Van Bittner, Chester Bowles, Sidney Hillman, James M. Landis, Eleanor Roosevelt, and James B. Carey.

Even more voluminous are the records of the West Virginia Labor Federation (WVLF), an organization created by the merger of the AFL and CIO state bodies in 1958. The WVLF archives comprise more than 200 linear feet and include the correspondence, speeches, and research files of longtime WVLF president Miles Stanley (116 boxes). In addition to about 35 boxes of files from the predecessor AFL and CIO federations, WVLF records contain correspondence with affiliated organizations (58 boxes), Committee on Political Education files (67 boxes), and legislative files (47 boxes).

Complementing these collections are files of *West Virginia AFL-CIO News and Views* (1959–70), *West Virginia AFL-CIO Observer* (1967–80), and the *West Virginia Federationist* (1948–57). The WVRHC also has several less complete collections of West Virginia state and local labor council records. Among these are the records of the West Virginia Building Trades Council, 2 feet (1946–57); the Harrison County Labor Federation, 9 feet (1958–69); the Mason-Jackson Labor Council, 4 feet (1949–77); and the Huntington District Labor Council, 2 feet (1943–65). These collections, although small, do contain interesting information on political activities at the local level.

One locality of special importance to West Virginia labor history, documented well by WVRHC holdings, is Wheeling. Particularly in the late 19th and early 20th centuries, Wheeling was a staunch union town and the backbone of the socialist movement in the state. Key for studying the Wheeling labor movement are the records of the Ohio Valley Trades and Labor Assembly (OVTLA). Begun in 1885, the OVTLA was the political voice of labor in Wheeling. The collection includes minutes (1888–1950), correspondence, and miscellaneous files which chronicle the Association's activities, from legislative lobbying to planning the annual Labor Day parade.

Wheeling craft unions that were members of the OVTLA are also quite well-represented in the WVRHC. Among the union locals for which the WVRHC has material are: International Typographical Union, Local 79 (minutes, 1904–07, 1918); Wheeling Tobacco Workers, Local 2 (minutes, 1890–1905); Brotherhood of Painters and Decorators, Local 91 (minutes, 1886–1970s, correspondence); American Federation of Musicians, Local 142 (minutes, 1894–1917); Brotherhood of Railway Trainmen, Local 13 (minutes, 1914–18); and the Amalgamated Association of Street and Electric Railroad Employees, Division 103 (minutes, 1901–32, correspondence, 1914–40s). There are also microfilm files of the *Wheeling Majority* (1908–16), the weekly paper of the local labor movement.

Many relevant collections at the WVRHC do not allow such coherent groupings but nevertheless contribute to a more rounded picture of the labor movement in the Mountain State. Particularly rich are the records of United Toy Workers, Local 149 of Glen Dale (1941–66). Included are minutes, contract negotiations, grievance files, and correspondence comprising 11 boxes. Other small but rich collections highlight International Association of Machinists Local 598 at the Union Carbide plant in Charleston, the Morgantown Newspaper Guild (1972–73), and Local 1199 of the National Union of Hospital and Health Care Employees, in Huntington, 1975–79.

In addition to the specific labor holdings in the WVRHC, there are many collections containing material related to work and workers. The WVRHC houses a large number of business archives and collections which often reveal much about wages, working conditions, labor turnover, and other matters. Aside from the material for the coal and glass industries already noted, there are records and account books for the iron, lumber, textile, salt, oil, and chemical industries which were important in the state's economic development. Such collections range in size from large corporate archives to individual ledgers, but all contain a wealth of information. For scholars interested in the social history of the West Virginia working class, the WVRHC holds microfilmed census manuscripts, hundreds of feet of county court records, a variety of directories, and the most substantial collection of West Virginia newspapers in the country. Add to this a 15,000-item pamphlet collection, more than 100,000 photos, well over 300 sound recordings and oral histories, and a substantial library (which contains a large number of labor and industrial history-related items) and it becomes easy to see that the specifically labor-oriented manuscript collections only scratch the surface of materials in the WVRHC for the study of labor and working-class history.

Access: The WVRHC is open 9 am to 5 pm, Monday through Saturday, but the hours do vary. For the best results, it is recommended that the researcher write in advance. Contact Ken Fones-Wolf, The West Virginia and Regional History Collection, Colson Hall, West Virginia Univ., Morgantown, WV 26505; phone: (304) 293-3536.

THE SOUTHERN LABOR ARCHIVES

by
Robert Dinwiddie and Leslie S. Hough

The year 1989 marks the 20th anniversary of the founding of the Southern Labor Archives in Atlanta. Much has been accomplished over those two decades. The years since 1982, when *Labor History* last published an article on American labor archives, have been particularly noteworthy ones for the Southern Labor Archives. Its holdings have expanded rapidly and its outreach activities have been diverse and successful.

In 1982, 1984, and 1986 the Southern Labor Archives sponsored the Southern Labor Studies Conference. In 1984 the Conference was held in Arlington, TX, in cooperation with the Southwestern Labor Studies Association. These conferences have served as a most useful forum for scholars and labor practitioners to share ideas on the past, present, and future of labor in the South and beyond.

Exhibits have been a major area of activity of the Southern Labor Archives since 1982. In 1984 the permanent exhibit, "Friends of Honest Labor," was opened. The materials in this display were for the most part taken from the holdings of the Archives. The exhibit highlights the lives of workers in the South, as well as the leaders of the labor movement in the region, and was made possible with the support of friends of the Archives in organized labor. Over the years thousands of students and other citizens have been educated by the exhibit regarding the vital role that labor has played in the development of the South and the nation.

In 1985 the Southern Labor Archives received support from the Georgia Humanities Council to create a traveling exhibit on the history of textile workers, nationally, regionally, and in two particular mill towns in Georgia. This project involved substantial field work in com-

Robert Dinwiddie is assistant director of the Southern Labor Archives. Leslie S. Hough has been director of the Southern Labor Archives since 1977.

munities where mills had closed. The evidence of the lives of textile workers is disappearing in many of these mill villages. This project both captured something of their vanishing heritage, and provided information on the history of the communities to both newcomers and others in surrounding areas.

In 1982 the Archives completed the Georgia Textile Workers Project, which involved the work of two notable labor historians, Mary Frederickson and Dale Newman. These intrepid researchers explored widely the development of the textile industry in Georgia, found hundreds of images of textile workers and their communities, and presented their findings to groups of interested people at five locations across the state. Their work made possible the 1985 exhibit that followed.

The year 1988 was a momentous one for the Archives. In January it opened new and expanded quarters on the 8th floor of a new library building on the Georgia State Univ. campus in Atlanta. This move was the second by the Southern Labor Archives since 1982, each time into space that provided more room for collections and an environment enabling the Archives' staff to better serve researchers.

The Southern Labor Archives also helped the International Association of Machinists and Aerospace Workers (IAM) celebrate its centennial in 1988. The IAM had been founded in Atlanta in 1888, and the union returned there to hold its centennial convention. The Archives created two major exhibits on the history of the IAM, which were seen by the thousands of delegates and guests in attendance at the convention. These exhibits were made possible by the IAM's decision in 1985 to designate the Archives as the official repository for its historical records.

The American Library Association honored the Southern Labor Archives in 1988 by giving it the John Sessions Memorial Award for outstanding service to the labor community. The year 1988 was also notable for the decision by the University and College Labor Education Association to designate the Archives as the official repository for its historical records.

The future of the Southern Labor Archives promises even greater successes to come. The Archives will soon be sponsoring, with the Bill Usery Labor Management Relations Foundation and the U.S. Department of Labor, a major conference on the past, present, and future of American labor policy. Opening at that time will be a major exhibit on labor from World War II to the present, also sponsored by the Usery Foundation. The Southern Labor Archives is privileged to have the personal papers of former U.S. Labor Secretary W. J. Usery, Jr., and its recent and future successes would not be possible without his help.

The Archives has since 1969 been collecting organizational records and personal papers pertaining to the history of trade unionism in the South.[1] Since previously little collecting of labor material had been done in the region, the staff of the Archives realized at the beginning that their aim had to be to collect broadly from the entire Southeast rather than to emphasize the history of one or two unions. Appropriately, the first significant collection acquired by the founding archivist, Dr. David B. Gracy II, was the records of Atlanta Typographical Union No. 48, the city's oldest trade union. Subsequent acquisitions came from city central bodies, regional union headquarters, and additional local unions.

With the acquisition of the records of the United Textile Workers of America in 1973, the Archives for the first time reached beyond its initial geographic focus.[2] While maintaining its goal of assembling a body of research materials pertaining to Southern unionism, the Archives began to pursue the records of selected international unions with historic ties to the South.[3] The Archives also acquired records from AFL-CIO regional offices, state AFL-CIO councils, independent labor organizations, local unions, and persons active in trade union activity. The following collections are illustrative of this acquisition process:

1. The records (1922–1976) of the UNITED FURNITURE WORKERS OF AMERICA include correspondence, minutes, proceedings, reports, legal documents, financial statements, printed items, and photographs. UFWA officers whose correspondence is included in the collection are Michael DeCicco, Fred Fulford, Jack Hochstadt, Ernest Marsh, Max Perlow, Morris Pizer, and Carl Scarbrough. The record series comprising this collection are: CIO (1945–1955); AFL-CIO (1956–1968); other international unions — particularly the Upholsterers International Union (1946–1973); the UFWA General Executive Board (1943–1952); the UFWA International Executive Committee (1953–1959); the UFWA Administrative Committee (1953–1959); the

---

[1]For an account of the founding of the Southern Labor Archives, see *Labor History*, 23 (1982), 502–512.

[2]The UTWA Records (1941–1956) were described in *Labor History*, 23 (1982), 504–505. The Archives now hold a large uncataloged addition to this collection.

[3]The article in the Fall 1982 issue of *Labor History* contained descriptions of five collections in the Southern Labor Archives: UTWA; International Woodworkers of America District No. 4; Atlanta Typographical Union (ATU) Local No. 48; IAM Lodge 1 (Atlanta); and the papers of Stanton Smith. In addition to the UTWA records mentioned in Footnote 2, three of these collections have been significantly augmented by recent accessions. Records from typographical unions in Birmingham, Jacksonville, Memphis, and Richmond now complement those of ATU No. 48; the IAM national office and many district and local lodges have donated historical materials; and the records of the Chattanooga Area Labor Council (CALC) complement the papers of Stanton Smith, who was a long-time president of the CALC.

UFWA Finance Committee (1948–1950); individual UFWA officers (1947–1970). Additional record series pertain to UFWA conventions, departments, regions, joint councils, districts, local unions, organizers, lost shops, and the pension fund. 65 linear feet.

2. The records (1947–1986) of the MISSISSIPPI AFL-CIO reflect the career of Claude Ramsay, who served as its president from 1959 until his retirement on January 1, 1986. Ramsay was employed in the paper-making industry on the Mississippi Gulf Coast when he helped organize the first local union of Paperworkers there in 1939. After serving in World War II and returning to his job and a shop steward position with the International Paper Company in Moss Point, Ramsay was elected president of the Jackson County Central Labor Union in 1950. The records of the Mississippi AFL-CIO are organized into five series — Series 1: correspondence, speeches, public statements, and biographical newsclippings (1959–1986); Series 2: unions affiliated with the Mississippi AFL-CIO (1957–1983); Series 3: CIO and AFL-CIO officers and departments (1952–1985); Series 4: government agencies (1960–1983); Series 5: subject files (1947–1986).

Series 1 contains the bulk of Ramsay's correspondence with among others: George Meany, Andrew J. Biemiller, Stanton Smith, Dan Powell, and Carl McPeak of the AFL-CIO; political figures Lyndon Johnson, Hubert Humphrey, Edmund Muskie, and William F. Winter; civil rights leaders Charles Evers, Roy Wilkins, and Coretta Scott King. Series 2 contains memoranda, newsclippings, printed items, and legal papers concerning unions affiliated with the Mississippi AFL-CIO. This series includes varying amounts of information on some 14 unions, with the most extensive coverage being on the American Federation of State County and Municipal Employees, the American Federation of Teachers, the Communication Workers of America, the United Brotherhood of Carpenters, the International Union of Electronic Workers, and the Jackson Police Officers Association. Series 3 includes correspondence and other materials pertaining to the CIO, the AFL-CIO and its departments, standing committees, and councils; other state labor councils; industrial and trade councils in Mississippi; and county and city central union councils in Mississippi. Series 4 is comprised of correspondence, news releases, memoranda, and printed items chronicling Ramsay's interest in and involvement with many local, state, and national governmental agencies and commissions. Series 5 is an extensive compilation of material arranged alphabetically by subject dealing with state and national political activity (civil rights activities predominate in this series). Non-manuscript material such as sound recordings and photographs complete the collection. 54 linear feet.

3. The records (1968–1973) of the ALLIANCE FOR LABOR AC-
TION (ALA) include correspondence, minutes, financial statements,
organizing reports, newsclippings, and pamphlets. The ALA was
founded in 1969 by the Teamsters and Autoworkers. Shortly thereafter
these two unions were joined by the Chemical Workers and the Distributive Workers. The ALA was dissolved in 1971. These records primarily contain files pertaining to the ALA's Atlanta organizing campaign, but also include information on other ALA concerns, such as
opposition to the Vietnam War and the Anti-ballistic Missile System
as well as activities in support of tax reform. Teamsters Local Unions
528 and 728 of Atlanta were the principal backers of the ALA efforts
in the Atlanta metropolitan area. 3 linear feet.

4. The records (1905–1971) of the ATLANTA EDUCATION AS-
SOCIATION contain correspondence, financial and legal documents,
minutes, photographs, and issues of the *Atlanta Teacher* for the years
1929–1945. These records are in fact the files of the defunct ATLANTA
PUBLIC SCHOOL TEACHERS ASSOCIATION (APSTA), which
surrendered its charter as Local 89 of the American Federation of
Teachers (AFT) in the mid-1960s. These records document APSTA's
relationships with the AFT; the National Education Association; the
Georgia Education Association; the Atlanta Board of Education; the
Atlanta Federation of Trades; Jerome Jones, editor of the *Journal of
Labor* in Atlanta; and numerous other individuals and organizations
interested in public education in Atlanta and Georgia. Mary C. Barker
served as president of APSTA from 1921 to 1923 and as AFT president
from 1925 until 1931. 16 linear feet.

5. The papers (1928–1979) of JOHN RAMSAY consist of six record
series: CIO (1939–1955); AFL-CIO (1956–1967); Community Relations
Departments of the United Steelworkers of America (USWA) (1936–
1974); International Unions (1937–1969); the National Religion and
Labor Council of America (NRLCA) (1942–1978); personal papers
(1928–1979). Born in 1902, Ramsay worked in the steel mills of Beth-
lehem, PA for 17 years, where he served as a vice-president of a local
of the Amalgamated Association of Iron, Steel and Tin Workers. He
joined the new Steel Workers Organizing Committee in 1936 and soon
was elected President of Steelworkers Local 1409. In 1940 Ramsay joined
the USWA organizing staff and in 1942 became an assistant to John
Riffe in a campaign in Columbus, OH. Soon Ramsay began to devote
all his energies to community relations work for USWA, an emphasis
he would later specialize in as part of the CIO's "Operation Dixie" in
the Southern states from 1946 to 1953. When Operation Dixie ended
in 1953, USWA head David McDonald asked Ramsay to continue his

community relations activities, working out of the CIO office in Washington, DC. Ramsay returned to USWA in 1956 and remained there until his retirement in 1964.

The bulk of the papers concern Ramsay's community relations work for the CIO in the South (1946–1953). Ramsay traveled extensively throughout the South to assist in organizing compaigns, typically through the establishment of "Religion and Labor Fellowship" discussion groups that brought together labor activists, religious leaders, and others, with the hope of creating a climate more favorable for the successful organization of industrial workers. Lucy Randolph Mason collaborated with Ramsay in many of these efforts. Prominent among those with whom Ramsay corresponded are Philip Murray, John Riffe, David McDonald, I. W. Abel, Witherspoon Dodge, Clair Cook, and Willard Uphaus. The NRLCA series and the personal papers illustrate Ramsay's long and deep involvement with such religious groups as the United Presbyterian Church and the National Council of Churches. 15 linear feet.

6. The papers (1933–1981) of STETSON KENNEDY are comprised of correspondence, subject files, typescripts of articles written by him, pamphlets, periodicals, and photographs. Kennedy began his literary career when he worked as a writer and editor with the Federal Writers Project in Florida. His initial interest in folklore soon broadened to encompass the social and political inequities evident to him there. Kennedy's work as a government informer inside the KKK led to the publication of *I Rode With the Ku Klux Klan* (1954). Following an unsuccessful campaign for the Senate seat from Florida in 1950 and several years traveling extensively in Asia, Africa, and Eastern Europe, Kennedy returned home in 1956 to resume his career as a writer and lecturer in the labor, civil rights, and peace movements, most consistently through his column entitled "Up Front Down South," which ran in the *Pittsburgh Courier* during the 1960s.

Kennedy's subject files pertain to economic conditions, violence against blacks and labor organizers, peonage, peace activities, Southern politicians, the Spanish Civil War, Mexico, and his 1950 Senate race. Articles, news clippings, and pamphlets concern most of these same issues. His correspondence includes activist student groups, peace groups, committees to aid Spanish loyalists, literary agents, publishers, government agencies, writers' organizations, and magazine editors. Kennedy also authored a syndicated column entitled "Inside Out" and published several other monographs, including *Jim Crow Guide to the U.S.A.* (1959) and *Southern Exposure* (1946). 8 linear feet.

7. The records (1933–1974) of AFL-CIO REGION 8 chronicle the

long career in the labor movement of Paul R. Christopher. He went to work as a silk weaver in South Carolina in 1925 aged 14. Ten years later he was elected president of the United Textile Workers in North Carolina and a vice-president of that state's Federation of Labor. Christopher allied himself with the fledgling Textile Workers Organizing Committee (TWOC) in 1937, and when TWOC became the Textile Workers Union of America (TWUA) within the CIO, he was named TWUA state director in South Carolina. He moved to Tennessee in 1940 as the state CIO director. In 1953 he was named director of the CIO's Fourth Region (TN, KY, NC, and VA). When the CIO and AFL merged in 1955, Christopher was named director of the new AFL-CIO Region 8, headquartered in Knoxville and encompassing Tennessee and Kentucky.

These records cover Christopher's career (except for the very early years) in extensive files of correspondence (and associated material) with CIO and AFL-CIO officers; international, regional, state, and local union leaders; state and local central body leaders; government departments; politicians; and organizations and persons interested in or related to the labor movement. These records also include sound recordings, photographs, pamphlets, and proceedings of state labor conventions. 61 linear feet.

Another significant adjustment in the collecting focus of the Southern Labor Archives occurred in 1976 when Gracy accepted the records of the Georgia Nurses Association, an old and large professional organization whose members shared many of the economic and job security concerns of trade unionists. Following Gracy's initiative, his successor has strengthened this area of interest by acquiring records of other nurses associations (including those of KY, MD, SC, and the District of Columbia). The nurses' associations records now total approximately 250 linear feet.

Many other collections have been opened for research during the past five years. These include:

International union regional offices—
Amalgamated Clothing Workers of America, Southern Region, 1939–1976
International Ladies Garment Workers Union, Southern Region, 1940s–1960s
Retail, Wholesale, & Department Store Union, Southeast Region, 1940–1968
Service Employees International Union, Southern Region, 1960–1972
United Steelworkers of America, District 35, 1940–1974
Textile Workers Union of America, Central North Carolina Joint Board, 1939–1979; Northwest Georgia Joint Board, 1949–1976

AFL-CIO Regions, Departments, and State and Local Councils—
AFL-CIO Region 5, 1941–1981
AFL-CIO COPE, Area 3, 1970–1979

AFL-CIO Civil Rights Dept., Southeast Office, 1963–1984
Florida State AFL-CIO, 1965–1971
Georgia State AFL-CIO, 1956–1975
North Carolina AFL-CIO, 1950s–1970s
South Carolina AFL-CIO, 1950s–1960s
Local labor councils: Asheville (NC), 1948–1975; Atlanta, 1956–1975; Birmingham, 1954–1965; Decatur (AL), 1953–1983; Jacksonville, 1956–1973; Newport News, 1899–1981; Savannah, 1946–1970; Tennessee Valley Trades & Labor Council, 1941–1974

Local Unions—
Carpenter Union locals in Atlanta, 1937–1938; Macon, 1887–1970; Savannah, 1899–1956; Newport News, 1901–1968; Ft. Myers, 1941–1978; St. Petersburg, 1900–1977; Tallahassee, 1951–1969; Tampa, 1892–1971. Also Florida State Council of Carpenters, 1952–1978
IBEW Local 613 (Atlanta), 1939–1977
Atlanta Fire Fighters Union, 1966
Glass Bottle Blowers Association Local 101 (Atlanta), 1953–1978
Laundry Workers Local 218, 1950–1971
Brotherhood of Locomotive Engineers, Simpson Division 210, 1884–1918
Meatcutters Local 525 (Asheville, NC), 1957–1975
Operating Engineers Local 926 (Atlanta), 1927–1971
Atlanta Printing Pressmen No. 8, 1940–1973
Atlanta Printing Specialities No. 527, 1954–1972
United Food and Commercial Workers Local Union No. 1063 (Atlanta), 1947–1974
Retail, Wholesale & Department Store Union, Local 15-A (Charleston), 1945–1973
Amalgamated Transit Workers No. 732 (Atlanta), 1940–1981

Law Firms—
Adair, Goldthwaite, Stanford & Daniel, 1955–1971
Jacobs & Langford, 1936–1984
D. Bruce Shine, 1928–1981

Individuals—
E.L. Abercrombie, 1942–1982
J.W. Giles, 1920–1979
Mrs. George Googe, 1946–1961
Mrs. Carey Haigler, 1933–1970
F.H. (Pug) King, 1937–1970
Carmen Lucia, 1927–1979
Andrew McElroy, 1884–1935
Frank Sgambato, 1936–1952
Leon Stamey, 1951–1972
Emory Via, 1955–1964

Miscellaneous —
Ellis Arnall Write-In Campaign for Governor (GA), 1966–1967
National Domestic Workers Union, 1965–1979
Georgia Democratic Party Forum, 1967–1972
Kingsport, Tennessee Press Strike, 1963–1967
National City Lines, 1942–1956

Access: The Southern Labor Archives is located on the Eighth Floor of Library South, 103 Decatur St., on the campus of Georgia State Univ. in downtown Atlanta. The Archives is open for research 9 am–5 pm, Monday–Friday, and at other times, including weekends, with advance notice. The telephone number is (404) 651-2477. Copying and telefacsimile facilities are available. The staff of the Southern Labor Archives welcomes research inquiries by letter or telephone, as well as in person. For further information contact Leslie Hough.

LABOR HISTORY RESOURCES AT THE OHIO HISTORICAL SOCIETY

by
Dan Ashyk and Wendy S. Greenwood

The Ohio Historical Society (OHS) began the Ohio Labor History Project in 1975 to locate, inventory, acquire, preserve, and provide access to labor union records and personal papers of Ohio labor leaders and to conduct oral history interviews. Initial funding came from the National Endowment for the Humanities, the Ohio AFL-CIO, the Labor Education Research Services of the Ohio State Univ., and the Ohio Historical Society. Since 1979 the Society's manuscripts department, through continuing support from the Ohio General Assembly, has expanded the collections and conducted extensive research into the history of Ohio labor. Several publications have resulted from this research, including Ray Boryczka and Lorin Lee Cary's *No Strength Without Union: An Illustrated History of Ohio Workers, 1803–1980*; the booklets, *United in Purpose, a Chronological History of the Ohio AFL-CIO, 1958–1983* and *The Unceasing Struggle—A Chronology of Ohio Labor History, 1803–1987*; the *Guide to Primary Sources in Ohio Labor History*, and *How to Preserve Local Union Records for Historical Purposes*. Except for the last, which is out of print, these publications may be purchased through the Society's sales office.

The project also has mounted a traveling photographic exhibit entitled "Vistas and Visions of Labor" and, most recently, has prepared a script on Ohio's labor history for a video production in cooperation with WBGU-TV of Bowling Green State Univ. In addition to continuing efforts in the collection of papers, records, and oral histories, project plans include publishing a history of labor in Toledo, Ohio.

Dan Ashyk has worked as a labor archivist at the Western Reserve Historical Society and is a researcher for the Ohio Labor History Project. Wendy S. Greenwood was archivist for the Ohio Labor History Project and is now a reference librarian in the Ohio Historical Society's Archives Library.

The *Guide to Primary Sources in Ohio Labor History*, published in 1980, is a bibliographic guide to sources inventoried and collected during the initial phase of the project. The wide range of records collected and unions represented in the Labor History Project reflects the diversity in Ohio's labor heritage. The project channeled union records in the state to eight regional repositories comprising the Ohio Network of American History Research Centers. The *Guide* includes descriptions of 207 collections housed at the eight Ohio library research centers, additional collections in union offices, 80 oral history interviews, and labor-related publications such as newspapers, proceedings, and journals held by the Ohio Historical Society. An addendum will soon be available to expand and update the original *Guide*. It will include records and oral histories accessioned since 1980 and will inventory the substantial photographic collections and other audio-visual materials dealing with labor at the Society and its network centers.

The majority of collections at the Ohio Historical Society are of local unions in the central Ohio area, but district and regional headquarters for many internationals are located in Columbus and larger central labor bodies also are included. The Ohio AFL-CIO Records for the years 1922–1984 cover nearly all aspects of organized labor in the state, including material on the important defeat of the right-to-work campaign in 1958. The Columbus-Franklin County AFL-CIO, Newark Area AFL-CIO Council, and the Columbus-Franklin County Building and Construction Trades Council Records also are at OHS.

Though not a major industrial region, the Columbus area has developed a growing industrial base since World War II. This growth is reflected in the number of industrial unions' records housed at OHS. These include the United Steelworkers, District 27, Subdistrict 5 in central Ohio, Subdistrict 3 covering east-central Ohio, and Locals 2342 and 2627. The Machinists also are well represented with collections from District 52, and Lodges 55, 1038, 1136, 1427, 1651, and 1847. Also represented are Local 487 of the Textile Workers, including records of a 1973 neuropathy outbreak which led to a strike and transfer of half of the struck plant's operations, and the United Industrial Workers which split from the Teamsters in 1961 shortly after James Luken led several Cincinnati locals to disaffiliate from the IBT.

Finally, the glass and pottery industries were particularly strong in much of Ohio. The OHS holds the records of the Glass Bottle Blowers Association Locals 33 and 244, and the United Glass and Ceramic Workers Local 20. The U.S. Potters Association records (1894–1977) also are housed at the Society. During its first 30 years, the USPA served as an informational and regulatory trade association, then assumed the role of an employers association and bargained collectively with the National Brotherhood of Operative Potters.

Columbus has been a political and commercial center for 150 years and the Ohio Historical Society's labor collections reflect this in the number of service and government union records held, and in the political records of the Ohio Socialist Labor Party (1936–68) which includes convention proceedings and minutes of meetings (1944–1955). Service employee records include the Food and Allied Workers, District 346; the Retail, Wholesale, and Department Store Union, Midwest Region and Local 379; the Retail Clerks International Union, District 22 and Local 1059; the Hotel and Restaurant Employees and Bartenders International Union Local 505; the Service, Hospital, Nursing Home, and Public Employees Union Local 47; the Transport Workers of America Local 208; and the Communication Workers of America Local 4371 in Marion, Ohio. Government employees are represented by the American Federation of Government Employees Local 1148; the Ohio Civil Service Employees Association (which affiliated with AFSCME in 1983 when Ohio enacted its first collective bargaining law for public employees); the Ohio Postal Workers Union; and the International Association of Fire Fighters Local 379 in Marion and Local 291 in Lancaster.

OHS also has concentrations among several unions in central Ohio, such as the printing trades. The Columbus Typographical Union No. 5 is one of the oldest in the country. Its records, 1859–1969, include minutes (1859–1960), financial records, correspondence, a black list (1869–1874) kept by the union to exclude "rats" and others, and a strike roll book (1917–1937). Other printing trades unions at OHS are ITU Local 675 and the Printing and Graphic Communications Union Local 15 representing the pressmen at *The Columbus Dispatch*. Another area of concentration is in the building trades, with collections of the Carpenters, Electrical Workers, Ironworkers, and Bricklayers, Masons, and Plasterers.

The Ohio Historical Society also holds collections of personal papers of prominent labor leaders. Among these collections are the Leland Beard Papers (1934–1965) pertaining to his work in the United Glass and Ceramic Workers; the Robert Dean Bollard Papers (1917–1972) regarding his work with the United Steelworkers and the Ohio AFL-CIO; the G. George DeNucci Papers (1934–1976) concerning the United Garment Workers, the United Steelworkers, the Ohio CIO, and the Ohio AFL-CIO; the John Gates Ramsay Papers (1936–1976) documenting his work on the Steelworkers Organizing Committee and his involvement in religion and community relations for the CIO; and the Pauline

Taylor Papers, pertaining to her participation in the Little Steel Strike, the International Workers Order, and the Progressive Party.

The Ohio Historical Society has an impressive collection of over 160 taped interviews on labor, most of which are transcribed. The interviews range from leaders such as the presidents of internationals (I. W. Abel of the Steelworkers and Jackie Presser of the Teamsters) to regional officers (William Kircher, George DeNucci, and Harry Mayfield) to rank-and-file unionists like coal miner Robert Guess. The content of these interviews varies greatly. Jackie Presser describes the difficulties and complexities of union leadership and provides some political views prior to his presidency of the IBT, while James Luken and William Kircher's interviews provide insight into the short but potentially threatening disaffiliation movement in the Teamsters during the early 1960s. George Addes, former UAW Secretary-Treasurer, discusses the working conditions and strike actions of the powerful Toledo autoworkers in the founding days of that union.

Some of the most fascinating material can be found in interviews with men like Robert Guess. He describes the 1930 Millfield Mine disaster in which 82 died in the Hocking Valley. Guess also describes mining town company stores, strikes, survival, his work in the mines and in shoe factories. Other oral histories at the Ohio Historical Society include Ione Biggs of the Cleveland Women Working Project, William Presser, former head of the Ohio Teamsters, and Jacob Clayman, former head of the AFL-CIO's Industrial Union Department. For information on the use of oral histories, contact the manuscripts department at OHS. Transcriptions and tapes are not available on interlibrary loan.

The Ohio Historical Society houses several photographic collections rich in labor history. The Youngstown Sheet and Tube Co. collection reveals working conditions of steel workers in Ohio from the turn-of-the century to the 1970s. Subjects of interest in this collection are men at work, machinery and construction, portraits of laborers both candid and posed, and company welfare work including safety campaigns, company sponsored athletics for men and women, housing, hospitalization, and locker rooms.

The files (1912–1919) of the Buckeye Steel Casting Co. of Columbus are another valuable photographic collection. It also contains photographs of men at work and of company welfare projects including shots of workers learning English, reading, and writing at a local YMCA. Jeffrey Mining Machine Division-Dresser Industries (1880–1949) of Columbus offers photographs of miners and mining equipment. The Ohio AFL-CIO collection (c. 1936–1980) features photos of members during conventions, meetings, and other activities. Additional collections include the Fisher Body Strike of 1939 in Cleveland; Adamson United Company of Akron (c. 1941-1960s) manufacturer of rubber plant equipment; local labor organizations; and several personal photograph collections of leading figures in Ohio labor history such as Max S. Hayes, Leland Beard, Joseph Slight, and Elmer F. Cope.

Small collections of photographs are also available to researchers and can be accessed by a variety of subject headings including specific local labor organizations, events, or prominent labor leaders in Ohio.

Sound recordings on reel, cassette, and disc enhance the Society's labor collections. Items of interest include a Farm Labor Organizing Committee strike meeting (September 1978) and Solidarity Day celebrations and rallies (c. 1981, Washington, DC). Other sound recordings include songs by artists such as Joe Glazer, Larry Penn, Bobbie McGee, and Earl Robinson, whose themes evolve around steelworkers, wobblies, working women, autoworkers, and anthracite miners, to name a few.

The Ohio Historical Society currently has 22 microfilmed labor collections. In addition to several local union records on microfilm, collections of importance include the William Green Papers (1891-1952) concerning his presidency of the AFL; the Max S. Hayes Papers (1891-1945) regarding his editorship of the Cleveland *Citizen*, his leadership in the AFL and his activities in the Socialist and National Labor Parties; the Joseph Slight Papers (1874-1957) concerning the National Window Glass Workers of America and the Knights of Labor; the papers of Jacob S. Coxey (1872-1975), labor reformer, who formed the "Commonweal of Christ"; and a scrapbook on Coxey (1894-1951), kept by Wilbur Miller, a reporter for the Cincinnati *Enquirer* and the Associated Press, who traveled with "Coxey's Army" from Massillon, OH in 1894 to its destination in Washington, DC; the Elmer F. Cope Papers (1921-1965) concerning his work with the Steel Workers Organizing Committee, the CIO, the Ohio AFL-CIO, and Brookwood Labor College; and the papers of John Samuel (1873-1907) recording his activities as secretary of the cooperative board of the Knights of Labor.

The Society has microfilmed 49 labor union newspapers from Bluffton, Springfield, East Liverpool, Cleveland, Columbus, Cincinnati, Heath, Lima, Lorain, Toledo, Marion, Dayton, Tiffin, Canton, Akron, Warren, and Youngstown. Among those of interest are the East Liverpool *Potter's Gazette* (1876-1884); the Cleveland *Citizen* (1891-1893); the *Toledo Union Journal* (1942-1983); the Cincinnati *Chronicle* (1892-1910 and 1916-1918); the Cincinnati *Labor Advocate* (1915-1934); and a strike newspaper the Lima *Bulletin* (1957).

These microfilmed titles and the labor collections on microfilm may be obtained from the Society by purchase or interlibrary loan. For additional information, contact the Society's Microfilm Department.

In addition to manuscripts, oral histories, photographs, and microfilmed collections, OHS holds a variety of miscellaneous collections, including ephemera, broadsides and posters, pamphlets, flyers, and vertical files. The Society also purchases dissertations and theses relating to Ohio labor history not available through interlibrary loan.

Access: The Ohio Historical Society's archives/library is open Tuesday through Saturday, 9 am–5 pm. For further information contact Research Services Dept. at the Society, 1982 Velma Avenue, Columbus, OH 43211; phone: (614) 297-2510.

THE DEBS COLLECTION AT
INDIANA STATE UNIVERSITY

by
David E. Vancil, Robert L. Carter, and Charles D. King

Renowned labor activist and socialist Eugene V. Debs (1855–1926) was born in Terre Haute, IN, where he resided throughout his life except for two periods when he was incarcerated for his labor and anti-war activities. Debs was the oldest son in a family of four daughters and two sons, and his brother, Theodore, was his lifelong personal secretary and booking agent. Theodore's daughter, Marguerite Debs Cooper, became the sole surviving family member left in Terre Haute and thus came into possession of Eugene V. Debs's and her father's private papers, including family and other correspondence. Eugene V. Debs's activities and high visibility as a five-time candidate for U.S. President on the Socialist Party ticket, not to mention his captivating speaking style and his anti-war efforts, certainly stirred up enough reaction to make his correspondence and papers informative and exciting. Yet, not until 1967 did Bernard J. Brommel, then a member of both the Speech Dept. at the university and the governing board of the Eugene V. Debs Foundation, persuade Marguerite Debs Cooper to deposit in the University Library the Debs papers which she had inherited, making them available to scholars with some stipulations.

In 1962 the Eugene V. Debs Foundation had been founded with the primary goals of historic preservation of the Debs Home and its utilization as a museum open to the public. Many charter members of the Foundation were professors at Indiana State Univ., whose campus now surrounds the Debs Home. Having faculty as members of the Foundation helped ensure from the start close and productive ties with Cunningham Memorial Library, where the Debs Collection is now located

David E. Vancil is head of the Dept. of Rare Books and Special Collections, Indiana State Univ. Robert L. Carter is reference librarian in that Dept. Charles D. King is a Prof. of Sociology at the Univ., and Secretary of the Eugene V. Debs Foundation.

in the Dept. of Rare Books and Special Collections. Interest in the preservation of the Debs Home extended also to deteriorating materials in the house, including some personal correspondence and copies of books autographed for Debs by famous authors such as Upton Sinclair, Jack London, Irving Stone, and Emma Goldman. The Debs Foundation recently discontinued the maintenance of a library research facility in the Debs Home not only to preserve deteriorating materials but also to make them accessible to serious researchers in a facility that already housed significant holdings. The execution of this plan in 1988 involved the donation to the University Library of more than 150 books, myriad newspaper clippings, scarce photographs, and a few other items. Among these items were bound volumes of *Locomotive Fireman's Magazine*, which Debs edited from 1880 to 1894. Thus, through the efforts of University librarians and members of the Foundation, the Dept. of Rare Books and Special Collections is now the sole repository of an extensive Debs Collection, which has experienced considerable growth in recent years.

Initially, both the History Committee of the Foundation and the Director of Libraries had to give permission to use or publish the contents of any of these materials, but in 1974, to facilitate access by scholars, Mrs. Cooper gave the Dean of Library Services or his appointed representative complete control of the collection. Nonetheless, the Eugene V. Debs Foundation maintains an active involvement in the Collection by providing funds for the acquisition of scarce or expensive materials. In addition, there are other important ways in which the Debs Collection remains closely tied to the Foundation. The Foundation is thus in an opportune position to provide the curators of the Collection with helpful advice both on acquisitions and on needed archival activities, including the preparation of bibliographies and guides.

The initial gift establishing the Debs Collection contained 3800 letters, 6000 speeches, 220 telegrams, 170 typescripts, 60 manuscripts, and 300 other items, including campaign memorabilia and photographs. A gift of particular significance came to the Collection through the efforts of J. Robert Constantine, a member of the university's Dept. of History, who for many years was Secretary of the Debs Foundation and was instrumental in the inception of the Debs Collection. Assisted by a grant from the National Endowment for the Humanities, Constantine collected, cataloged, and prepared a 21-reel microfilm edition of the papers of Eugene V. Debs (published by the Microfilming Corp. of America). Part of this project was to collect photocopies of all papers not already in the Debs Collection, and these photocopies were a most valuable addition to the materials already held, adding approximately 3000 letters to the original Debs Cooper gift.

As a corpus, these various published and unpublished materials trace Debs's public career as Socialist Presidential candidate, his work as a social reformer, and his life as a member of a family and community. Included among the thousands of original letters are exchanges between Debs and leading figures of the era, such as Upton Sinclair, Jack London, Margaret Sanger, Samuel Gompers, and William Haywood. The letters from Emma Goldman are particularly noteworthy because of her insight into conditions in the Soviet Union of the early 1920s. Similarly, heated exchanges of opinions with William Z. Foster, a noted American Communist, concerning the Third International reveal much about Debs's feelings on communism. As a final example of the richness of the Collection, Debs's letters about the plight of Sacco and Vanzetti are poignant and fascinating views of history as it occurred.

Soon after the Collection was formed, the Library received a large selection of the many thousands of "Little Blue Books" published in several series by E. Haldeman-Julius from 1919 through 1951 and by Henry J. Haldeman through 1976. These palm-size booklets, containing reprints of literary, philosophical, and social tracts, sold for pennies a copy and were intended for a receptive proletarian audience. Although the holdings of Little Blue Books is substantial, the Library still lacks many titles in this now scarce series. In 1986 John Feier, a resident of Staunton, IN, gave several hundred more of them to the Library, helping to fill in some of the gaps in the Collection's holdings. Another substantial donation came from Oscar K. Edelman, a resident of Dayton, OH, adding 3600 pamphlets of socialist, labor, and similar interest dating from the Debs period, including some written by Debs himself, through the 1960s.

Both the gifts of Marguerite Debs Cooper and Oscar Edelman helped to establish the scope and focus of the Collection. As the Collection has evolved, it has become not only a resource for the study of Debs's political career and his family life, including the contributions by Theodore Debs to his better known brother's social and political goals, but it has also become a resource for the study of American socialist-oriented political and labor movements. The format of materials in the Collection has expanded to include not only papers, pamphlets, booklets, and other fugitive items, but books and microforms as well. The books in the Collection now number 1500 volumes. The acquisition of books has been limited to scarce editions or materials written either by Debs himself or by members of his circle, including relevant works by literary figures sympathetic to Debs or to labor or socialism. Included also are particularly important historical or critical texts on Debs, American socialism, and progressive labor movements.

The number of rare, or scarce, books in the Collection is significant and has been enhanced recently by several large donations. One such gift included 400 social and political histories and analytical texts donated in 1984 by Oscar Edelman, who maintained an active interest in the Debs Collection until his death in 1987. Another acquisition was the gift from the Debs Foundation in 1988, mentioned previously, that included more than 150 books which had been kept in the Eugene V. Debs Home. Finally, the Collection received 150 volumes from the estate of Marguerite Debs Cooper, who died in late 1987. The books from the Debs Cooper estate are particularly noteworthy for volumes which are inscribed or privately printed in limited numbers, for example, books by Kate Crane-Gartz, a wealthy California socialist.

The Debs Collection includes limited but important holdings of non-print media. This includes the materials on microfilm collected by Constantine and a microfilm copy of the journal *Appeal to Reason*. These materials are kept in the Collection to provide better service to researchers, while microform collections relating to the general subject of the Debs tradition are housed in another department of the Library. These include microfilm editions of *The Socialist Party of America Papers* at Duke Univ. and *U.S. Military Intelligence Reports: Surveillance of Radicals in the United States, 1917–1941*.

Although limited to a relatively few items, the audio-visual materials are nevertheless consequential and include the following: a VHS-format videotape of a silent film on Eugene Debs's life produced by the American Socialist Party; a student videotape production on Debs's life prepared at Indiana State Univ.; a 50-minute documentary film in VHS-format on the life of Eugene Debs produced by Cambridge Documentary Films (MA); and a selection of audio-tapes of many of the speeches given at the annual award banquets of the Eugene V. Debs Foundation, including those of Walter Reuther, Pete Seeger, Michael Harrington, and Ed Asner.

No attempt has consciously been made to limit the size of the Collection, but an effort is being made not to duplicate holdings readily available in the general collection or easily obtainable from other college and university libraries on interlibrary loan. Thus the focus of the Collection on scarce materials has kept the complete holdings of the Collection to a manageable 18,000 items of which only a very few have been fully cataloged and made available through OCLC, an international shared-cataloging network.

Cunningham Memorial Library is a medium-sized research library of over 1,000,000 physical volumes, excluding documents, microforms, and other media. Holdings of labor history materials in the general collection of the Library are substantial. Care has been taken in building the serial and monographic holdings in this area. The curators welcome materials in various formats for addition to the Collection or to the Library's general holdings to bolster the study of Debs, American socialism, labor history, or other relevant topics.

Since the Debs Collection was formed only in 1967 and became easily accessible only in 1973 when the present facility opened, the Debs Collection did not begin making itself felt as a research facility until 1978 with the publication of Brommel's *Eugene V. Debs* which relied, in part, on the original gift of papers that Marguerite Debs Cooper had provided to begin the Debs Collection. Another volume that relied heavily on the original Debs Cooper gift was Nick Salvatore's *Eugene V. Debs: Citizen Socialist* (1982). The next year Constantine's microfilm edition of Debs's papers became available. Constantine's three-volume *The Correspondence of Eugene V. Debs, 1874–1926* (Univ. of Illinois Press, 1990), is based on original or photocopied materials found in the Debs Collection.

Until recently, studies of the Socialist Party of America and Debs as a labor activist have appeared without the researchers having been able to consult the primary or, in some instances, extremely scarce secondary research materials now made available through the Debs Collection. Neither the Collection nor the Library's general holdings can pretend to provide the same kind of depth of coverage of socialism or labor history as institutions or universities such as the Hoover Institution on War, Revolution and Peace, Wayne State Univ., Duke Univ., or the Tamiment Institute of New York Univ., to name only four important repositories of materials on these topics. Yet, with particular regard to Debs, his personal life, his interaction with his circle, and his public life as a labor activist and political leader, the Debs Collection has become an essential resource. The guide to Constantine's *The Papers of Eugene V. Debs, 1834–1945*, which he prepared with his associate, Gail Malmgreen, and his *The Correspondence of Eugene V. Debs, 1874–1926*, serve not only important scholarly purposes but also provide bibliographic access to many important fugitive materials held either in the original or in photocopy. Similarly, a bibliography compiled by Gene DeGruson of the Pittsburg State Univ. Library in Pittsburg, KS, lists the Little Blue Books, but provides only numerical access to them. Extensive card catalogs and an abstract file of the letters in the original Debs Cooper gift are available in the Dept. of Rare Books and Special Collections at Cunningham Memorial Library, where the materials are housed. A newsletter published under the auspices of the Friends of the Cunningham Memorial Library reports significant acquisitions, publications, and events in the Library, including the Debs Collection. The newsletter is available for a nominal annual membership fee, and sample issues are free on request. At the present time, no other printed or published guides to the Collection are available although a catalog of the monographic holdings in the Collection, including the Little Blue Books and the pamphlets, is in the planning stages.

Researchers wishing to use materials in the department will find a spacious reading room available for viewing materials and a knowledgeable staff on hand to assist them. All original and photocopied documents are available for use in the Dept. of Rare Books and Special Collections or in microfilm collections and books edited by Constantine; original documents owned by the Dept. may be photocopied with the permission of the department head or Dean of Library Services. Blanket approval has been given for quoting or photocopying microfilmed materials owned by the university; however, the researcher is responsible for obtaining the necessary permissions in order to copy or publish materials not owned by Indiana State Univ. but housed there in photocopy or on microfilm.

Access: the Collection's holdings of original and photocopied documents are available for use in the Dept. of Rare Books and Special Collections which is open 8 am–4:30 pm, Monday–Friday. Microform and other nonprint media materials housed in the Dept. may be used in the Library's Dept. of Teaching Materials, Microforms, and Media, which has extended hours. Originals and microfilm are not loaned outside the Library, and modest fees are assessed for photocopying original non-copyrighted research materials owned by the Collection. For further information contact David Vancil, Dept. of Rare Books and Special Collections, Cunningham Memorial Library, Indiana State Univ. Terre Haute, IN 47809; phone: (812) 237-2610.

THE ARCHIVES OF LABOR HISTORY AND URBAN AFFAIRS, WALTER P. REUTHER LIBRARY, WAYNE STATE UNIVERSITY

by
Philip P. Mason

The Archives of Labor History and Urban Affairs was established in 1960 to collect and preserve the records of the American labor movement, with special emphasis upon industrial unionism and related social, economic and political reform movements in the U.S., especially those relating to workers. A second major collecting theme has been workers, working and living conditions and the nature of work. Later, in 1970, the scope of the Archives was expanded to include urbanization, especially relating to Detroit and southeastern Michigan. Many of the union collections also contain extensive material on such issues as immigration, ethnicity, public housing, civil rights, health, education, and a variety of social programs and urban-related reform movements.

The majority of the archival collections relate to the period after 1920, though some collections like those of the Industrial Workers of the World, the American Federation of Teachers, and the personal papers of labor leaders date back to the turn of the century. As of 1989 the Archives contain 50,000 linear feet of records, nearly a million photographs, broadsides, posters and illustrations, 25,000 films and videotapes, and a reference library of 20,000 volumes.

The Archives is the official depository for eight major international unions: the United Automobile, Aerospace and Agricultural Implement Workers of America (UAW), the Industrial Workers of the World (IWW), The Newspaper Guild (TNG), the American Federation of Teachers (AFT), the American Federation of State, County and Municipal Employees (AFSCME), the Air Line Pilots Association (ALPA),

---

Philip P. Mason is Professor of History at Wayne State University and has been director of the Archives of Labor History and Urban Affairs since its establishment.

the Association of Flight Attendants (AFA), and the United Farm Workers of America (UFW).

Under the terms of deposit agreements with the eight international unions, additional files are systematically transferred to the Archives annually and are available to researchers after they have been processed and meet the terms of access.

It is not possible in this article to describe or even list the several thousand collections in the Reuther Library. The collecting policy of the Archives, especially for the official files of unions, will give the researchers a clear idea of the type of union records available in the Archives. From its beginning in 1960, the Archives has adopted a vertical collecting policy for union records. It collects the records of the key offices and departments of each international union and of the regional and state offices of the organization. In addition, the Archives collects the records of key locals, selected because of such factors as size, geographical location, type of employer, association with historic strikes and events, factional struggles, and other related criteria. This selective list of key union locals is under periodic review by the Archives staff and changes periodically. Some local unions which were important in the founding and early years of an international union decline in importance and often become defunct. Newer locals, such as the UAW Local in Lordstown, Ohio, which was founded in 1966, became leaders. In addition, the Archives has acquired the records of dissident and grass roots movements, such as the Dodge Revolutionary Union Movement (DRUM), Teamsters for a Democratic Union, Steelworkers Fight Back, Miners for Democracy and the Association for Union Democracy.

This vertical collecting policy differs sharply from the acquisitions policy of many archives that concentrate almost solely upon key offices of an international union and the personal papers of top union leadership. Although, to be sure, such records have great research value, they often fail to reveal the important role of local unions and rank and file movements within an international union.

Another major holding of the Archives is the voluminous files of the Congress of Industrial Organizations (CIO). The original installment of CIO files was received in 1966 and consists of 120 linear feet of records covering the years 1935 to 1955 and representing the office files of James B. Carey, Secretary-Treasurer from 1938 to 1956, and George L-P. Weaver, Assistant Secretary-Treasurer (1945–1950, 1953–1955). The internal operation of the CIO is reflected in these files as well as the organization's involvement in a wide variety of activities such as civil rights, social security, housing, universal military training, southern organizing campaigns, international affairs, World War II, communism, jurisdictional disputes, union racketeering, and the merger of the CIO and the AFL.

The files of Walter P. Reuther as president of the CIO (1952–1955) and later as president of the Industrial Union Department of the AFL-CIO, and the papers of Victor G. Reuther as Director of the CIO's International Affairs Department, have also been acquired by the Archives. They supplement the Carey-Weaver files and reflect the Reuthers' widespread domestic and international interests.

Other collections of personal papers also relate to the CIO, most notably those of Katherine Pollack Ellickson who was assistant to CIO President John L. Lewis in the first year of the organization. Her collection includes the most complete set of minutes available for the first 18 months of the CIO, summaries of CIO-AFL confrontations, correspondence, speeches, and special reports. Other CIO collections include the papers of August Scholle as CIO Regional Director in Michigan (1937–1954); Irwin L. DeShetler, CIO Regional Director in Ohio (1943–1946) and California (1946–1952); and Leo Goodman, Director of the CIO Housing Committee (1948–1955).

In 1987 and 1988 the Archives received an additional 75 linear feet of CIO records which were discovered in the basement of the IUE headquarters in Washington and an additional group of papers in the possession of John Carey, James Carey's brother.

Included in these acquisitions were the minutes of the CIO Executive Board from 1939 to 1955, including the hitherto missing ones of 1946; periodic field reports from CIO staff; James Carey's speeches and congressional testimony; and general correspondence files of the Secretary-Treasurer. In addition the collections included CIO scrapbooks and photographs. A recent installment of papers from George L-P. Weaver also relates in part to his CIO duties.

The papers of numerous reform organizations which have assisted the labor movements have been collected by the Archives, including the Workers Defense League, the Association of Catholic Trade Unionists, the National Farm Workers Ministry, National Sharecroppers Fund, the Peoples Song Library, Center for Community Change, Committee for National Health Insurance, Citizens Crusade Against Poverty, the Coalition of Labor Union Women, and the Urban Environmental Conference, Inc.

The Raya Dunayevskaya Collection on Marxist-Humanism was presented to the Archives in several installments between 1969 and 1988. The collection contains her extensive writings and her correspondence with Leon Trotsky, for whom she served as Russian Secretary from 1937 to 1938, and also her correspondence with Herbert Marcuse, Ralph Bunche, Max Schachtman, C. L. R. James, Erich Fromm and other philosophers and writers. The founding of *News and Letters*, a Marxist-Humanist newspaper is also documented in her collection. A superb collection of photographs including several of Ms. Dunayevskaya and Leon Trotsky in Mexico in 1937–1938 are also a part of the Collection.

The papers of John Dwyer and Martin Ahern, received in the Archives during 1987, add to the Archives holdings on socialism, communism, and other political movements in the United States.

Labor education is another theme which has been given attention by the Archives. The files of the education departments of the major depositing unions, and the personal papers of persons involved in labor education have been actively solicited. Two of our most extensive acquisitions are the records of Brookwood Labor College, which operated at Katonah, NY from 1921 to 1937; and Commonwealth College, which ran from 1923 to 1940 at Mena, AR. These collections provide in-depth information on all aspects of these schools — faculty, students, curriculum, political activities, and the like. The personal papers of faculty members and students of Brookwood and Commonwealth have been added to those holdings. Workers Education Local 189, which had its origin at Brookwood and was affiliated with the American Federation of Teachers for many years, has designated the Archives as its official depository and has placed all of its extant inactive files here. Finally, a number of labor educators teaching in university programs have given their papers to the Archives.

Michigan labor unions, community organizations, public figures, and labor leaders have been given a high priority in the Archives. The Michigan AFL-CIO, the Metropolitan Detroit AFL-CIO, the Trade Union Leadership Council, the Jewish Labor Committee, the Detroit Education Association, the Detroit Federation of Teachers and dozens of local unions and Local Central Bodies have placed their papers in the Archives. The state offices of many international unions, such as the Communications Workers of America, District 4; Michigan Postal Workers Union; Welfare Employees Union; Society of Engineering Office Workers; Amalgamated Clothing and Textile Workers Union, Chicago and Central States Joint Board; and Detroit Typographical Union #18, have taken similar action.

Typical of the urban related community organizations that have deposited their files are: United Foundation of Detroit, the International Institute of Metropolitan Detroit, the Detroit Commission on Community Relations, and the Michigan Citizens Lobby.

The personal files of labor leaders at the national, regional and local levels, and rank and file union members supplement the exten-sive files of labor unions and related support organizations. Many union leaders maintained duplicate union files at home for protection in in-ternal and factional struggles. In some cases union officials cleared out and maintained their complete office files at the end of their term of office or upon retirement. For example, when Homer Martin, the first elected president of the UAW, was removed from office in 1939, he took with him many official union records which were later placed in the Archives as part of his personal collection.

Space does not permit a listing or description of the hundreds of collections of personal papers in the Reuther Library. Such a list, fur-thermore, would be immediately out-of-date because the Archives re-ceives a continuous flow of new collections or installments to existing groups of papers. *A Guide to the Archives of Labor History and Urban Affairs* published in 1974 and subsequent lists of collections are avail-able to researchers.[1]

The personal papers of the leaders of the eight international unions are on deposit in the Reuther Library and represent a major section of the Archives' holdings. All UAW past and present members who have served as officers of the International and its Executive Board have been solicited for their personal papers. In addition, key regional and local UAW leaders have been contacted.

The largest collection of personal as well as official records was given to the Archives by Walter Reuther, his family, and the UAW. These papers cover all phases of his life including his boyhood in Wheeling, WV; his move to Detroit in 1927 and his employment at the Ford Motor Company; his education at the College of the City of Detroit (now Wayne State University); his trip to Russia and Asia, accompanied by his brother Victor, in the early 1930s; and his active role in the Auto Workers starting in 1935 and ending with his tragic death in a plane crash, May 9, 1970. Other major groups of papers in the Reuther Col-lection cover his activities as president of the CIO (1952–1955); vice president of the AFL-CIO (1955–1967), and president of the AFL-CIO Industrial Union Department (1955–1967). His service on various govern-ment and community boards and agencies is also documented in his papers.

Despite the size of the Reuther Collection, not all of his private

[1]Warner Pflug, *A Guide to the Archives of Labor History and Urban Affairs* (Detroit, 1974); Philip P. Mason, "Wayne State University—The Archives of Labor and Urban Affairs," *Archivaria*, No. 4 (1977), 137–156; Dione Miles. *Something in Common: An IWW Bibliog-raphy* (Detroit, 1986).

papers have been placed in the Archives. Some are still in custody of family and friends and are periodically added to his collection. In 1988, the Archives received a seven-page typed letter written by Walter to his brothers Victor and Roy on April 22, 1936. This unique document, edited by Kevin Boyle and published in *Labor History*, describes his early activities in the UAW and the Wayne County Farm Labor Party.[2] The letter reveals his socialist philosophy, his idealism and his driving ambition to be a leader of workers. This letter and thousands of other communications in his collection reveal the breadth of his interest in social, political and economic reform movements, politics, international affairs, and other key issues. Supplementing the Walter Reuther papers are collections of his brothers, Roy and Victor, who also held leadership positions in the union movement.

The personal papers of other UAW presidents, Homer Martin, R. J. Thomas, Leonard Woodcock, and Douglas Fraser are a part of the extensive official files of the UAW presidency.

A similar collecting program has been adopted for the other seven international unions which have placed their inactive records in the Archives. Special attention has been given not only to the records of the key officers of the international but also to key regional and local divisions on a selective basis. The personal papers of union officials have also been solicited and acquired. Several hundred such personal collections have been obtained since the 1982 issue of *Labor History* when the holdings of the Reuther Library were described.[3]

In 1983 the Archives acquired the personal papers of Jerry Wurf, who served as president of AFSCME from 1964 until his death in 1981. They supplement and fill in gaps in his official presidential files. Another related acquisition, obtained in 1987, was the personal papers of Arnold Zander, the founder and president of AFSCME from 1935 to 1964. Of particular interest and value are Zander's personal diaries, covering the years from 1940 to 1973. They not only shed new light on key controversial events in the development of the union, but they reveal the personal side of the dynamic union leader.

As a parallel strategy to the policy of vertical coverage of regional and local union organizational records, the Archives also collects the personal papers of individuals who served on the local level and in rank and file groups. This approach has not only enriched the labor holdings but has been the source of extremely valuable archival collections. The

[2]Kevin Boyle, "Building the Vanguard: Walter Reuther and Radical Politics in 1936," *Labor History*, 30 (1989), 433–448.
[3]Philip P. Mason, "The Archives of Labor and Urban Affairs, Walter P. Reuther Library, Wayne State University," *Labor History*, 23 (1982), 534–545.

first collection given to the Archives in 1959 by Nick Di Gaetano proved a valuable lesson in the potential source of historically valuable sources. Di Gaetano was an Italian immigrant who came to the U.S. in 1909 and joined the IWW, and later moved to Detroit and became an auto worker. Deeply conscious of the historical importance of unions and especially the role of local unions, he compiled a voluminous collections of union newspapers and publications, strike leaflets, and broadsides. As Chief Steward at the Chrysler plant in Detroit, he kept a detailed record of all worker grievances which he handled from 1937 to 1947. These records, the most complete grievance file for this early period, give a picture of the nature and conditions of work in an auto plant and the shop conflict between management and local union leaders. Di Gaetano did not have a formal education but he had a deeper understanding of the need to document the labor movement than many of his better educated colleagues.

Labor and international affairs is another identifiable grouping of records in the Archives. In addition to the international affairs departments of the CIO, the UAW, and other international unions, the personal papers of union officials who were assigned to foreign capitals have also been acquired by the Archives. The papers of William Gausmann, Newman Jeffrey, Jay Krane, William Kemsley, Victor Reuther, Allen Schroeder, D. Alan Strachan, Morris Weisz, George Lichtblau, Thomas Posey, Valery Burati and George L-P. Weaver contain rich accounts of labor's role on the international scene, especially in the years after World War II. The role of Jay Lovestone and Richard Deverall in undermining and removing key CIO unionists from government assignments in Europe and Asia is revealed in a dramatic way.

Collections relating to women's rights and the role of women in unions form another distinct research area.[4] Indeed, because of the interest of a large number of researchers in this subject, the Archives has established a high priority for such collections. The records of women's departments and women's auxiliary groups of the UAW and other unions have great research value, as do the personal papers of women. The Mary Heaton Vorse papers, for example, represent one of the largest and most important collections in the Archives. Ms. Vorse, who was born in 1874 and raised in Amherst, MA, achieved her initial success as a writer of light fiction and her published writings include 16 books and more than 400 articles and stories which appeared in more than 70 periodicals. She also wrote news articles for the International

---

[4]See "Women's History Sources at the Archives of Labor and Urban Affairs," available on request from the Reuther Library.

News Service, United Press, Labor Press Association, Federated Press and newspapers in New York, Washington, and Paris, France. From 1912 until her death in 1966, she traveled throughout the U.S. and abroad observing and reporting on strikes, civil disturbances, wars, revolutions, and political upheavals. Her activities, views, and interests, especially on women's rights, are described in her voluminous correspondence with political and literary intelligentsia during the first six decades of the 20th century.

Other important women's collections include those of: Ann Blanken-horn, Phyllis Collier, Edith Christenson, Katherine Pollak Ellick-son, Jean Gould, Lillian Hatcher, Dorothy Haener, Mildred Jeffrey, Dolores Huerte, Mary Herrick, Selma Borchardt, Mary Van Kleeck, Olga Madar, Loretta Moore, Matilda Robbins, Carrie Overton, Mary White Ovington, Moragh Simchak, Marjorie Stern, Mary Wheeler, and Raya Dunayevskaya.

Labor and politics represent another grouping of personal papers. The Archives has been extremely selective in collecting the papers of political figures, not only because of the staggering volume, but also because of the limited research value of such collections. On the Michi-gan political scene the Archives has obtained the public files of the late Senator Patrick McNamara, the late Mayor Jerome P. Cavanagh, Judge George Edwards, and about 20 state legislators. The papers of Ofield Dukes, who served as a member of the late Vice President Hubert Humphrey's staff, are typical of a number of collections relating to the Washington political scene. The papers of Aaron Henry of the Mis-sissippi Freedom Democratic Party are an excellent source on the civil rights movement and the Democratic Party in the south.

The Archives, from the time of its establishment, has utilized oral history to supplement its holdings of archival, manuscript, and library materials. The oral history program has been based upon clearly de-fined subject areas in which the Archives has a major interest. The first oral history project, co-sponsored by the University of Michigan and Wayne State University in 1959–1961, related to the unionization of the automobile industry. More than 140 persons active in the founding and early history of the UAW were interviewed, including rank and file members, as well as local, regional, and international union leaders. Although the oral history interviews are influenced by the preoccupa-tion with "factional" struggles within the UAW, the transcripts, if used in conjunction with archival collections, are an extremely important source for the history of the UAW.

In 1983 the Archives began a second major project, interviewing all former members of the UAW Executive Board. Some interviews supplement the earlier oral histories; others provide an account of the UAW for a more recent period.

Other oral history projects sponsored by the Archives relate to the role of blacks, women, and minorities in the labor movement, and to the history of the American Federation of State, County and Municipal Employees, the American Federation of Teachers, The Newspaper Guild, and the United Farm Workers. In 1982 the Archives became the depository for the interviews undertaken by the creator of the film *Rosie the Riveter.*

The audiovisual section of the Archives contains extensive resource material on labor. More than a million photographs have been collected from a variety of sources — unions, union members, and personal donors, newspapers, and commercial photographers. They document important strikes and other events, conventions, meetings, parades, Labor Day and related celebrations. Among the IWW related collections, for example, are unique photographs of the funerals of Joe Hill,[5] Frank Little, and other union martyrs, the Everett "massacre," the deportation of "Wobblies" from Bisbee, and the famous Wheatland, Patterson, and Lawrence strikes. A recent acquisition of 140 photographs of the distinguished artist Lewis W. Hine add immeasurably to the Archives' holdings.

The Ludlow Massacre is shown in 15 rare glass negatives given to the Archives in 1964. Interior scenes of mills and factories, stores and shops, mines and mining camps, as well as photographs of work in lumber camps, and other outdoor activities depict the work place, tools, and workers.

From its establishment in 1960, until 1975, the Archives was housed in the Purdy Library on the main campus of the university. In 1975 a new building, given to the university by the UAW, was opened and named the Walter P. Reuther Library of Labor and Urban Affairs in memory of the late president of the UAW. At the UAW Constitutional Convention in Anaheim, CA, in June 1989, delegates voted unanimously to give the university $3.4 million to build an addition to the Reuther Library, named in honor of Leonard Woodcock, who succeeded Reuther as president of the UAW in 1970. The recently completed facility provides another 20 years of storage space and includes a conservation laboratory and special facilities for the preservation of films, tapes, and photographs.

Access: Access to union and other records in the Archives is gov-

---

[5]See Philip P. Mason, "Joe Hill-Cartoonist," *Labor History*, 25 (1984), 553-555.

erned by legal agreements with each donor. Some donors restrict access to their collection for a specific period of time, or until the death of a donor. For the UAW, AFSCME, TNG, ALPA, and AFA the period of closure is 10 years; for the AFT, four years; and for the UFW, 15 years. Under these access agreements all archival material held for less than the specified closure period is not available to researchers without authorization from the donor union; those records which are older are available to researchers. Union newspapers, proceedings, contracts, brochures and pamphlets and other publications which are in the public domain are open without restriction.

The Reuther Library is open 9 am–5 pm, Monday, Tuesday, Thursday, Friday, 9 am–9 pm, Wednesday. Researchers are requested to call or write in advance describing their topics or subject interests. This will facilitate the location of relevant material. Contact Philip P. Mason at the Walter P. Reuther Library, Wayne State Univ., 5401 Cass, Detroit, MI 48202; phone: (313) 577-4024.

THE LABADIE COLLECTION IN THE UNIVERSITY OF MICHIGAN LIBRARY

by
Edward C. Weber

One of the oldest special collections of radical history in the United States, the Labadie Collection was accepted by the Regents of the University of Michigan, Ann Arbor, as a gift in 1911, and few collections have been consulted over the years by such a wide variety of scholars. More than 50 books acknowledge indebtedness to the Collection, and it receives constant use by students, classes, and the general public.

The history of the Labadie Collection is very largely the story of two individuals whose modest original writings in radical history would have merited no more than a mention in footnotes. Charles Joseph Antoine Labadie (1850–1933) documented his career as worker, union official, candidate for public office, writer, and editor as well as his widespread interests for social reform in the turbulent period when America was shaping its modern image. Agnes Inglis (1870–1952) organized labadie's donation, directed its course for almost 30 years, enormously enriched its holdings, and gave it the direction it has since kept as a fecund source of current as well as past radical protest movements.

The Labadies were an old French-Canadian family whose descendants had settled on both sides of the Detroit River by the late 18th century. However, it was at a frontier settlement in Western Michigan that Antoine Cleophas Labadie married his distant cousin Euphrosyne in 1849. Jo, born the following April, actually lived in the wilderness during his early childhood, but the discomforts of backwoods life decided Euphrosyne to return with her family to Canada and her native Windsor area. Antoine Cleophas, after serving in the Civil War and fathering his last child in 1869, took off with his guns and dogs to fend for himself in the virgin forests of northern Michigan. He is recalled nostalgically in one of Jo's best poems. The teen-ager Jo Labadie

Edward C. Weber is head of the Labadie Collection, University of Michigan Library.

became a printer's devil in South Bend, where his family was living for a while, and like Benjamin Franklin and Walt Whitman found this a stimulus to education and expression. In a day when every community of a certain size had a newspaper his calling was no obstacle to the adolescent urge to roam. At Kalamazoo, Jo's first stop, he had his initial experience in labor activism, organizing his fellow-workers. By the time he returned to Michigan in 1872, he had worked in Cincinnati, Erie, and Boston, with his longest stint, more than a year, on the New York *World*, not yet Pulitzer's paper.

We do not know when he differentiated his political view from the dominant political parties. Perhaps the stimulus came from his marriage in 1877 to his cousin, Sophie Archambeau, a schoolteacher, who is credited with having taught him to express his ideas succinctly. At any rate, shortly thereafter Labadie garnered a few hundred votes for the Detroit mayorality on the Greenback-Labor ticket. Working 60 hours a week for the Detroit *Post*, Labadie was nevertheless involved in the production of the Detroit *Socialist* and with his friends published a series of seven "Socialistic Labor Tracts," which bore out their allegiance to the party later dominated by Daniel De Leon.

In November 1878 Labadie and his circle were approached by a visiting shoemaker from Massachusetts, Charles Litchman, to discuss the formation of the Knights of Labor in Michigan. Labadie eagerly threw himself into organizing and chose the name of Washington Literary Society to disguise their activities. This was, of course, in keeping with the Knights' injunction of secrecy. Labadie was instrumental in creating the Detroit Council of Trades and Labor Unions in 1880, and served as its first president, attended the national conventions of his own International Typographical Union, and worked in state labor assemblies. His own papers, *The Three Stars, Labor Review,* the *Advance and Labor Leaf,* were pioneering labor journalism.

The concentration of state power under socialism and its potential threat to individual efforts and rights were issues not often considered by the parties professing this doctrine. Labadie's apprehensions were fortified by reading *Liberty*, the eloquent journal edited by the redoubtable anarchist Benjamin Ricketts Tucker. It was Jo's allegiance to anarchism which precipitated his break with the Knights of Labor. Terence Powderly, the Grand Master, stubbornly refused to join the protest against the death sentences of the Haymarket Anarchists in Chicago. Labadie's reaction was vehement. In any case, he had little temperamentally in common with Powderly and joined with great enthusiasm the new American Federation of Labor, headed by Samuel Gompers, who had advocated clemency for the Haymarket martyrs. In 1889 Labadie was elected the first president of the Michigan Federation of Labor.

Although he would remain an ardent proponent of any legislation that would "benefit the underdog," Labadie did not long continue his active association with the labor movement. Perhaps difficulties with his health led (1893) him to take a job with Detroit's Water Department. In 1908, Labadie, who liked to bait conventionality, affixed some anarchist stickers to his letters. Detroit Post Office Inspector J. J. Larmour took strong exception to these "bloodthirsty" maxims and, stating that they were unmailable, ordered Jo to retrieve them. It is hard to believe that there was no connection when only a month later Labadie was dismissed from his clerical job on the Water Board by Commissioner James Pound, who intoned, "I am teetotally opposed to any man who says he is against government continuing to draw payment from this board."

Jo, who was widely known as "the gentle anarchist," did not lack allies. This time the fray was joined by department store magnate J. L. Hudson, the manufacturer F. F. Ingram, and the Episcopal Bishop of Michigan, Charles D. Williams, all of whom stoutly supported Labadie's right to hold and publish anarchist opinions. Not only was Jo reinstated within two weeks, but one of those drawn to his cause was a wealthy tanner, Carl Schmidt, who invited Jo and Sophie to make his home their own and eventually gave them a 40-acre farm. There at 64 Jo retired to operate his "Bubbling Waters Press," on which he printed his poems and essays, and to carry out some of his anarchist convictions in utilizing his property for summer homes. This farm is now within the boundaries of Kensington Park, Huron-Clinton Metropolitan Authority, to which Labadie's heirs deeded it in 1945; an exhibit in the Nature Center Building commemorates his association.

Before embarking on this last phase of his long life, Labadie donated to the Univ. of Michigan his personal library — a huge accumulation of books, pamphlets, journals, personal records, and ephemera — which had gradually come to occupy the third floor of his Detroit home. Feelers to acquire it had already been made by John Hopkins Univ. and by the Univ. of Wisconsin, where John R. Commons and his staff were working on the first large history of American labor. Indeed, Richard T. Ely had utilized Labadie's library for his pioneering *The Labor Movement in America* (1886). Labadie, however, was a staunch Michigander and believed that the best use of his collection would be made in the region it most strongly reflected. The deed of gift (Jo actually did receive emoluments of $100 each from 15 well-wishers as some recompense) stipulated that his library be made available for students. As is unfortunately the case in many institutions the planning for immediate necessities year after year postponed the implementation of this pledge. In 1924, when his friend and fellow anarchist Agnes Inglis decided to use it for her research on the fight for the eight-hour day, Labadie's gift was still resting in its shipping wrappers in the attic of the University Library.

Agnes Ann Inglis would have seemed an unlikely person to adopt the principles of anarchism in a day when the American public loathed the name for its associations with bombings and assassinations. Her background was in strong contrast to Labadie's. She was the youngest daughter of a wealthy and socially prominent Detroit family and spent almost the first 30 years of her existence in domestic retirement, nursing her invalid sister and aging mother. After a year at the Univ. of Michigan she went to Chicago's Hull House, worked under Jane Addams, and returned to Detroit's Jefferson Street Settlement House. In 1905 she returned to Ann Arbor, bought a house, and immersed herself in community affairs. Working at the YWCA, she began to investigate the paths by which poor young women drifted into prostitution.

Her persistence in exploring the tabooed topics of prostitution and venereal disease probably led to the first serious strains with her conservative family, but it has been stated that Inglis's pioneering efforts led to the creation of the Michigan Social Hygiene Commission. The opposition Inglis encountered convinced her that religion and prudery were foes of human progress. Labor organizing drew her sympathetic attention, and by the time of the Lawrence Strike she was an ardent partisan of the IWW. A few years later Inglis was accused of fomenting a strike at Ann Arbor's Hoover Ball Bearing Plant.

Inglis considered herself a socialist for a brief period, but in 1915 a meeting with Emma Goldman, whose appearances she helped to arrange in Michigan, gave a strong new direction to her revolutionary zeal. In *Living My Life* Goldman pays tribute to Inglis's generous support, which grew into a lifelong commitment to the anarchist cause, a decision which needless to say strained or ruptured many ties of family and friendship. Inglis never regretted the step.

America's involvement in World War I not only divided and ultimately crushed socialism as a political force, but under the sedition laws passed during this period, the IWW and the anarchist movement as well suffered harassment, trials, and imprisonment. Inglis's energies were expended and her personal fortune dissipated in defending her beleaguered comrades. By the early 1920s she depended on her family for a small remittance, eventually living in reduced, even meager circumstances.

We do not know what paper resulted from Inglis's research on the eight-hour day, but as she rummaged through the Labadie donation she was thrilled to discover the documentation of a golden yesterday in radicalism. She requested the library for permission to put the collection in order, perhaps believing this to be a matter of weeks or months; but she had actually found her life's vocation. Obviously the gap between Labadie's donation in 1911 and her discovery of the collection in 1924 had to be covered, filled with drama and tragedy as it was. Agnes Inglis's wide acquaintance with radical activists of many descriptions prompted her to write of her plans and to request assistance: besides information she would welcome gifts and would exchange duplicates.

With no formal library experience or training she utilized rudimentary archival approaches instead of conventional cataloging to organize the collection. Information about her subjects was gathered on handwritten cards (still very valuable for research) and occasionally she would compile a bibliography. By the mid-1930s the Labadie Collection was becoming known not only nationally but throughout the world, while a succession of books crediting the Labadie Collection and Inglis for assistance began to appear. She was instrumental, for example, in giving aid to Henry David's pioneering study of the Haymarket tragedy. The Sacco-Vanzetti case, the ordeal of Tom Mooney, and the roles of anarchism and Trotskyism in the Spanish Civil War were issues of intense interest to Agnes Inglis.

Her zeal uncovered the later American career of the Englishman John Francis Bray, of whom previously the last known in standard histories had been the publication of his *Labour's Wrongs and Labour's Remedies* in Leeds (1839). Combing the countryside around Pontiac, Michigan, for traces of Bray, who had died 40 years before, Inglis discovered that his daughter-in-law was running a cider mill and, cherishing his memory, had saved a trunk full of pamphlets, manuscripts, and memorabilia of the old socialist.

From his grandchildren Inglis was able to obtain the papers of the 48er, Karl Heinzen, perhaps the most notable of her many acquisitions from German radicals.

Substantial acquisitions came to Labadie also when she re-established contact with the family of Benjamin Ricketts Tucker, who had spent the last four decades of his life in France and Monaco. One can only estimate how greatly she enlarged the Labadie Collection. It may have been 20 fold. Agnes Inglis never married and except for the suggestion of romance rather late in life in her association with a young Polish baritone her personal feelings poured out in warmly generous, unflagging, sensitively understanding friendships. For her loyalty, energy, and imagination the Labadie Collection is eternally in her debt.

After her death the collection was rearranged, and a few prominent items chosen for official cataloging; but even after 1960, when consistent efforts were made to catalog the most important books and serials, the flood of acquisitions was always much greater than the cataloging. Systems of local cataloging for serials, pamphlets, and books in the backlog were devised to give some measure of control for subjects, personal names, and groups, with a utilization for serials of geographic and time period approaches. Since the late 1970s a notable advance has been the careful cataloging of manuscripts, drawing together collections which a draconian approach had dispersed and reporting these to the National Union Catalog of Manuscript Collections. In 1982 R. Anne Okey, a librarian in the Labadie Collection since 1974, applied successfully for a grant from the National Endowment for the Humanities to establish a data base that would employ multiple approaches to the serials and pamphlets, for which there had been only imperfect and inconsistent local cataloging. This grant proposal stipulated also that the larger Labadie archival collections be inventoried with the assistance of the staff of the Bentley Library and that a guide to all manuscripts be published. Copies of the guide, which was published in 1987, can be purchased for $5.00 from the Labadie Collection (please make checks payable to the University of Michigan).

The Labadie Collection presently consists of approximately 7000 cataloged monographs, 8000 serials (of which 600 are currently received), 20,000 uncataloged pamphlets, 25 drawers of vertical files, 550 reels of microfilm, and 300 phonorecords, cassettes, and phonotapes. Although the archival holdings are not large (200 linear feet), they are rich in correspondence and other writings. Included are the records of the American Committee for Protection of Foreign Born and the papers of the contemporary writer William Reuben, who has worked on the Rosenberg, Sobell, Trenton Six, and Hiss-Chambers cases. The collection is notable for its ephemera, in which collecting field Labadie was a pioneer, and includes leaflets, flyers, scrapbooks, clippings, posters, photographs, cartoons, sheet music, buttons, badges, armbands, and bumper stickers. Although Americana is naturally strongest, coverage of subjects is international in scope.

As the lives of Joseph Labadie and Agnes Inglis would suggest, the outstanding feature of the collection is the in-depth documentation of the anarchist movement, perhaps the most comprehensive in this hemisphere. Other notable strengths are socialism, especially much rare early Americana and publications of groups in the Fourth International; Communism; early labor history; civil liberties, especially the plight of racial minorities and such causes célèbres as the Haymarket, Sacco-Vanzetti, and Mooney cases; cooperatives; free thought; sexual freedom; colonialism and imperialism; the radical right; monetary reform; single tax; the Spanish Civil War; youth and student protest, especially the ferment of the 1960s; and recent social activism, such as women's liberation and gay liberation.

The once-bruited title, Labadie Labor Collection, is actually a misnomer for the collection as a whole — perhaps it was an effort to forestall criticism of the radical content. Researchers in labor history are well served by a warning that the Labadie Collection is most useful for older materials, especially on a regional level. We do not, in fact, collect contemporary labor union serials or pamphlets: it has been said that once a labor organization becomes respectable, the Labadie Collection no longer has interest in it! Our few current accessions about labor concern radical caucuses or grassroots rebellions. Pamphlets totalling about 2000 discuss labor issues from the mid-19th century to the 1940s; likewise, the union reports, proceedings and minutes of conventions seldom extend into the post-World War II period. Expectedly, the auto workers' unions, based in Michigan, are the most fully represented; spottier are the records of labor unions in the mining, smelting, and steel industries and those of skilled workers, such as Labadie's own International Typographical Workers Union. A unique set contains the Protokol, or minutes (1859–1900) in German script, of the Internationale Möbel-Arbeiter Union, New York City, active in the First International. Other special strengths are the news sheets of CIO locals, mostly UAW, in Michigan in the 1930s and early 1940s; papers of groups, often Communist Party influenced, who endeavored to organize the unemployed; and Communist shop papers.

The material of the larger labor federations, the AFL, the CIO, and the merged body, are modest indeed. Understandably, it is the radical federations, the Knights of Labor and the Industrial Workers of the World, who have more notable representation in the Labadie Collection. The records of the Michigan Knights of Labor, which Labadie helped to engender, are slight but unique. The IWW materials, often rare originals, are rich in serials, pamphlets, and early ephemera. At one time unique for its coverage, the Labadie Collection still has perhaps the most varied and extensive holdings after the official repository at the Walter Reuther Library in Detroit.

In our manuscript and archival collections the correspondence of Joseph Labadie is the richest source for labor-oriented subjects, since he wrote over a period of 50 years to people as prominent in the movement as Eugene Debs, Samuel Gompers, William Green, and Terence Powderly, besides a host of minor figures. The correspondence of Agnes Inglis is especially noteworthy because of her interest in labor unrest and the IWW and for her efforts to track down material, as well as for her comments on her discoveries and her organization of the Labadie Collection. Other notable groupings are the papers of Henry Bool (1845–1922), labor theorist; John Francis Bray (1809–1898), socialist who had many labor affiliations; Judson Grenell (1855–1930), long-time Michigan labor activist; David A. Boyd (1868–1939), official of the Michigan Federation of Labor early in the century, and Ralph Chaplin (1887–1961), the IWW writer and editor.

Although the international coverage of the Labadie Collection needs to be stressed for most of its specialties, this is sadly not the case for labor. A few British labor serials do not contribute appreciably to the needs of the specialist; the early ones are readily found in the Greenwood reprints. Pamphlets and a scrapbook on the General Strike of 1926 and a substantial amount of material by the National Minority Movement, an effort by the Communist Party to infiltrate the British labor movement, merit a mention. Canadian materials are naturally more plentiful than those from other parts of the Commonwealth. Except where there might be a connection with anarchism, coverage of the labor movements in continental Europe, in Asia, Africa, and Latin America is sparse indeed.

Access: Since 1964 the Labadie Collection has been under the supervision of the Dept. of Rare Books and Special Collections, the Univ. of Michigan Library. The hours during regular academic sessions are 10 am–noon and 1–5 pm, Monday–Friday; 10 am–noon, Saturday. Photoreproduction services are available, depending on the condition of the material. Although only books in good condition may circulate on interlibrary loan, our program of preservation also makes possible the lending of some serials and pamphlets on microfilm. Filmed by the Chadwyck-Healey Corporation, the anarchist pamphlets of the Labadie Collection are available on microfiche. Because the staff is small, it is advisable to write ahead if you are planning a visit. Contact Edward C. Weber or Anne Okey, Labadie Collection, 711 Hatcher Library, Univ. of Michigan, Ann Arbor, MI 48109-1205; phone (313) 764-9377.

LABOR HISTORY MANUSCRIPTS IN THE CHICAGO HISTORICAL SOCIETY

by
Archie Motley

Established in 1856, the city's oldest cultural institution — the Chicago Historical Society — collects, preserves, and interprets the history of Chicago and selected aspects of American history through exhibitions, research collections, educational programs, and publications. Some 200,000 people view the Society's exhibitions and attend its programs annually; 10,000 more use its library and various archival research collections.

The Archives and Manuscripts Department (one of 7 curatorial departments in the CHS) holds about 14,000 linear feet of records on the city's history from its earliest days to the present, along with selected materials on the American Civil War, the American Revolution, Illinois prior to the Civil War, and other aspects of American history.

Materials of and about labor unions and working people are an important segment of the Society's holdings and an active area of collecting efforts. Labor history holdings include large archival collections from major American trade unions along with scattered individual items and small collections, the great majority of them emanating from the Chicago area.

Nineteenth century holdings are not extensive, but they do include the voluminous archives of Chicago Typographical Union No. 16 (the city's earliest trade union, formed in 1852) that date from after the Chicago Fire of 1871 through the 1970s; along with minutes and records (1889–90) of the Trade and Labor Assembly of Chicago, the forerunner of the present-day Chicago Federation of Labor. A stenographic transcription of the trial of the Haymarket martyrs is also present along with random items of interest by these famed labor activists.

Major 20th century collections include extensive files of the Chicago

Archie Motley is Curator of Archives & Manuscripts at the Chicago Historical Society since 1960.

Federation of Labor during the presidencies of John Fitzpatrick and William A. Lee (who together guided the Federation for over 75 years) along with minutes of the CFL from 1903–22. Fitzpatrick's papers, which date from 1910 through the early 1940s, are an uneven lot often consisting of incoming correspondence without copies of Fitzpatrick's replies and frequently silent on major issues of the day involving the Federation and Fitzpatrick's personal activities, but they are of considerable value on a wide variety of local and national issues. Lee's papers are a smaller lot, even more random in nature, but they, too, are worthwhile in understanding a number of issues, events and people, such as the Cook County Industrial Union Council, from the 1950s into the early 1980s.

The Society also houses Victor A. Olander's papers (chiefly 1925–33) relative to his service as Secretary-Treasurer of the Illinois State Federation of Labor, along with smaller amounts of material on his role as a member of the Illinois Emergency Relief Commission during the 1930s, and as a member and officer of the International Seaman's Union of America and other maritime unions in the teens and 1920s. A smaller collection of Olander's papers are at the University of Illinois at Chicago, and Reuben Soderstrom's papers as President of the Illinois State Federation of Labor are held by the Illinois State Historical Society in Springfield.

The voluminous archives of District 31 of the United Steelworkers of America are also on hand. These records are sparse through the 1940s but expand thereafter and offer considerable information on district, national and local affairs of the union through the 1970s — including many significant materials distributed by the international office in Pittsburgh. Additional small collections of papers of District 31 Presidents Edward A. Sadlowski (including "Steelworkers Fight Back" materials) and James Balanoff are also present. (Penn State University serves as the international repository for records of the USWA; Wayne State University has a significant collection of "Steelworkers Fight Back" papers.)

These USWA records are complemented by a small collection of papers of organizer George A. Patterson that are particularly important as regards organizing activities during the 1930s and include a copy of Patterson's unpublished autobiography.

The CHS also holds the vast archives of the Chicago Division of the Brotherhood of Sleeping Car Porters, the nation's foremost Afro-American trade union. This collection includes important A. Philip Randolph correspondence dating from the formation of the union in 1925, Chicago Division President Milton P. Webster's files relative to his service (1941–46) on the Fair Employment Practices Committee, and working files of the Brotherhood's Ladies Auxiliary 1931–56. Many of these records are being filmed and will be offered for sale by University Publications of America.

The Afro-American work experience (as well as civil liberties and civil rights concerns) are also covered in the voluminous records of the present-day Afro-American Police League, the nation's first organization of its kind, from the League's formation in 1968 into the 1980s.

Unions of a leftist political persuasion are represented in: papers (1936–74) of Ernest DeMaio, primarily in his capacity as President of District 11 of the United Electrical, Radio and Machine Workers of America (the University of Pittsburgh is the designated national repository for UE records); author and union organizer Sid Lens' papers concerning United Service Employees Local 329's efforts to organize grocery and department store workers 1941–56, and his participation in the Revolutionary Workers League 1935–47; records of Chicago Local 18B of the United Furniture Workers of America and various Midwestern locals from the 1940s through the 1960s, with the earlier materials being more significant.

Papers of attorneys who represented left-wing unions include extensive files from the 1940s through the early 1960s of David Rothstein and Irving Meyers (law partners during a good portion of their legal careers), particularly relative to their work with the United Auto Workers, the UE, and the Farm Equipment Workers unions; a small collection of records of Irving Meyers' brother, Ben Meyers, concerning Ben's work as counsel for the Chicago Newspaper Guild during the tumultuous 1940s strike against the Hearst Newspapers; and sundry records of attorney Max Naiman, whose files include International Labor Defense materials from the 1930s and '40s, along with a random lot of mailings received from many Communist and radical organizations into the 1960s. A small excellent collection of Chicago Newspaper Guild papers from the 1930s on working conditions and strikes is also available.

Teachers' unions are represented by the extensive records of the Chicago Teachers' Federation, the city's first teachers' organization, established in 1897 and of the current Chicago Teachers Union, which was formed in 1937 through the amalgamation of four earlier teachers' organizations. In addition to their documentation of teachers' efforts to become organized and obtain better working conditions and contracts, these collections contain information on the early history of the National Education Association and on leftist-right wing disputes within the American Federation of Teachers during the 1940s. These worthy collections, however, are not very informative on teaching and learning conditions within the schools and on the experiences of the students there. A small collection of files of American Federation of Teachers Local 1600 at Morton Junior College in Cicero during the 1950s and 1960s is also useful.

Other labor history holdings include a significant collection of papers (1900–1948) of Agnes Nestor of the International Glove Workers Union, who also served as President of the Women's Trade Union League, along with a complete microfilm copy of the entire collection of WTUL's papers across the country (including the Nestor papers) filmed by the Schlesinger Library at Radcliffe College; minute books (in English and Czech) of various Chicago locals of the Amalgamated Clothing Workers of America 1919–49; and minute books (in English, French, and German) of various locals of the United Brotherhood of Carpenters and Joiners in Chicago, 1887–1903.

The activities of various unemployed workers groups during the Great Depression as well as Labor Education at Roosevelt University in Chicago during the 1940s are documented in the papers of Frank W. McCulloch, assistant to Senator Paul H. Douglas and former Chairman of the National Labor Relations Board. A small collection of papers (1920–58) of teacher and workers' education activist Lillian Herstein is also present as is the 1912–14 minute book of the Chicago Building Trades Council.

Scattered significant labor history materials can also be found in the papers of: Claude A. Barnett, founder and Director of the Associated Negro Press; the Catholic Council on Working Life; Chicago Alderman and attorney Leon M. Despres; Senator Paul H. Douglas; the Illinois Manufacturers' Association; and attorney Donald R. Richberg. Two oral history projects undertaken in the 1970s and 1980s to document Chicago's Polish and Italian communities offer meaningful accounts of many interviewees' working experiences.

The Chicago Historical Society's Prints and Photographs Department contains many photographs, posters, handbills and film materials on unions and working conditions and experiences in Chicago, many of them received with the manuscript collections noted above.

The Society's library also contains various pertinent materials including two special sources worth noting: the Chicago Foreign Language Press Survey, which provides English translations of articles on a variety of subjects topically arranged from foreign language publications in Chicago from the 1860s through the 1920s; and the "Annals of Labor and Industry," another WPA Project that provides several hundred wallets of transcriptions of newspaper and journal articles, and legal materials from the 19th and early 20th century, chiefly relative to the Chicago area. These materials have been filed chronologically but, unfortunately, have not been indexed.[1]

Access: The Archives and Manuscripts Department and the Chicago Historical Society's Library are both open without appointment to researchers from 9:30 am–4:30 pm, Tuesday–Saturday. Prior appointments are required to use materials in the Prints and Photographs Department, which is open from 9:30 am–noon and from 1:00 pm–4:30 pm, Tuesday–Saturday.

The Chicago Historical Society is located at Clark Street at North Avenue, Chicago, Illinois 60614. The Society's automated-touch-tone system phone number is (312) 642-5035. The Archives & Manuscripts Department's Reference Desk Extension Number is 314; the Library Reference Desk Extension is 356; and the Prints and Photographs Department's Reference Desk Extension is 325. For further information contact Archie Motley.

---

[1] A useful overview is Steve Rosswurm, "Sources for the Study of Labor History at the Chicago Historical Society," *Labor's Heritage*, 2 (Jan., 1990), 64–75.

THE OZARKS LABOR UNION ARCHIVES AT SOUTHWEST MISSOURI STATE UNIVERSITY

by
J. David Lages and Neal Moore

The Ozarks Labor Union Archives is a multifaceted collection of primary documentary material from a number of unions in the Ozarks, primarily, at this time, from those organizations near Springfield, Missouri. It is housed in the Library Annex of the Meyer Library at Southwest Missouri State University in Springfield, Missouri. The Archives is an on-going project directed by J. David Lages, PhD, Professor of Economics, and Neal Moore, a long-time member of the International Typographical Union, former editor of the *Springfield Union Labor Record* and *The Kansas City Labor Beacon*, and president of the Ozarks Labor Historical Society.

Holdings in the Archives consist of 59 collections of primary documentary material from organizations and individuals, most of it in its original form but some microfilmed; a collection of about 150 photographs; memorabilia such as union charters, certificates of affiliation with the State Labor Council, banners, union seals and convention badges; and 18 taped interviews in an oral history project. The documentary material varies from collection to collection, but overall runs the full gamut of what one will find in the normal business operation of a union: by-laws, contracts, minute books, membership records and ledgers, correspondence, financial records, health and welfare fund records, and brochures and pamphlets on a large variety of subjects of interest to the trade union movement.

Individual collections of manuscript material vary in size from a single folder to much larger collections. A number of local organizations and unions have donated extensive holdings relating to their history and operations, including: the Springfield Central Labor Council —

J. David Lages is Professor of Economics, Southwest Missouri State University. Neal Moore oversees the Ozarks Labor Union Archives.

46 letter boxes (about 20 linear feet), Service Employees Local 50 — 21 letter boxes, Laborers Local 676 — 14 linear feet, Bakers Local 235 — 18 linear feet, Moving Picture Machine Operators Local 447 — 10 linear feet, and Garment Workers Local 216 — 28 linear feet. While the oldest document in the Archives is a membership ledger of the Brotherhood of Locomotive Engineers dated February 1871, most of the early records have been lost. The bulk of the collections date from the late 1930s.

A 27-minute slide-tape program of the history of the trade union movement in the Ozarks, narrated by Neal Moore, has been prepared by the Media Production Department of SMSU for use in classroom instruction and for showing to interested community organizations.

The Ozarks Labor Union Archives was an outgrowth of a fortuitous meeting of David Lages and Neal Moore. Springfield Attorney Ben Francka was presenting a paper before a joint meeting of the Ozarks Labor Historical Society and a graduate class in the Department of Economics at SMSU, on the subject, "Impact of Springfield City Employee Litigation on State Labor Law." The first three Missouri State Supreme Court cases relating to public employee bargaining came out of Springfield. "Springfield wrote the law for the state of Missouri," Francka said, and concluded that the first case, "Springfield vs. Clouse, was must reading for anyone interested in public employee bargaining."

At the conclusion of the discussion Lages, who in his undergraduate and graduate studies and later as a professor of labor economics realized that the greatest barrier to meaningful research was the lack of primary or original source material, commented that unions needed to save and preserve the records of their oganizations. Moore, who, as a long-time union member and labor editor, knew that even union members were unaware of their own history, responded that the unions had the records but there was no place to store them. A few months later SMSU, in its expansion program, built a new library annex. At Lages' request space for an archives was reserved in the new building, and on its completion, Lages and Moore set up an aggressive collections campaign to fill it.

In a section of the country where it was widely believed that few unions existed it was obvious that an aggressive education program was the first order of business. Few people were aware that there were over 50 union organizations headquartered in Springfield alone. To develop an archival collections program it was necessary to find these organizations and locate and identify the archival records that might be available to the archives. On the unions' part, there was little communication with the university and even less knowledge about the nature and purpose of archival collections. It was necessary to explain both the kinds of documents that make up an archival collection and how this material is used in the writing and interpretation of the history of the labor movement. At the same time, if union records were to be turned over to an archival holding, it was necessary to win the trust and confidence of union officials and members controlling those records. To carry this out in the early stages of the program, Lages and Moore made repeated visits to individuals and to organizations to explain the nature and purpose of the archives and to win union support.

Carpenters Local 978, chartered in 1901, joined the United Brotherhood of Carpenters and Joiners in the celebration of its 100th anniversary by making available the minute books of the local's first 40 years for microfilming. A visit to the Bakers hall resulted in the immediate collection of two cartons of records and the development of a strong personal interest in the archives program by Bakers Business Manager Milos Kukal, who later arranged for the donation of 13 more cartons of Bakers' records and assisted in locating and gathering important documentary material from other unions. Ronald Dean, general chairman of the Frisco division of the Brotherhood of Locomotive Engineers, took part in a two-hour interview for the oral history project and later arranged for the acquisition of a carton of Locomotive Engineers records, the earliest dated 1871. Likewise, a visit to the home of Essie DeCamp, an active leader in the women's auxiliary movement from the 1920s on, provided a large amount of material relating to the role of women in the Springfield trade union movement. As interest in the Archives grew, more and more union members began to take initiative in locating and bringing documentary material into the collection. In the absence of strong institutional support for a project of this kind, and without large financial backing, the importance of the personal involvement of local trade union officials and members cannot be over-emphasized.

Funding, though extremely limited, has come at crucial moments. The university, through its Faculty Development Fund, provided necessary early funding to organize the collections and to make the archives collections accessible. The Media Production Department provided necessary personnel and equipment to produce the slide-tape history program. The International Brotherhood of Electrical Workers (IBEW) at the behest of its president, Charles H. Pillard, and Jack F. Moore, then, vice-president for the 11th District, provided $1200.00 to pay for a summer graduate assistant in 1982 to work on the collections. The following year the Southwest Missouri State University Foundation granted the Archive $1538 for needed equipment and assistance. Additional funding came from the Springfield Central Labor Council, the Ozarks Labor Historical Society, and various individuals.

In 1987 a crucial pemanent funding program was initiated. Jack Moore, a local trade union member from the Ozarks, had been promoted to the office of secretary of the IBEW. At the request of local IBEW members, the International Union offered $25,000 as matching funds to establish a Jack F. Moore Labor Studies Endowment at Southwest Missouri State University to support the Ozarks Labor Union Archives. Later, Ray Edwards, another Ozarks native who succeeded Moore as vice president for the 11th district, headed a fund raising drive and at another dinner honoring Moore in Cedar Rapids, Iowa, in August 1989, presented SMSU President Marshall Gordon with another $25,000 check for the Jack Moore endowment.

At the present time top priority is being given to an aggressive collections program. With limited funding and personnel, the organizing and indexing of the collections has been proceding slowly. Every effort is being made to follow standard archival procedure in the storage, preservation, and organizing of the documents. Basically the collections have been grouped according to organizations, and these, then, organized according to successive years. Some limited indexing has been done. The goal, of course, is to have the whole collection indexed, and, preferably, on computer.

Because of the dominance of the craft unions in the building trades and the railroad industry, and because of the absence of mass production industry in the early years of Springfield history, there were no CIO organizations during the AFL-CIO split. Because of the variety of organizations represented in the Ozarks Labor Union Archives, such as garment workers, railroad workers, street car workers, government employees, rubber workers, and building trades workers such as carpenters, electricians, and laborers, there is presented here an overall view of a dynamic trade union movement existing in a supposedly nonunion area of rural Missouri. The role of the trade union movement in Ozark culture bears further study.

Given the central role of Springfield unions in the development of Missouri public employee bargaining, emphasis is being given to collecting as much material on this subject as possible. In the 1978 Right-to-Work amendment campaign many of these rural, supposedly antiunion counties in the Ozarks surprised many political pundits by turning in strong majorities for the union position, against right-to-work. In addition to local records, five cartons of Missouri State Labor Council material relating to this campaign have been donated. More material is anticipated.

Copying of specified documents can be arranged, at cost, on a limited basis. To obtain a copy of the latest catalog of holdings, or be included on the mailing list of the occasional Newsletter, write Prof. J. David Lages or Neal Moore.

Access: material in the Archives can be viewed at the present time only by appointment. For further information about the Ozark Labor Union Archives write Professor J. David Lages or Neal Moore, c/o Dept. of Economics, Southwest Missouri State University, 901 South National, Springfield, MO 65804; phone (417) 836-4933.

LABOR HISTORY RESOURCES IN THE UNIVERSITY OF IOWA LIBRARIES, THE STATE HISTORICAL SOCIETY OF IOWA/IOWA CITY, AND THE HERBERT HOOVER PRESIDENTIAL LIBRARY

by
John N. Schacht

Located within 12 miles of one another in east central Iowa, the three institutions named in the title, taken together, have long been known as a major repository of source materials concerning the politics of American agriculture, Iowa history, and the Hoover Presidency and Commerce Secretariat. Less well known are the institutions' materials bearing on other aspects of American history, among them original sources of potentially great value to historians of American labor. My main aims are to call attention to such sources and describe them briefly.

The University of Iowa Libraries (UIL)[1]

The UIL's Special Collections Department holds all the original UIL sources mentioned here. Pertinent oral history collections are the Communications Workers of America-University of Iowa Oral History Project, consisting of transcripts of 89 interviews, primarily with full time union officials who had helped build the union movement in Bell Telephone c. 1917–61 (2000 pp. with subject index, conducted 1969–72) and the Quad Cities (Davenport and Bettendorf, IA; Rock Island and Moline, IL) Oral History Project, containing transcripts of interviews with six local leaders in the Davenport-Moline area c. 1940–1970, along with a 1936 typescript history of the area's labor and radical movements by R.F. McNabney (107 pp., conducted 1973).

John N. Schacht is a reference librarian at the Univ. of Iowa Libraries and author of The Making of Telephone Unionism, 1920–1947 *(1985).*

---

[1] I thank Robert McCown and Earl Rogers, of the UIL Special Collections Department, for their help in familiarizing me with pertinent UIL collections.

All UIL collections listed below are accompanied by finding aids describing materials down to the folder level, except where otherwise noted. Trade unionism in Iowa is the principal focus of the papers of Leroy Jones, an official in the American Federation of Grain Millers (920 items, 1936–54); of Ben A. Henry, a United Mine Workers of America (UMWA) official, a packinghouse organizer, and an Iowa CIO staffer (3 ft., 1933–62); and of John C. Lewis, a UMWA official, packinghouse organizer, and in 1941 national president of the Packinghouse Workers Organizing Committee (4 ft., 1937–54). The records of the Univ. of Iowa Bureau of Labor and Management (40 ft., 1952–72) delineate labor education efforts in an agricultural state. Grievance arbitration proceedings in farm equipment manufacturing, food processing, and Iowa and Wisconsin public employment are the focus of the case files of arbitrators Clarence Updegraff (36 ft., 1940–70) and Anthony Sinicropi (80 ft., 1965–). Similar materials covering a wider range of industries are in the unpublished awards compiled in the American Arbitration Association Collection (50 ft., 1963–71). Finding aids for the latter three collections are rudimentary, though researchers may enter the Updegraff and Sinicropi files by company name and by union name.

UIL holds a rich vein of papers concerning 20th century agricultural organizations which sought alliances with organized labor and/or aspired toward collective bargaining — organizations such as the Farmers Holiday Association, the Iowa Farmers Union, the National Farmers Organization, and the U.S. Farmers Association. These include the papers of Milo Reno (3 ft., 1929–36); of Fred Stover (40 items, 1948–54); of Daniel W. Turner (2 ft., 1928–67); of Clyde Herring (2 ft., 1932–42); of Erik Bert (12 ft., 1918–77); of John L. Shover (200 items including oral history interviews, 1933–64); and of the U.S. Farmers' Association (2 ft., 1919–70).

The main appeal of the UIL's Henry A. Wallace papers (213 ft., 1888–1965), from a labor history standpoint, lies in their elucidation of Federal control of the war economy, in which Wallace was centrally involved from mid-1941 to mid-1943. A published guide/index to the Wallace papers is available at many locations, as is a microfilm edition of the papers themselves. UIL is a major repository of materials concerning the Progressive Party, the vehicle of Wallace's 1948 presidential candidacy. Along with the Wallace papers, UIL holds the Progressive Party Records (30 ft., 1946–54), consisting of materials assembled by Curtis MacDougall. These contain much printed material and occasional correspondence concerning those CIO unions which supported Wallace — and some which did not. The papers of C.B. Baldwin (30 ft., 1933–75), a CIO-PAC and Progressive Party official, are scant concerning labor support for Wallace, but their CIO-PAC materials are substantial.

Portions of the following individuals' papers are of potential interest: Harold E. Hughes, a member of the U.S. Senate Committee on Labor and Public Welfare, 1969–75 (200 ft., 1963–75); Nelson Kraschel, Iowa's governor during the famous 1938 UE-Maytag strike in Newton (4 ft., 1932–50); Robert Blue, Republican governor of Iowa during the Taft-Hartley era (42 ft., 1934–76); Gerald Bogan, executive director of Iowans for Right to Work from 1965 into the 1980s (7 ft., 1912–86); and Wayne Biklen, an industrial efficiency expert concerned with labor dimensions of quality control (3 ft., 1932–81). The papers of Mary Louise Smith (45 ft., 1972–77), head of the Republican National Committee from 1974 to 1977, contain much correspondence from rank and file Republicans concerning the Equal Rights Amendment and union political contributions. The papers of E.T. Meredith (38 ft., 1894–1928), a member of the American Labor Mission which visited France and England in 1918, contain two albums of photographs from the mission.

Institutional collections of interest are those of the Davenport-Besler Corporation (80 ft., 1901–56), a locomotive manufacturer, containing personnel and collective bargaining records from the 1950s; and the Chautauqua Collection (648 ft., c. 1907–1928), containing the largely unprocessed records of the Redpath Bureau of Chicago, booking-employment agents for the Chautauqua and lyceum circuits.

The State Historical Society of Iowa/Iowa City (SHSI)

The SHSI holds a magnificent and in some ways unparalleled collection which, due to staff shortages in recent years, remains largely unprocessed and therefore somewhat difficult to access. This is the collection gathered from 1977 to 1984 by the Iowa Labor History Oral Project, Inc. (ILHOP), a cooperative venture of the SHSI — which allocated space and much staff processing time — and the Iowa Federation of Labor, AFL-CIO (IFL), joined by Iowa's Teamsters and United Auto Worker state organizations — which committed over $196,000, drawn mostly from special per capita membership taxes.[2] Researchers with specific projects in mind may apply to view the collection, but

---

[2] I owe thanks to Mary Bennett and Merle Davis, of the SHSI, for introducing me to the ILHOP materials, and to H. Shelton Stromquist, of the Univ. of Iowa Dept. of History — a member of the ILHOP advisory committee and probably the historian most familiar with the ILHOP collection as a whole. My comments concerning the quality and monitoring of the ILHOP interviews, the unusual qualities of the collection, and attendant implications for research are based on an unpublished assessment by Professor Stromquist which he kindly shared with me.

the lack of descriptive aids has made the formulation of projects at a distance difficult and requests for access therefore rare. The collection consists of:

(a) 953 oral history interviews with Iowa trade union leaders and rank and file workers, representing 35 communities and 80 international unions. Of these, 819 have been transcribed, totalling some 40,000 typed pages; all tapes have been saved. The interviews were conducted by three labor historians, employed successively, who worked with an advisory committee that monitored the quality of the interviews. There was an effort to insure that toughminded questions were posed concerning divisions along race and gender lines, and to insure that comparable data for nearly all interviewees was drawn by means of a standard core of questions — while enough flexibility remained to allow a free flow of unique material. There are single-page, typed "summary sheets" for about half of the interviews, amounting to topical outlines or tables of contents. There is no subject index or other comprehensive finding aid. Shelving arrangements and typed lists do, however, confer access by community, by union, by broad chronological category, and by the interviewee's name.

(b) 125 discrete manuscript collections totalling 400 linear feet. The majority are the records of Iowa local unions — affiliates of 40 international unions. Also included are the papers of four individual activists, the records of 10 city central bodies, and the records of the IFL (80 ft., 1894–1988). Typical contents are minutes of meetings, scrapbooks, correspondence, memoranda, and grievance arbitration materials. Among the more important local union records are those of the Clinton local of the American Federation of Grain-elevator Employees (46.5 ft., 1937–80), the Ottumwa Carpenters local (12 ft., 1912–80), Waterloo United Packinghouse Workers of America (UPWA) Local 46 (8 ft., 1942–85), Ottumwa UPWA Local 1 (31 ft., 1940–73), Machinists locals in Des Moines (8 ft., 1953–1970s) and Sioux city (15 ft., 1945–82), and several Farm Equipment-United Electrical locals in the Quad Cities (32 ft., ca. 1930s–1950s). Of the 125 collections, only five are accompanied by detailed finding aids. (Among the five are the Waterloo and Ottumwa UPWA locals' records, which are grouped with the ILHOP materials but not formally a part of them — and not subject to the same restrictions.) The remainder have no finding aids or detailed subject access of any kind, even to the box level. Each collection is, however, usefully represented in a nearby card catalog, classified by union, employer, community, broad occupational grouping, and broad chronological period.

(c) Printed materials, drawn mostly from the manuscript collections. These have been shelved separately in categories: contracts and agreements (6 ft.) and constitutions and bylaws (3 ft.), both arranged by union name; a vertical file consisting mostly of flyers and pamphlets, arranged by subject (25 ft.); and books (25 ft.). These materials are unrestricted.

(d) More than 500 photographs, about half of which have been categorized; 50 films and videotapes; and over 100 sound recordings, drawn mostly from the manuscript collections.

Apart from the ILHOP, the SHSI holds substantial runs of eight Iowa labor newspapers: the *Iowa Unionist* (Des Moines, 1908–88, incomplete), *Labor Leader* (Dubuque, 1907–73, incomplete), *Labor Voice* (Muscatine, 1907–16, incomplete), *Tri City Labor Review* (Davenport/Rock Island, 1912–48), *Iowa Farm Labor News* (Cedar Falls, 1957–63), *Tribune* (Cedar Rapids, 1907–56), and *The Unionist and Public Forum* (Sioux City, 1907–51, incomplete).

Unusual in its public-private collaborative origins, the ILHOP materials are also unusual in the complementarity of their oral history and manuscript segments. Because the acquisition of the manuscripts held by unionists was ordinarily the direct outgrowth of interviewers' contacts with those unionists *as interviewees*, the manuscripts support the oral history to a degree seldom, if ever, found elsewhere. And the density of coverage is, of course, extraordinary. For example, more than 190 interviews and 10 manuscript collections deal in detail with the packinghouse industry in the state of Iowa. The implications for research possibilities are many. To mention one: materials permitting in-depth studies of several communities in a manner consonant with the aims of the "new labor history" are very likely present here.

The Herbert Hoover Presidential Library (HHPL)[3]

The HHPL, opened to scholars in 1966, holds the Hoover papers, totalling some 2450 linear feet, and the papers of more than 100 of Hoover's associates and contemporaries, totalling over 2200 linear feet. Most boxes contain a combination of correspondence, memoranda, and mimeographed and printed materials. The Hoover papers are at many points supplemented by photocopied files from the National Archives. Excellent finding aids, in most cases providing a subject approach, describe materials down to the folder level in all collections mentioned here, with one exception, noted below.

[3]I owe thanks to Dale Mayer and Mildred Mather, of the HHPL, for their guidance and other helpful labors, and to the Hoover Presidential Library Association, for its grant in support of the HHPL segment of this investigation.

The following subgroups of the Hoover papers are of particular interest:

(a) Pre-Commerce Period (78 ft., 1895-1921). From 1919 to early 1921 Hoover developed and articulated a vision in which improved labor-management relations would be a key element in a new, more efficient economic system. He did so mainly in two major forums for contemporary views concerning industrial relations and scientific management — President Wilson's Second Industrial Conference and the Federated American Engineering Societies — in both of which he emerged as the leading figure.[4] Boxes 33-40 and 43-46 illustrate the thinking of Hoover and other experts, along with their informational milieu.

(b) Commerce Period (385 ft., 1921-28). A proponet of moderation toward organized labor in the Harding and Coolidge cabinets, Secretary Hoover's vision of the worker as a central figure in building an efficient economic order prompted him to intervene often in labor matters (aided by the acquiescence of Secretary of Labor James J. Davis).[5] Substantial materials reflect Hoover's prominence during the 1922 railroad shopmen's strike and in subsequent railway labor relations (boxes 503-08); in the abandonment of the 12 hour day in steel (boxes 234, 614); in UMWA-operator relations in bituminous coal (boxes 99-113); and in the 1921 President's Conference on Unemployment (boxes 615-73). This conference engendered several useful studies, much unheeded exhortation, some ideas which arguably found later expression in New Deal legislation, and reports on unemployment from hundreds of cities, written mostly by local officeholders. The latter provide a mass of inchoate information and a huge mosaic of attitudes toward the unemployed. The HHPL holds extensive Hoover correspondence with Davis, Samuel Gompers, John L. Lewis, and other labor figures during the Commerce period (and other periods), some of it photocopied from other repositories.

(c) Presidential Period (693 ft., 1929-33). Sources of potential interest include those concerning the Labor Department and Administration relations with organized labor (boxes 27-32, 59, 193, 245); old age insurance (boxes 221-22), and efforts to maintain wage levels in 1929-30 (boxes 91-92). Materials concerning the bituminous coal industry (box 104) are typical of those concerning many industries in portraying depressed conditions among workers, with appeals for aid

---

[4] Robert Zieger, "Herbert Hoover, the Wage-Earner, and the 'New Economic System,' 1919-1929," *Business History Review*, 51 (1977), 162-73.

[5] *Ibid.*, 173-78. See also his *Republicans and Labor 1919-1929* (Lexington, KY, 1969), esp. pp 60-63, and his "Labor and the State in Modern America: The Archival Trail," *Journal of American History*, 75 (1988), 186.

and other countermeasures, and protests against cuts in employment and wages. Substantial materials concerning unemployment and Administration attempts to combat and allay it (boxes 76-77, 136-37, 324-48) include material on: the Federal Employment Stabilization Board; the Share the Work effort; reorganization of Federal-state employment services and handling of the related Wagner bill; the 1930-31 President's Emergency Committee for Employment (PECE); and the 1931-32 President's Organization on Unemployment Relief (POUR). These are supplemented by 32 linear feet of photocopies from the National Archives' PECE/POUR record group, with finding aids. Materials concerning ambitious studies whose origins lay in the Commerce period, most notably those of the Committee on Social Trends, are traced by adequate in-house finding aids.

PECE/POUR materials are also among the papers of Arthur Woods (diary, 1930-31), Fred C. Croxton (2 ft., 1871-1939), E. French Strother (7 ft., 1920-33), and Edward Eyre Hunt (3 ft., 1904-57). The latter two collections contain Committee on Social Trends materials, and the Hunt papers contain files on the U.S. Coal Commission (1922-23), employment stabilization (1931-32), and unemployment (1921-40). Further collections of note are the papers of:

(a) Westbrook Pegler (80 ft., 1908-69). The winner of a 1941 Pulitzer Prize for his columns on labor racketeering, Pegler collected some 15 linear feet of material (boxes 19, 77-105) on racketeering, Communist influence in unions, and such other targets of Pegler's attacks as union featherbedding, strike violence, and undemocratic internal governance. Most of the correspondence is an informative if biased post-1941 outpouring from anti-union businessmen and attorneys, and from persons best described as professional anti-communists; but a large minority flowed from unionists themselves aggrieved by the things Pegler was attacking.

(b) Karl Baarslag (4 ft., 1927-67). Baarslag was a marine radio operator, 1925-39, and a naval intelligence officer, 1941-45. His papers consist mostly of correspondence and printed and mimeographed minutes of local, regional, and national meetings of maritime labor organizations, particularly the American Radio Telegraphists Association. A major theme is resistance to Communist influence.

(c) Clark Mollenhoff (192 ft., 1947-76). These contain 21 boxes of material, mostly court and Congressional documents, used in preparing his book on Teamster corruption, *Tentacles of Power* (1965). They are closed pending processing and are unaccompanied by finding aids.

*   *   *

Proximity and cooperative relations among the UIL, SHSI, and HHPL extend the strength of all three institutions' collections. Users primarily focused on the manuscript collections of one institution will often find useful supporting material at another: the UIL and SHSI in combination are a major repository of federal and Iowa legislative and executive agency documents, along with Federal and Iowa census materials; the UIL and HHPL in combination hold extensive microform reproductions of manuscript and archival materials available from the National Archives and from commercial vendors; and the UIL maintains monograph, serial, and reference collections in the depth expected of a major research library. A somewhat outdated but still useful guide to the combined holdings, published by the UIL, is Boyd Keith Swigger, comp., *A Guide to Resources for the Study of the Recent History of the United States in the Libraries of the University of Iowa, the State Historical Society of Iowa, and in the Herbert Hoover Presidential Library* (283 pp., 1977).

Access: While most of the collections named above are open to researchers, some require special permission to view and/or are otherwise restricted. Researchers should write to the holding institution well before travelling any distance to use a collection. All three institutions will send general brochures upon request and, in response to specific requests, will reproduce at cost unpublished finding aids for their collections. Contact: Robert McCown, Special Collections Department, The Univ. of Iowa Libraries, Iowa City, IA 52242; phone: (319) 335-5921; hours, 9 am–noon, 1–5 pm, Monday–Friday. Mary Bennett, Special Collections, State Historical Society of Iowa, 402 Iowa Ave., Iowa City, IA 52240; phone: (319) 335-3916; hours, 9 am–4:30 pm, Tuesday–Friday. Dwight Miller, Herbert Hoover Presidential Library, West Branch, IA 52358; phone: (319) 643-5301; hours, 8:45 am–noon, 12:30–4:45 pm, Monday–Friday.

SOURCES FOR STUDY OF THE LABOR MOVEMENT AT THE STATE HISTORICAL SOCIETY OF WISCONSIN

by
James P. Danky and Harold L. Miller

The labor history resources at the State Historical Society of Wisconsin are, in part, the result of the first systematic attempt to document the rise of working-class movements and trade unionism in America. In the early 1890s, when Richard T. Ely joined the Univ. of Wisconsin faculty, the Society began assisting him in gathering source material for the study of the labor movement. When, in 1904, Ely formed the American Bureau of Industrial Research and brought John R. Commons to Madison, the Society began collecting labor material on a systematic basis.[1] Consequently the Society is today one of the preeminent repositories of labor history materials.

From the 1890s to the present, those collecting for the Society have had a very broad definition of the labor movement, including not only trade unions but also anarchism, communism, cooperation, socialism, utopianism, and other working-class movements. Combining this broad definition with Society collecting efforts in business history, civil rights and other social action movements, and Federal and state government publications and records means that the Society is rich in source material for those studying workers from the perspective of the shop floor

James P. Danky is the Newspaper and Serials Librarian at the State Historical Society of Wisconsin. Harold L. Miller is the Society's Reference Archivist.

[1] For background on the Society's labor collecting efforts, see Harold L. Miller, "The American Bureau of Industrial Research and the Origns of the Wisconsin School of Labor History," *Labor History,* 25 (1984), 166-188; John Calvin Colson, *Academic Ambitions and Library Development: The American Bureau of Industrial Research and the State Historical Society of Wisconsin 1904-18,* University of Illinois Graduate School of Library and Information Science Occasional Papers, 159 (1983). The collections acquired in this early period are summarized in *Collections on Labor History and Socialism in the Wisconsin State Historical Library* (Madison, 1915).

or the union office, and for those interested in ethnicity, as well as minority group and women's participation in the labor movement.

Society research collections are divided functionally into three major areas: Library, including newspapers, pamphlets, books, and state and Federal government publications; Archives, including organizational records, personal papers, and Wisconsin governmental records; and Visual and Sound Archives, including photographs, posters and other graphics, motion pictures, and recorded sound collections.

Library

The Library's holdings of labor materials form the foundation of the Society's labor resources. The size and scope of the library holdings defy concise description. Comprehensiveness in time and subject coverage, not any particular title or group of titles, is the key to the value of the Library collections. Of particular importance is the Society's collection of labor newspapers and periodicals. First in conjunction with the American Bureau of Industrial Research and later with the aid of the John R. Commons Memorial Labor Research Library, the Society has attempted to collect practically every known labor newspaper and journal on a systematic basis. This collection attracts scholars from around the world and has been described by one labor education expert as "undoubtedly the most extensive and complete collection in this country of old and current journals issued by internationals, local unions and state labor bodies, and of local labor newspapers." As scholars become more interested in contemporary labor topics the printed, public word — for all its defects of bias and omission — grows in value.

To preserve the pulp newspapers and make them more readily available to researchers, the Library began in the 1940s to microfilm its labor papers. This effort increased and was extended to other national repositories in the late 1940s and early 1950s at the suggestion of the Committee of University Industrial Relations Librarians (now the Committee of Industrial Relations Librarians). The Society Library also participated in a cooperative project to produce a comprehensive guide to the location of labor periodicals. This project resulted in a preliminary edition (1953), *A Union List of American Labor Union Periodicals,* and a final edition (1956), *American Labor Union Periodicals, A Guide to Their Location.* The latter work compiled by Bernard G. Naas and Carmelita S. Sakr, is a guide to over 1700 labor union periodicals published in the United States and Canada. In addition to basic bibliographic information about each publication, there is a record of the holdings of the State Historical Society and 19 other cooperating libraries, and an indication of the availability of negative microfilm. All of the negative microfilm citations in Naas and Sakr refer to titles preserved by the Society's extensive preservation program. This pioneering work was welcomed at the time of its publication and has remained the basic work in the field for over 20 years.

In 1965, the Society published *Labor Papers on Microfilm: A Combined List,* which lists 804 microfilm titles of labor and allied titles held by 13 cooperating institutions. The Society holds master negatives to 80% of the titles listed in the 1965 publication, and this forms the basis for a continuing program of microfilming labor periodicals. Unfortunately, since publication of this list in 1965, information on the labor press in America has only been available though occasional lists produced by individual libraries or as part of a more general project on periodicals. In all cases there has only been access by title and not, for example, by union or trade group. As titles are cataloged on OCLC by the Society and other libraries, the information is made significantly more accessible and can be the basis for a revised national bibliography.

In addition to its notable collection of labor periodicals, the Society's library also maintains a comprehensive book and pamphlet collection on U.S. and Canadian labor, trade unionism, and related subjects. These materials include union proceedings, journals, reports, and such occasional publications as constitutions and bylaws, research studies, and educational material; general labor histories and biographies; labor conference reports; books on the sociology of labor; and state and federal government documents pertaining to labor. The collecting policies in effect at the Society's Library over 100 years have produced collections that are broader than even experienced researchers might imagine. Pamphlet items have been collected since the mid-19th century and continue to be a significant portion of the Library's total holdings of some 2.2 million items. Contemporary pamphlets, as well as older items, are added to the holdings on a regular basis, with a total pamphlet collection of some 600,000 items. Approximately 50% of these pamphlets are unique to the Society's collections.

Archives

Society Archives collections related to labor are described in more detail in two available printed sources.[2] Since 1984, newly acquired and

---

[2] F. Gerald Ham and Margaret Hedstrom, eds., *A Guide to Labor Papers in the State Historical Society of Wisconsin* (Madison, 1978); Harold L. Miller, "Labor Records at the State Historical Society of Wisconsin," *Labor History*, 23 (1982), 546–552. Other collections related to civil rights, anti-war, or radical or reform movements are described in Menzi L. Behrnd-Klodt and Carolyn J. Mattern, eds., *Social Action Collections at the State Historical Society of Wisconsin: A Guide* (Madison, 1983).

newly processed collections have also been described in the Research
Libraries Information Network (RLIN). For descriptive purposes, several areas of concentration can be identified, including trade unions
and trade-union leaders; working-class political, radical, and reform
movements; labor law; labor education; and labor economics and
regulation.

The Archives has major collections of records from the AFL and
from 12 national labor organizations. The AFL collection contains small
numbers of papers from the 1880s and 1890s and much more complete
records of Federation activities from about 1904 to the early 1950s. International union collections include: Amalgamated Association of
Street, Electric Railway and Motor Coach Employees, 1889–1959*;
Amalgamated Meat Cutters and Butcher Workmen, 1900–1979; American Communications Association, 1934–1966; American Federation
of Hosiery Workers, 1923–1964; Associated Unions of America, 1940–
1972; Boot and Shoe Workers' Union, 1958–1977; International Association of Machinists and Aerospace Workers, 1901–1974; International Brotherhood of Pulp, Sulphite and Paper Mill Workers,
1906–1966; International Brotherhood of Teamsters, Chauffeurs, Warehousemen and Helpers, 1904–1952; Retail Clerks International Union,
1900–1980; Textile Workers Union of America, 1934–1974; and the
United Packinghouse Food and Allied Workers, 1937–1968. These collections provide comprehensive documentation on the unions, generally including their relations with local affiliates, organizing efforts,
political involvement, bargaining, and relations with the rest of the labor
movement. Certain collections have additional strong points. The AFL
collection contains a good deal of information on Federation activities in Europe, particularly during and immediately after World War
II. The Packinghouse Workers collection demonstrates that union's concerns with civil rights and minority workers and contains large numbers
of grievance files which could be used to reconstruct conditions on the
shop floor. The Textile Workers and Boot and Shoe collections contain files on competing unions in the same trades. The Textile Workers'
records also document the flight of that industry from New England,
and the problems of organizing in the South.

Collections of state and local labor organizational records are extensive but are almost exclusively related to Wisconsin. Included are
records of the Wisconsin State AFL-CIO, 1941–1977, the Industrial
Union Council, 1937–1958, and central bodies from Milwaukee,

---

*Date spans used in this article refer to dates covered by collections, not life spans of individuals
  or organizations.

Madison, and other cities. Also in the holdings are records of over 200 local unions representing many different trades and communities. Collections of the State Federation and some Milwaukee area organizations are especially interesting due to the strong ties with the Wisconsin Socialists which existed at least through the 1930s.

Closely related to the organizational collections are papers of notable trade-union leaders. Among these are papers of Adolph Germer, 1898-1966; Hilton Hanna, 1919-1980; Ralph Helstein of the United Packinghouse Food and Allied Workers, 1942-1985; Charles P. Howard of the International Typographical Union, 1917-1938; Harvey Kitzman, 1938-1972; John L. Lewis, 1879-1969; and Arnold Zander, founder of the American Federation of State, County and Municipal Employees, 1921-1975.[3] The Germer papers are particularly rich in covering his leadership roles in the Socialist Party, United Mine Workers, and the CIO. Kitzman was a CIO regional director intimately involved with a pre-World War II strike at the J.I. Case Co. and with postwar conflicts at Case, Allis Chalmers, and the Kohler Co. Hanna, who is black, was the long-time assistant to Patrick Gorman of the Amalgamated Meatcutters and has also been active in civil rights issues.

Perhaps stronger than the Archives' trade union collections are holdings related to working class political, radical, and reform movements. Through the records of the International Workingmen's Association (IWA), 1871-1876, the Workingmen's Party, 1876-1878, and the Socialist Labor Party (SLP), 1877-1974, the Society holdings document the origins of Marxism in the U.S. The SLP collection is especially useful for studies based in ethnicity because the foreign language federations associated with the Party. Arrangement of the collection, which is by state and city after 1909, facilitates locality-based research. The SLP collection also contains valuable information on other working class organizations, particularly New York City Knights of Labor District Assembly 49, and the IWW. Other collections prominently associated with socialism include the papers of Morris Hillquit, 1895-1943; Harry Laidler, 1913-1959; Clarence Senior, 1924-1945; Algie M. Simons, 1894-1951; and William English Walling, 1871-1962. The Society is also the repository of the records, 1928-1985, of the Socialist Workers Party. American communism is documented by papers of Fred Bassett Blair, 1923-1981; Eugene and Peggy Dennis, 1923-1985; Betty Gannett, 1929-1970; and Liston Oak, 1910-1970. Other collections prominently associated with labor-oriented reform or radical movements include

---

[3]Unfortunately the Zander papers are now split since the Archives of Labor and Urban Affairs at Wayne State Univ. recently acquired Zander's personal diaries.

Stephen P. Andrews, a radical reformer with IWA connections, 1869–1925; Henry Demarest Lloyd, author of *Wealth Against Commonwealth*, 1840–1937;[4] Joseph P. McDonnell, labor editor and one-time IWA and NJ Federation of Trades and Labor Unions official, 1869–1906; Haymarket martyr Albert R. Parsons, 1876–1893; Thomas Phillips, a Knights of St. Crispin official and cooperationist, 1866–1909; Raymond and Margaret Dreir Robins, 1878–1954; Edward H. Rogers, a ship-carpenter and eight-hour day advocate, 1865–1908; John Samuel, active in the Knights of Labor and cooperative movement, 1868–1907; and Ira Steward, credited by John R. Commons with formulating "the first philosophy springing from the American Labor Movement."[5]

Worker education and labor law are two additional areas of strength. The American Labor Education Service collection, 1921–1961, contains records of several institutions serving particularly women workers: the Bryn Mawr Summer School for Women Workers in Industry, the Hudson Shore Workers School, the Vineyard Shore Workers School, and the Barnard Summer School for Workers. Another excellent collection is the Highlander Research and Education Center records, 1917–1978. The Highlander school had its origins in labor education and since the 1950s has changed its orientation more toward civil rights and community organizing. In labor law the Society has the papers of William B. Rubin, 1908–1950, and Joseph A. Padway, 1916–1946, both of whom served as chief legal counsel for the AFL; Herbert Thatcher, 1950–1966, who did work for the Teamsters and other unions; and historian-turned-labor lawyer Staughton Lynd, 1940–1977.

Labor related oral history was practiced at the Society as early as 1952, and in the 1970s and early 1980s was used extensively to supplement major union collections. The 1952 project interviewed workers who entered Milwaukee leather tanneries between 1890 and 1910 and provides a rare glimpse into factory work in that era and later. Two other worker-focused projects involve retail meatcutters and chain-store workers, and packinghouse workers. The former is limited to Southern Wisconsin workers, 1930–1980, and covers topics such as productivity, employee-management relations, and male-female working relationships. The latter involves rank and file members of the United Packinghouse Workers, 1930–1980, and concentrates on minority and women's issues as well as working conditions. Oral history projects con-

---

[4] A recent acquisition of Lloyd papers by the Chicago Historical Society means that this collection is also split between two repositories.

[5] John R. Commons, Ulrich B. Phillips, Eugene A. Gilmore, Helen Sumner, and John B. Andrews, eds., *A Documentary History of American Industrial Society* (Cleveland, 1910–1911), ix, 24.

centrating on union leadership relate to the Amalgamated Meatcutters, Retail Clerks, Textile Workers Union of America, and the United Packinghouse Workers.

In the late 19th and 20th centuries individuals, not from the labor movement, but often with academic backgrounds, working through government agencies and private organizations have had profound effects on the working classes and society as a whole. Society holdings include papers of many such individuals including Arthur Altmeyer, Wilbur Cohen, John R. Commons, Richard T. Ely, William Leiserson, Charles McCarthy, David J. Saposs, Edwin Witte, and Helen Sumner Woodbury. These collections are useful to the labor historian in many ways. The Ely and Commons collections document the origins of the field of labor history in this country, and contain correspondence with numerous labor and radical leaders. The Saposs papers contain his interviews with union officials concerning immigrant workers conducted as part of a Carnegie Corporation Americanization study in 1918-1919, and summaries of his interviews with hundreds of workers who participated in the 1919 steel strike. All these collections shed light on bodies such as the U.S. Commission on Industrial Relations and the NLRB, and on efforts to turn working-class concerns into workable economic and social reforms such as social security, workers' compensation, and unemployment compensation.

Wisconsin was among the first states to actively regulate and study working conditions in factories and shops. A state Bureau of Labor Statistics was formed in 1887, and was succeeded by the Industrial Commission in 1911. The state initiated the nation's first unemployment compensation plan in 1934, and has had employment relations and fair employment practices boards since 1937. The publications and records of these and other agencies provide valuable sources for the labor historian. For example, during World War I the Industrial Commission studied working conditions of street car drivers to determine if women were suited to that type of employment. Seeking unemployment benefits or filing complaints with boards or commissions sometimes results in extensive hearings which describe job content, labor-management conflicts, or other work situations. Such regulatory agencies are a largely untapped source, awaiting imaginative researchers. A recent study of labor spies, for example, made valuable use of registration and licensing records of private detectives in Wisconsin.[6]

[6]Darryl Holter, "Labor Spies and Union-Busting in Wisconsin, 1890-1940," *Wisconsin Magazine of History,* 68 (1985), 243-265.

Visual and Sound Archives

Photographs, motion pictures, posters, broadsides, and ephemeral materials such as buttons, banners, membership cards, time cards, labels, letterheads, union membership cards, and strike stamps are administered through the Society's Visual and Sound Archives. Major collections of photographs are associated with some of the large organizational collections held in the archives. Thus the Visual and Sound Archives has many photos which originated with the Meatcutters, Packinghouse Workers, and Textile Workers unions. Given the Society's early emphasis on documenting working class movements, the Visual and Sound archives has excellent poster, broadside, and ephemeral material from the 19th as well as the 20th century. Also in the holdings are two major collections of newspaper cartoons, with heavy emphasis on working class issues. These are editorial cartoons from *The People*, the publication of the Socialist Labor Party, and the collection, 1972–1984, of Mike Konopacki.

Perhaps more significant are the thousands of photographs showing people at work from the last half of the 19th century to the present. Most are arranged in a topically arranged file designed by Paul Vanderbilt who, before coming to the Society, organized the photograph collection of the Farm Security Administration. The classification scheme includes over 100 categories of work, from agricultural to white collar, and from service industries to manufacturing, and lends itself to research on job content and working conditions.

Closely related to the Visual and Sound Archives are the holdings of the Wisconsin Center for Film and Theater Research. These include films, scripts, and other production documentation from thousands of feature films and television programs; and scripts, musical scores and production files from hundreds of theatrical productions from the 1920s through the early 1980s. Working-class-theme films documented in the holdings include *Our Daily Bread* and *Salt of the Earth*. Particularly well covered are feature films from Warner Brothers, known in the 1930s for films on contemporary social issues. Also noteworthy are the papers of composer Marc Blitzstein, who created several musical works about attempts of workers to organize, including *The Cradle Will Rock*.

While the Society concentrates on the resources of American labor history, the Univ. of Wisconsin-Madison's Memorial Library continues to develop holdings in such allied areas as foreign labor and socialist movements, economic theory, industrial relations, and collective bargaining. Still other Madison campus libraries — the Law School Library, the Business Library, and the School for Workers Library—house smaller, more specialized collections in this area.

Access: The State Historical Society of Wisconsin is located on the Univ. of Wisconsin-Madison campus. Society holdings are open to all researchers, although collections may occasionally be unavailable due to donor imposed restrictions or administrative needs such as cataloging or microfilming. Many collections of both the Library and Archives have been microfilmed. Filmed collections are available for sale, and microfilm and parts of the Library's book collection may be borrowed on interlibrary loan. It is advisable for researchers to call or write in advance to determine if collections they wish to use will be available at the time of their visit.

The Library is open 8 am–9 pm, Monday–Thursday, and 8 am–5 pm, Friday and Saturday when the University is in session. Otherwise the hours are 8:00 am–5 pm, Monday–Saturday. At the Archives, the reading room is open 8 am–5 pm, Monday–Friday, and 9 am–4 pm on Saturdays; the visual and sound archives are open 11 am–5 pm, Monday–Friday. For information about the Library contact James Hansen, the Reference Librarian; for information about the Archives contact Harold L. Miller, the Reference Archivist. They can be reached at the State Historical Society of Wisconsin, 816 State Street, Madison, WI 53706; phone: (608) 262-3266.

THE IMMIGRATION HISTORY RESEARCH CENTER AS A SOURCE FOR LABOR HISTORY RESEARCH

by
Joel Wurl

In the Fall 1982 issue of *Labor History*, Rudolph Vecoli summarized the holdings of the Immigration History Research Center (IHRC) pertaining to labor issues.[1] Using that earlier report as a point of departure, the following essay essentially provides new information on materials acquired over the last eight years. Certain basic points on the overall services and programs of the IHRC, as well as descriptions of key sources received prior to 1982, are restated or amplified for the reader's convenience.

The IHRC is approaching its 26th year of work in the acquisition, preservation, and provision of archival and library resources on the experiences of some 24 European and Near Eastern ethno-linguistic groups in the U.S.[2] The Center also serves as an active agent in stimulating research and activity in immigration and ethnic studies. Since its establishment, the IHRC has sponsored numerous conferences, symposia, and lectures and has published various descriptions of collections, bibliographies, and conference proceedings. The 1986 Center-sponsored symposium, "A Century of European Migrations, 1830–1930: Comparative Perspectives," emerged as a milepost for research on migra-

Joel Wurl is curator, Immigration History Research Center.

[1]Rudolph J. Vecoli, "Labor Related Collections in the Immigration History Research Center," *Labor History*, 23 (1982), 568–74.
[2]For general descriptions of the IHRC see Rudolph J. Vecoli, "The Immigration Studies Collection of the University of Minnesota," *American Archivist*, 32 (1969), 139–145; Rudolph J. Vecoli, "Diamonds in Your Own Backyard: Developing Documentation on European Immigrants to North America," *Ethnic Forum*, 1 (1981), 2–16; Susan Grigg, "A World of Repositories, a World of Records: Redefining the Scope of a National Subject Collection," *American Archivist*, 48 (1985), 286–295; and Joel Wurl, "The Immigration History Research Center: A Historical Profile and Prospective Glimpse," *Ethnic Forum*, 7 (1988), 73–85.

tion history, drawing together leading scholars from 10 countries whose work sounded a number of themes, including labor issues.[3]

The Center's holdings document those immigrant groups most commonly associated with the great trans-Atlantic migration to the U.S. from roughly the 1880s to the 1920s.[4] These were the "new immigrants" whose experiences, while extremely diverse, were on the whole linked closely with those of America's industrial working class. The collections span the period between the mid-1800s to the present, reflecting more recent migration activity and manifestations of ethnicity as well as the mass migration period. Materials include the written records of American-born generations as well as immigrants. The collection is national (indeed, international) in scope, with strengths of geographic coverage relating closely in most cases to concentrations of immigrant settlement.

One of the nation's largest repositories of immigration and ethnic source material, the IHRC holds over 45,000 monographs and bound periodicals, nearly 900 newspaper files and 3000 serial titles, and over 800 manuscript collections amounting to some 4000 linear feet. The Center's 5000 reels of microfilm consist mainly of newspapers, along with several significant manuscript collections reproduced from archives in Europe and from ethnic organizations in the U.S. The bulk of these holdings were created by the ethnic communities and individuals themselves; much of it is in the original languages of these groups. Documentation overall (not exclusively labor-related) is especially abundant for the Finnish, Italian, Polish, and Ukrainian groups and, to a slightly lesser degree, for the Czech, Hungarian, Greek, Slovak, and Slovenian groups as well as for the Center's "general" section.

As stated in the 1982 Vecoli article, newspapers constitute perhaps the best source of primary evidence on immigrant involvement in labor struggles, unionism, and leftist political activism. A landmark reference guide for researchers wishing to pursue these materials systematically is the 3 volume *Immigrant Labor Press in North America, 1840s–1970s: An Annotated Bibliography* (edited by Dirk Hoerder and published

---

[3]Proceedings from this symposium are currently being prepared for publication. A good deal of research has been carried out at the IHRC in recent years on the role of immigrants in the American labor force and the labor movements. Some of these researchers and topics include: Ivan Cizmic, South Slavs in the American Labor Movement; Dirk Hoerder, International Labor Markets and Community Building by Migrant Workers in Atlantic Economies; William Pratt, Finnish Radicalism in the Northern Plains; Neil Basin, Kate Richards O'Hare; Varpu Lindstrom-Best, Finnish Radical Women; and John Roberts, Attitudes of U.S. Labor Toward Foreign Affairs, 1932–1945.

[4]See Velcoli, *op. cit.*

by Greenwood Press in 1987). The periodical holdings of the IHRC are prominently represented in the chapters covering its constituent immigrant groups. In addition to the newspapers listed in the 1982 article, the following publications are of value for labor studies:[5]

Czech
  Slavie (Slavia, Racine, WI, c. 1861–1918)
Finnish
  The Cooperative Builder (Superior, WI, c. 1931–82)
  Sosialisti (The Socialist, Duluth, MN, 1914–16)
  Toveritar (The Woman Comrade, Astoria, OR, 1914–30)
Hungarian
  A Teny (The Fact, Los Angeles; 1947–51, 1954, 1968, 1970)
Italian
  L'Asino (The Jackass, New York, 1906–08)
  L'Aurora (The Dawn, Paterson, NJ, 1899–1930)
  Il Martello (The Hammer, New York, 1922–25, 1927, 1935–36)
  Il Risveglio (The Awakening, Denver, 1906–17, 1920–24, 1927–36)
  L'Unione (The Union, Pueblo, CO, 1897–1900, 1907–08, 1916–17, 1931–47)
Lithuanian
  Laisve (Liberty, Brooklyn, 1929, c. 1938–84)
  Koleivis (Traveler, Boston, 1931, c. 1944–79)
  Moteru Balsas (The Women's Voice, Philadelphia, 1916–22)
  Sviesa (The Light, Ozone Park, NY, 1934–37, 1940–43, 1946–58, 1962–79)
Polish
  Straz (The Guard, Scranton, PA, c. 1897–present)
Romanian
  America (Cleveland, 1906–66)
Slovak
  Amerikansko Slovenske Noviny (American Slovak News, Pittsburgh and New York, 1893–1904)
Ukrainian
  Hromads'kyi Holos (Voice of the Commonwealth, New York, c. 1941–68)
  Robitnychyi Holos (Voice of the Worker, Akron, OH, 1925–26)

---

[5]The data given here for individual newspapers are abbreviated. They do not indicate title changes, mergers, or changes in place of publication. The years given are for the inclusive holdings of publications by the IHRC. Most of the files are not complete, with issues and often entire years missing.

One of the IHRC's most important recently-acquired newspapers is the Estonian *Uus Ilm* (New World). This paper, published in NYC beginning in 1909 and later in Monroe, NY, served initially as the organ of the American Estonian Socialist Association. As a result of political disputes among its publishers following the Russian Revolution, *Uus Ilm* became more closely affiliated with the Estonian American communist movement. The IHRC's holdings (1912, 1919–20, 1923–27, 1930), which are the only known early issues of this title available, are in the process of being microfilmed.

A number of other newspapers have been preserved on microfilm through the cooperative efforts of the IHRC and other institutions. With the Center for Research Libraries, the IHRC coordinated the Carpatho Ruthenian Microfilm Project and the Polish Microfilm Project; both endeavors resulted in IHRC-published guides identifying titles available for on-site research use, interlibrary loan, or purchase.[6] More recently, the IHRC has directed similar projects for Italian-American and Finnish-American newspapers.

In addition, the IHRC holds several thousand volumes of autobiographies, polemical tracts, translations of radical works, poetry, plays, anniversary volumes, proceedings of conventions, almanacs, and pamphlets pertaining to all phases of labor and radical involvement among various ethnic groups. For the Finns, for example, there is a rather complete set of publications documenting the strong cooperative movement which they established, while the struggle of the Italian-American left against fascism is reflected in many publications. Also available are commentaries and historical narratives of the Industrial Workers of the World, the International Ladies Garment Workers Union (ILGWU), the American Committee for the Protection of the Foreign Born, and other labor and political groups.

The IHRC's manuscript collections furnish unique documentation on the intertwining of immigration and the labor movement at the turn of the century and beyond. The 1982 article highlighted manuscript materials for the Finnish, Italian, and South Slavic groups. Among the key collections cited were: records of the Finnish Socialist Federation, the IWW-affiliated Work People's College, and the Tyomies Society (Finnish); records of the ILGWU (Local 48), ILGWU-related papers of Angela Bambace and Antonio Crivello, and papers of labor activists Anthony Capraro, Emilio Grandinetti, Guiseppe Procopio, Alberico

[6]Frank Renkiewicz, comp., *The Carpatho-Ruthenian Microfilm Project: A Guide to Newspapers and Periodicals* (St. Paul, 1979), and Frank Renkiewicz and Anne Bjorkquist Ng, comp., *A Guide to Polish American Newspapers and Periodials in Microform* (St. Paul, 1988).

Caselli, and Egidio Clemente (Italian); and records of the Yugoslav Socialist Federation, the Croatian drama society "Nada," and the pub-
lisher of the Slovenian paper *Glas Naroda* (South Slavic).

Since 1982, the IHRC has received several additional labor-related
manuscript materials. Among the recent additions to the Finnish collection are the records of Finnish Socialist Federation chapters and
related organizations in Minnesota, Wisconsin, Massachusetts, Oregon,
and California. These documents cover the period from roughly 1905
to the mid-1970s and include minutes, financial records, membership
materials, and playscripts. Documentation on the Finnish-American
cooperative movement includes the papers of Kaarle Lehtinen, which
contain correspondence and other items from the Wayne Produce Association and the Fairfield Cooperative Farm Association of Jesup,
GA. Also available are voluminous files of the Farmer's Cooperative
Mercantile Association of Kettle River, MN.

In the early 1980s, the IHRC co-sponsored a major project to gather
memoirs, oral history recordings, photographs, and other documents
chronicling the experiences of Finnish immigrants and their descendants in Minnesota. The resulting Minnesota Finnish American Family
History Collection contains firsthand accounts on a wide variety of
topics, including trade union activities in the mining and lumber industries of Minnesota's Iron Range area as well as the programs and
objectives of various cooperatives. A published guide to this collection
of over 100 files and interviews can be purchased from the IHRC.[7]

Important additions to the Italian American section in recent years
include the papers of prominent labor activists and anti-facists Vincent Massari and Pasquale Mario De Ciampis. Massari, whose father
was involved in the 1914 Ludlow Massacre in Colorado, was himself
a mine union organizer in the Pueblo area. His papers span the dates
1895 to 1976 and cover particularly his work as editor of the Pueblo
newspaper L'UNIONE, local civic leader, and Colorado legislator. De
Ciampis was active in labor affairs in Italy before migrating to the U.S.
in 1912. He served as editor of the syndicalist paper, IL PROLETARIO,
from 1922 to 1933 and again from 1936 to 1937. His files include a
lengthy draft history and related notes on IL PROLETARIO. The IHRC
is currently preparing for publication abstracts of De Ciampis' extensive summaries of the newspaper's contents. The Center also recently
obtained the papers of New York labor figure Howard Molisani. These
materials cover the years 1920–1987 and include minutes, financial

[7]This collection is further described in Mary Koske, comp., Suzanna Moody, ed., *Guide to the Minnesota Finnish American Family History Collection* (St. Paul, 1985).

records, and correspondence on the Italian American Labor Council, the Italian Labor Center, the ILGWU (Local 48), and the AFL-CIO.

In 1988, the IHRC completed a 3-year project to acquire, preserve, and make available documentation on the Order Sons of Italy in America (OSIA), the nation's largest and oldest Italian fraternal organization. Over 600 linear feet of organizational records and personal papers documenting a multitude of topics were transferred to the Center. Various OSIA files and periodicals enable an examination of the organization's perspective on labor and political affairs during the 20th century. The papers of OSIA leader Giovanni DiSilvestro, for example, furnish unique information in the Sacco Vanzetti case.[8]

Significant labor-related collections were also added to the Center's holdings for other ethnic groups. Among these are the unpublished autobiography and reading library of Anthony Bimba (1894–1982), journalist, key figure in the Lithuanian Communist League of America, and author of 22 books and pamphlets, including *History Of The American Working Class* (1927) and *The Molly Maguires* (1932). The extensive papers and library of the late eminent Greek American historian Theodore Saloutos were acquired by the Center in 1982. These materials cover the years 1932–82 and deal with a wide spectrum of Greek American subjects. Included are written notes from Saloutos' interviews with numerous Greeks in various segments of the work force.[9] The Center also holds the papers of Ukrainian emigré Myroslav Sichynsky (1887–1979), president of the Ukrainian Workingmen's Association in the 1930s. (Prior to his arrival in the U.S. in 1914, Sichnysky assassinated the governor of Galicia in retaliation for mistreatment of Ukrainian peasants.)

Although the preceding pages point to materials of considerable research value, it is clear that much work remains to be done by the IHRC and other repositories in gathering and preserving the labor-related records of immigrant groups. The IHRC remains actively interested in building its labor-related holdings and in working with other repositories to improve documentation in this subject area.

Access: The IHRC is open to all qualified researchers 8:30 am–4:30 pm, Mondays–Fridays. Materials do not circulate; however, in most cases photocopies or photographic reproductions can be obtained within customary limits, and microfilm for which the IHRC holds the master negative can be purchased or borrowed through inter-library loan.

---

[8]For a description of this project and summaries of OSIA records available at the IHRC and elsewhere, see John Andreozzi, comp., *Guide to the Records of the Order Sons of Italy in America* (St. Paul, 1989).

[9]Louise Martin, comp., *Guide to the Theodore Saloutos Collection* (St. Paul, 1989).

Cataloging descriptions for a large percentage of the Center's book collection are accessible through the Research Libraries Information Network (RLIN). In addition, all manuscript collections have been described in automated form, and the microcomputer data base can be put to use for on-site research visits or for mail inquiries. The Center's first comprehensive guide to collections is currently being published by Greenwood Press and will be available in 1990.[10] For further information contact Joel Wurl, Immigration History Research Center, Univ. of Minnesota, 826 Berry St., St. Paul, MN 55114; phone: (612) 627-4208.

[10]Suzanna Moody and Joel Wurl, comp., *The Immigration History Research Center: A Guide to Collections* (Westport, CT, forthcoming in 1990). Earlier descriptions of holdings include: *Immigration History Research Center: Guide to Manuscript Holdings* (St. Paul, 1976); Bonnie Meon, comp., *Periodicals and Newspapers in Microform* (St. Paul, 1978); Halyna Myroniuk and Christine Worobec, comps., *Ukrainians in North America: A Select Bibliography* (St. Paul, and Toronto, 1981); Joseph Szeplaki, ed., *Hungarians in the United States and Canada: A Bibliography* (St. Paul, 1977); and Robert P. Gakovich and Milan M. Radovich, comps., *Serbs in the United States and Canada: A Comprehensive Bibliography* (St. Paul, IHRC, 1976). The Center publishes information on current acquisitions in its publications *Spectrum* and *IHRC News*.

LABOR COLLECTIONS IN THE WESTERN HISTORICAL COLLECTIONS, AT THE UNIVERSITY OF COLORADO, BOULDER

by
Cassandra M. Volpe

The University of Colorado's Western Historical Collections originated with its history faculty. Professor James F. Willard, head of the Dept. of History from 1907 to 1935 and history professor Frederick L. Paxson devoted much of their time to collecting manuscripts throughout Colorado. They also endeavored to inform their colleagues and state officials that historical preservation was an important function. During World War I, Willard received the first financial support specifically for historical records development. This period was the official beginning of the Western Historical Collections.

With the decline during the 1920s of the West's hardrock mining industry, collecting of materials from the fading bonanza towns resulted in major groups of records being found. Some of those collections of papers were: D. R. C. Brown (1880–1920), mining entrepreneur in Aspen, CO; Senator Henry M. Teller and his legal partner, Harper M. Orahood (1861–1877), Central City, CO; J. J. Blow, Henry Moody and W. W. Old (1880s–1890s), mining speculators and businessmen from Leadville, CO.

In 1935 with the death of Willard a new era began with shared responsibility between the history department and the university library. Several history professors continued to personally collect historically relevant manuscripts for the Western Historical Collections. Those foresighted professors included Carl C. Eckhardt, department chairman, 1935–1945; Percy S. Fritz, Colorado and mining history specialist; Colin B. Goodykoontz, American social and cultural historian; and Robert G. Athearn, an authority on the Trans-Mississippi West and the American frontier. Their collection areas were diverse.

Cassandra M. Volpe is archivist and acting head of the Western Historical Collections.

The University Library accepted complete responsibility for the development of the Western Historical Collections in 1959, and with this change, a full-time, permanent, and qualified staff was hired. In 1964, the curator, John A. Brennan, a PhD in History, began to change the direction of acquisition from frontier and pioneer era material to 20th century manuscripts concerning political, social, and economical history emphasizing labor, politics, women, and non-profit organizations.

In 1968 the emphasis on labor archives began with the acquisition of the Western Federation of Miners and International Union of Mine, Mill and Smelter Workers Archive. The WFM/IUMMSW merger with the United Steelworkers of America in 1967 marked the date span for the collecting efforts for this hard-rock miners union, 1893–1967. The WFM's national records contain the executive board minutes (1902–1916), convention proceedings (1893–1916), *The Miners Magazine* and subsequent publications (1900–1967), financial and membership records (1894–1916), defense records of the Haywood-Moyer-Pettibone trial, and the Clarence Darrow and Michigan Defense funds records. The records of the IUMMSW are more extensive and document the years 1916–1967, especially the period from 1940 to 1967. These records include executive board minutes, convention proceedings, election and referendum materials, correspondence, memoranda, and publications.

District and local union materials included in the WFM/IUMMSW Archive are from Southwestern District #2; Eastern District; Montana locals #1 (Butte), #16 (Great Falls), #18 (Coeur d'Alene), and #117 (Anaconda); and various locals in Utah, Kansas, Texas, Nevada, Arizona, and California. In addition to the above mentioned locals, the Archive contains a fairly complete set of records of Local #890 (Bayard, NM) and its predecessor locals. These records include minutes, roll books, negotiation files, contracts, and correspondence for the years 1941 to 1975. The Bayard Local #890 was the subject of the controversial film *Salt of the Earth*.

The WFM/IUMMSW Archive is open for qualified researchers and has a detailed and indexed finding aid to assist staff and visitors to gain access to this approximately 800 box collection.

Another major labor collection is the Archive of the Oil, Chemical and Atomic Workers International Union (OCAW). This collection includes the records of the national, District I (California) and Local #1-128 (Long Beach, CA). The national papers include convention proceedings (1937–1973), district strike files, executive board minutes (1940–1974), contracts (1940–1970), and financial records. District I deposited extensive files of Verlin L. McKendree (1926–1975) consisting largely of: Grievance and Arbitration Training School files; grievance and arbitration case files (1941–1979); negotiations case files (1949–1981); and contracts (1940s–1980s). The records of Local #1-128, Long Beach, CA, include: constitutions (1937–1970s); convention proceedings (1938–1970s); membership records (1922–1970s); general files arranged by company names (1927–1978); grievance, negotiation and contract files (1928–1970s); strike files (1960s–1970s); election records (1960s–1970s); unit minutes (1922–1970s); and financial records (1943–1970s).

The National Farmers Union (NFU), founded in Texas in 1902 and headquartered in Denver since 1940, was the voice of small farm operators. Its archive spans the years from 1902 to the present. The NFU maintains offices not only in Denver, but also in Washington, DC, and many state capitals throughout the Midwest. The papers reflect the NFU's advocacy role in promoting legislation beneficial to the family farm.

The James G. Patton Papers complement the NFU Archive. Patton was a native of western Colorado who became interested in organizing farmers in the early 1930s. He held various offices in the Colorado Farmers Union and later served as president of the National Farmers Union (1940–1966). This collection contains correspondence, published materials, and topical files on Patton's wide-ranging agricultural, political, and social interests from 1930 to 1985.

Additional smaller collections concerning the labor movement divide into three categories: national, state, and local. The collections from national groups include the following: The International Mailers Union (IMU) formed in 1943 from the International Typographical Union (ITU) and re-merged with it in 1978 because of presssures from automation and reduced employment in the printing trades. This collection includes the IMU president's office correspondence, bargaining agreements, secretary-treasurer's membership and financial records, union publications and related materials from the 1940s to 1978. The ITU, the oldest labor union in continuous existence, began in 1852. Colorado Springs was the headquarters for the ITU as well as the location for the union's Printers' Home for retired typographers. After the ITU's merger in 1987 with the Communication Workers of America, a small portion of the printing union's records remained in Colorado. The materials held by the Western Historical Collections include primarily published journals, proceedings, newspapers, newsletters, and the library of the union (1889–1986). Also included are the legal files of several NLRB cases (1950s–1960s) and photos of the Printers' Home.

There are also collections from various state organizations. Brotherhood of Railroad Trainmen (BRT) contains the grievance files of the union in Colorado with the Denver & Rio Grande Western Railroad Co. (1929–1965). Three collections which relate to each other are the

Colorado State Federation of Labor (1896–1955), the Colorado Labor
Council (1955–1973), and the Herrick Roth Collection (1950s–1970s).
The Colorado State Federation of Labor was affiliated with the AFL
in 1905 and in 1955 merged with a CIO branch to form the Colorado
Labor Council (CLC). The State Federation and the CLC collections
provide important information on labor, social, and political problems
and concerns in Colorado between 1896 and 1973. Record groups included are correspondence, record books, convention proceedings,
reports, periodicals, and pamphlets. Herrick Roth was a founder of
the American Federation of Teachers (AFT) and served as president
of the Colorado Labor Council (1962–1973). His papers contain correspondence, clippings, and pamphlets and reflect his efforts on behalf
of the AFT and CLC.

Another labor collection with state-wide interest is the Hefferly
Papers. Frank Hefferly (1902–1960) along with his son, Fred K. Hefferly
(1938–1972), were both organizers and officials of the United Mine
Workers of America (UMWA), District #12 (IL) and #15 (CO and NM),
and staunch supporters and trusted colleagues of John L. Lewis. The
collection consists of an incomplete record (1902–1972) of both men's
careers. It contains important correspondence, reports, newsletters, and
photographs of organizing in the coal fields of the West.

The local records of various Colorado unions comprise the final
group of labor collections. These are the Denver Typographical Union
Local #49 (1864–1960) containing general records, meeting minutes,
officers' reports, convention proceedings, membership rolls, Chapel
reports, and apprenticeship files; International Brotherhood of Elec-
trial Workers Local #111 (1950s–1980s) consisting of meeting minutes,
membership and financial data, collective bargaining agreements, contracts, correspondence, and publications; International Moulders and
Foundery Workers Union Local #188 (1878–1970) includes meeting
minutes, membership and financial records; and finally the United
Brotherhood of Carpenters and Joiners Local #55 (1886–1975) comprises minutes of meetings, financial, and other records including ledgers
from absorbed locals.

The Western Historical Collections have additional manuscript collections which complement and relate to labor union issues. Some examples of those manuscript collections follow.

The Edward P. Costigan Papers contain the personal, business, and
political papers of this progressive Colorado lawyer and senator.
Costigan represented the United Mine Workers during the Colorado
coal field strikes from 1913 to 1916. His papers contain correspondence,
reports, and legal records concerning this struggle plus hearings before

the 63rd Congress' Subcommittee of the Committee on Mines & Mining, and the U.S. Commission on Industrial Relations.

The papers of Edward Keating contain information on the Adamson Eight-Hour law, the first Federal child labor law, and minimum wage laws for women and children. Keating served in the U.S. Congress from 1913 to 1919 and was editor and manager of *LABOR*, the official newspaper of the associated railroad labor organizations from 1919 until his death in 1953.

The Josephine Roche Papers tell labor's story from both the management and union sides. Ms. Roche was director and president of the Rocky Mountain Fuel Co. in Colorado from 1927 to 1950. She was also Director of the United Mine Workers of America's Welfare and Retirement Fund beginning in 1948 and worked very closely with John L. Lewis to promote better conditions in the coal mining industry. Her papers contain records of the Rocky Mountain Fuel Company and the UMWA including correspondence with John L. Lewis.

Lastly, the Rocky Mountain Fuel Company (RMF) Collection contains information on the Columbine and Vulcan mines, the Rocky Mountain Stores, and the Employer's Mutual Insurance Co. which dealt with the RMF employees. The period covered is from the 1920s through the 1940s, a portion of the period Josephine Roche was the president and director. Taken together, the Josephine Roche Papers and the Rocky Mountain Fuel Company records give an interesting insight into management and labor working for common goals.

Access: the Western Historical Collections is located in Norlin Library on the Univ. of Colorado's Boulder Campus. The facilities are open to the public 10 am–5 pm, Monday–Friday. A letter of introduction stating your topic or research interest will be useful before an on-site visit. Personal identification is required in order to use the repository. Some collections have restrictions on use as requested by the donors. Finding aids are available and individual assistance is provided for visiting researchers. Because the staff is small, phone and written reference questions are handled only on a limited basis. Photoduplication service is available but nothing circulates on interlibrary loan. For further information contact Curator, Western Historical Collections, Box 184, Univ. of Colorado, Boulder, CO 80309-0184; phone: (303) 492-7242.

---

1. John A. Brennan, "The University of Colorado's Western Historical Collections," *Great Plains Journal*, Spring 1972, 154–160.

2. John A. Brennan and Cassandra M. Volpe, "Sources for Studying Labor at the Western Historical Collections of the University of Colorado, Boulder," *Labor's Heritage*, Jan. 1989, 68–74.

LABOR RESOURCES AT THE NEVADA STATE LIBRARY AND ARCHIVES

by
Guy Louis Rocha

The Division of Archives and Records (State Archives) was created in 1965 by the legislature and transferred to the State Library from the Secretary of State's office in 1979. The State Archives is not a traditional labor archives and does not possess or acquire collections per se as they relate to workers, organized or unorganized. What the State Archives does have in the way of resources for the study of labor is a vast array of governmental records from the executive, legislative, and judicial branches of state government that document work, workers, and labor union activity. The making of law, the implementation and enforcement of law, and the adjudication of law have touched the life and defined the rights of every worker in Nevada and throughout the country.

Nevada was created as a territory on March 2, 1861 and admitted as a state on October 31, 1864. In the intervening time, there have been three territorial legislative sessions, 65 state sessions, and 16 special sessions. The legislature is bicameral and has met biennally for most of its existence. Practically every session has passed some legislation affecting labor. Under the title of Labor and Industrial Relations in the Nevada Revised Statutes are chapters entitled: Labor Commissioner; Compensation, Wages and Hours; Employment of Minors; Apprenticeships; Employment Agencies and Offices; Unemployment Compensation; Employment Practices; Organized Labor and Labor Disputes; Vocational Rehabilitation; Industrial Insurance; Occupational Diseases; and Occupational Safety and Health. As one might expect, much of Nevada's labor law dates from the Progressive Era, the New Deal period and post World War II.

Publications related to the legislative process in Nevada include the

Guy Louis Rocha is state archives and records administrator, Nevada State Library and Archives.

Statutes of Nevada; Journal of the Senate; Journal of the Assembly;
bound bill books dating back to 1915; and numerous legislative studies
since the creation of the Legislative Council Bureau in 1945. Compiled
laws and supplements were produced in 1873, 1885, 1900, 1912, 1919,
1929, 1938, 1942 and 1950. The current *Nevada Revised Statutes*, which
dates back to 1957, is annotated and includes citations to pertinent state
Attorney General's opinions, district court, State Supreme Court, and
federal court cases.

Among the holdings of legislative records at the State Archives are
the original bills, including those not enacted into law; Senate and Assembly floor tapes beginning in 1961; and standing committee minutes
dating from 1965. Not all standing committees kept minutes from 1965
through 1973. The Assembly adopted a standing rule in 1973 to keep
minutes of standing committees and the Senate adopted a similar rule
in 1977.

Nevada's court system also dates to the territorial period. Surviving
records of the Territorial and State Supreme Court are housed in the
State Archives including docket books, transcripts, and opinions. The
publication, *Nevada Reports*, contains all the opinions for the State
Supreme Court. Among the notable labor cases heard in the Supreme
Court are *Ex parte* Boyce (1904) and *Ex parte* Kair (1905). The rulings
in these two cases upheld Nevada's eight-hour law in mines, mills and
smelters (1903), one of the first such laws in the West, as a valid exercise of the police power and no violation of the state constitution or
the 14th amendment to the U.S. Constitution. The Western Federation
of Miners (WFM) was instrumental in the passage of the eight-hour
law in Nevada and other mining states.

Other significant cases include *L. C. Branson* v. *Industrial Workers
of the World* (1908), which focused on the common law doctrine defining
conspiracy in relation to a Wobbly boycott of newspapers in Tonopah
and Goldfield; and *State of Nevada* v. *M. R. Preston and Joseph Smith*
(1908), which dismissed an appeal and denied a rehearing for murder
and manslaughter convictions stemming from the Goldfield labor
troubles of 1907. The WFM defended labor officials Preston and Smith
in their district and supreme court cases. The Socialist Labor Party
nominated Morrie Preston as its candidate for the presidency of the
U.S. in 1908.

Executive branch records of state government are among the richest
resource for the writing of labor history. Executive agencies implement
and enforce labor laws and generally have more direct contact with
workers and unions than the legislative and judicial branches of
government.

The State Legislature created the Adjutant-General's office in 1865 and named the Governor Commander-in-Chief. The State Militia, renamed the National Guard in 1893, was used on a number of occasions in Nevada's history to "keep the peace" during a labor disturbance or strike action. Adjutant-General records housed at the State Archives include reports and official correspondence which relate to policing labor unrest. Among the noteworthy labor-management conflicts where the Governor called out the State Militia must be noted the so-called Charcoal Burners' War of 1879 in Eureka County and the American Railway Union boycott and strike in 1894, which impacted Nevada's communities on the Central Pacific Railroad.

The National Guard was disbanded by the Governor in 1906 because the state's chief executive had been advised that the guard units, many of them composed of union miners, railroad employees, and other laborers, could not be relied upon for strike duty. When the National Guard was reorganized in 1929, state law specifically prohibited the use of the guard to police "any labor trouble, strike or lockout within this state . . . public peace shall be preserved by the Nevada state police."

The State Police was created in January 1908 with the absence of a National Guard for strike duty. The Governor had called a special session of the state legislature and requested that the legislators create a state constabulatory to replace Federal troops assigned to keep the peace in the WFM strike and management lockout in Goldfield. Records and reports maintained by the State Archives document the use of the State Police in scores of labor-management clashes through the mid-1920s, including the national railroad strike of 1922. The State Police evolved into the Highway Patrol in the 1940s.

Strikes and labor actions sometimes led to violence which more often than not resulted in arrests and court trials. Union members and labor officials were also arrested and tried for breaking criminal anarchy and syndicalism laws, labor racketeering, and a host of other charges. Felony convictions many times meant sentences in the State Prison. The State Archives has in its legal custody inmate files dating from 1863 through 1955. Public disclosure laws limit access to some of these records, but generally most files more than 50 years old are open for research. The records of the Board of Pardons and Board of Parole Commissioners are also valuable when examining how workers fared in Nevada's penal system

The state's chief legal officer is the Attorney-General. As such, the Attorney-General represented the state in labor cases appealed to the Supreme Court such as *Ex parte* Boyce, *Ex parte* Kair, and *State of Nevada* v. *M. R. Preston and Joseph Smith*. The Attorney-General's records group includes case files dating from the 1880s through the 1970s. In addition, the Attorney General sits on the Board of Pardons with the justices of the Supreme Court and the Governor, and prior to 1957 served on the Board of Parole Commissioners.

Like the Attorney-General, the Secretary of State is a constitutional officer in Nevada and an elected position. The office is primarily ministerial and is the office of record for state filings. Of particular importance to the labor researcher are the initiative petitions filed with the Secretary of State. Among the petitions transferred to the Archives are the "Right-to-Work" petitions which resulted in Nevada's voters narrowly passing a "Right-to-Work" law in November 1952. Organized labor circulated petitions in 1954 and 1956 to repeal the law but the electorate voted to keep "Right-to-Work" on the books where it still remains.

The Progressive Era produced a number of regulatory offices and agencies concerned with conditions of labor, worker's compensation and labor relations. Many of the records of these governmental entities are now housed in the State Archives. In 1909, the office of Inspector of Mines was created by the legislature. The Inspector was required to produce an annual report which included a list of all accidents including fatalities; number of mines both operational and idle; number of men employed, wages paid, and nationality; conditions in the mines; compliance with recommended improvement; and licensing of hoisting engineers among other information. The Inspector of Mines was originally an elected office but since 1973 has been an executive branch agency.

The Industrial Insurance Commission was created statutorily in 1913. The "workman's compensation" law defines and regulates the liability of employers to their employees. Injured workmen, or their dependents when injuries result in death, are compensated from employers' contributions to a fund administered by the Industrial Commission unless the employer is self-insured. Records and reports of the commission include lists of contributors by class of business or industry; rates and premiums collected; and compensation paid. The IIC was renamed the State Industrial Insurance System in 1981.

Among the most valuable record groups as a resource for labor history are the records and reports of the State Labor Commissioner. The office was created in 1915. Duties outlined in the statutes include the generating of statistics by industry or occupation for length of work day; average length of time employed yearly; net wages; apprenticeships; unemployment; conditions of labor; ethnicity and race of workers; prison labor; health care; employment bureaus; and labor unions. Particularly important are the reports on labor difficulties which provide background on the disputes and outlines any government action including the deployment of the State Police, intervention by the Governor, and the Labor Commissioner's role in mediating or arbitrating a settlement.

The Governor's executive records are probably the single most important body of governmental records relating to labor housed at the State Archives. Every state executive office communicates with the Governor on any significant matter affecting labor relations. Correspondence between the Governor's office and the state official or agency head provides insights into the chief executive's stance on a labor issue that generally will not find its way into a government report, press story, or formal message. So too, one will find correspondence from business leaders, labor unions and workers to the Governor expressing their points of view and his response.

Unfortunately, most of Nevada's 19th-century Governor's records have been lost with the exception of Territorial Governor James W. Nye. The 20th century is well-documented and includes the records of Governor John Sparks and his call to President Theodore Roosevelt for Federal troops to occupy Goldfield in 1907; the records of Governor Tasker L. Oddie which demonstrate his liberal use of State Police in labor disputes including their utilization in the strike at the White Pine County copper camps in 1912 where two workers were killed; the records of Governor Emmet Boyle, which provide substantial insights into labor relations during World War I and its aftermath, and particularly his support of anti-syndicalist legislation targeting the IWW; and the records of Governor Fred Balzar which give some indication of the state's position in labor difficulties associated with the construction of Hoover (Boulder) Dam and other Federal projects in the early 1930s.

Other governmental records that have value as labor resources include those of the State Councils of Defense for World Wars I and II, particularly as they relate to radicals, enemy aliens, and Japanese-Americans; the Employment Security Dept.; and the Nevada Administrative Code which contains all agency regulations.

Access: Currently, there is no published guide to the overall holdings of the State Archives, but there are in-house inventories to the various records groups which can be used by researchers on-site. Information about the State Archive's holdings is being fed to the RLIN data base on an on-going basis.

The research facilities are open 8 am to 5 pm, Monday–Friday. Staff limitations mandate research and photocopy fees for any large scale search and photocopying. For further information write to Jeff Kintop, State Archives Manager, at the Nevada Division of Archives and Records, 3579 Highway 50 East, Carson City, NV 89710; phone: (702) 687-5210.

THE TEXAS LABOR ARCHIVES

by
George N. Green

During the Southern Historical Association convention in Memphis, November 1966, some 20 young participants, including the author, organized the Association of Southern Labor Historians. Its purpose was to promote the neglected field of Southern labor history by encouraging the collection of labor records in various states and the presentation of scholarly labor papers at annual meetings concurrent with the Southern Historical Association.

In January 1967 I conferred with John Hudson, head librarian at the Univ. of Texas at Arlington (UTA), about the absence of primary resource materials for graduate and undergraduate study in history at the university and about the lack of labor research in the South and Southwest. When I mentioned this to one of my colleagues, Dr. Howard Lackman, he joined in the series of conversations. We learned that no university in the Southwest was soliciting labor records. And we learned that unions possessed tons of noncurrent records, many of which were destroyed from time to time. In late January Hudson and I sallied forth to our first labor meeting, a sub-regional gathering of United Auto Worker leaders in Grand Prairie. They thought the creation of a labor archives was a great idea. Encouragement to launch an archives also came from various Fort Worth and Dallas labor leaders whom we approached at random in the next month or so, particularly from former Mayor Willard Barr of Forth Worth, a typographer.

Professor Dick Shuttee, a labor economist at UTA, was an old friend of the secretary to the president of the Texas AFL-CIO in Austin; she was enthusiastic about the idea of an archives. This was our first of many experiences with secretaries who are strongly in favor of an archives. They are the ones who are sometimes inundated by records and

---

George N. Green is Professor of History at the University of Texas at Arlington.

are frequently charged with managing them. In this instance secretary Lynita Naughton was also keenly aware of the historical need to preserve records. In March or April, Hudson, Lackman, Shuttee, and I made the final decision to attempt to create a labor collection. We decided not to ask the campus administration if we could launch a labor archives, since we believed that "no" was its customary response to academic requests.

Our first overture to the president of the Texas AFL-CIO, Hank Brown, did not succeed. He was not impressed by a letter from three professors and a librarian whom he had never heard of. Hudson then informed UTA President Jack Woolf that the library had an archives and that it needed his signature on a letter and some modest financing. Our second approach to the AFL-CIO included a letter from Woolf, pledging his support, and was enhanced by the active backing of Mrs. Naughton and AFL-CIO Education Director Harold Tate. Brown and the other state leaders then informally agreed to encourage the establishment of a labor archives at UTA.

With the permission of the History Dept., Professor Lackman and I were given a half-summer salary to solicit records in the field, to contact individuals, locals, labor councils, and regional offices, and to begin the process of collecting union non-current materials. Mayor Barr informed us of the M.M. McKnight Memorial Fund of Forth Worth, designed to perpetuate the memory of the late labor leader and Mayor Pro-Tem of that city. The McKnight trustees had intended to establish a labor library, but they had not received enough money and the project had foundered. The trustees, along with Reecy McKnight, donated $800 for travel and mailing expenses for the summer of 1967.

Our initial strategy was to concentrate on seeking the endorsements of the various central labor councils in Texas' cities and the official stamp of approval at the Texas AFL-CIO convention in August. Lackman and I, and occasionally Hudson and Shuttee, addressed 15 or more central labor councils in June and July 1967. Remarks at each meeting stressed the need to preserve the spirit of unionism, the uniqueness of the collection in the Southwest, the capacity of UTA to accommodate the archives (given our new and empty library building), and the need for statewide cooperation. We also gently lobbied for the councils' assistance for a resolution of endorsement at the state convention. At several of the meetings Texas AFL-CIO leaders were present and they helped us secure favorable votes from some of the councils. Every council was receptive. One potent Houston labor leader, however, objected to our speaking to the labor councils before receiving the formal convention blessings of the Texas AFL-CIO. He probably had a point, but we were so deeply involved in the project by then that all I could do was alter the standard remarks in Houston. There I described the archives as a tentative effort that awaited the state body's endorsement; I asked for no records.

In July each of the 2500 or so local unions in the state received a letter of solicitation from UTA's labor archives and a brochure, hopefully to be displayed on the local bulletin board. These items were endorsed in the Texas AFL-CIO Secretary-Treasurer's monthly report to the membership. This mailing, the appearances before the central labor councils, and publicity in the labor press advertised UTA's labor collection throughout the state. By August we had acquired a considerable amount of historical labor records.

The donated materials included minutes of meetings, correspondence, contracts, bylaws, constitutions, financial records, broadsides of strikes and boycotts, scrapbooks, pamphlets, photographs, newspaper clippings, books, films, tapes, phonograph records, newssheets, ledgers, court cases, grievance records, arbitration reports, and labor newspapers.

From these materials we gleaned display items for a "History of Texas Labor" booth at the state AFL-CIO convention. The booth was eye-catching and very well attended. It evoked high compliments from labor leaders and from such guests as Senator Ralph Yarborough, who later contributed some congressional labor hearings, and Congressman Jim Wright, who sent us some 150 volumes of out-of-print NLRB decisions. The 1800 convention delegates voted unanimously to endorse UTA's Texas Labor Archives as the state body's official labor depository. All Texas locals and labor councils were urged to cooperate in the enterprise.

In 1968 the McKnight trustees provided Lackman and me with $1200 to make a more comprehensive tour of Texas and collect more records. In 1969 I was granted $400 by the School of Liberal Arts at UTA to tour central and coastal Texas for the purpose of collecting records and also interviewing labor leaders.

In April 1967 I had begun taping interviews. A major shortcoming, of course, was that so few people were involved in our project and we did not have the time to conduct the considerable research necessary for proper interviews. By the summer of 1969 only a half dozen people had been interviewed on tape. The pace picked up considerably in 1971, when a grant from the Zale Foundation allowed me to tape some 20 veteran labor leaders. Most were from the hispanic and black communities in which the Foundation was particularly interested. Over the years others have participated in the oral history project. People's His-

tory in Texas, an Austin-based research group, contributed 22 interviews, mostly of women, in a cooperative venture with UTA. Graduate
students Carr Winn, Jan Hart, Jim Reed, and David Ledel each conducted four or five oral histories as part of their thesis research.

In 1987 Bernard Rapoport, CEO of the American Income Life Insurance Company (which sells only to union members), put up $1250
for the oral history program, providing the archives could match it.
The Texas AFL-CIO, Dallas ironworkers, Fort Worth machinists, and
longshoreman Bill Follett did match it, and 20 unionists have since been
interviewed in various parts of the state. The oral history program is
ongoing, of course, and as of this writing some 115 labor leaders and
rank and file members have been interviewed, and 61 have been
transcribed.

The Texas labor movement is not rich or powerful, and all of us
most intimately associated with the archives through the years — archivist
Bob Gamble, 1969–1984, archivist Jane Boley, 1984–present, and myself — have not made a habit of asking unions for money. The Texas
AFL-CIO, Reecy McKnight, and the Forth Worth typographers local
have nevertheless contributed generously over the years.

The largest collections — filled with minutes and correspondence —
have been donated by the Texas AFL-CIO (well over 400 archival boxes),
the Packinghouse Workers (about 280 boxes), the Professional Air
Traffic Controllers Organization (PATCO) (about 250 boxes), the Amalgamated Meat Cutters (over 190 boxes), the Mullinax-Wells law firm
which specializes in labor issues (105 boxes), and the Machinists (over
90 boxes). The Packinghouse and Meat Cutter collections include regional files as well as local records. The PATCO records are national,
regional, and local. Other sizeable collections, in the 20 to 75 box range,
have been contributed by five Typographer locals, eleven Carpenter
locals, three Longshoremen locals, two Rubber Worker locals, seven
Electrician locals, three Building and Construction Trades Councils,
the Sam Houston Clinton law firm, which also has an active labor law
practice, George and Latane Lambert — representing the Ladies Garment Workers and political activity, the Fort Worth IATSE local, the
Texas Brotherhood of Locomotive Engineers, the West Texas district
of the Operating Engineers, and two Oil Worker locals and the district
office. Central labor councils from 11 cities donated trades assembly
and industrial union council records.

Smaller, but rich collections, ranging from 7 to 18 boxes, represent
the AFL-CIO Regional Office, American Federation of Government
Employees, United Farm Workers, Painters, Communications Workers,
Brotherhood of Railroad Trainmen, American Newspaper Guild, United

Sugar Workers, Ironworkers, Hatters, Office and Professional Employees, Retail Wholesale Department Store Clerks, and the State, County, and Municipal Employees.

Some records date back to the late 19th century. Typographical locals' minutes from Austin and Dallas, carpenters' minutes from Waco, San Antonio, and Austin, a few items on the Knights of Labor and on Eugene Debs, Brotherhood of Locomotive Firemen minutes from Temple, Longshoremen's minutes from Galveston, materials from the Brotherhood of Locomotive Firemen and Enginemen Legislative Board, Dallas Trades Assembly minutes, and San Antonio brewery workers' minutes (in German) are the oldest collections. The oldest single record is the Austin typographical minute book, which begins in 1870. Three collections extending back to the late 19th century were microfilmed from other archives — the Houston Street Railway Employees, the John L. Lewis Papers, and the American Federation of Labor-Sam Gompers Papers. Photographs are scattered throughout the holdings, but the most historic single collection is a dozen or so originals taken at the Thurber coal mines in the 1910s.

Some locals did not want to part with their original records, so the library began paying for microfilming in the fall of 1967. With a $1000 donation from the McKnight trustees and some initiative on the part of the head librarian, the library acquired its own microfilm camera in the fall of 1968. Sixteen collections were filmed before the camera was diverted to filming Yucatecan and Central American records, then was retired from service.

About three dozen Texas labor newspapers and newsletters have been collected or have been purchased from other archives' microfilmed holdings. They are published by locals, by regional and state bodies, and by the labor movements in various cities. They are housed with the library's newspapers rather than in the archives.

As of December 1989, there are over 220 processed labor collections totaling over 800 linear feet, and 18 political ones amounting to about 335 linear feet. There is a backlog of some 650–700 linear feet for both collections. Under current staffing arrangements, Jane Boley handles all labor and political records by herself, usually assisted by part-time students.

Political collections were added in the late 1960s, as it became obvious that the unions were constantly involved in political activity. The papers of former Congressman Dale Milford, a conservative Democrat, are the second largest collection in the archives, with over 370 boxes. Several liberal and conservative state senators and representatives and various political activists and political action groups have donated their correspondence and related materials. So has Bernard Rapoport, a major financier of liberal, Democratic candidates and causes in Texas.

The Texas Labor Archives of UTA is currently the only depository in the Southwest that actively seeks union records. In the late 1960s in this conservative state the mere presence of the labor archives was cited as a justification for the UT Austin archives to collect some papers of radicals, and it also helped inspire the establishment of the Southern Labor Archives at Georgia State Univ. in Atlanta. The collections are used primarily by undergraduate students writing term papers and graduate students writing theses, but also by occasional faculty and scholars from around the nation. Most of the usage comes from UTA history students, and, in fact, the first two history MA Essays written at UTA came from the labor archives. These records can also be used by students in political science, economics, urban studies, sociology, and business, but not many have done so.

Access: The Texas Labor Archives is open Monday-Friday 8 am to 5 pm, and Saturday 10 am to 2 pm, except holidays. The files are open to all researchers, though a few holdings have been restricted by request of the donor and unprocessed materials are not generally available to undergraduate researchers. Selected items may be photocopied. Subject lists describing the holdings of the archives in various fields of current interest include the contributions of blacks, Mexican-Americans, and women to Texas labor history, and significant strikes of the 19th and 20th centuries in the state. These lists are available upon request. Inquiries are welcomed and should be directed to Jane Boley, Head of the Archives, UTA Library, Box 19497, Arlington, Texas 76019; phone: (817) 273-3393.

SOURCES ON LABOR HISTORY AT THE SOUTHERN CALIFORNIA LIBRARY FOR SOCIAL STUDIES AND RESEARCH

by
Sarah Cooper

Labor history sources at the Southern California Library for Social Studies and Research in Los Angeles are part of a larger collection on 20th century social and political history developed by Library founder Emil Freed who died in 1982. When Freed opened the Library in 1963, he brought into being an institution that would house much of the material he had collected during a lifetime on the Left and in the labor movement. Though Los Angeles was Freed's base, the Library's holdings, particularly of books and pamphlets, reflect his zealous acquisition of a wide range of published and unpublished material dealing with regional, national, and international labor, minorities, Marxism, Communism, immigration, civil rights, and other social movements.

The idea of a Library to preserve the history of labor and the Left took firm hold in Freed's mind in the 1950s, when Freed rescued the personal libraries of friends who, vulnerable to the repression of the Cold War era, were on the verge of destroying their political books and pamphlets. To these collections Freed added his own accumulation of documents from various struggles in which he had been closely involved: the Unemployed Councils of the 1930s, the Hollywood studio strikes of the 1940s, and the Civil Rights Congress (CRC) of the late 1940s and early 1950s (he had served as the Los Angeles CRC's organizational director). His long, active membership in the Communist Party also meant that he amassed a voluminous collection of pamphlets and periodicals issued either by the Party or by organizations and unions that had close ties to it.

Beyond the 25,000 volume book collection, of which U.S. labor

---

Sarah Cooper has been director of the Southern California Library for Social Studies and Research since mid-1983.

history is a particular emphasis, the Library's 20,000 item pamphlet collection is a rich source for labor research. Labor organizations whose pamphlets are well represented in the Library's holdings include the Congress of Industrial Organizations; the Industrial Workers of the World, especially pertaining to the Los Angeles "Red Squad's" assault against the Wobblies on the San Pedro waterfront in the early 1920s; the International Ladies' Garment Workers' Union; the International Longshoremen's and Warehousemen's Union; the International Mine, Mill, and Smelter Workers; the Marine Workers Industrial Union; the United Auto Workers; the United Electrical, Radio, and Machine Workers of America (UE); and the United Steel Workers of America. While not comprehensive, there is some documentation from each for most decades since the 1930s. Labor pamphlets are complemented by a separate file, arranged alphabetically by union, of newsletters, publications, and in some cases proceedings for an even wider range of international unions, spanning the 1930s to the 1980s.

There are few collections of union records per se in the Library's holdings. Several special collections, however, are concerned with labor issues or labor activists. There are also fragmentary records from the Los Angeles office of the California CIO Council, which occupied a building during the 1940s not far from the Library's current site in South Central Los Angeles. James Daugherty, West coast regional director for the Utility Workers Organizing Committee in the late 1930s and the last president of the California CIO Council before the national CIO revoked the state council's charter in 1950, donated these records to the Library. He also gave the Library a vast collection of labor pamphlets and periodicals accumulated during his many years as an organizer for UE and Mine, Mill.

The Library's collection on the Hollywood studio strikes of 1946 and 1947 contains short-lived strike newspapers (e.g., the *Hollywood Atom*, the *Hollywood Sun*, the *Picket Line*) and other ephemera issued by the International Alliance of Theatrical Stage Employees and the Conference of Studio Unions. Complementing this collection is *Hollywood Lockout*, a 20 minute black and white silent film on the 1947 strike which shut down production at Republic, Columbia, Warner Brothers, and MGM.

Several organizational collections, legal records, and personal papers held by the Library are important sources for labor history, particularly for researchers looking at the struggles of immigrant labor activists whose livelihoods and organizing activities were threatened by the Smith Act and later the McCarran-Walter Act. The Harry Bridges Legal Collection is the most notable example in the Library's holdings of an immigrant labor activist's legal battle to avoid deportation. The

Bridges legal records are the voluminous files of lawyer Richard Gladstein, documenting the long and ultimately successful battle to prevent the U.S. government from deporting the famous longshore leader to his native Australia.

The Library's holdings of papers include those of Robert W. Kenny, civil liberties lawyer, counsel to the Hollywood Ten, California attorney general in the 1940s, and first president of the Library board. Kenny's papers provide documentation on the defense of foreign-born labor activists. Of special note in the Kenny Collection is the series on Guatemalan-born Luisa Moreno Bemis, a regional director of the Food, Tobacco and Agricultural Workers Union and a vice-president of the California CIO. The Moreno files document the efforts by Kenny, Carey McWilliams, and others to prevent Moreno from being deported following her appearance in 1948 before the Tenney Committee, California's Un-American Activities Committee. Under government pressure, Moreno left the U.S. the following year and subsequently settled in Mexico. The collection contains her correspondence with Kenny and his partner Robert Morris into the 1950s.

Papers of Leo Gallagher, another important Southern California civil liberties lawyer, include files about his defense of labor activists, particularly in his capacity as a lawyer for the International Labor Defense. The collection documents his works, under ILD auspices, as an advocate for labor organizers being prosecuted in the late 1920s and early 1930s under California's Criminal Syndicalism law. There is also correspondence between Gallagher and J. B. McNamara, who had been convicted of the 1910 *Los Angeles Times* bombing. These letters, exchanged during the 1930s, pertain primarily to McNamara's treatment in prison.

Organizational collections which shed light on the convergence between labor and civil liberties in Southern California are records of the Los Angeles Committee for the Protection of the Foreign Born and the Los Angeles Civil Rights Congress. In the late 1940s and early 1950s, both organizations continually came to the defense of immigrant or minority workers whose civil rights were being undermined, especially after the passage of the McCarran-Walter Act.

Finally, a large collection of personal papers from composer Earl Robinson offers researchers a source for examining the cultural dimension of labor and progressive movements since the 1930s. The collection contains documentation on Robinson's work as a songwriter (*Joe Hill, Ballad for Americans, The House I Live In*) and correspondence with his associates and friends, including Woody Guthrie, Pete Seeger, and others in the People's Song movement.

The Library's films, especially from the 1930s, are another valuable source for research on labor, particularly in California. Most of the 1930s films were produced by the Los Angeles Film and Photo League and document or dramatize poverty in Los Angeles during the Depression (e.g., *Conditions in Los Angeles*), farmworker strikes (El Monte berry pickers; Kern County cotton workers), and labor demonstrations in San Pedro and San Diego. There are several short films on the campaign to free Tom Mooney, the California labor hero imprisoned for his unjust conviction in connection with a bombing of a 1916 Preparedness Day Parade in San Francisco. There is footage of the scene at the 1932 Olympics when several Mooney supporters dashed from the crowd at the Los Angeles Coliseum onto the track and pulled off their shirts to reveal "Free Tom Mooney" banners. Other footage documents victory rallies in San Francisco and Los Angeles when California Governor Culbert Olson pardoned Mooney in 1938.

Through a series of grants from the American Film Institute/National Endowment for the Arts Film Preservation program, the Library has in recent years been able to have preservation work done on about 20 of its documentary films, including virtually all the 1930s and 1940s films on labor. These preservation projects have made it possible for the Library to make its holdings more accessible both to academic researchers and to the many contemporary documentary filmmakers seeking footage of strikes and demonstrations from those decades.

While the Library has not developed as a full-fledged *archive* that preserves the records of trade union locals, it is keenly interested in providing more documentation on and stimulating interest in Los Angeles labor history. To that end, it has sponsored several programs pertaining to California labor history and selectively undertaken documentation projects on local unions. The pilot was a major Library project on the history of the Los Angeles International Ladies' Garment Workers' Union (ILGWU). This effort was begun in late 1986; project staff conducted primary research on the history of the ILGWU locally, organized a public conference which involved past and present garment workers as both audience and participants, and produced a short history of the Los Angeles ILGWU, coauthored by UCLA labor historian and Library board member John Laslett and Library Assistant Director Mary Tyler — *The ILGWU in Los Angeles, 1907–1988* (Inglewood, CA: Ten Star Press, 1989). This publication is the first in a projected Library series of *Occasional Papers in Los Angeles Working Class History*. Under consideration for the future are a tour of Los Angeles labor history landmarks and a project on the Los Angeles CIO.

The Library's efforts in recent years to bring more attention to the history of the Los Angeles labor movement fits with a gradual narrowing of the broad collecting scope that characterized the Library during most of its existence. In 1988, six years after Emil Freed's death and 25 years after the Library's founding, the Library board explicitly endorsed a *regional* collecting and education mission centered on labor, minority, and grassroots social movements *in* Southern California, particularly the Los Angeles metropolitan area. With the core Freed collection consolidated, appraised, and partially organized, the Library today is in a position to more clearly turn its attention to the great need for a regional institution to focus its documentation efforts on Southern California labor history.

Access: The Library is open to the public five days a week, Tuesday through Saturday, 10 am–4 pm. Registers or finding aids exist for most of the special collections. Copies of them, as well as the Library brochure and quarterly newsletter, *Heritage,* can be obtained by calling the Library at (213) 759-6063, or by writing Sarah Cooper, Director, Southern California Library for Social Studies and Research, 6120 South Vermont Avenue, Los Angeles, California 90044.

THE URBAN ARCHIVES CENTER
AT CALIFORNIA STATE UNIVERSITY,
NORTHRIDGE

by
Robert G. Marshall

The Urban Archives Center (UAC) at California State Univ., North-ridge (CSUN), is located at the north end of the San Fernando Valley approximately 30 miles from downtown Los Angeles. The Center was established in 1979 through the efforts of university faculty and con-cerned community organizations and leaders. The primary purpose of the Center has been to collect the historically significant records of voluntary associations and prominent citizens who have directed growth in Los Angeles County and influenced government and public thinking since the beginning of the 20th century.

One of the first major subject areas of concern in establishing a detailed collecting policy for the Archives was the scarcity of research sources available in the field of Southern California labor history. Other major subject areas developed during the Center's first 10 years of oper-ation include: trade, tourism, and urban development; education; minority and ethnic organizations; politics; social services; women of Los Angeles; and recreation, sports and leisure studies.

In cooperation with the Los Angeles County Federation of Labor, AFL-CIO, the UAC undertook a comprehensive survey of labor records in Los Angeles County in the spring of 1979 under a partial grant re-ceived through the National Endowment for the Humanities. The Center sent out 800 questionnaires inquiring about materials being stored in union halls and administrative offices. The responses revealed the ex-istence of a wealth of untapped historical documents as well as the will-ingness of many labor organizations to participate in an archival pro-gram. Out of these efforts the Urban Archives Center was able to acquire

Robert G. Marshall is archivist at the Urban Archives Center.

substantial collections for labor research and to make available copies of the *Survey of Labor Collections in Los Angeles County*, a guide that directed researchers to local resources.

The Urban Archives' labor collections document many important events in the nation's labor movement since the early 1930s. The union struggle to organize, participation in wartime industry, the separation and later merger of the AFL and the CIO, the post-war strike of Holly-wood directors and Disney's animators, the struggle for organizing California's farm workers, racial conflict within the union movement, labor's growing concern about automation, and the 1967 *Los Angeles Herald Examiners* strike are only a few of the subject areas covered in the Center's extensive labor holdings, which include:

ASSOCIATED TEACHERS OF LOS ANGELES
Papers, 1966–1971; 5 cubic feet (unprocessed)

Associated Teachers of Los Angeles (ATLA) was formed in 1932 as a federation of organizations representing elementary and high school teachers, principals, counselors, nurses, and truant officers. It was organized to provide a unified representation to the Board of Education. In the late 1960s ATLA merged with other Los Angeles teachers organizations, first becoming the Associated Classroom Teachers of Los Angeles, and later, the United Teachers of Los Angeles in association with American Federation of Teachers, Local 1079.

The collection, donated by Harold Corbin, former ATLA official and long-time Los Angeles school teacher, is an excellent resource for research into the Los Angeles teachers' strike of 1971. Materials include agreements, conference programs, correspondence, fact sheets, handbooks, journals, minutes, newsclippings, reprints, and speeches. Several audio-tapes from ATLA conferences are also included in the collection.

CALIFORNIA FEDERATION OF TEACHERS, AFT, AFL-CIO
Papers, 1947–1974; 45 linear feet (semi-processed)

The California Federation of Teachers (CFT) was formed in 1919 to help facilitate the process of collective bargaining in public and private education. Its program is to improve salaries and working conditions for teachers, and to lobby for improved public support for education in California. CFT is the California affiliate of the American Federation of Teachers. CFT lobbying efforts and legislative advocacy in Sacramento are well represented in this extensive collection. Correspondents in the papers include governors Edmund G. Brown Sr. and Ronald Reagan. The collection includes agendas, annual conference proceedings, by-laws, committee and officer reports, constitutions, correspondence, financial records, grievance case files, legislative bills and acts pertaining to education, minutes, policy statements, press releases, speeches and numerous publications of the CFT and local affiliates like the United Teachers of Los Angeles.

DIRECTORS GUILD OF AMERICA, INC.
Papers, 1939–1978; 185 linear feet (semi-processed)

The Screen Directors Guild (SDG) was formed in 1936 by ten notable motion picture directors. It sought to promote closer cooperation among individual directors, to bring greater professional recognition to directors and to preserve the creative freedoms of the director in film making. In 1940 the Guild won its first collective bargaining agreement with a producers association. During WWII many directors joined the military and made newsreels and films promoting the war effort. In 1948 the SDG inaugurated the annual "Best Direction" award.

The SDG extended its membership to include television directors in the 1950s and became the Screen Directors Guild of America, then SDGA merged with the Radio and Television Directors Guild to form the Directors Guild of America, Inc.

The DGA Collection consists of the organizational records of the DGA and its predecessor organizations. Holdings include bylaws, minutes of executive and local council meetings, election returns, guild history, labor agreements, merger agreements, property records, arbitration and grievance case files, deceased member files and proceedings. Also included are general subject files which document censorship, cable TV, foreign broadcasting, film festivals, minorities, women directors and cruelty to animals in the movies.

GOLDNER, PAUL J. (UNITED AUTO WORKERS, LOCAL 645)
Papers, 1937–1977; 12.5 linear feet (processed)

Paul Goldner is former president of United Auto Workers Local 645, representing workers of the General Motors Assembly Plant in Van Nuys, CA. The records cover selected aspects of his union activities. Material includes correspondence, educational handbooks, grievance settlements, meeting summaries, minutes, national agreements, negotiation proposals and demands, press releases, speeches and related documents. The collection also includes various issues of *The Valley Auto and Air News, Monthly Labor Review* and *Our Union Heritage.*

INTERNATIONAL ASSOCIATION OF MACHINISTS AND AEROSPACE WORKERS, AFL-CIO, DISTRICT LODGE 727
Papers, Bound Volumes, Photographs, 1941–1977; 19 linear feet (semi-processed)

This Burbank, California IAM local was formed in the 1930s. It was highly successful during World War II in improving working conditions for the 30,000 workers employed at the Lockheed-Vega Plant. Also during the war, the union actively recruited women and made leadership positions available to them. The collection consists of 36 bound volumes of the *American Aeronaut*, District 727's weekly publication and an extensive collection of press photographs. Manuscript material in the collection includes transcripts from proceedings of the National War Labor Board for 1944, president's reports, pamphlets, shop-steward manuals and news clippings.

INTERNATIONAL LONGSHOREMEN'S AND WAREHOUSEMEN'S UNION, LOCAL 13, AFL-CIO

Papers, 1933–1989; Audio tapes, 1966–1987; 52 linear feet (processed); 10 linear feet (unprocessed)

ILWU Local 13 of Wilmington, CA was established in 1933 and has since become the largest longshoremen local on the West Coast, representing the dock workers at Los Angeles Harbor. In 1937, Local 13 actively supported other Pacific Coast longshoremen for separation from the AFL, joining the CIO. The collection includes extensive materials on the internal structure and procedures of the union, race relation problems faced by the union immediately following the end of World War II, and the change-over to automation on the docks which directly affected ILWU membership. The collection consists of correspondence, executive board meeting minutes, committee minutes, arbitration proceedings, membership ledgers and records, rulings of the Pacific Coast Maritime Industry Board, strike bulletins, labor agreements and contracts, and proceedings of the Longshore, Ship Clerks and Walking Bosses' Caucus. Audio tapes of regular local meetings, strike meetings, and over 60 oral histories of individual ILWU members are recent additions.

LEONARD, NORMAN, AND WILLIAM H. CARDER COLLECTION

Papers, 1942–1983; 10 linear feet (processed)

Attorney Norman Leonard has represented the ILWU, other unions and left-wing movements since the 1930s. Over the years, Leonard has served as counsel in many labor disputes over civil rights, racial discrimination, hiring and registration issues, and unfair labor practices. During the McCarthy era of the early 1950s, he represented several members of the Communist Party. The collection consists of case documents pertaining specifically to ILWU Local 13 and other Southern California longshore labor issues, hearings before the National Labor Relations Board and internal conflicts within the union itself. The materials include correspondence, evidential and research papers, trial proceedings and related legal records. Leonard's papers for Northern California are located at San Francisco State Univ.

LOS ANGELES COUNTY FEDERATION OF LABOR, AFL-CIO

Papers, 1937–1975; Microfilm, 1937–1971; 35 linear feet; 19 microfilm reels (semi-processed)

In 1959, four years after the national AFL and CIO merged in 1955, the Los Angeles affiliates of both organizations—the Los Angeles Central Labor Council and the Los Angeles Council of the CIO—merged with five other area AFL affiliates. This organization became the Los Angeles County Federation of Labor. LACFL is comprised of delegates from AFL-CIO locals. It is not a governing body, but rather a unifying force in the Los Angeles labor movement. Among the County Federation's concerns are strike coordination, labor education, health and welfare of union members, fair employment practices and civil rights, industrial safety and accident prevention, employment and disability insurance, housing, Labor Day observances and organizing non-union workers. The bulk of the collection consists of the CIO Council's office files through 1958 and includes correspondence, minutes, pamphlets, scrapbooks, and news clippings. *The L.A. Citizen*, the major voice of the Los Angeles County Federation of Labor, is available on microfilm. The papers also include extensive files of the Save Our State Committee formed in 1958 to defeat the California Right-to-Work Initiative.

LOS ANGELES NEWSPAPER GUILD, AFL-CIO
Papers, 1936–1974; 60 linear feet (unprocessed)

The Los Angeles Newspaper Guild, AFL-CIO (LANG), was formed in 1936. It represents a large multilevel work force in the newspaper industry which today includes deliverers, drivers, pressmen, reporters, and rollers. During the Guild's over 50-year history, it has launched three significant strikes against the *Los Angeles Herald-Examiner*, the Hearst owned newspaper: in 1947, 1951 and 1967. The 1967 strike was the most bitter, lasting almost seven years, until 1973. The collection provides extensive documentation of the 1967 *Herald-Examiner* strike. It includes issues of the guild newsletter *On the Line* that chronicled the strike, correspondence between the guild and management, administrative and correspondence files for its Los Angeles locals, and four publicity films.

LOS ANGELES TYPOGRAPHICAL UNION, LOCAL 174, AFL-CIO
Photographs, 1967–1972; 1979; 1 linear foot (processed)

Founded in 1875, Local 174 of the International Typographical Union is the oldest continuously functioning labor organization in Los Angeles. The major papers of the local are still located in the union's offices. The UAC holdings consist mainly of photographs depicting the *Los Angeles Herald-Examiner* strike from 1967 to 1972 and two short films, *Support Strikers Versus* Herald-Examiner and *Return to Tyranny*. Printed materials in the collection include handbills and a manual for picketers.

MILLER, RUTH
Pamphlets, 1930–1970; 14 linear feet (unprocessed)
Not opened until processing completed

Ruth Miller was assistant to the vice-president of the Amalgamated Clothing and Textile Workers Union (ACTWU). Formerly, Miller served as ACTWU's education director in Los Angeles. As education director, she actively collected labor pamphlets and literature on a variety of union-related subjects including automation, right-to-work laws, adult education, and the farm workers movement. She has also held leadership positions in the Coalition of Labor Union Women.

The collection consists of leaflets, newsletters, pamphlets, and reports published by ACTWU, other unions, and federal and state agencies concerned with the textile industry as well as some correspondence and newsclippings.

MONT, MAX
Papers, 1960–1976; 13 linear feet (processed)

In 1951, Max Mont was Western Regional Director for the Los Angeles Jewish Federation-Council's Jewish Labor Committee [JLC]. In addition to his involvement with JLC, Mont participated in the struggle for equal rights on behalf of racial minorities, farm workers, the elderly, and women. In the 1960s, he played an important role in developing and coordinating the activities of the Emergency Committee to Aid Farm Workers, the California Committee for Fair Practices, Californians Against Proposition 14, and the Los Angeles County Federation of Labor's Committee on Student Integration as well as working closely with Governor Edmund Brown's office conducting lobbying efforts on behalf of civil rights issues.

Mont's personal collection documents local labor and agricultural labor history during the 1960s and 1970s, the civil rights movement, fair housing and integration battles and similar concerns of the Jewish Labor Committee. The collection includes agendas and minutes, campaign material, correspondence, flyers, news clippings, pamphlets, policy statements, reports, speeches, and photographs.

MOTION PICTURE SCREEN CARTOONIST GUILD, LOCAL 839, AFL-CIO
Papers, 1937–1949; 2.5 linear feet (processed)

The Hollywood screen cartoonists held their first union meeting in 1937, and drafted a formal constitution in 1939, adopting the name, Screen Cartoonist Guild (SCG). A year later the guild won recognition at MGM and Walter Lanz studios, and launched its first major strike for union recognition at the Walt Disney Studios, an effort that lasted into 1941. Disney strike documents include leaflets which depict Mickey Mouse, Donald Duck and other famous Disney characters in the guise of union militants; an address from Walt Disney on labor matters; correspondence of strike organizers Herb Sorrell and Pepe Ruiz; and strike cartoons and photographs.

NATIONAL ASSOCIATION OF LETTER CARRIERS, NORTH HOLLYWOOD LADIES AUXILIARY, BRANCH #1094
Papers, 1941–1986; 2 linear feet (semi-processed)

No Restrictions

RETAIL CLERKS UNION, LOCAL 770, OF THE UNITED FOOD AND COMMERCIAL WORKERS INTERNATIONAL UNION, AFL- CIO
Non-manuscript material, 1942–1949; 6 scrapbooks; 24 photographs (processed)
No Restrictions

The Retail Clerks Union, Local 770 represents organized workers in the retail food-processing and grocery industry. For many years Local 770 was led by Joseph De Silva, one of the most charismatic labor leaders in Southern California history. The collection includes scrapbooks and photographs mostly commemorating De Silva's years in office.

VAN BOURG, VICTOR
Papers, 1965–1969; 1.2 linear feet (processed)

Victor Van Bourg is a noted California labor attorney. He represented the United Farm Workers, AFL-CIO, and its predecessor organizations since 1947 and the California Federation of Teachers. His legal case files reflect his dedicated involvement in the farm worker's struggles of the 1960s and the period of transition in farm worker union history. The Van Bourg collection begins in 1965 before the merger of the United Farm Workers' Union and the Agricultural Workers Organizing Committee, and covers its subsequent affiliation with the AFL-CIO. Significant legal battles documented through correspondence, court proceedings, memorandums, news clippings and related records include: AWOC vs. Di Giorgio Fruit Corporation, Di Giorgio Corporation vs. Cesar Chavez, et al., and Edmundson; Purity Market vs. San Francisco, the 1966 Delano Strike, and CFT vs. Oxnard Elementary School District.

Additional labor collections acquired by the Urban Archives Center include the following: Associated Teachers of Los Angeles (papers, 1966–1971), California Shipbuilding Corporation (published material, 1941–1945), Directors Guild of America, Inc. (papers, 1939–1978), Los Angeles County Employees Association (1 engraving plate), Los Angeles Typographical Union, Local 174, AFL-CIO (papers, 1967–1972, 1979), Ruth Miller Collection (pamphlets, 1930–1970 [Ruth Miller was assistant to the vice-president of the Amalgamated Clothing and Textile Workers Union]), Retail Clerks Union, Local 770, of the United Food and Commercial Workers International Union, AFL-CIO (6 scrapbooks, 24 photographs, 1942–1949), Union Temple Association (11 items, 1918–1919; 1957–1958). The UAC has also been slowly gathering together the union papers of several CSUN faculty organizations during the past year.

Many of the labor collections include audio tapes, broadsides, maps, photographs and like non-manuscript materials. Oral History collections at the Urban Archives Center include audio-cassette, reel-to-reel tapes, and transcriptions of interviews that compliment our manuscript and non-manuscript holdings. Among the more interesting:

Agricultural Workers – Van Bourg, Victor
Communication Workers of America – Stada, Robert
Longshoremen and Warehousemen – Leonard, Norman; ILWU
Los Angeles Teachers' Strike – Patino, Peter; Purcell, Tim
United Auto Workers – Goldner, Paul
Valley State College Teachers' Strike – Labovitz, Larry

More comprehensive descriptive finding guides to each collection are available upon request to the Archives. There are some confidentiality restrictions. The collections are non-circulating.

Access: The Urban Archives Center is located in Oviatt Library, Room 4, California State Univ., Northridge, Northridge, CA 91330. The hours are 9 am–4:30 pm, Monday–Friday, also 6–9 pm on Wednesdays. The Center is also open the last 10 Saturdays of every semester from 10 am–4 pm. For additional information write Robert Marshall or call (818) 885-2487.

THE LABOR ARCHIVES AND RESEARCH CENTER AT SAN FRANCISCO STATE UNIVERSITY

by
Lynn A. Bonfield and Leon J. Sompolinsky

The Labor Archives and Research Center was established in 1985 as part of the library system of San Francisco State Univ. Previously, despite San Francisco's reputation as a labor town, no archival repository in Northern California had actively collected the records relating to working people and their organizations even though there was a substantial body of published scholarship on the labor history of the San Francisco Bay Area.[1] Unfortunately, no comprehensive California labor oral history projects had been undertaken either, although some outstanding individual oral histories of labor leaders had been completed mainly through the Regional Oral History Office at The Bancroft Library and the Institute of Industrial Relations (both part of the Univ. of California, Berkeley) and the International Longshoremen's and Warehousemen's Union (ILWU).

The founding of the Center stems from the activities of three interested parties — each with a vital stake in its establishment and each essential to the effort. First, there was a dedicated group of labor leaders whose garages and closets held files, photographs, banners, and other historical material documenting their lives and local labor's past. Supporting these men and women were a group of local unions with boxes of noncurrent records crowding needed storage areas. Second, there was at San Francisco State Univ. a president, Paul F. Romberg, who with his close advisors recognized the importance of labor history. They

---

Lynn A. Bonfield, who has been an archivist at the California Historical Society, has served as director of the Center since its establishment. Leon J. Sompolinsky served as archivist at the Center from 1986 to 1989 when his status changed to consultant.

[1]See Mitchell Slobodek, *A Selective Bibliography of California Labor History* (Los Angeles, CA, 1964). Gordon Webb has compiled a bibliography of MA Essays and PhD diss. on the San Francisco Bay Area labor history.

wanted a research center devoted to its study. Supporting the University administration was a group of faculty members, particularly from the history department and special collections in the library, who recognized the danger of losing the accumulated records of an important part of local history.

The third component involved the financial backing for the proposed center. From the start it was obvious that neither the labor movement nor the University could divert funds from other programs. In 1984 labor representatives devised a plan to go directly to the California State Legislature with a strong lobbying effort. It began with an approach to a carefully selected group of labor-backed legislators by a team of representatives from organized labor and scholars from the Southwest Labor Studies Association and the Bay Area Labor History Workshop. Within months the effort was successful and a $60,000 line item was added to the budget allocation for the San Francisco State University library to establish a labor archives in 1985. An annual continuing allocation was assured.

By coincidence, at the same time, the University offered land near the campus border to the California State Library for the location of a branch known as The Sutro Library. Within this building, a wing was reserved for the use of the university, and this eventually became the home of the Labor Archives and Research Center. The space includes a reading room, work room, office space, and a stack area accommodating 5000 linear feet of shelving.

The final piece to fall into place was the decision by the director of the University library that the Center must be administered by an archivist with a professional library degree. This meant that the head of the Center would be on an equal footing with the faculty within both the library system and the teaching departments. At first this decision caused some distress in the labor community, but when the labor movement was given an active role in the national search for the best candidate, the problem soon dissipated. In addition to the director, the Center's staff includes a half-time archivist who is also part of the library faculty, a part-time consultant for visual collections and exhibits, and a half-time archival assistant at the beginning level.

The first issue for the Center was the acceptance of a collecting policy. A compromise was worked out in which the six counties surrounding San Francisco are specified in the collecting policy, and nothing from Northern California is explicitly excluded. Currently, over 90% of the records collected have originated in the San Francisco and Oakland areas.

Material of national origin is collected only if it helps reveal local labor history. Under this last provision, the Center has collected printed histories of international unions and visuals such as the CIO Political Action Committee posters by Ben Shahn.

In determining the types of records to collect, top priority has been given to primary sources: the archives of labor organizations and the personal papers of working men and women. These include labor leaders and the rank-and-file, union and nonunion workers. Special circumstances have made some subjects a low priority for collection. Among these are agricultural labor because the United Farm Workers archives are collected by the Reuther Library at Wayne State Univ., and the motion picture industry, whose union records are maintained in the Los Angeles area.

Labor periodicals caused another problem, because they are space-consuming and can be found elsewhere. It was finally decided that if a title were collected by the Univ. of California, Berkeley, or was included in the labor newspaper microfilm project of the Historical Society of Wisconsin, the Center would not add it to the shelves. We have made exceptions, in particular for the San Francisco Labor Council's *Clarion* (1902–1937) which came with the Council's archives, and the *Western Worker* (1932–1937) which came with the *People's World* Collection. Of course the Center does collect many local newsletters, both union and nonunion, and in some cases it holds rare copies of shop papers such as *Taxi Worker* (1935–1937) of the San Francisco Bay Area Teamsters. From the beginning the Center has emphasized the acquisition of visual materials suitable for exhibits. In particular we have sought out photographs, posters, handbills, picket signs, record album covers, prints, and other non-textual materials. A series of well-publicized exhibits has been carried out at the Center, at The Sutro Library, and at the J. Paul Leonard Library on campus. A traveling exhibit is available for labor heritage and union events. The publicity these exhibits have brought to the Center is far reaching and has educated workers and labor leaders as well as potential researchers about our collections.

In early 1987 the Center was designated as the official history participant in the Golden Gate Bridge's 50th Anniversary Celebration. A major exhibit on the building of the Bridge was produced by the Center and seen by over 20,000 viewers. A public program honoring the original workers and their families was held during the May anniversary events. "A Directory to Resources on the Building of the Golden Gate Bridge" was published, listing material in 35 collections across the nation. One result was to enhance the Center's Collections. We were given scores of snapshots by various donors of iron workers, laborers, teamsters, electricians, and painters hanging from half completed towers. A compelling scrapbook recording the experiences of a bridge builder who died in an accident on the Bridge three months before its opening was donated by the family. This album was put together in the late 1930s by the mother of bridge worker Fred Dummatzen as she mourned her son. It would be hard to find a better example of a public program which enriched an archives.

Over the years the Center has planned a range of special programs. In 1986 we held three; in 1987, five; in 1988, two; and in 1989, four, including a major exhibit on "150 Years of Photography, a Celebration." In 1988 with foundation help, the Center and the local chapters of the Coalition of Labor Union Women co-sponsored a two-day conference on "California Working Women in the Decade of the Forties." The video of the sessions is being edited to a half-hour program for classroom use, so students can understand the historical context of some of the perennial issues of the female workplace including child care, equal pay and advancement, and union representation of women's issues. In June 1989 the Center sponsored an exhibit and program on "Chinese and Japanese Workers in California — the Pioneers" with funding from the California Lottery. Material from six different libraries was on display including a 1906 diary of a Japanese immigrant from the Center's collection.

Also in 1989 the Center published "The San Francisco Labor History Tour," a map and brochure describing events and places in the downtown area which are significant in labor history.[2] Contributions from local unions and individuals paid for the complete production of the well-illustrated hand-out. Since 1985 the Center has accessioned over 400 donations. These include 612 books, 262 volumes of 16 serial titles, 130 casssette tapes, 19 films and videos, 112 long playing records, and 61 posters. The primary focus, however, is the archives of labor organizations and the papers of individual labor leaders and workers. In total, 11 unions have transferred their archives to the Center.

Since gold rush days, the Bay Area has been a major center for the print industry on the West Coast. Bay Area Typographical Union Local 21 obtained a charter from the National Typographical Union in 1885 and thus claims to be San Francisco's oldest union still in existence. Unfortunately, the archives at the Center (39.5 cubic feet) are primarily from after the 1906 earthquake. Membership cards are particularly complete and rich in immigration and genealogical detail.

Another ITU chartered union, the San Francisco-Oakland Mailers

---

[2]Individual copies of "San Francisco Labor History Tour" and catalogs from the different exhibits mentioned in this article can be obtained by writing the Labor Archives and Research Center.

Union #18, recently deposited its records. Mailers are responsible for the bundling and delivery of print shop products, primarily newspapers and other periodically distributed publications. Minutes are complete since 1901, and the early arbitration records document economic and working conditions during the Progressive Era. Chapel reports also articulate specific shop conditions.

The most requested collection (56 cubic feet) has been the San Francisco Labor Council (1965–1988). The Council serves as a central clearing house for organizing efforts, and its files are crucial for understanding the intimate ties between the labor movement and the social justice community. Although most of the Council's early records are at The Bancroft Library (Univ. of California, Berkeley), the Center has been designated as the Council's official repository for records created since 1965 and these reflect its interest in civil rights, housing and urban development, poverty programs, education, the criminal justice system, and changes in the economic base and government of the city. Office files are made up of correspondence to and from the affiliates and the secretary-treasurer's files document the Council's representation on the boards of county, city and grassroots community groups.

Files relating to organizing on the California State Univ. campuses have been placed in the Center. In the collection are minutes from the 1920s of the Association of State College School Instructors, the predecessor of the current faculty union. Both the United Professors of California (1965–1984, 19 cubic feet) and the California Faculty Association (1983–1987, 3 cubic feet) have made the Center their official repository. Organizing records from the 1960s forward are strong as well as papers defining the current issues in higher education such as work load, lectureship designation, and most recently, the cost of on-campus parking.

The commitment to worker and trade union education is seen in the historical files (2 cubic feet) of the California Labor School (1936–1956). Not a month goes by that a new donor does not add to the collection of class catalogs, theater and music programs, art works, and photographs. This unusual educational program closed in the 1950s, a victim of the Cold War, but the memories of its students continue.

Case files of attorney Norman Leonard record the activities of workers on the waterfront, in the factories, and in the fields. Since the New Deal, Leonard and his partners have represented unions such as the ILWU; Marine Cooks' and Stewards' Association of the Pacific Coast; the International Federation of Architects, Engineers, Chemists and Technicians; and the United Cannery, Agricultural, Packing and Allied Workers of America. Only two series of cases have been processed: those of the Smith Act defendants and the various deportation/denaturalization trials of ILWU official Harry Bridges. Besides legal documents, the Bridges case files include minutes, speeches, local police and FBI documents, broadsides, posters, and press clippings from mainstream, labor, and radical newspapers. The practice of government spies infiltrating the labor movement is clear from papers retrieved from the wastebasket of the American Legion by a building janitor sympathetic to labor. The Bridges' case files were collected and meticulously cross-indexed on cards in order to provide the defense with immediate access to information regarding any person who might be called as a witness, whether sympathetic or not. Therefore, the cards give information on almost everyone involved in the West Coast labor movement in the 1930s. A recent researcher found over 100 cards on civil liberties attorney Leo Gallagher who was accused of participating in the successful plot to run a "Free Tom Mooney" banner around the track during the opening ceremonies of the 1932 Olympics in Los Angeles.

The Bay Area's service economy includes many so-called women's employment positions which the Center is committed to documenting. Some of the earliest source materials on women workers are to be found in a scrapbook from the turn of the century on cooks, waiters, and waitresses. Yet to be explored by researchers are the records (5 cubic feet) of the Bookbinders and Bindery Women's Union (1902–1970) which illustrate gender-related labor issues. Organizing labor in Chinatown sweatshops is a topic of research in the records (1.5 cubic feet) of the San Francisco Joint Board of the International Ladies Garment Workers Union (1931–1947) the bulk of whose papers are at Cornell Univ. Store clerks are documented in the collections from Retail Store Employees Union Local 410R (1909–1984, 17 cubic feet) and Department Store Employees Union Local 1100 (1937–1981, 1 cubic foot).

More recent women's collections include the archives (5 cubic feet) of WAGE, the Union Women's Alliance to Gain Equality (1971–1982) which tried to place women's issues on the agendas at union halls, government hearings, and among the unorganized in the 1970s. Household Workers Rights, a project of Union WAGE, has placed its papers at the Center. These documents address problems faced by domestic servants, the majority of whom are minority women.

With the acquisition of the records (20 cubic feet) of the United Electrical, Radio and Machine Workers of America in the East Bay, San Jose, and Sunnyvale (1944–1981), researchers now can study the workers who built and repaired the dynamoelectric machines powering modern industry. These records, arranged by shop locations, include minutes, financial information, organizing drives, pay and fringe benefits, printed material, work rules issues, and photographs. The jurisdictional disputes with the rival AFL-CIO union (the International Brotherhood of Electrical Workers) is evident as is the tragic tale of runaway shops which have drained labor membership roles and community coffers.

Over 70 feet of West Coast arbitration records dating from 1934–1939 and 1944–1949 were transferred from the Institute of Industrial Relations Library in Berkeley. Prominent arbitrators represented in the collection are Clark Kerr, Wayne Morse, and Paul Elliel.[3] An oral history interview with Tom Nicolopulos also adds to the Center's arbitration files.

Researchers looking for waterfront material still will want to begin with the Anne Rand Memorial Library of the ILWU. But the Center does have the archives (33.5 cubic feet) of the Maritime Federation of the Pacific (1935–1942). This federation of maritime and waterfront unions grew out of the unity forged in the 1934 General Strike and documents the difficult transition from craft to industrial unionism in the New Deal era. Eventually it dissolved and the maritime workers concentrated their energies toward building industrial unionism through the national CIO Maritime Committee.

The Center has a fine collection of printed items in its ephemera files including handbills, leaflets, cards, published articles, and other material which at the time of origin was produced in large numbers, quickly handed out, and soon thrown away (35 cubic feet have been processed to date). In addition, the Center has received the labor and radical pamphet collection of lawyer Walton Duvall Phillips, which includes material from the IWW and Socialist Party going back to the turn of the century. Another unusual collection of printed material came to the Center when the research library of the California Dept. of Industrial Relations, Division of Labor Statistics, closed in 1986. The preliminary guide which came with the collections pinpoints material on health issues as well as State statistics on workers through the years 1930–75.

The Center has over 16 cubic feet of photographs, almost half are from the *People's World* newspaper morgue which covered the 1930s through the 1970s. In addition to subjects one would expect in these files, such as Tom Mooney's triumphant parade up Market St. 50 years ago, there are unexpected gems such as Dorothea Lange photographs with her scribbled comments on the back and many informal shots of workers' social events.

---

[3]For more detail on these records see Frances Gates, "Labor History Resources in the Libraries of the University of California, Berkeley," *Labor History*, 1 (1960), 197–204.

A life-size hand-tinted photograph of Mayor P. H. McCarthy, who founded the Building Trades Council in the Bay Area, was donated in 1986 when the Center held an exhibit and program on his life and times. The granddaughter of "Pinhead," as he was fondly called, has placed this photograph on loan with the Center along with other material from his career including his two years as San Francisco mayor (1909–1911).

There are also extensive portrait files whose examination can be rewarding. The common grin-and-shake photographs of labor leaders are there, but so also are pictures which depict the workplace, tools, and working conditions.[4]

Although preserving collections and sponsoring outreach programs are the Center's primary activities, other services are provided. Unions and labor organizations may request help with records management and in particular with the identification of historical material. Technological advances have allowed archivists to create and utilize data bases, and the Center is putting its information on collections in OCLC using the MARC format. The Center collects descriptive guides and inventories to all collections relating to Northern California labor, no matter what library in the country and Canada houses them.

The Center has been a leading force in exchanging archival information among the archivists and librarians in the West who administer labor collections. In 1989 the Center sponsored a workshop so that these specialists could exchange and raise questions about archival techniques and it is planned to continue such meetings.

As is the case with other archival repositories, the Center's main users are not academic historians. Today's researchers are often media specialists from TV news programs, or filmmakers with a documentary script in hand. They are lawyers looking for statistics on asbestos or city employees wanting information on how an underground transit tunnel was dug. In the past year, the Center's users have included union members searching for photographs of the first cannery assembly lines, genealogists wanting birth dates of draymen, nurses looking for their roles in the passage of the women's suffrage referendum, and students researching Chinese laundry workers and the Asiatic exclusion laws.

Access: The Center, located at 480 Winston Drive, San Francisco, CA 94132, is open 1–5 pm, Monday–Friday, and by appointment (including evening and weekend hours). For further information contact Lynn Bonfield. Phone: (415) 564-4010.

---

[4]A copy of the holdings of the Labor Archives and Research Center is available with annual updates. See also Lynn A. Bonfield, "To the Source: Archival Collections for California Labor History," *California History*, 56 (1987), 286–99. Send $5.00 to the Center to receive a copy.

INDEX

Abel, I. W., 99, 151, 158
Abelson, Paul, 72
Abercrombie, E. L., 153
Academy of Management, 72
Accidents, industrial, 77, 243. *See also* Occupational safety
Actors' Equity Association, 57, 58
Actors' Fund, 57
ACTU. *See* Association of Catholic Trade Unionists
ACTWU (Amalgamated Clothing and Textile Workers Union of America), 30, 35, 91, 170, 244, 246; in Greater Albany, 63–64
ACWA. *See* Amalgamated Clothing Workers of America
Adair, Goldthwaite, Stanford & Daniel (law firm), 153
Adams, Leonard, 73
Adamson Eight-Hour law, 223
Adamson United Co., 159
Addams, Jane, 180
Addes, George, 158
Advance and Labor Leaf, 178
AFA (Association of Flight Attendants), 168, 176
Affiliated School for Workers, 81
Affleck, Diane L. Fagan, 29
AFGWU (American Flint Glass Workers Union), 143
AFL (American Federation of Labor), 74, 105, 122, 124, 134–37, 138, 206; abroad, 206; in California, 243; and Cigar Makers Union, 130; CIO and, 37 *(see also* AFL-CIO); in Colorado, 222; Committee on Women in Industry of, 109; and federal labor unions, 64; focuses of, 109; ILWU and, 243; ITU and, 128; Labadie in, 178; lawyers of, 208; Metal Trades Department of, 108; in Michigan, 183; Rockefeller Foundation support for, 76; sleeping-car porters and, 106; in Texas, 233. *See also* AFL-CIO; Gompers, Samuel; Green, William

AFL-CIO, 124, 133, 135, 136–37, 138, 171, 217; Atomic Energy Technical Committee of, 109; in California, 240, 242–44, 245–46; Committee on Political Education (COPE) of, 136; in Connecticut, 42–45; in Detroit, 170; formation of, 110, 169, 241, 243; and George Meany Memorial Archives, 13; in Greater Albany, 65; international relations of, 124; Kemp and, 24; Latin American interests of, 73; in Michigan, 170, 183; in Mississippi, 149; in New York state, 57, 65; in Ohio, 155, 156, 157, 158, 159; in Pennsylvania, 97, 99; record-keeping of, 14; in South, 148–53; in Texas, 229, 230–32, 233; in textile industry, 34; in Wisconsin, 206; and WVLF, 144. *See also* Meany, George; Reuther, Walter
Africa, AFL-CIO activities in, 24
Afro-American Police League, 187
AFSCME (American Federation of State, County, and Municipal Employees), 37, 58, 149, 167, 172, 175, 176, 207, 233; and CSEA, 65; and Ohio Civil Service Employees Association, 157; paperwork problems of, 14. *See also* Zander, Arnold
AFT (American Federation of Teachers), 60, 65, 71, 103, 149, 167, 175, 176; and APSTA, 150; in Chicago, 187–88; in Colorado, 222; ideological conflict within, 187; in Los Angeles, 241; and Workers Education Local 189, 170
Agricultural Workers Organizing Committee (AWOC), 246
Ahern, Martin, 170
Air Line Pilots Association (ALPA), 167, 176
ALA (Alliance for Labor Action), 150
Alabama, University of, 81
Albany Allied Printing Trades Council, 65
Albany Typographical Union, 62–63
Albrier, Frances Mary, 24
Alexander, Frank, 137
Alexander, Gabriel, 72

Aliquippa, Pa., 98
Allegheny County, Pa., 103
Allen, Henry J., 107
Alliance for Labor Action (ALA), 150
Allied Printing Trades Councils, 44, 59
Allis Chalmers Co., 122, 207
ALPA (Air Line Pilots Association), 167, 176
Altmeyer, Arthur, 209
Aluminum Workers of America, 99
Amalgamated Association of Iron, Steel and
  Tin Workers, 99, 150
Amalgamated Association of Street and Elec-
  tric Railroad Employees, 144
Amalgamated Association of Street, Electric
  Railway and Motor Coach Employees, 206
Amalgamated Clothing and Textile Workers
  Union of America. See ACTWU
Amalgamated Clothing Workers of America
  (ACWA), 34–35, 44, 70, 91, 152, 188;
  merger of TWUA and, 34 (see also ACTWU
  [Amalgamated Clothing and Textile Workers
  Union of America])
Amalgamated Food and Allied Workers Union,
  84
Amalgamated Lithographers of America, 99
Amalgamated Meat Cutters and Butcher Work-
  men of North America, 84, 206, 209, 232
Amalgamated Transit Workers, 153
A. M. Byers Company, 104
America (Romanian-American newspaper), 214
American Aeronaut, 242
American Arbitration Association, 19, 69, 91,
  196
American Association for Labor Legislation,
  71, 79
American Association for Social Security, 71
American Bosch, 36
American Committee for the Protection of the
  Foreign Born, 182, 215, 237
American Communications Association, 206
American Communist Party, 54, 183, 235,
  243. See also Communism
American Council on Education—American
  Youth Commission, 81
American Estonian Socialist Association, 215
American Federation of Government Employ-
  ees, 157, 232
American Federation of Grain-elevator Employ-
  ees, 198
American Federation of Grain Millers, 196
American Federation of Hosiery Workers, 89,
  206

American Federation of Labor. See AFL
American Federation of Musicians, 58, 90,
  144
American Federation of State, County, and
  Municipal Employees. See AFSCME
American Federation of Teachers. See AFT
American Film Institute, 238
American Flint Glass Workers Union
  (AFGWU), 143
American Folklife Center, 113
American Friends Service Committee, 105
American Guild of Musical Artists, 58
American Guild of Variety Artists, 57
American Income Life Insurance Company,
  232
American Institute of Banking, 91
Americanization study, by Carnegie Corpora-
  tion, 209
American Labor Archives and Research Insti-
  tute, 55
American Labor Conference on International
  Affairs, 55
American Labor Education Service, 23, 71,
  208
American Labor Mission, 197
American Labor Party, 85
American Labor Who's Who, 53
American Labor Year Book, 53
American Legion, 253
American Library Association, 147
American Newspaper Guild, 232
American Postal Workers Union, 13
American Radio Telegraphists Association, 201
American Railway Union, 226
American Red Cross, 119
American Revolution, 185
American Socialist Party. See Debs, Eugene V.;
  Socialist Party of America; Socialist Labor
  Party (SLP); Socialist Workers Party
American Socialist Society (ASS), 52
American Writing Paper Co., 38
American Youth Commission, 81
Amerikansko Slovenske Noviny, 214
Anarchism, 178–81, 182, 203. See also Hay-
  market Square incident
Anderson, Mary, 19
Andrews, Stephen P., 208
Angevine, Erma, 86
Animators, strike of Disney, 241, 245
"Annals of Labor and Industry" (WPA), 188
Anne Rand Memorial Library, 254

Anthracite Coal Strike Arbitration Commis-
  sion, 108
Anti-communism, 22, 34; of Catholic CIO
  members, 123-24; "professional," 201. *See
  also* Cold War; McCarthy, Joseph; Red-bait-
  ing; Red Scare; Smith Act
Appalachia, 80, 140
Appeal to Reason, 164
Apprentices, printers', 62
APSTA (Atlanta Public School Teachers Asso-
  ciation), 150
Arbitration, 72, 86, 254. *See also* American
  Arbitration Association
Archambeau, Sophie. *See* Labadie, Sophie
  Archambeau
Archivaria, 13
Archives: access to, 15, 16n; municipal, 17;
  public-records, 16-17
Arkansas, University of, 81
Armaments industry, 118
Army, U.S.: "radicals" monitored by, 164; use
  of, during railroad strikes, 110, 111. *See
  also* War, U.S. Department of
Arnall, Ellis, 154
Aronson, Robert, 73
Arthur and Elizabeth Schlesinger Library on
  the History of Women in America. *See*
  Schlesinger Library
Asino, L', 214
Asner, Ed, 164
Aspen, Colo., 219
Assembly of Governmental Employees, 71
Associated Actors and Artistes of America, 58
Associated Classroom Teachers of Los Ange-
  les, 241
Associated Negro Press, 188
Associated Teachers of Los Angeles (ATLA),
  241, 246
Associated Unions of America, 206
Association for Improving the Condition of the
  Poor, 109–10
Association for Union Democracy, 168
Association of Catholic Trade Unionists
  (ACTU), 124, 169
Association of Colored Railway Trainmen and
  Locomotive Firemen, 108
Association of Flight Attendants (AFA), 168,
  176
Association of Southern Labor Historians, 229
Association of State School Instructors (Calif.),
  252

AT&T (American Telephone and Telegraph).
  See Bell System
AT&T Longlines, 59
Athearn, Robert G., 219
ATLA (Associated Teachers of Los Angeles),
  241, 246
Atlanta, Ga., 146–50, 153
Atlanta Board of Education, 150
Atlanta Education Association, 150
Atlanta Federation of Trades, 150
Atlanta Fire Fighters Union, 153
Atlanta Printing Pressmen, 153
Atlanta Printing Specialties, 153
Atlanta Public School Teachers Association
  (APSTA), 150
Atlanta Teacher, 150
Attorneys general, U.S., 112
Aurora, L', 214
Austria, AFL host to unionists of, 76
Automation, 221, 241, 243, 244
Automobile industry, 17, 117, 173, 174. *See
  also* UAW
Avery Fisher Center for Music and Media, 60
A. W. Burritt Co., 47
AWOC (Agricultural Workers Organizing Com-
  mittee), 246

Baarslag, Karl, 201
Bacon, Emory, 98
Baer, John, 74
Baker Library, 31, 33, 39
Bakers, 191, 192
Bakery, Confectionery and Tobacco Workers
  International Union, 44, 131
Bakery and Confectionery Workers Interna-
  tional Union, 100, 130, 131
Bakke, Edward Wight, 72
Balanoff, James, 186
Baldwin, C. B., 196
"Ballad for Americans," 237
Balzar, Fred, 228
Bambace, Angela, 215
Bancroft Library, 248, 252
Banking industry, 22, 108
Barker, Mary C., 150
Barkin, Solomon, 34
Barkley, Alben, 34
Barnard College, 86, 208
Barnes Textile Associates, 31
Barnett, Claude A., 188
Barnum, P. T., 46

Barr, Willard, 229, 230
Basin, Neil, 213n
Bayard, N. M., 220
Bay Area Labor History Workshop, 249
Beard, Charles, 54
Beard, Leland, 157, 159
Beaudry, Raymond, 38
Beaver Valley Labor History Society, 104
Bebel, August, 51
Becker, Henry, 44
Beer industry, 103–4
Beirne, Joseph A., 125–27
Belanger, J. William, 34
Belknap Manufacturing, 48
Bell, Daniel, 54
Bellamy, Edward, 51
Bellanca, Dorothy, 70
Bell System, 125, 126, 127, 128, 195
Bellush, Bernard, 58
Bellush, Jewel, 58
Bennett, Mary, 197n
Bentley Library, 182
Berkowitz, Monroe, 84
Bernstein, Meyer, 98, 99
Bert, Erik, 196
Beyer, Clara Mortenson, 25
Beyer, Otto S., 107
Biemiller, Andrew J., 149
Biggs, Ione, 158
Biklen, Wayne, 197
Billings, Warren K., 107
Bill Usery Labor Management Relations Foundation, 147
Bimba, Anthony, 217
Bisbee, Ariz., 175
Bishop, Merlin D., 44
Bittner, Van, 141, 144
Blacklisting, 30, 157
Black lung disease, 94
Blacks, U.S. labor movement and, 39, 106, 111, 119, 175, 187, 231, 234. *See also* Brotherhood of Sleeping Car Porters; Racism
Black Women's Oral History Project, Schlesinger Library, 24
Blair, Fred Bassett, 207
Blankenhorn, Ann, 174
Blewett, Mary, 39
Blitzstein, Marc, 210
Block, Harry, 99
Blow, J. J., 219

Blue, Robert, 197
Bobst Library, 50, 60
Bogan, Gerald, 197
Boley, Jane, 232, 233
Bollard, Robert Dean, 157
Bookbinders, 63
Bookbinders and Bindery Women's Union, 253
Bool, Henry, 184
Boot and Shoe Workers' Union, 206
Borah, William E., 107
Borchardt, Selma, 174
Borrup, Roger N., 44
Boston, Mass., 23, 39. *See also* Schlesinger Library
Boston Central Labor Union, 40
Bosworth, Louise Marion, 23
Boulder Dam, 228
Bowles, Chester, 144
Bowling Green State University, 155
Boycotts, union, 35, 225, 226
Boyd, David A., 184
Boyle, Emmet, 228
Boyle, Kevin, 172
Boyle, Tony, 111
Brass Worker's Federal Labor Union, 48
Bray, John Francis, 181, 184
"Bread and Roses" strike. *See* Lawrence, Mass.
Brennan, John A., 220
Brewery workers, 233
Bricklayers, Masons, and Plasterers International of America, 157
Bricklayers Union, 48
Bridgeport, Conn., 46–49
Bridgeport Brass Co., 46, 47, 48
Bridgeort Herald (Conn.), 49
Bridgeport Times Star (Conn.), 49
Bridges, Harry, 110, 236–37, 253
Brissenden, Paul Frederick, 71
Brockton Boot and Shoe Workers, 40
Brommel, Bernard J., 161, 165
Brooks, John Graham, 21
Brookwood Labor College, 159, 170
Brophy, John, 94, 109, 123
Brotherhood of Carpenters and Joiners. *See* United Brotherhood of Carpenters and Joiners of America
Brotherhood of Locomotive Engineers, 153, 191, 192, 232
Brotherhood of Locomotive Firemen and Enginemen, 70, 233

Brotherhood of Painters and Allied Trades, 57
Brotherhood of Painters and Decorators, 144
Brotherhood of Railroad Signalmen of America, 70
Brotherhood of Railroad Trainmen (BRT), 70, 144, 221, 232
Brotherhood of Railway, Airline and Steamship Clerks, Freight Handlers, Express and Station Employees, 70
Brotherhood of Sleeping Car Porters, 106, 111, 186–87. See also Randolph, A. Philip
Brown, D. R. C., 219
Brown, Edmund G., Sr., 241, 245
Brown, Hank, 230
BRT. See Brotherhood of Railroad Trainmen
Brubaker, Otis, 98
Bryn Mawr College, 23, 24, 86, 208
Bubbling Waters Press, 179
Buckeye Steel Casting Co., 158
Bucki, Cecelia, 42
Building and Construction Trades councils, 65, 232, 255
Building trades, 35, 36, 59, 63, 65
Bullard Co., 46, 47, 49
Bulletin (Lima, Ohio), 159
Bunche, Ralph, 170
Burati, Valery, 173
Bureau of Agricultural Economics, U.S., 117
Bureau of Employment Security, U.S., 119
Bureau of Foreign and Domestic Commerce, 120
Bureau of Indian Affairs, U.S., 119
Bureau of Industrial Research, 109
Bureau of Labor Statistics, U.S., 119
Bureau of Mines, U.S., 118
Bureau of Part-Time Work, 80
Bureau of Vocational Information, 23
Burke-Hartke law, 143
Burt, Sam, 71
Burton, Dennis, 119
Byrd, Robert C., 143

Cabin Creek, W.Va., 140
Cable television, DGA and, 242
CALC (Chattanooga Area Labor Council), 148 n3
California. See Hollywood; Los Angeles; San Francisco; San Pedro
California, University of, 248, 250
California Committee for Fair Practices, 245
California Faculty Association, 252

California Federation of Teachers (CFT), 241, 246
California Labor School, 252
Californians Against Proposition 14, 245
California Shipbuilding Corporation, 246
California State University, 252
Call Off Your Old Tired Ethics (COYOTE), 22
Camp Tamiment, 53, 56
Canada: archival institutions of, 13, 15; unions of, 205 (see also FOTLU [Federation of Trades and Labor Unions of the United States and Canada])
Capital District Labor History Project (N.Y.), 61, 62, 65
Capitalism, Catholic Church and, 121
Capraro, Anthony, 215
Carder, William H., 243
Carey, James B., 83, 124, 144, 168, 169
Carey, John, 169
Carnegie, Andrew, 107–8
Carnegie Corporation, 108, 209
Carpenters, 48, 153, 157, 193, 198, 232, 233. See also United Brotherhood of Carpenters and Joiners of America
Cartoons, labor-related newspaper, 74, 210, 245. See also Animators, strike of Disney
Caselli, Alberico, 215–16
Cass, Melnea, 24
Catherwood, Martin P., 67, 73
Catholic Council on Working Life, 188
Catholic Interracial Council of New York, 122
Catholicism, U.S. labor and, 121–24
Cavanagh, Jerome P., 174
Censorship, in entertainment industry, 242
Center for Community Change, 169
Center for Human Resources, IMLR, 86
Center for Popular Economics, 38
Center for Research Libraries, 215
Central City, Colo., 219
Central Labor Union (Bridgeport, Conn.), 48
Central Pacific Railroad, 226
Chaikin, Sol C., 71
Chain stores, workers in Wisconsin, 208
Chambers, Whitaker, 182
Chamber(s) of commerce: Connecticut, 48; Rockefeller interest in, 79
Chaplin, Ralph, 184
Chapman Valve Company, 37
Charcoal Burners' War, 226
Chattanooga Area Labor Council, (CALC), 148 n3

Chautauqua circuit, 197

Chavez, Cesar, 246

Chemical industry, 145

Chemical Workers union, 150

Chicago, Ill., 185. *See also* Haymarket Square incident

Chicago Building Trades Council, 188

Chicago Federation of Labor, 185–86

Chicago Foreign Language Press Survey, 188

Chicago Historical Society, 208 n4

Chicago Newspaper Guild, 187

Chicago Teachers' Federation, 187

Chicago Teachers Union, 187

Child labor, 21, 29, 85, 100, 106, 110, 113; Catholic Church focus on, 122; Cigar Makers Union vs., 130; federal focus on, 223; Sentinels of the Republic and, 22. *See also* National Child Labor Committee; Robinson, Harriet Hanson

Children, of working mothers, 251

Children's Bureau, U.S., 119

Chinatown, union organizing in San Francisco, 253

Chinese-Americans, 251

Christenson, Edith, 174

Christopher, Paul R., 152

Chrysler Corporation, 173

Cigar Makers International Union, 74, 130. *See also* Gompers, Samuel

Cinaglia, Leo, 84

Cincinnati Medical College, 78

CIO (Congress of Industrial Organizations), 58, 72, 124, 137–38, 168–69, 173; and AFL, 37 *(see also* AFL-CIO); in California, 236, 237, 238, 243, 244; in Colorado, 222; communism in, 108, 109, 123–24, 169; CWA and, 126; Fair Labor Standards Committee of, 34; Germer and, 207; in Greater Albany, 65; ILWU and, 243; international concerns of, 169, 173; in Iowa, 196; literature of, 236; Maritime Committee of, 254; in Michigan, 183; in Missississippi, 149; in New Jersey, 84; in New York City, 59; in Ohio, 157, 159; Political Action Committee of, 84, 110, 123, 144, 196–97, 250; Rockefeller Foundation grant to, 76; in South, 148, 149, 150, 151, 152, 169 *(see also* "Operation Dixie"); state employees union of, 109; and textile industry, 33, 34, 90, 152; (Henry) Wallace, support for, 196–97; in West Virginia *(see* West Virginia Industrial Union Council); in Wisconsin, 207. *See also* AFL-CIO; Brophy, John; Carey, James B.; Lewis, John L.; Murray, Philip; Reuther, Walter

Citizens Crusade Against Poverty, 169

Civilian Conservation Corps, 117

Civil liberties, 182, 187, 237

Civil rights, 111, 174, 187, 203, 235, 243, 245, 252; CIO and, 34, 168; Highlander Center and, 208; (Stetson) Kennedy and, 151; labor movement and, 84–85; Mississippi AFL-CIO and, 149; Mont for, 245; Packinghouse Workers and, 206. *See also* Equal employment opportunity; Handicapped, employment of; Racism

Civil Rights Congress, 235, 237

Civil Service Employees Association (CSEA), 64

Civil Service Forum, 58

Civil Service Technical Guild, 60

Civil War, American, 185

Civil Works Administration, 117

Cizmic, Ivan, 213n

Clarion, 250

Clark, B. M., 93

Clark, Heath S., 93

Clark, Samuel H., 108

Clay, Lucius, 124

Clayman, Jacob, 158

Clement Co., 38

Clemente, Egidio, 216

Clerical workers, 22

Cleveland, Grover, 110

Cleveland Women Working Project, 158

Clifford, Arthur, 48

Closed shop, 111

Clothing, manufacture of. *See* Textile industry

Coalition of Labor Union Women, 169, 244, 251

Coal miners, 94, 100. *See also* Mining industry; UMWA (United Mine Workers of America)

Coal regions: of Illinois, 141; of Kentucky, 105; NRA and, 117; of Pennsylvania, 94; Rocky Mountain, 222, 223; Texas, 233; of West Virginia, 140–41. *See also* Mining industry

Coal Strike Zone, Colorado, 79

Cohen, Wilbur, 209

Cold War, 235, 252

Cole, David, 72

Collective bargaining, employer opposition to, 115

College of the City of Detroit. *See* Wayne State University

Collier, Phyllis, 174

Collins, Justus, 142

Colorado, 79, 220–23. *See also* Ludlow Massacre

Colorado Farmers Union, 221

Colorado Fuel and Iron Company, 79, 82

Colorado Industrial Plan, 79

Colorado Labor Council, 222

Colorado State Federation of Labor, 222

Columbia Pictures, 236

Columbus, Ohio, 156–57, 158

Columbus Dispatch (Ohio), 157

Columbus-Franklin County Building and Construction Trades Council (Ohio), 156

Columbus Typographical Union (Ohio), 157

Commerce and Industry Association of New York, 79

Commission on Industrial Relations, U.S., 118, 209, 223

Committee on Fair Employment Practice, U.S., 119

Committee of Industrial Relations Librarians, 204

Committee for Industrial Organization. *See* CIO

Committee for National Health Insurance, 169

Committee on Social Trends, 201

Committee of University Industrial Relations Libraries, 204

Committees, U.S. congressional, 115–16

Commons, John R., 74, 179, 203, 208, 209

"Commonweal of Christ," 159

Commonwealth College, 170

Commonwealth Fund, 75, 80

Communications Workers of America. *See* CWA

Communism, 170, 182, 187, 203, 207, 235; in Britain, 184; Debs and, 163; Estonian-American, 215; Rand School and, 52; and U.S. unions, 34, 201 (*see also* CIO, communism in). *See also* American Communist Party; Anti-communism; Marxism; Radicalism; Red Scare; Socialism

Community College of Allegheny County, 103

Company stores, 94, 142, 158

Computers, organized labor and, 14

Conditions in Los Angeles (film), 238

Conference of Studio Unions, 236

Congress, Costigan before U.S., 222–23. *See also* Committees, U.S. congressional; House of Representatives, U.S.; Senate, labor and U.S.

Congress of Industrial Organizations. *See* CIO

Connecticut, 35. *See also* Bridgeport

Connecticut, University of, 41, 43, 44, 45

Connecticut Foreign Trade Association, 48

Connecticut Labor Relations Board, 69

Connecticut State Labor Council, 43

Connecticut Workers and Technological Change project, 45

Conscription, 52, 109. *See also* Universal military training

Conspiracy, IWW accused of, 225

Constantine, J. Robert, 162, 164, 165, 166

Construction. *See* Building trades

Consumerism, 85–86

Consumers' League of Massachusetts, 21, 22

Consumers League of New Jersey, 85

Consumers' League of New York, 71

Consumers Research, Inc., 85

Consumers Union, 85–86

Cook, Alice, 73

Cook, Clair, 151

Cook County Industrial Union Council (Ill.), 186

Cooks, professional, 253

Coolidge, Calvin, 112, 200

Cooper, Marguerite Debs, 161, 162, 163, 164, 165

Cooperative Builder, The, 214

Cooperatives, labor, 208; of Finnish-Americans, 215, 216

Cope, Elmer F., 159

COPE. *See* AFL-CIO, Committee on Political Education of

Copper mining, Nevada, 228

Corbin, Harold, 241

Cordwainers, 111

Cornehlsen, John H., 72

Cornell University, 12, 23, 56, 57–58, 61, 138, 253

Cornwell, John J., 140

Cortelyou, George B., 108

Costigan, Edward P., 222

Cotton workers, California, 238

Coulter & McKenzie Machine Co., 47

Counselors, unionization of school, 241

Court of Industrial Relations (Kans.), 107

Coxey, Jacob S., 159
COYOTE (Call Off Your Old Tired Ethics), 22
Cradle Will Rock, The (Blitzstein), 210
Crafts. *See* Building trades
Crane Company, 37
Crane-Gartz, Kate, 164
Crescent Steel Co., 69
Crivello, Antonio, 215
Croatians, in U.S., 216
Cross, James, 131
Croxton, Fred C., 201
CSEA (Civil Service Employees Association), 64
Cunningham Memorial Library, 161, 164, 165
Curtiss, Howard, 99
Cutlery industry, 38
CWA (Communications Workers of America), 13, 58, 59, 103, 125–28, 149, 157, 170; in California, 246; Committee on the Future of, 127; in Iowa, 195; and ITU, 221; in Texas, 232. *See also* Beirne, Joseph A.
Czechs, in U.S. labor movement, 213

Dallas Trades Assembly (Tex.), 233
"DALUs" (directly affiliated local unions), 135
Daniels, Andrew Frank, 44
Daniels, Wilbur, 71
D'Arienzo, Daria, 42
Darrow, Clarence, 51, 108, 220
Daugherty, James, 236
Davenport-Besler Corporation, 197
David, Henry, 181
Davis, Henry Gassaway, 140
Davis, James J., 108, 200
Davis, Merle, 197n
D. Bruce Shine (law firm), 153
Dean, Ronald, 192
Dearborn Conference Group, 72
Debs, Eugene V., 51, 52, 54, 118, 183, 233
Debs, Theodore, 161, 163
DeCamp, Essie, 192
De Ciampis, Pasquale Mario, 216
DeCicco, Michael, 148
DeForest, Robert, 79
DeGruson, Gene, 165
Delano, Calif., 246
De Leon, Daniel, 178
De Leon, Solon, 52
Deliverymen, newspaper, 244
Delman, A. G., 129
DeMaio, Ernest, 187

Dennis, Eugene, 207
Dennis, Peggy, 207
DeNucci, G. George, 157, 158
Denver, Colo., 222
Denver & Rio Grande Western Railroad Co., 221
Department Store Employees Union, 253
Department stores, unionization of, 187
Depression, Great, 89, 116–17, 188, 238; work relief programs during, 25, 119. *See also* New Deal; Roosevelt, Franklin D.
DeShetler, Irwin L., 169
De Silva, Joseph, 245
Despres, Leon M., 188
Detroit, Mich., 167, 170, 172–75; Labadie in, 178–79. *See also* Wayne State University
Detroit Commission on Community Relations, 170
Detroit Council of Trades and Labor Unions, 178
Detroit Education Association, 170
Detroit Federation of Teachers, 170
Deverall, Richard, 124, 173
Dewey, John, 54
Di Gaetano, Nick, 173
Di Giorgio Fruit Corporation, 246
Diocesan Labor Institute (Hartford), 44
Directly affiliated local unions ("DALUs"), 135
Directors, strike of Hollywood, 241
Directors Guild of America, Inc., 242, 246
Disability insurance, 244
Discrimination. *See* Racism
Disease, occupational, 77–78, 224. *See also* Black lung disease; Neuropathy
DiSilvestro, Giovanni, 217
Disney, Walt, 241, 245
Distributive Justice (Ryan), 121
Distributive Workers, 150
Dix, Keith, 141
Doctors, corporate, 77
Dodge, Witherspoon, 151
Dodge Revolutionary Union Movement (DRUM), 168
"Done in Oil" (Lynd), 79
Donovan, Raymond J., 116
Douglas, Paul H., 188
Draft. *See* Conscription; Universal military training
Draper, Ernest G., 108
Dreier, Dorothea, 19
Dreier, Henry Edward, 19

Dreier, Katherine, 19
Dreier, Mary E., 19, 20, 22
Dresser Industries, 158
Driscoll, Jeremiah, 44
Driscoll, John, 43
Drivers, newspaper-truck, 244
Drug and Hospital Workers Union, 71, 73
DRUM (Dodge Revolutionary Union Movement), 168
Dubinsky, David, 22
Dublin, Thomas, 39
Du Bois, W. E. B., 39
Dukes, Ofield, 174
Duke University, 81, 134, 136, 164, 165
Dummatzen, Fred, 251
Dunayevskaya, Raya, 169–70, 174
Duncan, James, 105
Dwyer, John, 170
Dye, Nancy Schrom, 19

Eagle A. Unity, 38
Earthquake, San Francisco, 251
Eberhardt, Mae, 24
Eckhardt, Carl C., 219
Edelman, Oscar K., 163, 164
Edison, Thomas Alva, 63
Edison Machine Works, 63
Edmonston, Gabriel, 135
Education: of adult workers, 208, 244, 252; labor, 170, 243; L.A. County and integrated, 245; Ohio steel-mill workers and, 158; Rockefeller support of U.S., 80–81; unions and California, 241
Edwards, George, 174
Edwards, Ray, 193
Eight-hour day, 79, 118, 180, 208, 225. *See also* Adamson Eight-Hour law; Haymarket Square incident
Elderly, Mont efforts for, 245
Electrical workers, 63, 157. *See also* IBEW; IUE; UE
Electricians, 193, 232. *See also* IBEW; IUE; UE
Electrotypers, 63
Elkins, Stephen S., 140
Ellickson, Katherine Pollack, 169, 174
Elliel, Paul, 254
Ely, Richard T., 179, 203, 209
Emergency Committee to Aid Farm Workers (Calif.), 245
Emerson, Harrington, 72, 100

Eminent domain, steel conference use of, 96
Empire Typographical and Mailer Conference, 65
Employee associations, 64, 127
Employee Retirement Income Security Act, 85
Employers associations, 157
Employer's Mutual Insurance Co., 223
Employe's Provident and Loan Association, Pennsylvania Railroad, 89
Employment and Adjustment Program, 81
Engineering, and Professional Guild, 58
Engineers Association of ARMA, 58–59
Engineers and Electrical Society, 72
Environmentalists for Full Employment, 104
Equal employment opportunity, 119
Equal Rights Amendment, 197
Equity Library Theater, 57
Erlich, Mark, 35
Espionage Act, U.S., 52
Essex Institute, 39
Estonians, in U.S. labor movement, 215
Ethnicity, 204, 213
Eugene V. Debs Foundation, 161–62, 164
Europe: American Labor Mission in, 197; Catholic labor movement of, 121. *See also* Germany
Evans, Elizabeth Glendower, 21
Evening Bulletin (Philadelphia), 91, 91 n6
Everett, Wash., 175
Evers, Charles, 149
Exclusion laws, California, 255
Ex parte Boyce, 225, 226
Ex parte Kair, 225, 226

Fair employment practices, 144, 209, 243
Fair Employment Practices Commission, 85
Fair Employment Practices Committee, 111, 122, 186
Fairfield Cooperative Farm Association, 216
Fair Labor Standards Act, 85
Fall River, Mass., 33
Fall River Yarn Finishers Union, 33
Farm equipment industry, 187, 196, 198
Farm Equipment Workers Union (FE), UAW vs., 123
Farmers, Rockefeller Foundation focus on, 80
Farmer's Cooperative Mercantile Association, 216
Farmers Federation, 80
Farmers Holiday Association, 196
Farm Security Administration, 210

Farmworkers, 39, 85, 106, 117, 159; California, 239, 241, 244, 245, 246; federal focus on, 116; imported, 109. *See also* UFW (United Farmworkers of America)
Farrell, James T., 39
Fascism, 182; Italian-American left's opposition to, 215, 216
FCC (Federal Communications Commission), 127
FE (Farm Equipment Workers Union), UAW vs., 123
Federal Bureau of Investigation (FBI), 22, 118, 253
Federal Communications Commission (FCC), 127
Federal Emergency Relief Administration, 117
Federal Employment Stabilization Board, 201
Federal Extension Service, 117
Federal Industrial Relations Committee, 109
Federal Labor Relations Authority, 69
Federal Mediation and Reconciliation Service, 116
Federal Mine and Safety Act, 85
Federal Reserve System, 108
Federal Writers' Project, 107, 151
Federated American Engineering Societies, 200
Federation of Flat Glass Workers, 142
Federation of Organized Trades and Labor Unions of the United States and Canada (FOTLU), 135
Federation of Telephone Workers of Pennsylvania, 103
Feier, John, 163
Feinberg, I. Robert, 72
Feinglass, Abraham, 71
Feiss, Richard A., 72
Fernbach, Frank, 99
Films: labor-related, 113, 238, 244; WWII promoted in, 242
Finnish Socialist Federation, 215, 216
Finns, in U.S. labor movement, 213, 213n, 215
Firemen, 86
Fisher Body Strike, 159
Fishing industry, 39
Fitcher's Trades Review, 68
Fitzpatrick, John, 186
Florida, University of, 19
Florida International University, 13
Florida State Council of Carpenters, 153
Florio, James J., 85

Flynn, Elizabeth Gurley, 56
Follett, Bill, 232
Foner, Henry, 71
Food and Allied Workers Union, 157
Food processing industry, 196
Food, Tobacco and Agricultural Workers Union, 237
Ford Motor Co., 171
Foreign policy, labor unions and U.S., 38
Foster, William Z., 163
Fostoria Glass Company, 143
FOTLU (Federation of Organized Trades and Labor Unions of the United States and Canada), 135
Francka, Ben, 191
Frank, Adelaide Schulkind, 22
Frankfurter, Felix, 108
Franklin D. Roosevelt Library, 23, 112
Fraser, Douglas, 172
Frederickson, Mary, 147
Freed, Emil, 235, 239
Free Trade Union Committee, 76
Frey, John P., 108
Friedman, Clara, 72
Friedman, Harvey, 37
Fritchman, H. Vernon, 93
Fritz, Percy S., 219
Fromm, Erich, 170
Fuel Administration, U.S., 119
Fulford, Fred, 148
Fund for the Republic, 54
Furniture industry, 39

Galicia, Sichnysky in, 217
Gallagher, Daniel J., 44
Gallagher, Leo, 237, 253
Gamble, Bob, 232
Gannett, Betty, 207
Gardiner, Elizabeth. *See* Evans, Elizabeth Glendower
Garfield, James R., 108
Garment industry, 18, 24, 57, 191, 193. *See also* ILGWU (International Ladies Garment Workers Union)
Gates, Frederick T., 82
Gausmann, William, 173
Gay rights, 183
Gelotte, Dominick, 94
General Education Board, 80–81
General Electric Company, 48, 64, 103
General Motors, 103, 242

George H. Gilbert Co., 38–39
George Meany Center for Labor Studies, 133
George Meany Memorial Archives, 36, 56, 57
Georgia, 146–50, 216. *See also* Atlanta
Georgia Democratic Party Forum, 154
Georgia Education Association, 150
Georgia Humanities Council, 146
Georgia Nurses Association, 152
Georgia State University, 147, 234
Georgia Textile Workers Project, 147
Germany: AFL host to unionists of, 76; post-
    WWII unionism in, 124
Germer, Adolph, 207
Giles, J. W., 153
Gladstein, Richard, 237
Glas Naroda, 216
Glass Bottle Blowers Association, 72, 153, 156
Glass industry, 142–43, 145, 156
Glass Workers' Protective League, 143
Glazer, Joe, 159
Gleason, Arthur H., 109
Gloversville, N.Y., 64
Gloves, manufacture of, 64
Gold, Ben, 71
Goldberg, Arthur, 98
Golden, Clint, 99
Golden Gate Bridge, 250–51
Goldfield, Nev., 225, 226, 228
Goldman, Emma, 162, 163, 180
Goldner, Paul J., 242, 246
Gompers, Samuel, 53, 56, 105, 130, 134–35,
    136, 233; and Allen debate, 107; and Debs,
    163; and Haymarket incident, 178; Hoover
    and, 200; and Labadie, 183. *See also* Sam-
    uel Gompers Papers Project
Goodman, Leo, 109, 169
Goodykoontz, Colin B., 219
Googe, Mrs. George, 153
Gordon, Marshall, 193
Gorman, Patrick, 207
Gould, Jean, 174
Government Printing Office, U.S., 114
Gracy, David B., II, 148, 152
Grandinetti, Emilio, 215
Granite Cutters International Association, 36
Graphic Arts Industrial Union, 99
Graphic Communications International Union,
    37–38, 63, 99, 100
Grayson, Martin, 99
Greater Hartford Building and Construction
    Trades Council, 43

Greater Hartford Industrial Union Council, 43
Greater Hartford Labor Council, 43
"Great Madness, The" (Nearing), 52
"Great Vacation." *See* Fall River, Mass.
Greeks, in U.S. labor movement, 213, 217
Green, George N., 229, 230–31, 232
Green, William, 53, 55, 74, 105, 130, 135,
    136, 159; Labadie and, 183
Greenback-Labor Party, 178
Grenell, Judson, 184
Grievances, 15, 173
Grocery stores, unionization of, 187
Gross, James, 72
Guess, Robert, 158
Guides, NARA, 115, 116, 117, 119
*Guide to Manuscripts in the Presidential
    Libraries,* 119
Guthrie, Woody, 237
Gutman, Herbert, 60

Haas, Joseph, 121, 122
Hackney, Ray, 127
Haener, Dorothy, 174
Haigler, Mrs. Carey, 153
Hall, G. K., 68
Hall, Keppele, 72
Handicapped, employment of, 119
Hanna, Hilton, 207
Harding, Warren G., 200
Hardy, J. Hazen, 91
Harkness, Mrs. Stephen V., 80
Harriman, Florence J., 109
Harriman, W. Averell, 109
Harrington, Michael, 164
Harrison, Gilbert, 109
Harrison, Nancy Blaine, 109
Harrison County Labor Federation (W.Va.),
    144
Harry Van Arsdale, Jr., Labor History Project,
    61
Hart, Jim, 232
Hartford Central Labor Union, 43
Harvard University, 21, 78, 81
Hatcher, Lillian, 174
Hatfield, Henry D., 140
Hatmaking, 39
Hatters union, 233
Hayes, John, 122
Hayes, Max S., 159
Haymarket Square incident, 178, 181, 182,
    185, 208

Haywood, William, 107, 108, 163, 220
Health insurance, 77, 109
Hearst Press, 187, 244
Hefferly, Frank, 222
Hefferly, Fred K., 222
Heinzen, Karl, 181
Helfgott, Simon, 73
Helstein, Ralph, 207
Henry, Aaron, 174
Henry, Ben A., 196
Henry Flynt Library, 39
Herrick, Mary, 174
Herring, Clyde, 196
Herstein, Lillian, 188
Higgins, George, 122, 124
Highlander Research and Education Center, 208
Hildebrand, George, 73
Hill, James, 72
Hill, Joe, 175
Hillman, Bessie, 70
Hillman, Sidney, 70, 144
Hillquit, Morris, 51, 207
Hilpert, E. E., 72
Hine, Lewis, 113, 175
Hines, Lewis G., 109
Hispanics, in U.S. labor unions, 231. See also Mexican-Americans
Hiss, Alger, 182
Historical Society of Wisconsin. See State Historical Society of Wisconsin
Hochstadt, Jack, 148
Hoerder, Dirk, 213, 213n
Hoffman, Alice, 137
Hofstadter, Richard, 39
Hoisting engineers, 227
Hollywood, Calif., 235, 241, 245
Hollywood Lockout (film), 236
Hollywood Ten, 237
Holt, Rush Dew, 140
Holyoke, Mass., 37
Home for Aged Women (Boston), 24
Homework, industrial, 21, 85
Hook, Sidney, 54
Hoopes, Darlington, 99
Hoover, Herbert, 195, 199–201
Hoover Ball Bearing Co., 180
Hoover Dam, 228
Hoover Institution on War, Revolution and Peace, 165
Hospitals, unions in, 82

Hotel and Restaurant Employees and Bartenders International Union, 157
Household Workers Rights, 253
"House I Live In, The" (song), 237
House of Representatives, U.S., 115–16
Housing, worker, 168, 244
Howard, Charles P., 207
Howe, Elias, 46
Howe, Irving, 39
Hromads'kyi Holos, 214
Hudson, J. L., 179
Hudson, John, 229, 230
Hudson, N.Y., 64
Hudson Coal Co., 100
Hudson Shore Workers School, 86, 208
Hudson Valley District Council of Carpenters (N.Y.), 63
Hudzinski, Stanley, 94
Huerte, Dolores, 174
Hughes, Harold E., 197
Hull House, 180
Humboldt County, Calif., 13
Humphrey, Hubert, 149, 174
Hungarians, in U.S. labor movement, 213
Hunt, Edward Eyre, 201
Huntington District Labor Council, 144

IAM (International Association of Machinists and Aerospace Workers, 42–44, 59, 145, 147, 148n3, 206, 242
IATSE. See International Alliance of Theatrical Stage Employees
IBEW (International Brotherhood of Electrical Workers), 36, 45n, 59, 153, 192, 222; CWA and, 126; UE vs., 253–54
IBT (International Brotherhood of Teamsters, Chauffeurs, Warehousemen and Helpers). See Teamsters
Ickes, Harold L., 93, 109
Idaho State Historical Society, 107
ILA (International Longshoremen's Association), 111
ILD. See International Labor Defense
ILGWU (International Ladies Garment Workers Union), 20, 71, 73, 152, 215, 217; in California, 238, 253; literature of, 236; in Texas, 232
Illegality, unions and, 16. See also Racketeering, labor
Illinois, 141. See also Chicago
Illinois, University of, 186

Illinois Central Gulf Railroad, 70
Illinois Emergency Relief Commission, 186
Illinois Manufacturers' Association, 188
Illinois State Federation of Labor, 186
Illinois State Historical Society, 186
ILO (International Labor Organization), 20, 68
ILWU (International Longshoremen's and
   Warehousemen's Union), 243, 246, 248,
   252, 254; literature of, 236. *See also*
   Bridges, Harry
IMLR. *See* Rutgers University, Institute of
   Management and Labor Relations of
Immigrant City Archives, 39
Immigrant Labor History Project (NYC), 60
Immigrants, in U.S. labor movement, 121,
   122, 209, 213, 213n, 215–17, 235, 236–37;
   in California, 251; female, 23
IMU (International Mailers Union), 59, 221,
   251–52
Index of Labor Periodicals, 53
Industrial Commission of Minnesota, 82
Industrial hygiene, 77–78
Industrial insurance, 224
Industrial Insurance Commission (Nevada), 227
Industrial Personnel Problem Conference, 80
Industrial relations, 80
Industrial Relations Counselors Program, 79
Industrial Union Council, 206
Industrial Union Council of New Jersey, 84
Industrial Union of Maritime and Shipbuilding
   Workers of America (IUMSWA), 129–30,
   131
Industrial Workers of the World. *See* IWW
Inglis, Agnes Ann, 177, 179–81, 182, 183–84
Ingram, F. F., 179
"Inside Out" (S. Kennedy newspaper column),
   151
Institute of Industrial Relations, UCAL, 248
Institute of Industrial Relations Library, 254
Institutions, Canadian archival, 13, 15
Insurance industry, 22
Insurance Workers of America, 72–73
International Alliance of Theatrical Stage
   Employees (IATSE), 232, 236
International Association of Fire Fighters, 48,
   157
International Association of Machinists and
   Aerospace Workers. *See* IAM
International Brotherhood of Electrical Work-
   ers. *See* IBEW
International Brotherhood of Pulp, Sulphite,

and Paper Mill Workers, 73, 206
International Brotherhood of Teamsters, Chauf-
   feurs, Warehousemen and Helpers. *See*
   Teamsters
International Confederation of Free Trade
   Unions, 69
International Congress of Women, 19
International Congress of Working Women, 19
International Education Board (IEB), 81
Internationale Möbel-Arbeiter Union, 183
International Federation of Architects, Engi-
   neers, Chemists and Technicians, 252
International Federation of Working Women,
   19–20
International Fur and Leather Workers' Union,
   70–71
International Glove Workers Union, 188
International Harvester, 103
International Institute of Metropolitan Detroit,
   170
International Labor Defense (ILD), 187, 237
International Labor Organization (ILO), 20, 68
International Ladies Garment Workers Union.
   See ILGWU
International Longshoremen's and Warehouse-
   men's Union. *See* ILWU
International Longshoremen's Association
   (ILA), 111
International Mailers Union (IMU), 221
International Moulders and Foundry Workers
   Union, 222
International Paper Company, 149
International Photoengravers' Union of North
   America, 99
International Seaman's Union of America, 186
International Typographical Union. *See* ITU
International Union of Bricklayers and Allied
   Craftsmen, 63
International Union of Electrical, Radio and
   Machine Workers. *See* IUE
International Union of Electrical Workers. *See*
   IUE
International Union of Electronic Workers, 149
International Union of Electronic, Electrical,
   Salaried, Machine and Furniture Workers,
   64
International Union of Mine, Mill, and Smelter
   Workers (IUMMSW), 73, 100, 220, 236
International Union of Operating Engineers,
   153, 232
International Union of Steam Engineers, 44

International Woodworkers of America, 148 n3
International Workers Order, 73, 158
International Workingmen's Association (IWA), 74, 207, 208
Iowa, University of, 112, 125
Iowa Farmers Union, 196
Iowa Federation of Labor, 197, 198
Iowa Labor History Oral Project, Inc. (ILHOP), 197, 197n, 198–99
Iowans for Right to Work, 197
I Rode With the Ku Klux Klan (S. Kennedy), 151
Iron City Legal Assistance Workers, 103
Iron industry, 100, 145
Ironworkers, 157, 232, 233. *See also* IUMMSW; UMWA
Irvine, David, 94
Italian American Labor Council, 217
Italian Labor Center, 217
Italians, in U.S. labor movement, 213, 216–17
Ittleson, Blanche, 23
ITU (International Typographical Union), 44–45, 62, 125, 128, 178, 183, 207, 221; in Atlanta, 148, 148 n3; in California, 244, 246, 251; in Chicago, 185; and CWA, 221; decline of, 128; in Denver, 222; in Detroit, 170; and IMU, 221; in Ohio, 157; in southern U.S., 148 n3; strike techniques of, 128; in Texas, 232, 233; in West Virginia, 144
IUE (International Union of Electrical, Radio and Machine Workers), 24, 36–37, 48, 59, 99, 124, 232; vs. GE/Schenectady, 64; and UE, 83. *See also* International Union of Electronic, Electrical, Salaried, Machine and Furniture Workers
IUMMSW (International Union of Mine, Mill, and Smelter Workers), 48, 73, 100, 220, 236
IUMSWA (Industrial Union of Maritime and Shipbuilding Workers of America), 129–30, 131
IWA (International Workingmen's Association), 74, 207, 208
IWW (Industrial Workers of the World), 72, 167, 173, 175, 215; California vs., 236; and Colorado Fuel and Iron, 79; FBI vs., 118; Inglis and, 180; in Kansas, 107; literature of, 236, 254; in Michigan, 183; in Nevada, 225, 228; songs celebrating, 159

Jack F. Moore Labor Studies Endowment, 193

Jackson County Central Labor Union (Miss.), 149
Jackson Police Officers Association (Miss.), 149
Jacob and Bessye Blaufarb Videotape Library of the American Labor Movements, 56, 60
Jacobs & Langford (law firm), 153
Jacoby, Robin Miller, 19
James, C. L. R., 170
James, Edward T., 19
Japanese-Americans, 228, 251
JDR 3rd Fund, 81
Jefferson Street Settlement House (Detroit), 180
Jeffrey, Mildred, 174
Jeffrey, Newman, 173
Jeffrey Mining Machine Division. *See* Dresser Industries
Jennings, Paul, 83
Jensen, Vernon, 73
Jewish Labor Committee (JLC), 57, 170, 245
J. I. Case Co., 207
Jim Crow Guide to the U.S.A. (S. Kennedy), 151
Joe Hill (song), 237
John and Mary Markle Foundation, 75
John R. Commons Memorial Labor Research Library, 204
John Sessions Memorial Award, 147
Johns Hopkins School of Hygiene and Public Health, 78
Johns Hopkins University, 179
Johnson, Ethel McLean, 20, 24
Johnson, Lyndon, 149
Johnstown, N.Y., 64
Joint Board of Fur, Leather and Machine Workers, 70–71
Joint State Labor Board of New Jersey, 84
Jones, Jerome, 150
Jones, Leroy, 196
Jones, Mark M., 82
Jones, Mary Harris ("Mother"), 94, 122, 141
Jones & Laughlin Steel Co., 98, 104
Jordan, Wilbur K., 18
Josephson, Ben, 56
Journal of the Knights of Labor, 68
J. Paul Leonard Library, 250
J. P. Stevens & Co., 27 n2, 124
Judiciary, papers of U.S., 112. *See also* Supreme Court, U.S.
Jurisdictional disputes, 169

Justice, U.S. Department of, 118, 127

Kaufman, Morris, 71
Kaufman, Stuart B., 129
Kautsky, Karl, 51, 52
Keating, Edward, 223
Keenan, Joseph, 124
Kellor, Frances, 19
Kemp, Maida Springer, 24
Kemsley, William, 173
Kennedy, John F., 24, 34
Kennedy, Stetson, 151
Kenny, Robert W., 237
Kentucky, 105, 141
Kerr, Clark, 254
Keyserling, Mary Dublin, 25
Kilgore, Harley, 140, 143
Kimmel, E. Logan, 137
King, Coretta Scott, 149
King, F. H., 153
King, W. L. MacKenzie, 79, 80
Kingsbury, John A., 109
Kircher, William, 158
Kirkland, Lane, 134
Kitzman, Harvey, 207
Knights of Labor, 18, 69, 122, 142, 159, 208;
    journal of, 68; and Massachusetts cutlery
    industry, 38; in Michigan, 178, 183; in
    NYC, 207; in Texas, 233. See also Pow-
    derly, Terence
Knights of St. Crispin, 208
Knowles, John H., 82
Kohler Company, 124, 207
Koleivis, 214
Konopacki, Mike, 210
Konvitz, Milton, 73
Kosik, Michael, 99
Krane, Jay, 173
Kraschel, Nelson, 197
Kroll, Jack, 110
Kukal, Milos, 192
Ku Klux Klan, 151

Labadie, Antoine Cleophas, 177
Labadie, Charles Joseph Antoine, 177–81, 182,
    183
Labadie, Sophie Archambeau, 178, 179
Label, union, 130
Labor: executive branch and U.S., 116; war and
    U.S., 117. See also Unions, labor
Labor, U.S. Department of, 74, 116

Labor, 70, 74, 223
Labor and Human Resources Committee, U.S.
    Senate, 85
Labor and Industry, Pennsylvania Department
    of, 82
Labor boards, NRA, 117
Labor Day, 175, 244
Laborers, 63, 193
Labor History, 55
Labor and Human Resources Committee, U.S.
    Senate, 85
Labor law, 85, 208, 225–26, 228
Labor Movement in America, The (Ely), 179
Labor press, 100, 173, 204–5, 210, 220, 223,
    231, 236, 242, 250, 253; foreign-language,
    213–15, 216; of Iowa, 199; of Ohio, 159;
    strike-oriented, 159; of Texas, 233; tobacco-
    union, 130; of West Virginia, 144
"Labor priests," 121, 122
Labor Review, 178
Labor's Heritage, 138
Labor's Non-Partisan League, 97, 123
Labor spies, 106, 209, 253
Labor standards, AFL focus on, 109
Labor Theater, The, 58
Labovitz, Larry, 246
Lackman, Howard, 229, 230, 231
La Follette, Philip F., 110
La Follette, Robert M., Jr., 110
La Follette, Robert M., Sr., 107, 110
La Follette family, 110
Lages, J. David, 190, 191–92
Laidlaw, Harriet, 23
Laidler, Harry, 207
Laisve, 214
Lake Torpedo Boat Co., 47
Lambert, George, 232
Lambert, Latane, 232
Lamont, Corliss, 21
Land, Emory S., 110
Landis, James M., 110, 144
Lange, Dorothea, 113, 254
Larmour, J. J., 179
Laslett, John, 238
Latin America, labor patterns in, 120
Laundry Workers union, 153
Laura Spelman Rockefeller Memorial, 81
Lawrence, Mass., 21, 33, 175, 180
L. C. Branson v. Industrial Workers of the
    World, 225
Leadville, Colo., 219

League for Mutual Aid, 22
Leather industry, 39, 64, 208
Le Blanc, Gaston, 103
Ledel, David, 232
Lee, Ivy, 80
Lee, William A., 186
Legal Research Program, Commonwealth Fund, 80
Lehman, Herbert, 110
Lehtinen, Kaarle, 216
Leiserson, William, 209
Lenin, Vladimir, 52
Lens, Sid, 187
Leonard, Louis, 99
Leonard, Norman, 243, 246, 252
Lever, E. J., 99
Lewis, John C., 196
Lewis, John L., 74, 94, 141, 142, 169, 200, 207, 222, 223, 233; Brophy vs., 123; Sifton exposé of, 112
Lewis, Joseph, 130
Liberty, 178
Liberty loans, Rand School opposition to, 52
Lichtblau, George, 173
Lincoln, Alexander, 22
Lindstrom-Best, Varpu, 213n
Litchman, Charles, 178
Lithographers, 59, 63
Lithuanian Communist League of America, 217
Little, Frank, 175
Little Blue Books, 163, 165, 166
Little Steel Strike, 158
Living My Life (Goldman), 180
Living Wage, A (Ryan), 121
Living Wage of Women Workers, The (WEIU), 23
Lloyd, Henry Demarest, 208, 208n4
Lobbying, 241
Lockheed-Vega Plant, 242
Lockouts, 107, 120, 128
Locomobile Co., 47, 49
Locomotive Fireman's Magazine, 162
Logan County, W.Va., 140
London, Jack, 162, 163
London, Meyer, 51
Longshoremen, 110, 232, 233. See also ILA; ILWU
Longshore, Ship Clerks and Walking Bosses' Caucus, 243
Loom Fixers Association, 33

"Lord's Acre" program, 80
Los Angeles, Calif., 235, 237–39, 240–41, 243–46
Los Angeles Citizen, The, 244
Los Angeles County Employees Association, 246
Los Angeles County Federation of Labor, 243–44
Los Angeles Film and Photo League, 238
Los Angeles Herald Examiner, 241, 244
Los Angeles Newspaper Guild (LANG), 244
Los Angeles Times, 237
Lovestone, Jay, 124, 173
Lowell, A. Lawrence, 21
Lowell, Josephine Shaw, 18
Lowell, University of, 31
Lowell, Mass., 20–21, 30, 31
Lowell Offering, 20–21
LTV Steel Corporation, 104
Lucchi, Pietro, 71
Lucia, Carmen, 153
Ludlow Massacre, 175, 216
Luken, James, 156, 158
Lumber industry, 145, 216
Luscomb, Florence, 22
Lusk, Clayton R., 52, 53
Lyceum circuit, 197
Lydia E. Pinkham Medicine Company, 24
Lynd, R. S., 79
Lynd, Staughton, 208
Lynn, Mass., 33, 40
Lyon, A. E., 70

McAdoo, William G., 110
McBride, John, 105
McCabe, Glen, 142
McCarran-Walter Act, 236, 237
McCarthy, Charles, 209
McCarthy, Joseph, 243
McCarthy, P. H., 255
McConnell, John, 73
McCreary Tire and Rubber, 96
McCulloch, Frank W., 188
McDonald, David, 98, 99, 150, 151
McDonnell, Joseph P., 208
MacDougall, Curtis, 196
McElroy, Andrew, 153
McGee, Bobbie, 159
McGowan, Raymond, 122
McGranery, James P., 110
Machine tool industry, 36–37, 47

Machinists, 156, 198, 232. *See also* IAM
McKelvey, Jean, 72
McKelway, Alexander J., 110
McKendree, Verlin N., 220
McKersie, Robert, 73
McKnight, M. M., 230
McKnight, Reecy, 230, 232
McLaurin, Benjamin F., 106
McLevy, Jasper, 48
McNabney, R. F., 195
McNamara, J. B., 108, 237
McNamara, Patrick, 174
McPeak, Carl, 149
McWilliams, Carey, 237
Madar, Olga, 174
Maids, Pullman, 24
Mailers Union. *See* IMU
Mailly, Bertha, 53
Malmgreen, Gail, 165
Management theory, 72
Manhattan Trade School for Girls, 19
Manufacturers Association of Southern Connecticut, 48
March on Washington Movement, 111
Marcuse, Herbert, 170
Margolius, Sidney, 86
Marine Cooks' and Stewards' Association of the Pacific Coast, 252
Marine Workers Industrial Union, 236
Maritime Federation of the Pacific, 254
Maritime Labor Board, 118
Mark, James, 94
Marsh, Ernest, 148
Martello, Il, 214
Martin, Albert, 73
Martin, Homer, 171, 172
Martyrs, U.S. labor, 175. *See also* Haymarket Square incident; Ludlow Massacre; Mooney, Tom
Marx, Karl, 51
Marxism, 207, 235. *See also* Communism; Socialism
Marxist-Humanism, 169–70
Mason, Lucy Randolph, 151
Mason-Jackson Labor Council, 144
Massachusetts, 35. *See also* Boston; Fall River; Holyoke; Lawrence; Lowell; Lynn; New Bedford
Massachusetts Commission on Collective Bargaining, 37
Massachusetts Historical Society, 40

Massachusetts Institute of Technology, 78
Massachusetts Society of Professors, 37
Massachusetts State Employees Association, 37
Massachusetts Teachers Association (MTA), 37
Massari, Vincent, 216
Match workers, 64
Matewan, W. Va., 140
Mather, Mildred, 199n
Mayer, Dale, 199n
Mayfield, Harry, 158
Maytag Co., 197
Meany, George, 34, 130, 133, 135, 136, 137, 149. *See also* George Meany Center for Labor Studies; George Meany Memorial Archives
Meany Archives. *See* George Meany Memorial Archives
Meatcutters, 153, 208, 210
Mechanic's Free Press, The, 68
Medical care, 142. *See also* Disease, occupational
Medrick, George, 99
Merchant Shipbuilding Corporation, 109
Meredith, E. T., 197
Merrimack Valley Textile Museum, 27
Metcalf-Adams papers, 30
Mexican-Americans, 234
Meyer Library, 190
Meyers, Ben, 187
Meyers, Irving, 187
Meyerscough, Tom, 141
MGM (Metro-Goldwyn-Mayer), 236, 245
Michigan, 167, 170, 172–73, 178. *See also* Detroit
Michigan, University of, 70, 174
Michigan Committee on Civil Rights, 122
Michigan Federation of Labor, 178, 184
Michigan Postal Workers Union, 170
Michigan Social Hygiene Commission, 180
Midwest Refining Company, 79
Migrant labor, 113
Milford, Dale, 233
Military Spending Peace and Justice Campaign, 95
Miller, Frieda, 20, 24
Miller, Ruth, 244, 246
Miller, Wilbur, 159
Millfield Mine, 158
Mills, C. Wright, 39
Mine, Mill, and Smelter Workers International Union. *See* IUMMSW

Miners for Democracy, 141, 168
Mines and Mining, U.S. House of Representatives Committee on, 79
Minimum wage, 85, 223
Mining industry, 118–19, 122, 183; in Colorado, 219, 223; Finns and Minnesota, 216; Hoover and, 200; in Nevada, 225, 226, 227, 228; in Ohio, 158; in Texas, 233. *See also* Coal regions; Iron industry
Minnesota, 77, 216
Minnesota Finnish American Family History Collection, 216
Minorities, U.S. labor movement and, 15, 175, 182, 204, 206, 208, 235; DGA and, 242; Mont efforts for, 245. *See also* Blacks; Chinese-Americans; Hispanics; Japanese-Americans; Migrant labor; Women
Mississippi Freedom Democratic Party, 174
Missouri, 190–94. *See also* Springfield
Mitch, William, 99
Mitchell, John, 122
M. M. McKnight Memorial Fund, 230, 231, 233
Molisani, Howard, 216
Mollenhoff, Clark, 201
Molly Maguires, 107
Monongah Mine Relief Fund, 141
Mont, Max, 245
Montana, 79, 220
Mon Valley Grievance Council, 95
Mon Valley Unemployed Committee, 104
Moody, Henry, 219
Mooney, Fred, 141
Mooney, Tom, 107, 181, 182, 238, 253, 254
Moore, Arch, 143
Moore, Jack F., 192, 193
Moore, Loretta, 174
Moore, Neal, 191–92
Moreno Bemis, Luis, 237
Morgantown Newspaper Guild (W. Va.), 145
Morris, James O., 73
Morris, Robert, 237
Morrison, Alice Angus, 25
Morrison, Frank, 135–36
Morse, Wayne, 254
Morton Junior College, 188
Moses T. Stevens & Sons Co., 27n2
Moteru Balsas, 214
Motion picture industry, 236, 245, 250
Motion Picture Screen Cartoonist Guild, 245
Moving Picture Machine Operators, 191

Moyer, Charles, 220
MTA (Massachusetts Teachers Association), 37
Mullinax-Wells law firm, 232
Munitions industry, 47
Murray, Philip, 34, 55, 99, 123, 137, 151
Muskie, Edmund, 149
Museum of Safety (NYC), 78
Musical Mutual Protective Union, 58

NAACP (National Association for the Advancement of Colored People, 19, 106
NAACP Legal Defense and Education Fund, 106
Naas, Bernard G., 204–5
"Nada" (Croatian drama society), 216
Naiman, Max, 187
NARA (National Archives and Records Administration), 114–15, 116
Nathan, Maud, 21
National Academy of Arbitrators, 72
National Archives and Records Administration (NARA), 114–15, 116
National Association for the Advancement of Colored People (NAACP), 19, 106
National Association of Cotton Manufacturers, 31
National Association of Letter Carriers, 13, 245
National Association of Railway Postal Clerks, 106
National Association of Wool Manufacturers, 31
National Brotherhood of Operative Potters, 157
National Bureau of Economic Research, 80
National Capital Area Trade Union Retirees Club, 138
National Catholic War Council, 122
National Catholic Welfare Conference, 121, 122
National Child Labor Committee (NCLC), 76, 81, 106, 110
National City Lines, 154
National Civic Federation, 122
National Coal Association, 93
National Commission on Product Safety, 86
National Conference of Catholic Charities, 122
National Consumers League (NCL), 21, 79, 86, 106
National Council of Catholic Women/National Council of Catholic Men, 122
National Council of Churches, 151

National Domestic Workers Union, 154
National Education Association, 150, 187
National Employment Exchange, 80, 81
National Endowment for the Arts, 238
National Endowment for the Humanities, 42, 55, 87, 98–99, 133, 137, 155, 162, 182, 240
National Farmers Organization, 196
National Farmers Union (NFU), 112, 221
National Farm Workers Ministry, 169
National Federation of Telephone Workers (NFTW), 125, 126, 127–28
National Guard (Nevada), 226
National Historical Publications and Records Commission, 56
National Industrial Conference Board, 80
National Institute of Industrial Psychology, 81
National Institute for Labor Education, 71
National Labor Board, 108, 122
National Labor Party, 159
National Labor Relations Act, 56, 85, 112
National Labor Relations Board (NLRB), 71, 73, 116, 188, 209; ILWU before, 243; ITU and, 221; IUE before, 83
National Maritime Union of America, 73, 84
National Mediation Board, 69, 107, 118
National Miners Union (NMU), 141
National Minority Movement (Brit.), 184
National Negro Congress, 111
National Negro Labor Council, 85
National Planning Association, 34
National Progressive Republican League, 110
National Railway Labor Conference, 70
National Recovery Administration (NRA), 34, ·117
National Religion and Labor Council of America, 150
National Sharecroppers Fund, 169
National Tobacco Workers Union, 130
National Typographical Union, 62, 251
National Union of Hospital and Health Care Employees, 145
National Union of Journeymen Bakers of North America, 131
National Urban League, 106
National War Labor Board (NWLB), 73, 117, 118, 242
National Window Glass Workers of America, 142, 159
National Woman's Suffrage Association, 20
National Women's Trade Union League of

America (NWTUL), 19, 106, 111, 113
National Writers Union, 59
National Youth Administration, 119
Naughton, Lynita, 230
Navy, U.S. Department of, 118
NCLC (National Child Labor Committee), 76, 81, 106, 110
Nearing, Scott, 52
Neeley, Matthew, 140
Negro American Labor Council, 111
Neill, Charles Patrick, 122
Nestor, Agnes, 188
Nettleton, Joseph C., 84
Neufeld, Maurice, 73, 110
Neuropathy, in Columbus textile mills (Ohio), 156
New Bedford, Mass., 34
New Deal, 31, 109, 122, 200; and coal miners' families, 105; effectiveness of, 119; unionism during, 36, 254. See also Civilian Conservation Corps; Civil Works Administration; Federal Emergency Relief Administration; National Recovery Administration (NRA); Roosevelt, Franklin D.; WPA (Work Projects Administration)
New Democratic Coalition of New York, 85
New Harmony Gazette, 68
New Jersey, 83–85, 86, 122. See also Paterson
New Jersey Bell Telephone Co., 84
New Jersey Federation of Trades and Labor Unions, 208
New Jersey Industrial Council, 24
New Jersey League of Women Voters, 85
New Jersey Public Employment Relations Commission, 86
New Jersey State Federation of Labor, 84
New Jersey Statutory Board of Arbitration, 84
New Leader, 55
Newman, Dale, 147
Newman, Pauline, 20
News and Letters, 170
Newspaper Guild, The (TNG), 59, 63, 124, 167, 175, 176
Newspapers: IWW boycott of, 225; labor (see Labor press)
New York, state of, 61. See also Cornell University; Gloversville; Hudson; Johnstown
New York Central Railroad, 100
New York City Central Labor Council, 55, 56, 57, 60
New York City Labor Records Survey, 56

New York Committee on Occupational Safety and Health, 57
New York Consumers' League, 18
New Yorker Volkzeitung, 68
New York Household Placement Association, 80
New York Labor Heritage, 60
New York Metro Area Postal Union, 58
New York-New Jersey Port Authority Employment Relations Panel, 86
New York Public Library, 134
New York State AFL-CIO Central Council, 71
New York State Board of Mediation, 71
New York State Council on the Arts, 60
New York State Industrial Commission, 122
New York State Public Employees' Fair Employment Act, 64
New York State Public Employment Relations Board, 71
New York State United Teachers (NYSUT), 65, 71
New York Women's Trade Union League (NYWTUL), 19, 20
NFTW (National Federation of Telephone Workers), 125, 126, 127–28
NFU (National Farmers Union), 112, 221
Nicolopulos, Tom, 254
9to5: Organization for Women Office Workers, 22
NLRB. *See* National Labor Relations Board
NMU (National Miners Union), 141
Noble, William, 46
Norfolk & Western Railroad, 108
Northampton Cutlery Co., 38
North Bennet Street Industrial School (Boston), 23, 24–25
Northern Textile Association, 31
Norton, Mary T., 85
NRA (National Recovery Administration), 34, 117
NRA Code Authority, 31
Nuclear energy, Mass. IBEW and, 36
Nurses, unionization of school, 241
Nurses' associations, 152
NWLB (National War Labor Board), 73, 117, 118, 242
NWTUL (National Women's Trade Union League of America), 19, 106, 111, 113
Nyden, Linda, 141
Nyden, Paul, 141
Nye, James W., 228

NYWTUL (New York Women's Trade Union League), 19, 20

Oak, Liston, 207
OCAW (Oil, Chemical and Atomic Workers International Union), 220–21, 232
Occupational safety, 38, 85, 86, 224, 243; in coal mines, 94, 141–42; in steel mills, 158. *See also* Disease, occupational; Radiation
Occupational Safety and Health Act, 85
Oddie, Tasker L., 228
Office and Professional Employees International Union, 59, 233
Office of War Information, U.S., 124
O'Hare, Kate Richards, 213n
Ohio Civil Service Employees Association, 157
Ohio Labor History Project, 155–56
Ohio Postal Workers Union, 157
Ohio Socialist Labor Party, 157
Ohio State University, 78, 155
Ohio Valley Trades and Labor Assembly (OVTLA), 144
Oil, Chemical and Atomic Workers International Union (OCAW), 220–21, 232
Oil industry, 145
Okey, R. Anne, 182
Olander, Victor A., 186
Old, W. W., 219
Old-age insurance, 200
Olney, Richard, 110
Olson, Culbert, 238
Olympics, pro-Mooney demonstrations during 1932, 238, 253
On the Line, 244
Operating Engineers. *See* International Union of Operating Engineers
"Operation Dixie," 144, 150
Orahood, Harper M., 219
Oral History of the American Left, 59
Order of Railway Conductors and Brakemen, 70
Order Sons of Italy in America (OSIA), 217
O'Reilly, Leonora, 18–19, 20
Organizers, labor, 99, 196, 216, 244; CWA, 126; prosecution of California, 237; Quaker, 105; in southern U.S., 151, 206 *(see also* "Operation Dixie"); TWIU, 130; UE, 102, 253; UMWA, 222; USWA, 186
O'Sullivan, Mary Kenney, 19
Our Daily Bread (film), 210
Overton, Carrie, 174

Ovington, Mary White, 174
OVTLA (Ohio Valley Trades and Labor
  Assembly), 144
Oxnard, Calif., 246
Ozarks Labor Historical Society, 190, 193

Pacific Coast Maritime Industry Board, 243
Packinghouse Workers Organizing Committee,
  196
Packinghouse Workers union, 208, 210, 232.
  See also United Packinghouse Food and
  Allied Workers; United Packinghouse Work-
  ers; United Packinghouse Workers of Amer-
  ica (UPWA)
Padway, Joseph A., 208
Paint Creek, W.Va., 140
Painters, 59, 63, 232
Palmer, Gladys, 89, 90
Palmquist, David, 46, 47
Pancallo, Ralph J., 44
Panels, presidential, 119
Paperhangers, 59
Paper industry, 38
*Papers of the Women's Trade Union League
  and Its Principal Leaders, The,* 19
Paperworkers, 149
Pardon Attorney, U.S., 118
Parsons, Albert R., 208
PATCO (Professional Air Traffic Controllers
  Organization), 232
Paterson, William, 85
Paterson, N.J., 175
Patino, Peter, 246
Patterson, George A., 186
Patton, James G., 221
Paxson, Frederick L., 219
PECE (President's Emergency Committee for
  Employment) (1930–31), 201
Pegler, Westbrook, 201
Penn, Larry, 159
Penn Central Railroad Appraisal Project, 88
Pennsylvania, University of, 78, 81
Pennsylvania Federation of Labor, 97
Pennsylvania Industrial Union Council, 97
Pennsylvania Railroad Co., 88–89, 100
Pensions: for Bell System employees, 128; for
  coal miners, 142
Peonage, 151
People, The, 210
People's History, 231–32
People's Legislative Service, 107

People's Song movement, 169, 237
People's World, 250, 254
Pepper, Claude, 130
Performing arts, union efforts in, 57–58. *See
  also* Motion picture industry
Perkins, Frances, 18, 20, 22, 24, 110
Perlow, Max, 148
Peterson, Esther, 24
Petroleum. *See* Oil industry
Pettibone, George, 220
Pettis, Andrew A., 131
Philadelphia, Pa., 87–88, 89, 90–92
Philadelphia Board of Education, 87
Philadelphia Federation of Teachers, 100
Philadelphia Labor Market Study, 89–90
Philadelphia Orchestra, organizing of, 90
Phillips, Thomas, 208
Phillips, Walton Duvall, 254
Photoengravers, 59, 63
Picketing: informational, 35; manual on, 244
Pillard, Charles H., 192
Pinchot, Amos R. E., 111
Pinchot, Cornelia, 111
Pinchot, Gifford, 111
Pinkerton's National Detective Agency, 107
Pittsburg State University (Kans.), 165
Pizer, Morris, 148
Plekhanov, Georgi, 52
Plumbers, 63
PMWA (Progressive Mine Workers of Amer-
  ica), 141
Pocahontas, W.Va., 142
Poisons, industrial, 21
Poles, in U.S. labor movement, 213
Policemen, 86
Polisar, Eric, 73
Politics, data on U.S., 85
Porters, 24
Posey, Thomas, 173
Post Office Department, U.S., 118
Potofsky, Jacob, 70
Potter, Charles J., 93
Pottery industry, 156–57
Pound, James, 179
POUR (President's Organization on Unemploy-
  ment) (1931–32), 201
Poverty programs, organized labor's creation
  of, 252
Powderly, Terence, 122, 178, 183
Powell, Dan, 149
Pratt, William, 213n

Preparedness Day parade, San Francisco, 107, 238
President's Commission on Pension Policy (1970–80), 73
President's Conference on Unemployment, 81, 200
President's Emergency Committee for Employment (PECE) (1930–31), 201
President's Mediation Commission (1917–18), 80, 118
President's Organization on Unemployment Relief (POUR) (1931–32), 201
Presser, Jackie, 158
Presser, William, 158
Pressman, Lee, 98
Pressmen, 63, 244
Preston, Morrie, 225
Price fixing, in coal industry, 142
Principals, unionization of school, 241
Printers, 39, 62
Printers' Home, 221
Printing and Graphic Communications Union, 157
Printing industry, 59
Prison labor, 130, 227. See also Peonage
Private detectives, licensing of, 209. See also Labor spies; Pinkerton's National Detective Agency
Procopio, Guiseppe, 215
Professional Air Traffic Controllers Organization (PATCO), 232
Professional Staff Congress, 58
Progressive Mine Workers of America (PMWA), 141
Progressive Party, U.S., 158, 196
Progressivism, 110, 111, 121, 227, 252
Proletario, Il, 216
Prostitutes: Inglis study of, 180; organized U.S., 22
Prostitution, 22–23
Protests, 1960s, 183
Protoindustrialization, era of, 39
Provost Marshall General, Office of the, 118
Public Charities of New York City, 110
Public employees, organizing of, 37, 58, 64–65, 71, 146, 191, 193
Publishing industry, 22
Pullman Company, 24
Purcell, Tim, 246
Purdue University, 81
Purk, Maud Wood, 18

Quakers. See American Friends Service Committee
Quill, Michael J., 58
Quinn, Thomas, 103

Race. See Ethnicity; Minorities; Racism
Racism, U.S. labor movement and, 39, 85, 91, 119, 130, 151, 241, 243
Racketeering, labor, 110, 169, 201, 226
Radiation, risk of industrial, 109. See also Occupational safety
Radicalism, 116, 118, 228. See also Anarchism; Communism; Marxism; Socialism; Syndicalism
Radio stations, AFM vs. Philadelphia, 90
Radio and Television Directors Guild, 242
Railroad Administration, U.S., 118
Railroads, 110, 111, 112, 118
Railroad workers, 70, 193, 200
Railway Labor Executives Association, 70
Ramsay, Claude, 149
Ramsay, John Gates, 150–51, 157
Rand, Carrie, 50
Randolph, A. Philip, 22, 106, 111, 186
Rand School of Social Science, 50–56
Rapoport, Bernard, 232, 234
Rauh, Joseph L., 111
Raya Dunayevskaya Collection on Marxist-Humanism, 169
RCA, 103
Read, Harry, 124
Reagan, Ronald, 241
Recreation, for workers, 25, 30, 77, 90, 158
Red-baiting, 22
Redpath Bureau, 197
Red Scare, post-WWI, 107
"Red Squad" (L.A.), 236
Reed, Jim, 232
Referenda, Mass. anti-labor, 34
Rehabilitation, vocational, 224
Reiss, Sam, 59
Religion, labor activism and, 151, 157. See also Association of Catholic Trade Unionists; "Labor priests"; National Council of Churches; National Farm Workers Ministry; National Religion and Labor Council of America, 150; United Presbyterian Church
Remington Arms, 47, 49
Remington Rand, 103
Reno, Milo, 196

Reporters, unionized newspaper, 244
Republic Pictures, 236
Republik Der Arveiter, 68
Rerum Novarum, 121
Research Libraries Group, 10
Retail, Wholesale and Department Store Union,
     130, 152, 153, 157, 233
Retail Clerks International Union, 157, 206,
     209, 245, 246
Retail industry (NYC), 59
Retail Store Employees Union, 253
Return to Tyranny (film), 244
Reuben, William, 182
Reuther, Roy, 172
Reuther, Victor, 169, 171, 172, 173
Reuther, Walter, 34, 164, 169, 171, 172, 175.
     See also Walter P. Reuther Library
Reuther Library. *See* Walter P. Reuther Library
Revolutionary Workers League, 187
Rhoads, James B., 119
Rice, Charles Owen, 99
Richberg, Donald R., 188
Riel, Dennis, 37
Riffe, John, 150, 151
"Right to Work" movement, 156, 193, 197,
     227, 244
Riker trucks, 47
Risveglio, Il, 214
R.J. Reynolds, 130
RLIN (Research Libraries Information Net-
     work), 10, 25, 55, 57, 60, 68, 92, 101,
     206, 218, 228
Robbins, Matilda, 174
Robert F. Wagner Labor Archives, 55, 61
Robert Morris College, 103
Roberts, John, 213n
Robins, Margaret Dreier, 19–20, 208
Robins, Raymond, 208
Robinson, Earl, 159, 237
Robinson, Harriet Hanson, 20–21
Robinson, Lucius Waterman, 93
Robitnychyi Holos, 214
Roche, Josephine, 223
Rochester & Pittsburgh Coal Co., 93–94
Rockefeller, David, 82
Rockefeller, John D., Jr., 75, 76, 78, 79, 80,
     81
Rockefeller, John D., Sr., 75, 78, 80
Rockefeller, John D., III, 81, 82
Rockefeller, Laurance S., 82
Rockefeller, Nelson A., 82

Rockefeller, Winthrop, 82
Rockefeller Brothers Fund, 82
Rockefeller Center, 79
Rockefeller Foundation, 75, 76–80, 81, 82
Rockefeller Institute for Medical Research, 80
Rockefeller University, 75, 80
Rocky Mountain Fuel Co., 223
Rodney Hunt Co., 38
Rogers, Caroline Stevens, 27
Rogers, Edward H., 208
Rogin, Lawrence M., 71
Rollers (newspaper workers), 244
Romberg, Paul F., 248
Romualdi, Serafino, 73
Roosevelt, Eleanor, 144
Roosevelt, Franklin D., 20, 108, 109, 112,
     117. *See also* Franklin D. Roosevelt Library;
     New Deal
Roosevelt, Theodore, 112, 228
Roosevelt University, 188
Rosenberg case, 182
Rosie the Riveter (film), 175
Roth, Herrick, 222
Rothstein, David, 187
Rourke, Joe, 43
Royal Industrial Union, 43, 44
Rubber industry, 193, 232
Rubin, William B., 208
Rubinow, Isaac M., 71
Ruiz, Pepe, 245
Rush Medical College, 78
Ruskin College, 50
Russell Sage Foundation, 75, 81
Russia, Reuther visit to, 171
Rutgers University, 13, 23, 83; Institute of
     Management and Labor relations of, 86
Rutland Corner House, 23
Ruttenberg, Harold, 99
Ryan, John, 121–22
Ryan, Joseph P., 111

Sacco, Nicola, 21, 163, 181, 182, 217
Sadlowski, Edward, 111, 186
Safety. *See* Occupational safety
Sage, Margaret Olivia, 81
St. Pierre, Eugene J., 45
Sakr, Carmelita S., 204–5
Salerno, Joseph, 35
Saloutos, Theodore, 217
Salt industry, 145
Salt of the Earth (film), 210, 220

Salvatore, Nick, 165
Sam Houston Clinton (law firm), 232
Sampson, William, 111
Samuel, John, 159, 208
Samuel Gompers Papers Project, 129
San Francisco, Calif., 238, 246; 1916 Preparedness Day parade in, 107
San Francisco Labor Council, 250, 252
San Francisco State University, 243
Sanger, Margaret, 163
San Pedro, Calif., 236
Santoianni, Louis J., 48
Saposs, David J., 209
Save Our State Committee (Calif.), 244
Scarbrough, Carl, 148
SCG (Screen Cartoonist Guild), 245
Schachter, Leon B., 84
Schachtman, Max, 56, 170
Schenectady Building and Construction Trades Council, 65
Schlesinger, Arthur M., Sr., 18
Schlesinger Library, 40, 188
Schlossberg, Joseph, 70
Schmidt, Carl, 179
Schnitzler, William F., 137
Schofield, John M., 111
Scholle, August, 169
Schonfeld, Frank, 59
Schroeder, Allen, 173
Schwellenbach, Lewis B., 111
Scientific management, 100
Screen Actors' Guild, 58
Screen Cartoonist Guild (SCG), 245
Screen Directors Guild (SDG), 242
Screen Directors Guild of America (SDGA), 242
Second Industrial Conference, Wilson's, 200
Security and Law Enforcement Employees, 65
Seeger, Pete, 164, 237
Seidenberg, Jacob, 72
Seitz, Peter, 72
SEIU. See Service Employees International Union
Seligman, Ben, 39
Senate, labor and U.S., 115–16
Seneca Crystal, Inc., 143
Senior, Clarence, 207
Sentinels of the Republic, 22
Service, Hospital, Nursing Home, and Public Employees Union, 157
Service Employees International Union, (SEIU), 103, 152, 191

Seward, Ralph T., 72
Sgambato, Frank, 153
Shahn, Ben, 250
"Share the Work" effort, 201
Sheet Metal Workers' International Association, 63
Sheetworkers, 44
Shipbuilding Stabilization Committee, 118
Shipping Board, U.S., 118
Shirtmakers, 35
Shishkin, Boris, 136
Shoemakers, 39, 40
Shover, John L., 196
Shuttee, Dick, 229, 230
Sichynsky, Myroslav, 217
Sierra Club, 104
Sifton, Claire G., 111
Sifton, Paul F., 111–12
Sikorsky Aircraft, 47
Simchak, Moragh, 174
Simkin, William E., 72
Simons, Algie M., 207
Sinclair, Upton, 162, 163
Singer, Morton, 72
Single tax, 183
Sinicropi, Anthony, 196
Skemer, Don C., 61
Slater Mill Historic Site, 31
Slavie, 214
Slavs, in U.S. labor movement, 213n
Slight, Joseph, 159
Slovaks, in U.S. labor movement, 213
Slovenians, in U.S. labor movement, 213
Smelting industry, 183
Smith, Clarence Edwin, 140
Smith, Hilda Worthington, 23
Smith, Joseph, 225
Smith, Margaret Earhart, 24
Smith, Mary Louise, 197
Smith, Stanton, 148 n3, 149
Smith Act, 236, 252
Smock, Raymond W., 119
Smokeless Coal Operators Association, 142
Sobell, Morton, 182
Social Democrats, German, 51
Socialism, U.S., 50–52, 165, 170, 182, 203, 207; Catholic Church opposition to, 121; perils of, 178; in West Virginia, 142, 144; in Wisconsin, 207; World War I and, 180. See also American Estonian Socialist Association; American Socialist Society; Debs,

Eugene V.; Finnish Socialist Federation;
Labadie, Charles Joseph Antoine; Reuther,
Walter; Socialist Labor Party (SLP); Social-
ist Party of America; Socialist Workers
Party; Tamiment Institute; Yugoslav Socialist
Federation
Socialist Call, 55
Socialist Labor Party (SLP), 207, 210, 225
Socialist Party of America, 20, 50, 51, 54,
111, 157, 159, 161, 163, 164, 165, 178,
207; literature of, 254. *See also* Socialist
Labor Party (SLP); Socialist Workers Party
Socialists, female, 19, 20
Socialist Workers Party, 207
Social Reform Club (NYC), 18
Social Science Research Council, 76
Social security, 168, 209
Society of American Archivists, 134
Society of Engineering Office Workers, 170
Solicitors general, U.S., 112
Solidarity Day, 159
Songs, labor, 73, 113, 159. *See also* People's
Song movement; Robinson, Earl
Sorrell, Herb, 245
Sosialisti, 214
South, labor patterns in U.S., 110. *See also*
Georgia; Mississippi; Texas; West Virginia
Southern Conference for Education and Indus-
try, 81
Southern Exposure (S. Kennedy), 151
Southern Historical Association, 229
Southern Labor Studies Conference, 146
South Vietnam, Keenan mission to, 124
Southwestern Labor Studies Association, 146
Southwestern Telephone Workers Union, 127
Southwest Labor Studies Association, 249
Sozialist, Der, 68
Spanish Civil War, 151, 181, 183
Sparks, John, 228
Special Services Committee (Detroit), 24
Speed-ups, 30
Spelman Fund of New York, 81–82
Sposato, Joseph, 45
Sprague Meter Co., 47
Springfield, Mo., 190, 191–94
Springfield Central Labor Council (Mo.), 190,
193
Stada, Robert, 246
Stamey, Leon, 153
Standard, William L., 73
Standard Oil, 69, 79

Stanley, Miles, 144
Starr, Mark, 56
Stasik, Margaret Darin, 103
State Charities Aid Association (N.Y.), 109
State Historical Society of Wisconsin, 24, 134,
136, 250
State of Nevada v. *M. R. Preston and Joseph
Smith,* 225, 226
Steel industry, 39, 95–96, 98, 157–58, 183,
209; NRA and, 117; 12-hour day in, 200
Steel Valley Unemployed Council, 104
Steel Valley United for Economic Development
Group, 95
Steelworkers. *See* USWA (United Steelworkers
of America)
Steelworkers Fight Back, 168, 186
Steel Workers Organizing Committee, 73, 98,
144, 150, 157, 159
Steinkraus, Herman W., 48
Stereotypers, 63
Stern, Marc, 46
Stern, Marjorie, 174
Stevens, Nathaniel, 27
Steward, Ira, 208
Stokowski, Leopold, 90
Stone, Irving, 162
Stout, Mike, 96
Stover, Fred, 196
Strachan, D. Alan, 173
Strachey, John, 54
Straus, Oscar S., 112
Strauss, Leon, 71
Straz, 214
Street car workers, 193, 209
Stretch-outs, 30
Strike(s), 15, 107, 120, 175; abroad, 120, 184;
AFM Philadelphia, 90; autoworkers, 158,
159; in California, 235, 238, 241, 244, 246;
consumer, 85–86; coordination of, 243; at
Disney Studios, 241, 245; general, 254; at
Hoover Ball Bearing, 180; IWW-led, 175; at
J. I. Case Co., 207; Justice Dept. and, 118;
Kingsport Press (Tenn.), 154; by miners, 94,
122, 140, 158, 222, 226, 228; N.Y. public
employees denied right to, 64; Nevada
National Guard vs., 226; Philadelphia transit,
91; railroad workers', 110, 111, 200, 226;
steel workers', 209; of Teamsters, 122; telephone workers', 126; in Texas, 234; of textile workers, 21, 156; UE-Maytag, 197; and
violence, 201. *See also* Boycotts; Lockouts

Strikebreakers, 100
Stromquist, H. Shelton, 197n
Strother, E. French, 201
Subversion, wartime, 117, 118
Summer schools, CIO-run, 76
Support Strikers Versus Herald-Examiner
    (film), 244
Supreme Court, U.S., 112, 120
Sutro Library, 244, 250
Sviesa, 214
Swados, Harvey, 39
Sweatshops, 21, 51, 253
Switchmen's Union of North America, 70
Sylvania, 103
Syndicalism, 226, 228, 237. *See also* IWW
    (Industrial Workers of the World)

Taft, Philip, 73
Taft, Robert A., 112
Taft-Hartley Act, 31, 109, 144
Tamiment Camp, 53, 56
Tamiment Institute, 165
Tanning. *See* Leather industry
Tate, Harold, 230
Taxi Worker, 250
Tax reform, ALA for, 150
Taylor, Pauline, 157–58
Taylorism, 30
Taylor Law, 64, 65
Teachers, organizing of, 58, 59, 187, 241
Teachers Union of the City of New York, 71
Tead, Ordway, 72
Teamsters (International Brotherhood of Team-
    sters, Chauffeurs, Warehousemen and Help-
    ers [IBT]), 13, 37, 84, 91, 103, 197, 206,
    250; ALA and, 150; corruption within, 201;
    CWA and, 126; disaffiliation movement
    within, 158; lawyers of, 208; United Farm
    Workers and, 124; United Industrial Workers
    and, 156
Teamsters for a Democratic Union, 168
Telecommunications industry, 127
Telecommunications International Union, 73
Telephone Guild of Wisconsin, 127, 128
Telephone Workers Union of New Jersey, 84
Television industry, 242
Teller, Henry M., 219
Temple University, 91; Center for Public His-
    tory of, 87
Temporary Home for Working Women (Bos-
    ton), 23

Ten Hour Movement, 29
Tennessee Valley Authority, 107
Tennessee Valley Trades & Labor Council, 153
Tenney Committee, 237
Tentacles of Power (Mollenhoff), 201
Teny, A, 214
Tepperman, Jean, 22
Textile industry, U.S., 27–32, 63–64, 122, 156,
    244; in New England, 33–35, 38–39, 106;
    NRA and, 117; in South, 145, 146–47, 152
Textile Workers' Organizing Committee
    (TWOC), 90, 152
Textile Workers Union of America. *See*
    TWUA; ACTWU
Thatcher, Herbert, 208
Thomas, J. Parnell, 22
Thomas, R. J., 172
Thompson, Ernest, 84
Thompson, Huston, 112
Thompson, Sanford E., 72
Three Stars, The, 178
Tianti, Betty, 43
Tichenor, George, 73
Timber. *See* Lumber industry
TNG. *See* Newspaper Guild, The
Tobacco industry, 130
Tobacco Workers International Union (TWIU),
    130
Toledo, Ohio, 155, 158
Tomassetti, Nicholas J., 45
Totten, Ashley L., 106
Toveritar, 214
Trachtenberg, Alexander, 52
Trade associations, 31
Trade and Labor Assembly of Chicago, 185
Trades councils. *See* Building and Construction
    Trades councils
Trade Union Leadership Council, 170
Transit strike, Philadelphia (1944), 91
Transport Workers Union of America, 58, 123,
    157
Transport Workers Union of Philadelphia, 91
Trenton Six, 182
Triangle Shirtwaist Company, 20
Tri-City Employment Stabilization Committee,
    77
Tri-State Conference on Steel, 46
Trotsky, Leon, 169–70
Trotskyism, 181
Truant officers, unionization of, 241
Truman, Harry S., 112

Tucker, Benjamin Ricketts, 178, 181
Tunnelworkers, 59
Turner, Daniel W., 196
TWIU (Tobacco Workers International Union), 130
TWUA (Textile Workers Union of America), 44, 90, 210; merger of ACWA and, 34 (see also ACTWU [Amalgamated Clothing and Textile Workers Union]); in New England, 30, 31, 33–34; in Philadelphia, 90–91; in South, 152, 206; in Wisconsin, 209
Tyler, Mary, 238
Tyomies Society, 215
Typographers, home for retired, 221
Typographical Journal, 128

UAW (United Automobile, Aerospace and Agricultural Implement Workers of America), 44, 59, 91, 111, 124, 167, 168, 171–73, 174–76, 183; ALA and, 150; archives of, 17; in California, 242, 246; in Chicago, 187; FE vs., 123; in Iowa, 197; literature of, 236; paperwork problems of, 14; in Texas, 229; in Toledo, 158; and Wayne State U., 175; women of, 173. See also Reuther, Walter; Royal Industrial Union; Woodcock, Leonard
UE (United Electrical, Radio and Machine Workers Union), 37, 45, 48, 99, 100, 187; Fair Practices Committee of, 85; IBEW vs., 253–54; in Iowa, 197, 198; IUE and, 83; labor archives of, 102–4; literature of, 236; and Mass. cutlery industry, 38
UELA. See UE (United Electrical, Radio and Machine Workers Union), labor archives of
UFW (United Farm Workers of America), 124, 168, 175, 176, 232, 246, 250
UFWA (United Furniture Workers of America), 148–49, 187
Ukrainians, in U.S. labor movement, 213, 217
Ukrainian Workingmen's Association, 217
UMWA (United Mine Workers of America), 73, 94–95, 99, 122, 123, 137, 200; anti-Boyle faction of, 111; in Colorado, 79, 222, 223; Germer and, 207; in Iowa, 196; miner opposition to, 141; in West Virginia, 140–42. See also Brophy, John; Jones, Mary Harris ("Mother"); Lewis, John L.
Unemployed Councils, 235
Unemployment, 96, 183, 188, 200–201; Depression-era, 89; Draper on, 108; Rocke-

feller Foundation focus on, 77, 80
Unemployment and Relief, Colorado State Committee on, 79
Unemployment compensation, 111, 209, 224
Unemployment insurance, 243–44
Union Carbide, 145
Unione, L' (Pueblo, Colo.), 214, 216
Union for Democratic Action, 112
Union Label and Service Trades of Greater New York, 57
Union Leadership Academy, IMLR, 86
Union Metallic Cartridge Co., 46–47
Union of State Employees, 58
Union Pacific Railroad, 109
Unions, labor: Canadian (see FOTLU [Federation of Trades and Labor Unions of the United States and Canada]); communist influence in, 54 (see also CIO, communism in); craft vs. industrial, 108; declining membership of, 14; federal, 64, 135; left-wing, 187; Massachusetts, 33–38, 40; of NYC, 57–60; political contributions of, 197; racism in, 39; rank-and-file protest in, 15, 37–38; runaway, 254; unions vs., 15–16 See also Directly affiliated local unions ("DALUs"); Employee associations; Labor
Union Temple Association, 246
Union Women's Alliance to Gain Equality (WAGE), 253
United Aircraft Corporation, 44
United Association of Plumbers and Steamfitters, 44
United Automobile, Aerospace and Agricultural Implement Workers of America. See UAW
United Brewery Workers, 103
United Brotherhood of Carpenters and Joiners of America 35–36, 43, 44, 149, 188, 192, 222
United Brotherhood of Telephone Workers, 127, 128
United Cannery, Agricultural, Packing and Allied Workers of America, 252
United Community Services of Metropolitan Boston, 24
United Electrical, Radio and Machine Workers of America. See UE
United Farm Workers of America. See UFW
United Federation of Teachers, 58, 60
United Food and Commercial Workers International Union, 37, 153, 245. See also Retail Clerks International Union

United Foundation of Detroit, 170
United Furniture Workers of America (UFWA), 148–49, 187
United Garment Workers, 157
United Glass, Ceramic and Silica Sand Workers of America, 142
United Glass and Ceramic Workers of North America, 156, 157
United Industrial Workers, 156
United Mine Workers of America. *See* UMWA
United Packinghouse Food and Allied Workers, 206, 207
United Packinghouse Workers, 40, 209
United Packinghouse Workers of America (UPWA), 198
United Paperworkers International Union, 38
United Presbyterian Church, 151
United Professors of California, 252
United Scenic Artists, 57, 58
United Service Employees, 187
United States: in ILO, 20; vs. Rand School, 52
United States Catholic Conference, 122, 124
United States Coal Commission, 201
United States Commission on Industrial Relations, 74, 81
United States Employment Service, 82
United States Farmers Association, 196
United States Industrial Commission, 79, 80
United States Potters Association (USPA), 156–57
United States Steel, 96, 104. *See also* USX Corporation
United Steelworkers of America. *See* USWA
United Stone Workers of America, 103
United Sugar Workers, 232–33
United Teachers of Los Angeles, 241
United Technologies, 36–37
United Telegraph Workers International, 44
United Textile workers of America (UTWA), 34, 45, 148, 152
United Toy Workers, 145
United Transportation Union (UTU), 70, 73
United University Professors (UUP), 65
Unity House, 53
Unitypo, Inc., 128
Universal military training, 168
Universities, Working Women vs. U.S., 22
University and College Labor Education Association, 147
University of Massachusetts Employees Association, 37

University Publications of America, 118
Unterberger, S. Herbert, 72
Updegraff, Clarence, 196
"Up Front Down South" (newspaper column), 151
Uphaus, Willard, 151
Upholsterers International Union, 148
UPWA (United Packinghouse Workers of America), 198
Urban Environmental Conference, Inc., 169
Urbanization, 167
Usery, W. J., Jr., 147
USPA (United States Potters Association), 156–57
USWA (United Steelworkers of America, 91, 95, 96, 97–99, 103, 123, 137, 150, 156; in Chicago, 186; insurgents of, 111; literature of, 236; in Ohio, 157; in Pittsburgh, 186; Sierra Club and, 104; WFM, IUMMSW absorbed by, 220. *See also* Abel, I. W.; McDonald, David; Murray, Philip; Steel Workers Organizing Committee
USX Corporation, 104
Utility Workers Organizing Committee, 236
Utopianism, 203
UTU (United Transportation Union), 70, 73
UTWA (United Textile Workers of America), 148
UUP (United University Professors), 65
Uus Ilm, 215

Valentine, Ethel, 19
Valley State College, 246
Van Bourg, Victor, 246
Vanderbilt, Paul, 210
Van Kleeck, Mary, 81, 174
Van Norman Machine Company, 37
Vanzetti, Bartolomeo, 21, 163, 181, 182, 217
Vecoli, Rudolph, 212, 213
Veterans, AFL concern for WWII, 109
Via, Emory, 153
Vietnam War, ALA opposition to, 150. *See also* South Vietnam
Vineyard Shore Workers School, 208
Vladeck Stephen, 55
Vocational Adjustment Bureau for Girls (NYC), 23
Vocational guidance, 23
Vocational readjustment, 77
Vocational training, 25
Voice of Labor, 68

Voluntary Relief Department, Pennsylvania
  Railroad, 88–89
Vorse, Mary Heaton, 22, 173–74

Wade, Betsy, 59
WAGE (Union Women's Alliance to Gain
  Equality), 253
Wages and Hours Act, 85
Wages and Hours Divsion (U.S. Department of
  Labor), 112
Wagner bill, 201
Waiters, 24, 253
Waitresses, 253
Wallace, Henry A., 112, 196–97
Wallen, Saul, 72
Walling, William English, 207
Wallpaper Craftsmen and Workers of America,
  99
Walsh-Healey, 31
Walt Disney Studios, 241, 245
Walter Lanz Studio, 245
Walter P. Reuther Library, 250. See also Wayne
  State University
War Labor Board, 123
War Labor Policies Board, 117
War Manpower Commission, 107, 112, 117–18
Warnaco, Inc. See Warner Corset Co.
Warner, DeVer H., 48
Warner Brothers, 46, 210, 236
Warner Corset Co., 47, 49
War Production Board, 34
War Shipping Administration, 110
War, U.S. Department of, 118
Washington, George, 112
Washington, D.C., 106, 129–31; "Coxey's
  Army" in, 159
Washington Industrial Conference of 1919, 80
Washington Literary Society. See Knights of
  Labor, in Michigan
Watts, Glenn, 125, 127
Watts Labor Community Action Committee, 76
Wayne County Farm Labor Party (Mich.), 172
Wayne Produce Association, 216
Wayne State University, 165, 186, 207n
WBGU-TV (Bowling Green), 155
Weaver, George L-P., 168, 169, 173
Webb, Gordon, 248n
Webster, Milton P., 186
Wechsler, Robert, 60
Weinstock, Louis, 59
Weir, Stan, 39

Weisen, Ron, 96
Weisz, Morris, 173
WEIU (Women's Educational and Industrial
  Union), 22, 23, 80
Welborn, J. F., 79, 80
Welfare Employees Union, 170
Western Federation of Miners. See WFM
Western Worker, 250
Westinghouse, 103
West Virginia. See Matewan; Pocahontas;
  Wheeling
West Virginia Building Trades Council, 144
West Virginia Federation of Labor, 143
West Virginia Industrial Union Council, 143
West Virginia Labor Federation, 144
WEVD (Socialist Party radio station), 51
WFM (Western Federation of Miners), 73,
  107, 225, 226; and USWA merger, 220. See
  also Haywood, William
Wheatland, Wyo., 175
Wheeler, Mary, 174
Wheeler and Wilson Sewing Machines, 46
Wheeling, W.Va., 144
Wheeling Majority, 145
Wheeling Tobacco Workers, 144
White-collar workers, union organizing of, 58–
  59
Wholesale industry, CIO and NYC, 59
Whyte, William F., 73
Wickens, Aryness Joy, 25
Widener Library, scrubwomen of, 21
Wiesman, Margaret, 21
Wilkins, Roy, 149
Willard, James F., 219
Williams, Charles D., 179
Williams, Harrison A., Jr., 85
Willkie, Wendell, 109
Wilson, William B., 116
Wilson, Woodrow, 110, 112, 200
Winant, John G., 20
Window Glass Cutters and Flatteners Protec-
  tive Association, 142
Window Glass Cutters League of America,
  142–43
Winn, Carr, 232
Winstead, Ralph, 73
Winter, William F., 149
Wisconsin, 206–7, 208–9
Wisconsin, University of, 179, 203; libraries
  of, 210–11. See also Commons, John R.;
  State Historical Society of Wisconsin

Wisconsin Bureau of Labor Statistics, 209
Wisconsin Center for Film and Theater
  Research, 210
Wisconsin Industrial Commission, 209
With These Hands (Erlich), 35
Witte, Edwin, 209
Wobblies. *See* IWW (Industrial Workers of the
  World)
Wolf, Benjamin, 72
Wolff, Sidney, 72
Wolfson, Theresa, 71
Woman's Rights Collection (WRC), 18
Women: in ACTWU, 244; black, 24; equal pay
  for, 251; Finnish, 213n; in IAM, 242; labor
  movement and, 15, 18, 40, 122, 173–74,
  175, 192, 204, 208, 232, 234, 251, 253;
  minimum wage for, 223; Mont support of,
  245; as radio/film/TV directors, 242; as
  street-car drivers, 209; union activity on
  behalf of, 64
Women in the Federal Government Oral His-
  tory Project (Schlesinger Library), 25
Women's Archives. *See* Schlesinger Library
Women's Bureau, (U.S. Dept. of Labor), 20,
  24, 74, 119
Women's CIO League of New Jersey, 84
Women's Educational and Industrial Union
  (WEIU), 22, 23, 80
Women's Educational-Industrial Alliance, 81
Women's liberation movement, 183
Women's Service Club (Boston), 24
Women's suffrage, 18, 19, 21
Women's Trade Union League, 188
Woodbury, Helen Sumner, 209
Woodcock, Leonard, 172, 175
Woods, Arthur, 201
Woodworkers' Conspiracy Trial, 108
Woolf, Jack, 230
Woolis, Ben, 71
Workers Defense League, 169
Workers Education Bureau of America, 71, 81

Workingman's Advocate, 68
Working Man's Advocate, 68
Workingmen's Party, 207
Working Women, 22
Working Women's Protective Union, 76
Working Women's Society, 18
Workmen's compensation, 77, 85, 119, 209,
  227
Work People's College, 215
Work Projects Administration (WPA), 107, 117
World Confederation of Labour, 69
World Federation of Trade Unions, 68, 69, 73
World War I, 47, 117, 209, 228, 238; Catholic
  Church social action during, 122; labor
  reform during, 107, 122; opposition to, 52,
  161; U.S. railroads seized during, 110; U.S.
  socialism affected by, 180
World War II, 47, 117–18, 228, 242; Holly-
  wood support of, 242; House of Representa-
  tives focus after, 116; labor patterns during,
  110, 119, 130, 169, 206; labor problems
  after, 111
WPA (Work Projects Administration), 107, 117
WRC (Woman's Rights Collection), 18
Wright, Jim, 231
Writers, union organizing of, 59
Wurf, Jerry, 172
Wyoming, 79. *See also* Wheatland

Yagoda, Louis, 72
Yale Club (NYC), 77
Yale University, 78
Yarborough, Ralph, 231
Young America, 68
Youngstown Sheet and Tube Co., 158
Youth Task Force, JDR 3rd Fund, 81
Yugoslav Socialist Federation, 216

Zack, Arnold, 72
Zale Foundation, 231
Zander, Arnold, 172, 207